VAMPIRELLA

Hollywood Horror

Hollywood Horror

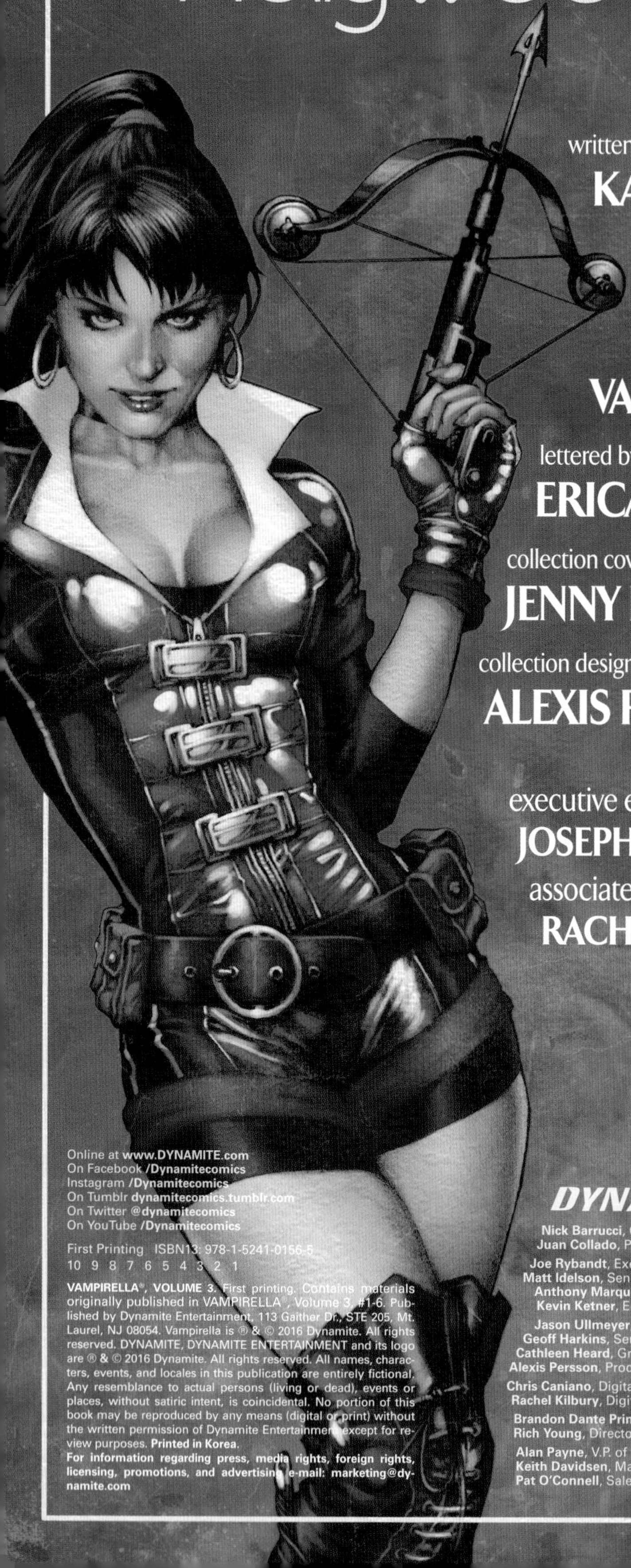

written by
KATE LETH

illustrated by
EMAN CASALLOS

colored by
VALENTINA PINTO

lettered by
ERICA SCHULTZ

collection cover by
JENNY FRISON

collection design by
ALEXIS PERSSON

executive editor
JOSEPH RYBANDT

associate editor
RACHEL PINNELAS

Online at www.DYNAMITE.com
On Facebook /Dynamitecomics
Instagram /Dynamitecomics
On Tumblr dynamitecomics.tumblr.com
On Twitter @dynamitecomics
On YouTube /Dynamitecomics

First Printing   ISBN13: 978-1-5241-0156-5
10 9 8 7 6 5 4 3 2 1

DYNAMITE.

Nick Barrucci, CEO / Publisher
Juan Collado, President / COO

Joe Rybandt, Executive Editor
Matt Idelson, Senior Editor
Anthony Marques, Assistant Editor
Kevin Ketner, Editorial Assistant

Jason Ullmeyer, Art Director
Geoff Harkins, Senior Graphic Designer
Cathleen Heard, Graphic Designer
Alexis Persson, Production Artist

Chris Caniano, Digital Associate
Rachel Kilbury, Digital Assistant

Brandon Dante Primavera, V.P. of IT and Operations
Rich Young, Director of Business Development

Alan Payne, V.P. of Sales and Marketing
Keith Davidsen, Marketing Director
Pat O'Connell, Sales Manager

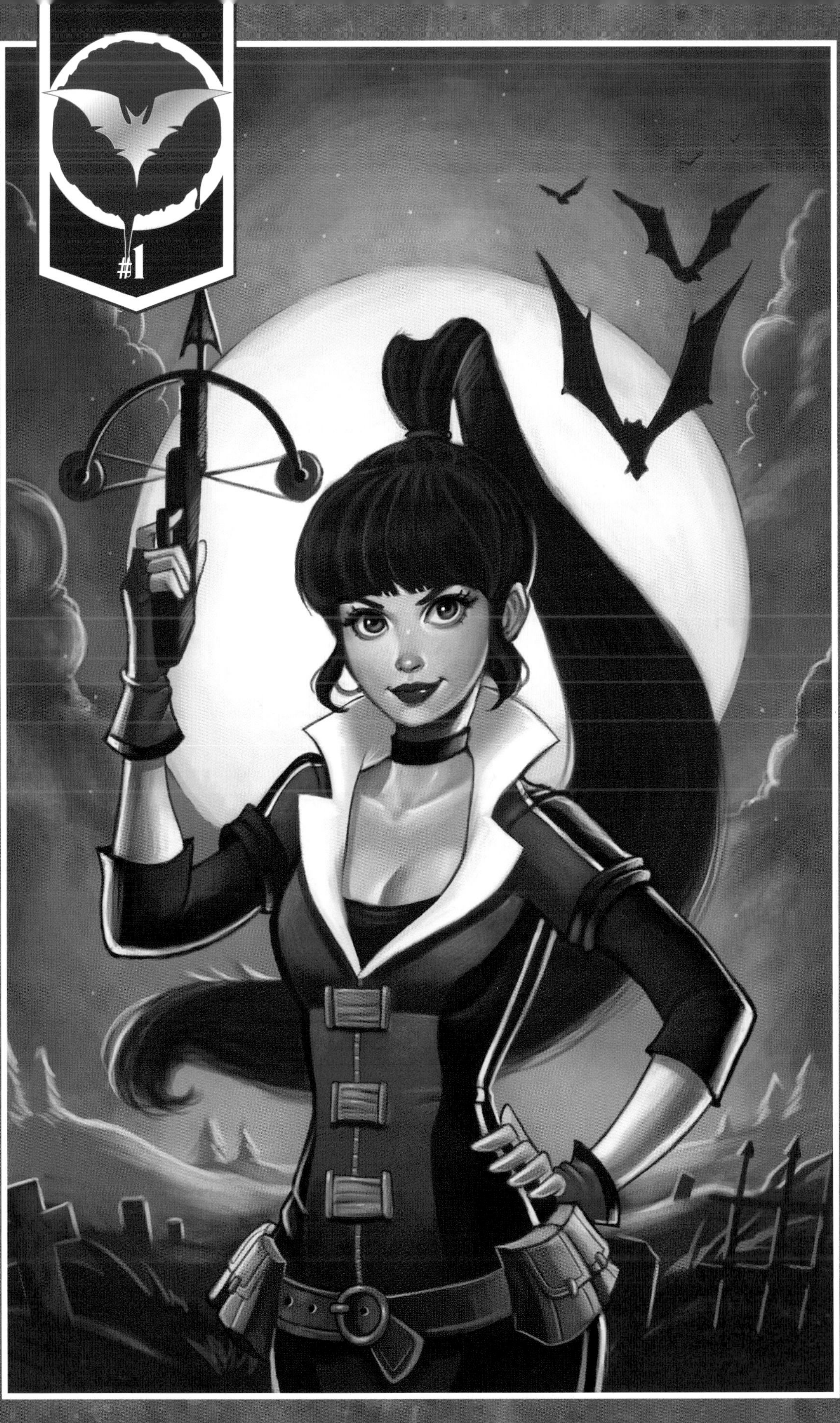
#1

cover by **Chrissie Zullo**

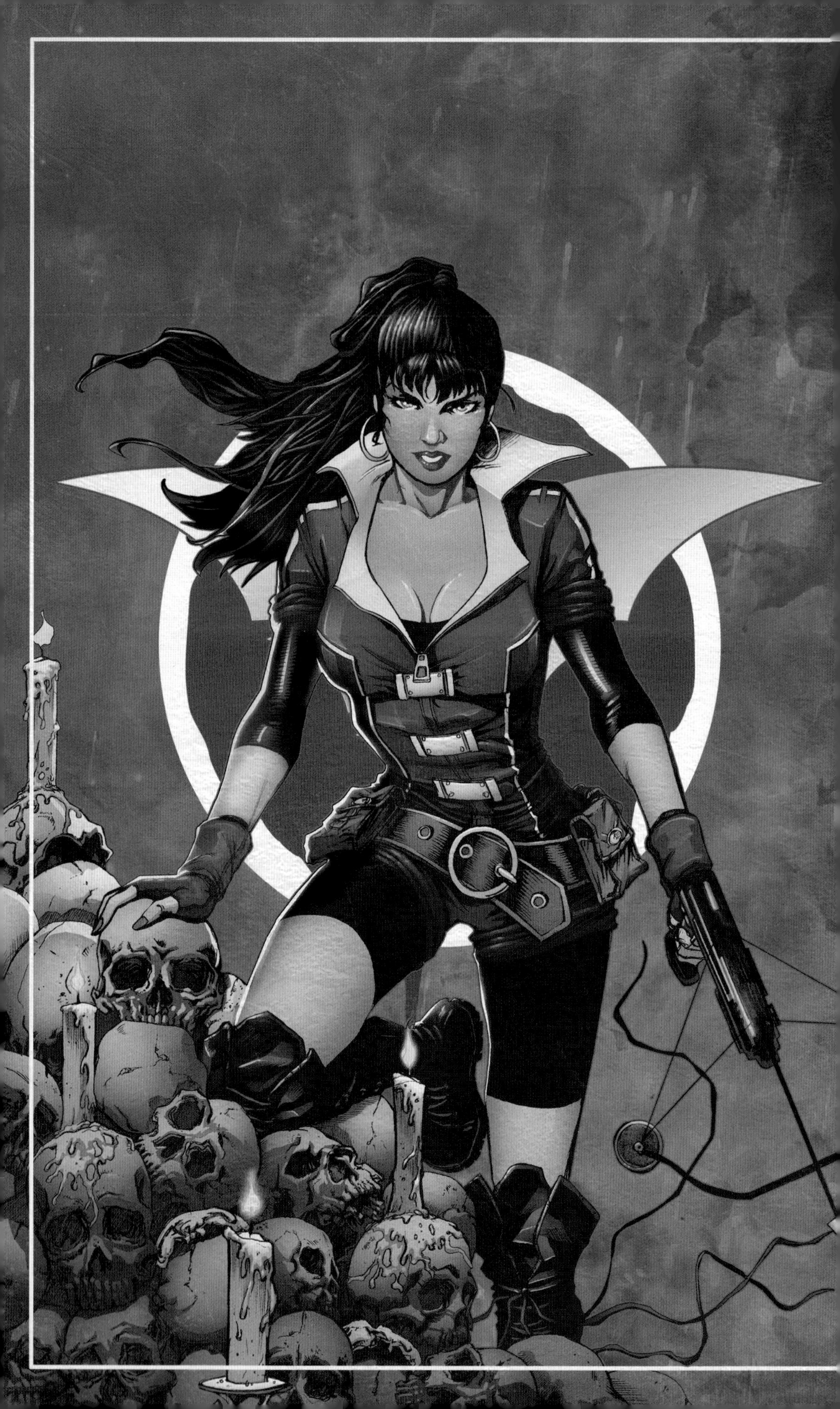

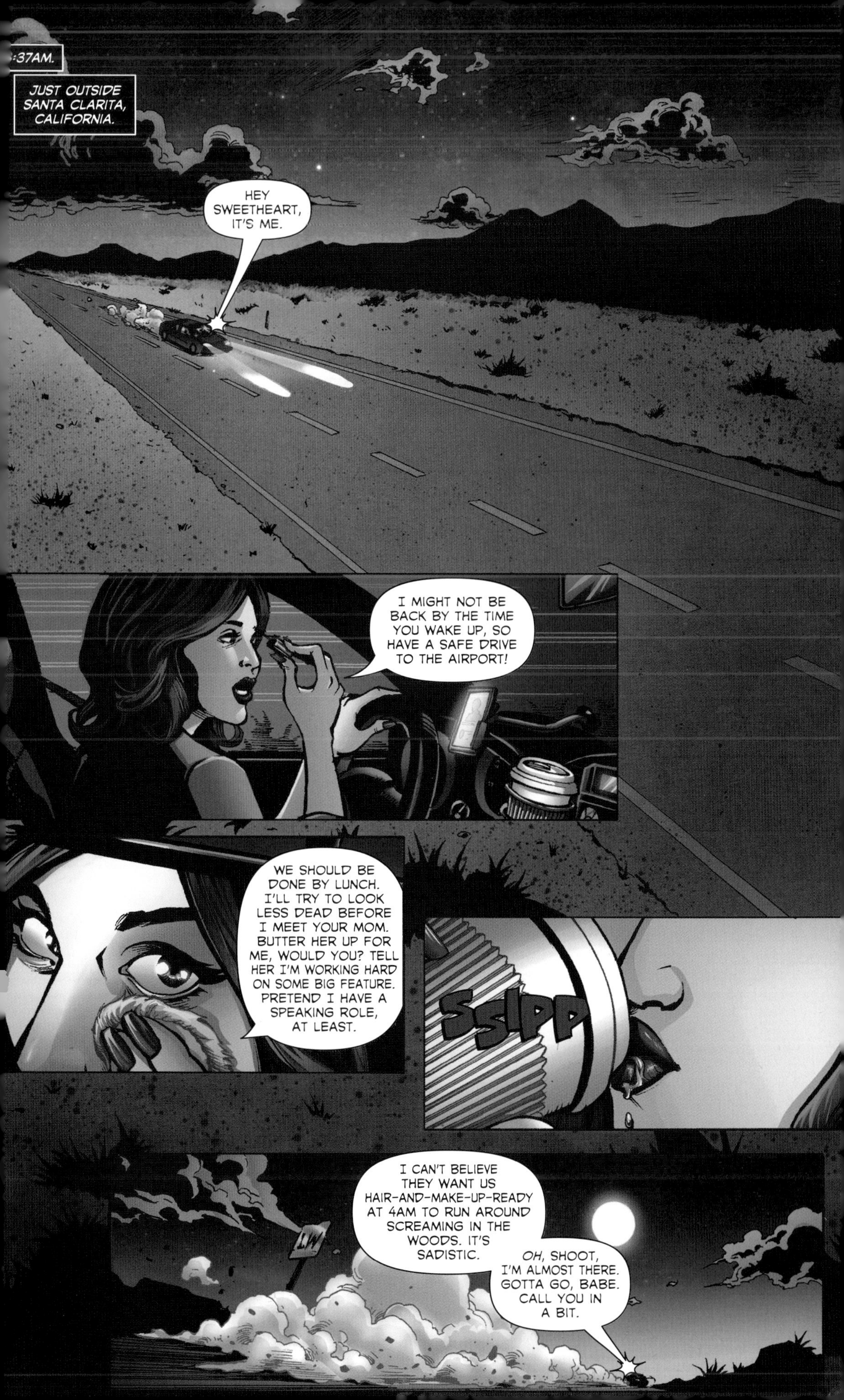

:37AM.
JUST OUTSIDE SANTA CLARITA, CALIFORNIA.
HEY SWEETHEART, IT'S ME.
I MIGHT NOT BE BACK BY THE TIME YOU WAKE UP, SO HAVE A SAFE DRIVE TO THE AIRPORT!
WE SHOULD BE DONE BY LUNCH. I'LL TRY TO LOOK LESS DEAD BEFORE I MEET YOUR MOM. BUTTER HER UP FOR ME, WOULD YOU? TELL HER I'M WORKING HARD ON SOME BIG FEATURE. PRETEND I HAVE A SPEAKING ROLE, AT LEAST.
SSIPP
I CAN'T BELIEVE THEY WANT US HAIR-AND-MAKE-UP-READY AT 4AM TO RUN AROUND SCREAMING IN THE WOODS. IT'S SADISTIC.
OH, SHOOT, I'M ALMOST THERE. GOTTA GO, BABE. CALL YOU IN A BIT.

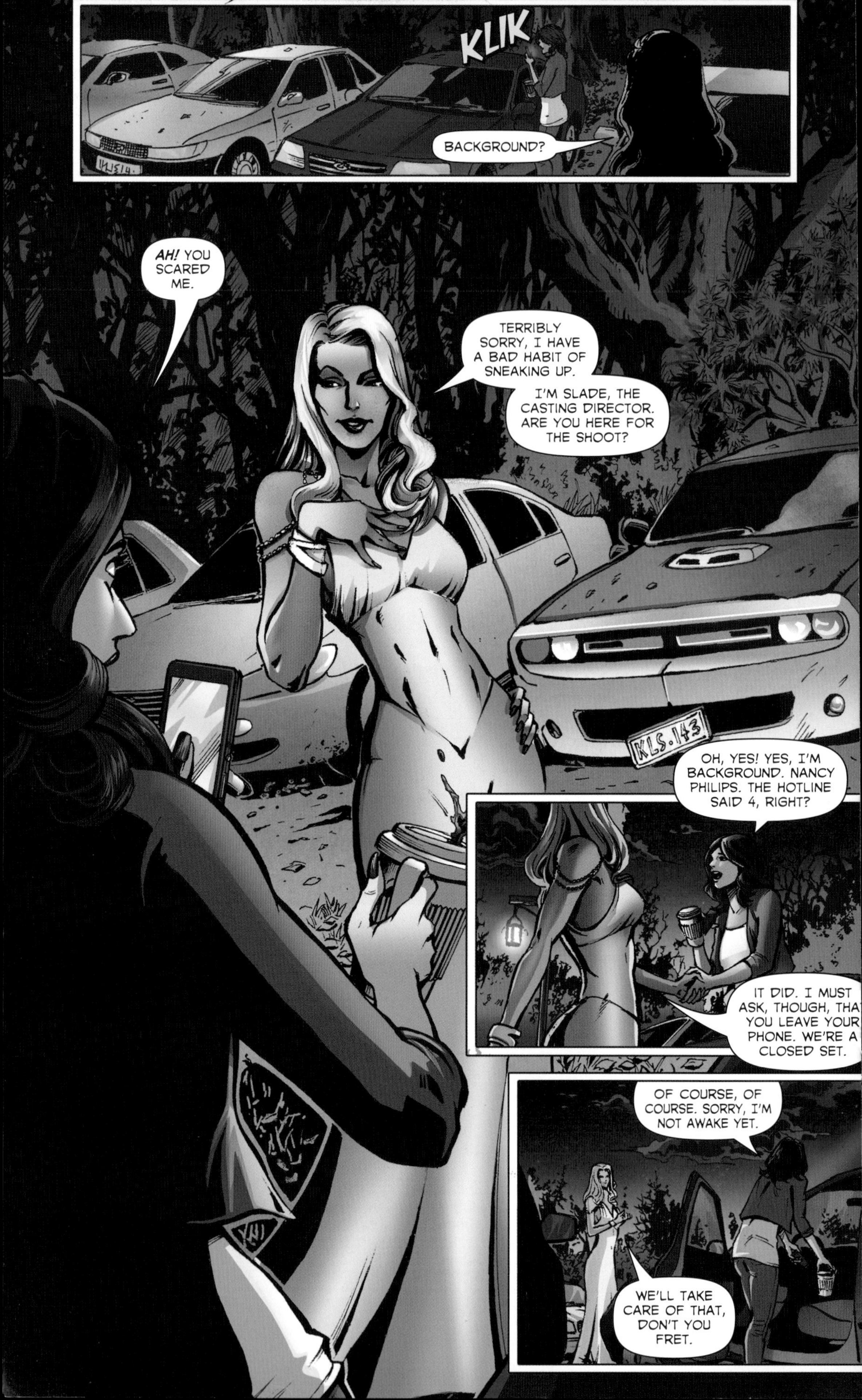
KLIK
BACKGROUND?
AH! YOU SCARED ME.
TERRIBLY SORRY, I HAVE A BAD HABIT OF SNEAKING UP.
I'M SLADE, THE CASTING DIRECTOR. ARE YOU HERE FOR THE SHOOT?
KLS.143
OH, YES! YES, I'M BACKGROUND. NANCY PHILIPS. THE HOTLINE SAID 4, RIGHT?
IT DID. I MUST ASK, THOUGH, THAT YOU LEAVE YOUR PHONE. WE'RE A CLOSED SET.
OF COURSE, OF COURSE. SORRY, I'M NOT AWAKE YET.
WE'LL TAKE CARE OF THAT, DON'T YOU FRET.

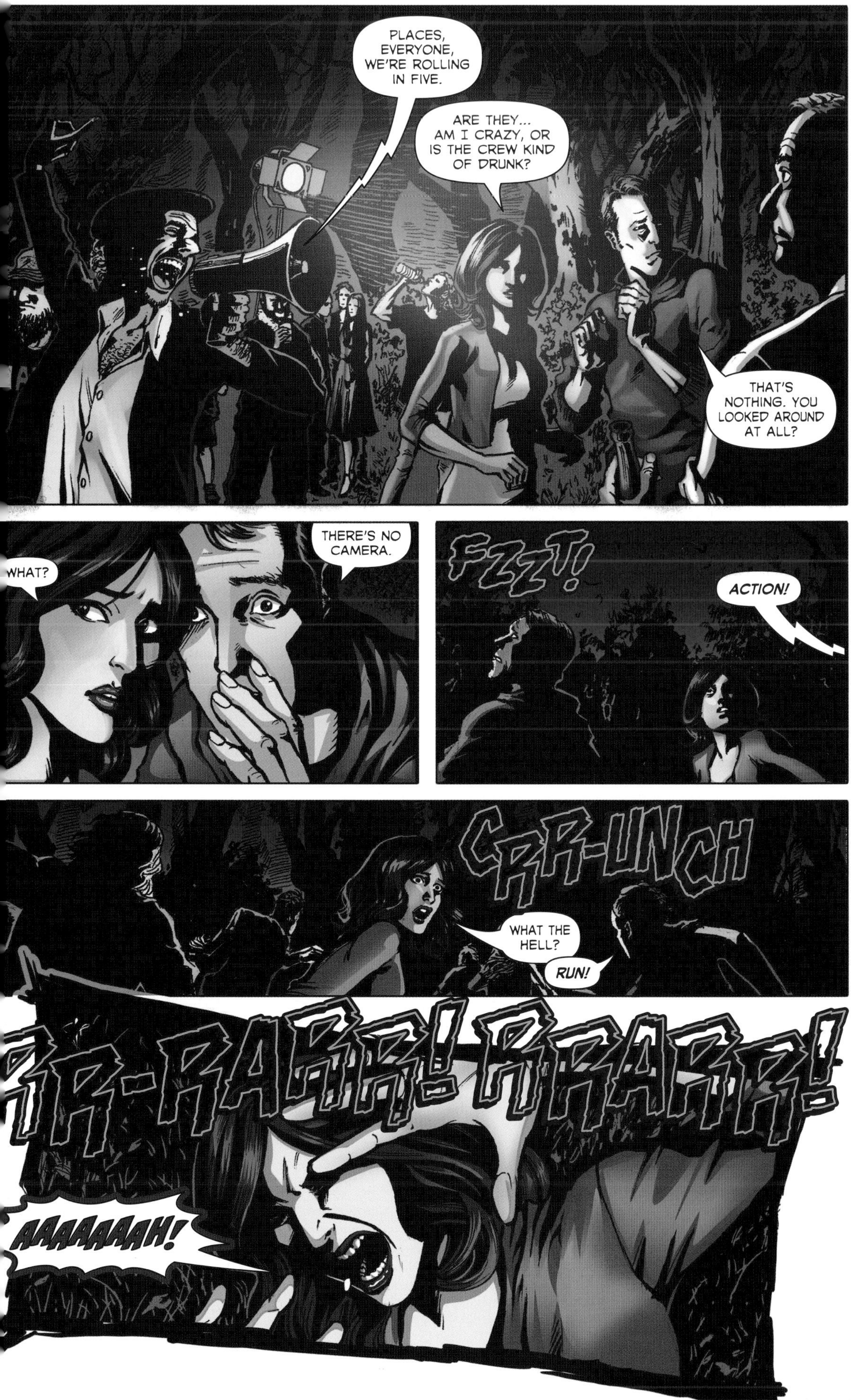
PLACES, EVERYONE, WE'RE ROLLING IN FIVE.
ARE THEY... AM I CRAZY, OR IS THE CREW KIND OF DRUNK?
THAT'S NOTHING. YOU LOOKED AROUND AT ALL?
WHAT?
THERE'S NO CAMERA.
FZZT!
ACTION!
CRR-UNCH
WHAT THE HELL?
RUN!
RR-RARRR! RRARR!
AAAAAAAH!

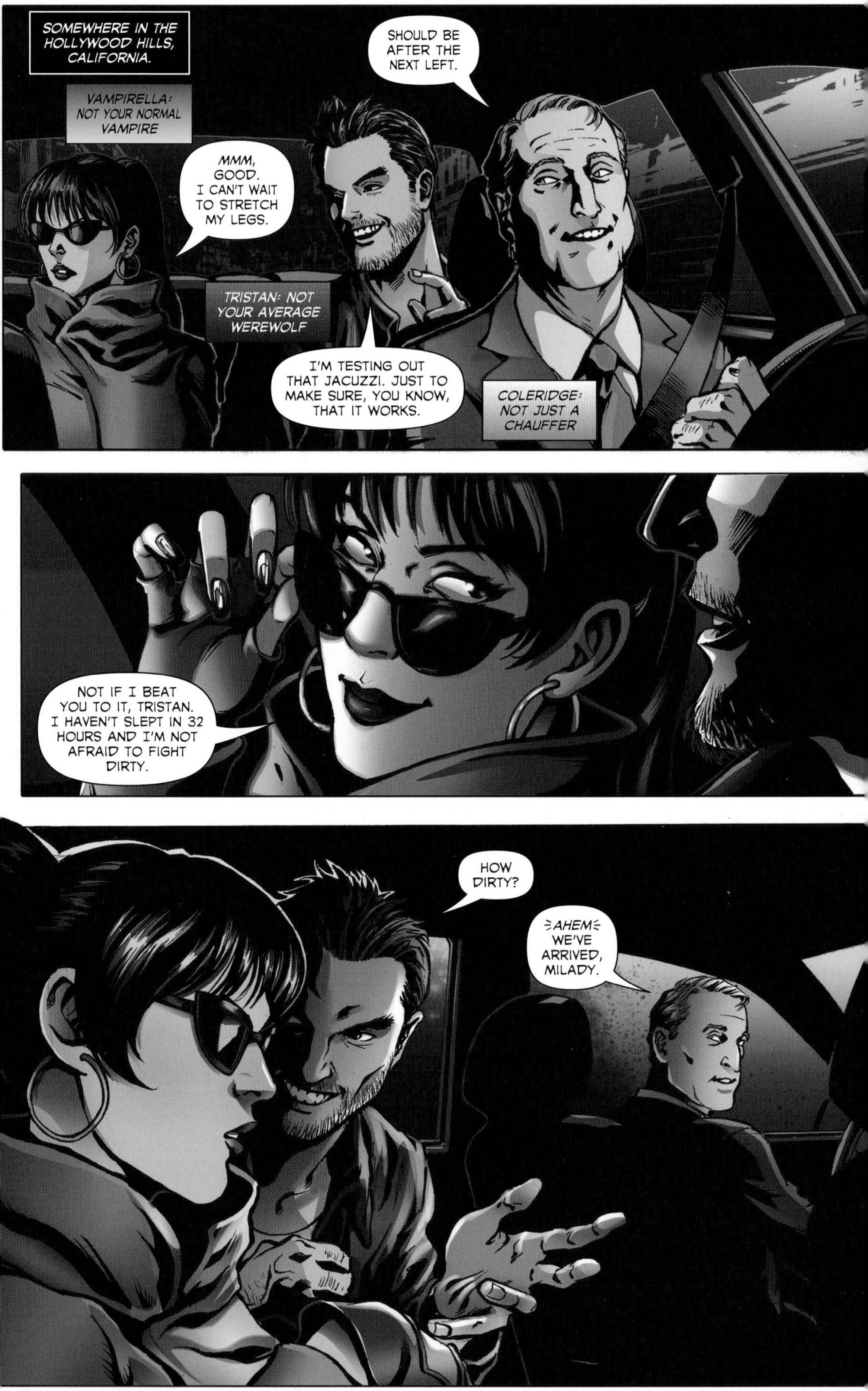
SOMEWHERE IN THE HOLLYWOOD HILLS, CALIFORNIA.
VAMPIRELLA: NOT YOUR NORMAL VAMPIRE
SHOULD BE AFTER THE NEXT LEFT.
MMM, GOOD. I CAN'T WAIT TO STRETCH MY LEGS.
TRISTAN: NOT YOUR AVERAGE WEREWOLF
I'M TESTING OUT THAT JACUZZI. JUST TO MAKE SURE, YOU KNOW, THAT IT WORKS.
COLERIDGE: NOT JUST A CHAUFFER
NOT IF I BEAT YOU TO IT, TRISTAN. I HAVEN'T SLEPT IN 32 HOURS AND I'M NOT AFRAID TO FIGHT DIRTY.
HOW DIRTY?
AHEM WE'VE ARRIVED, MILADY.

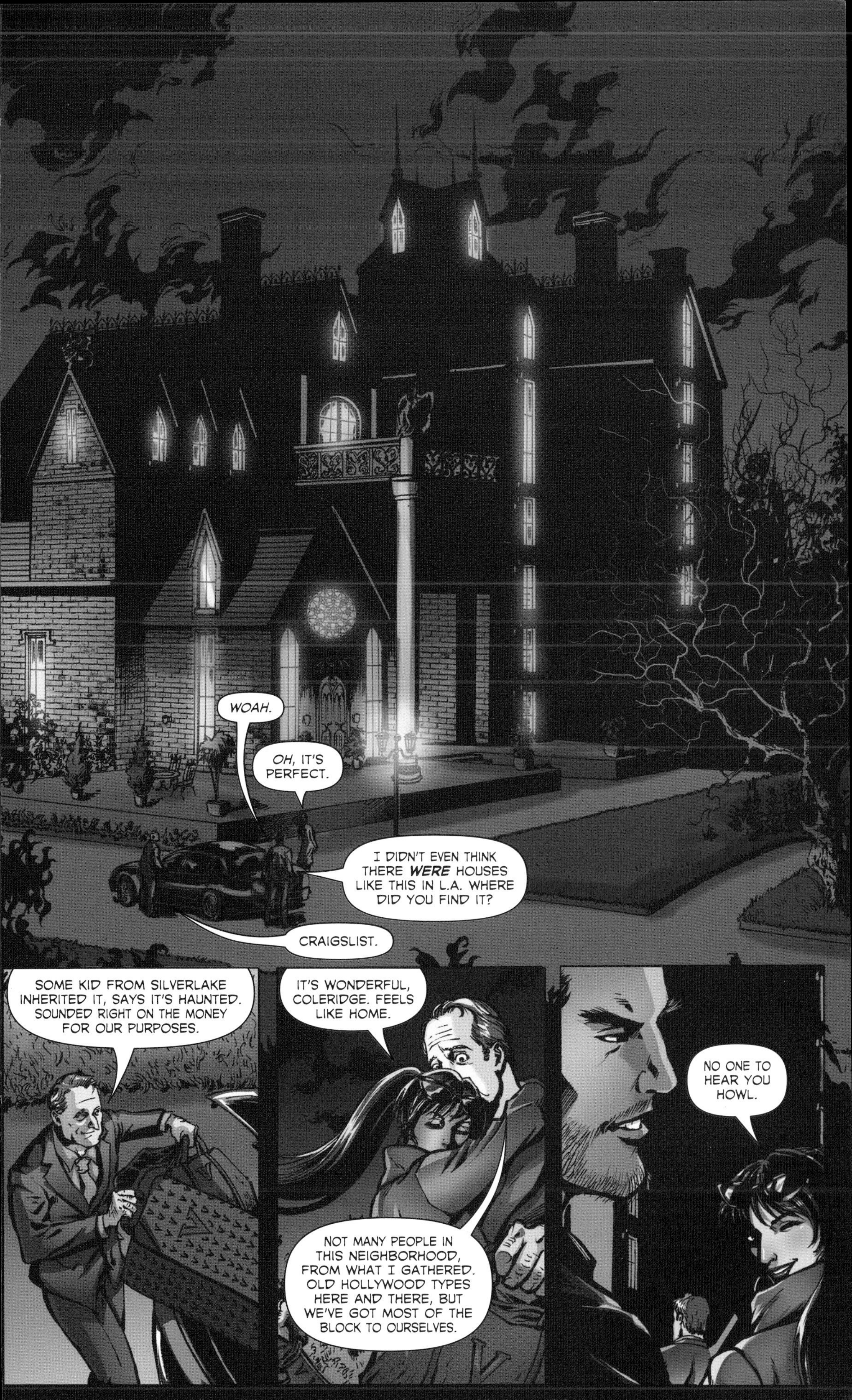

WOAH.
OH, IT'S PERFECT.
I DIDN'T EVEN THINK THERE WERE HOUSES LIKE THIS IN L.A. WHERE DID YOU FIND IT?
CRAIGSLIST.
SOME KID FROM SILVERLAKE INHERITED IT, SAYS IT'S HAUNTED. SOUNDED RIGHT ON THE MONEY FOR OUR PURPOSES.
IT'S WONDERFUL, COLERIDGE. FEELS LIKE HOME.
NOT MANY PEOPLE IN THIS NEIGHBORHOOD, FROM WHAT I GATHERED. OLD HOLLYWOOD TYPES HERE AND THERE, BUT WE'VE GOT MOST OF THE BLOCK TO OURSELVES.
NO ONE TO HEAR YOU HOWL.

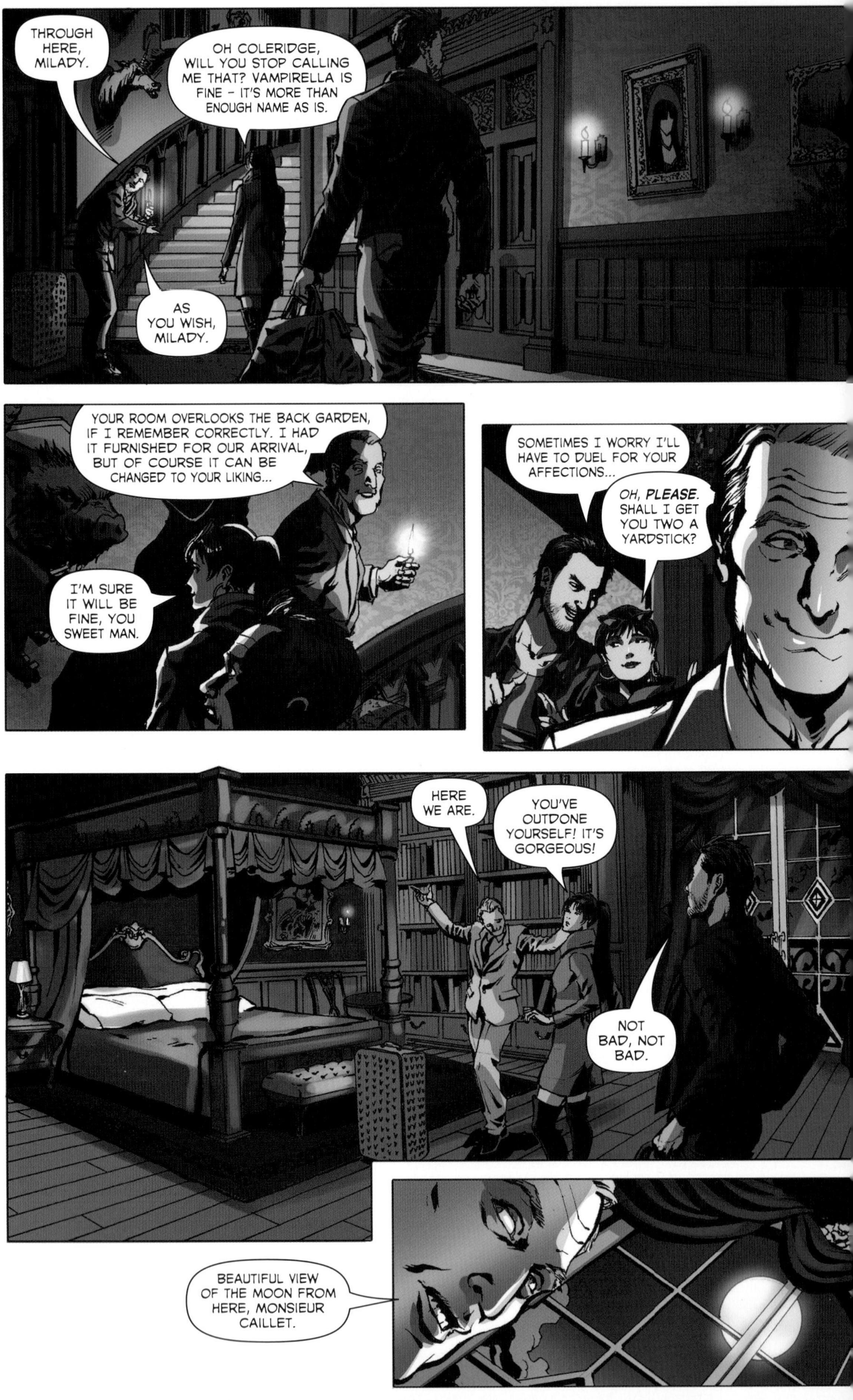
THROUGH HERE, MILADY.
OH COLERIDGE, WILL YOU STOP CALLING ME THAT? VAMPIRELLA IS FINE - IT'S MORE THAN ENOUGH NAME AS IS.
AS YOU WISH, MILADY.
YOUR ROOM OVERLOOKS THE BACK GARDEN, IF I REMEMBER CORRECTLY. I HAD IT FURNISHED FOR OUR ARRIVAL, BUT OF COURSE IT CAN BE CHANGED TO YOUR LIKING...
I'M SURE IT WILL BE FINE, YOU SWEET MAN.
SOMETIMES I WORRY I'LL HAVE TO DUEL FOR YOUR AFFECTIONS...
*OH, **PLEASE**.* SHALL I GET YOU TWO A YARDSTICK?
HERE WE ARE.
YOU'VE OUTDONE YOURSELF! IT'S GORGEOUS!
NOT BAD, NOT BAD.
BEAUTIFUL VIEW OF THE MOON FROM HERE, MONSIEUR CAILLET.

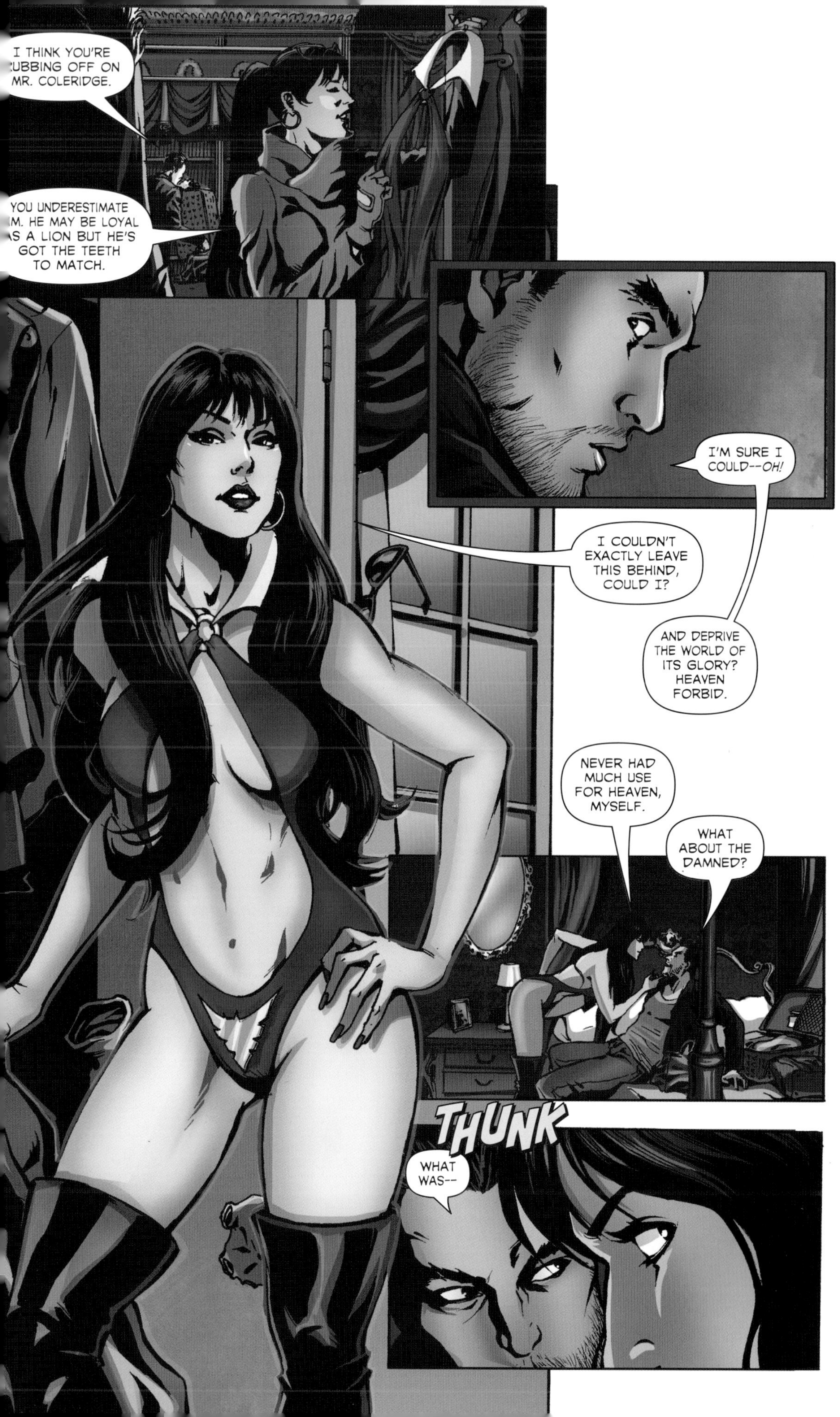

I THINK YOU'RE RUBBING OFF ON MR. COLERIDGE.
YOU UNDERESTIMATE HIM. HE MAY BE LOYAL AS A LION BUT HE'S GOT THE TEETH TO MATCH.
I'M SURE I COULD--OH!
I COULDN'T EXACTLY LEAVE THIS BEHIND, COULD I?
AND DEPRIVE THE WORLD OF ITS GLORY? HEAVEN FORBID.
NEVER HAD MUCH USE FOR HEAVEN, MYSELF.
WHAT ABOUT THE DAMNED?
THUNK
WHAT WAS--

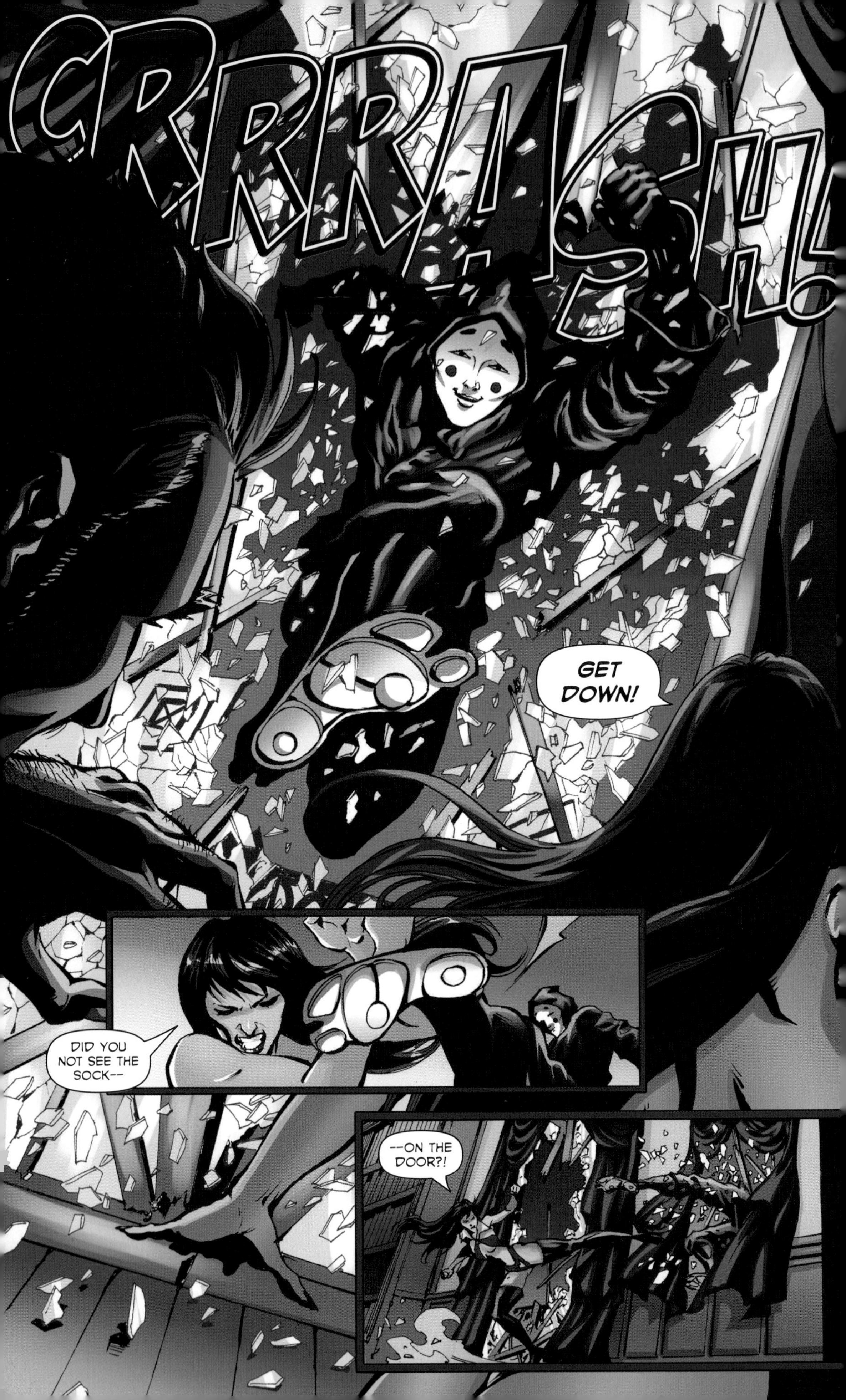
CRRRASH!
GET DOWN!
DID YOU NOT SEE THE SOCK--
--ON THE DOOR?!

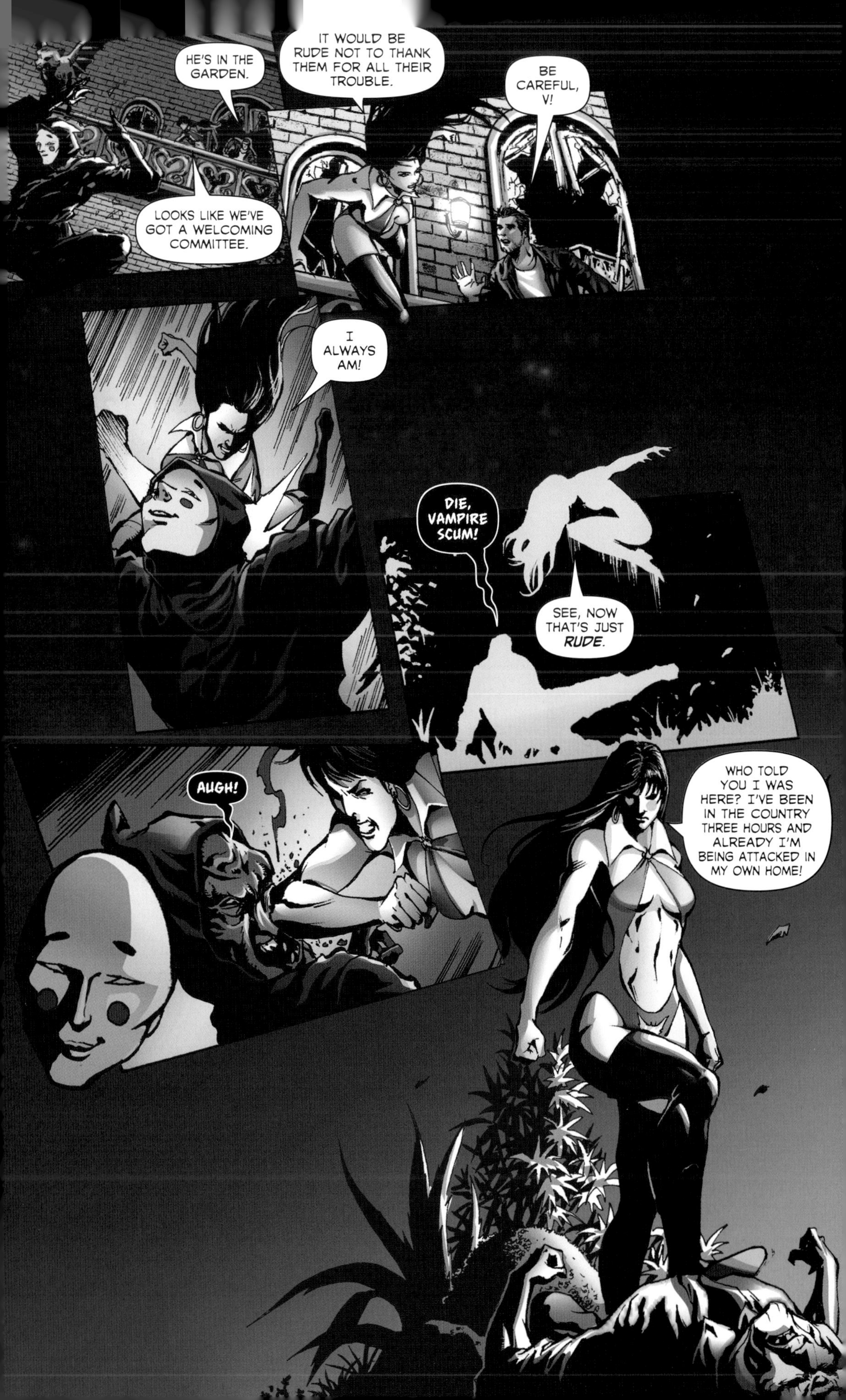
HE'S IN THE GARDEN.
LOOKS LIKE WE'VE GOT A WELCOMING COMMITTEE.
IT WOULD BE RUDE NOT TO THANK THEM FOR ALL THEIR TROUBLE.
BE CAREFUL, V!
I ALWAYS AM!
DIE, VAMPIRE SCUM!
SEE, NOW THAT'S JUST RUDE.
AUGH!
WHO TOLD YOU I WAS HERE? I'VE BEEN IN THE COUNTRY THREE HOURS AND ALREADY I'M BEING ATTACKED IN MY OWN HOME!

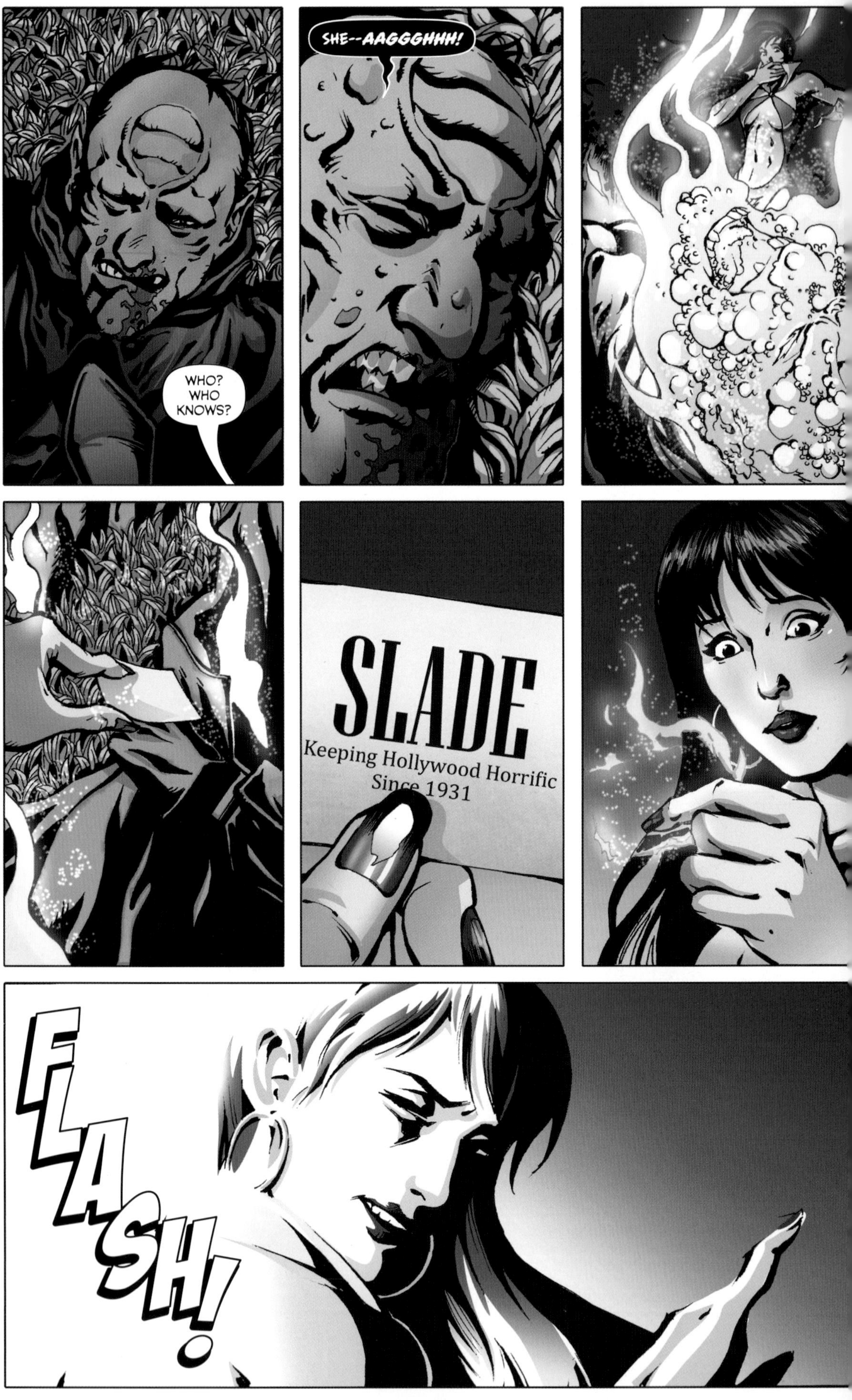
WHO? WHO KNOWS?
SHE--AAGGGHHH!
SLADE
Keeping Hollywood Horrific Since 1931
FLASH!

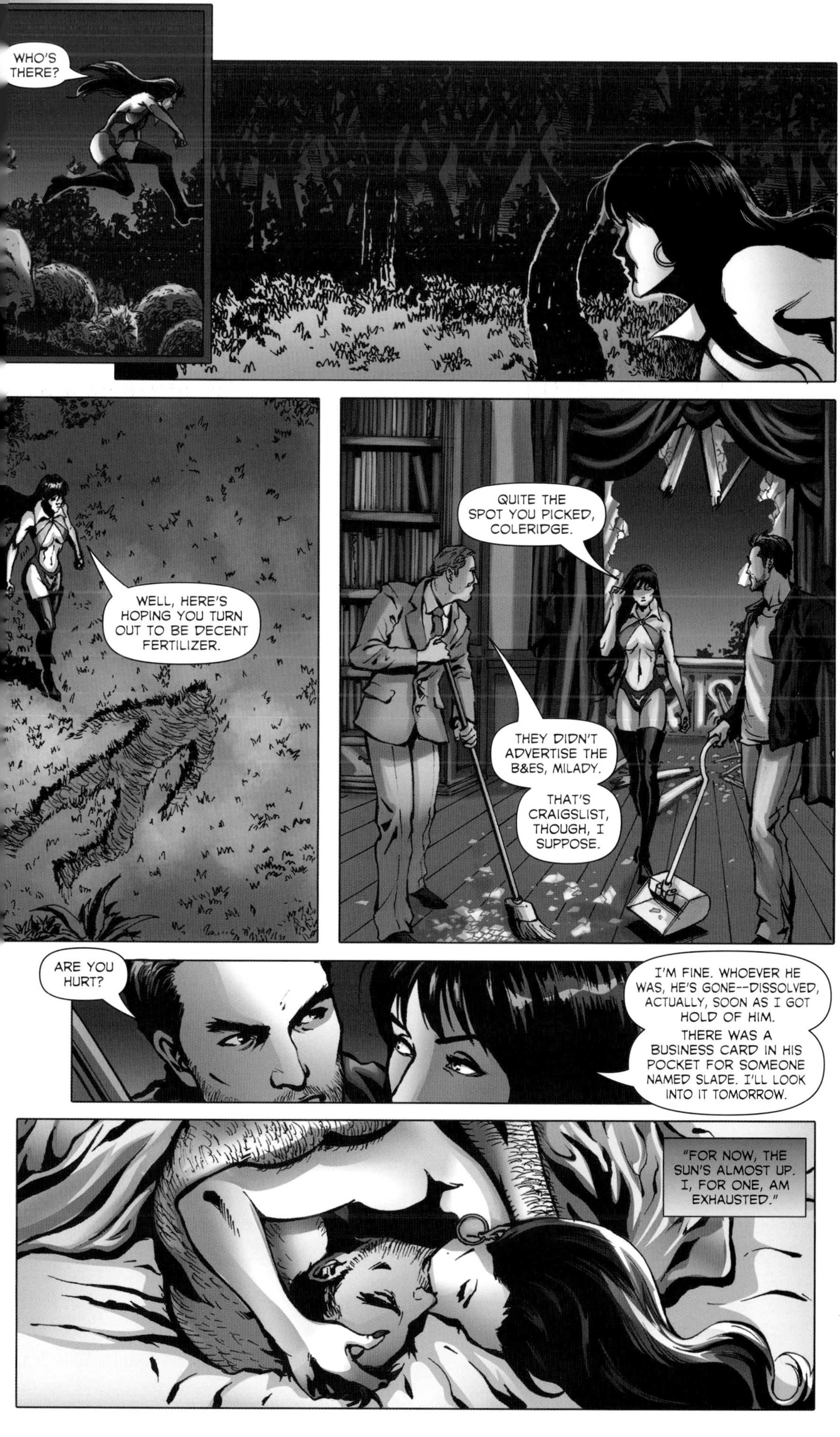
WHO'S THERE?
WELL, HERE'S HOPING YOU TURN OUT TO BE DECENT FERTILIZER.
QUITE THE SPOT YOU PICKED, COLERIDGE.
THEY DIDN'T ADVERTISE THE B&ES, MILADY.
THAT'S CRAIGSLIST, THOUGH, I SUPPOSE.
ARE YOU HURT?
I'M FINE. WHOEVER HE WAS, HE'S GONE--DISSOLVED, ACTUALLY, SOON AS I GOT HOLD OF HIM.
THERE WAS A BUSINESS CARD IN HIS POCKET FOR SOMEONE NAMED SLADE. I'LL LOOK INTO IT TOMORROW.
"FOR NOW, THE SUN'S ALMOST UP. I, FOR ONE, AM EXHAUSTED."

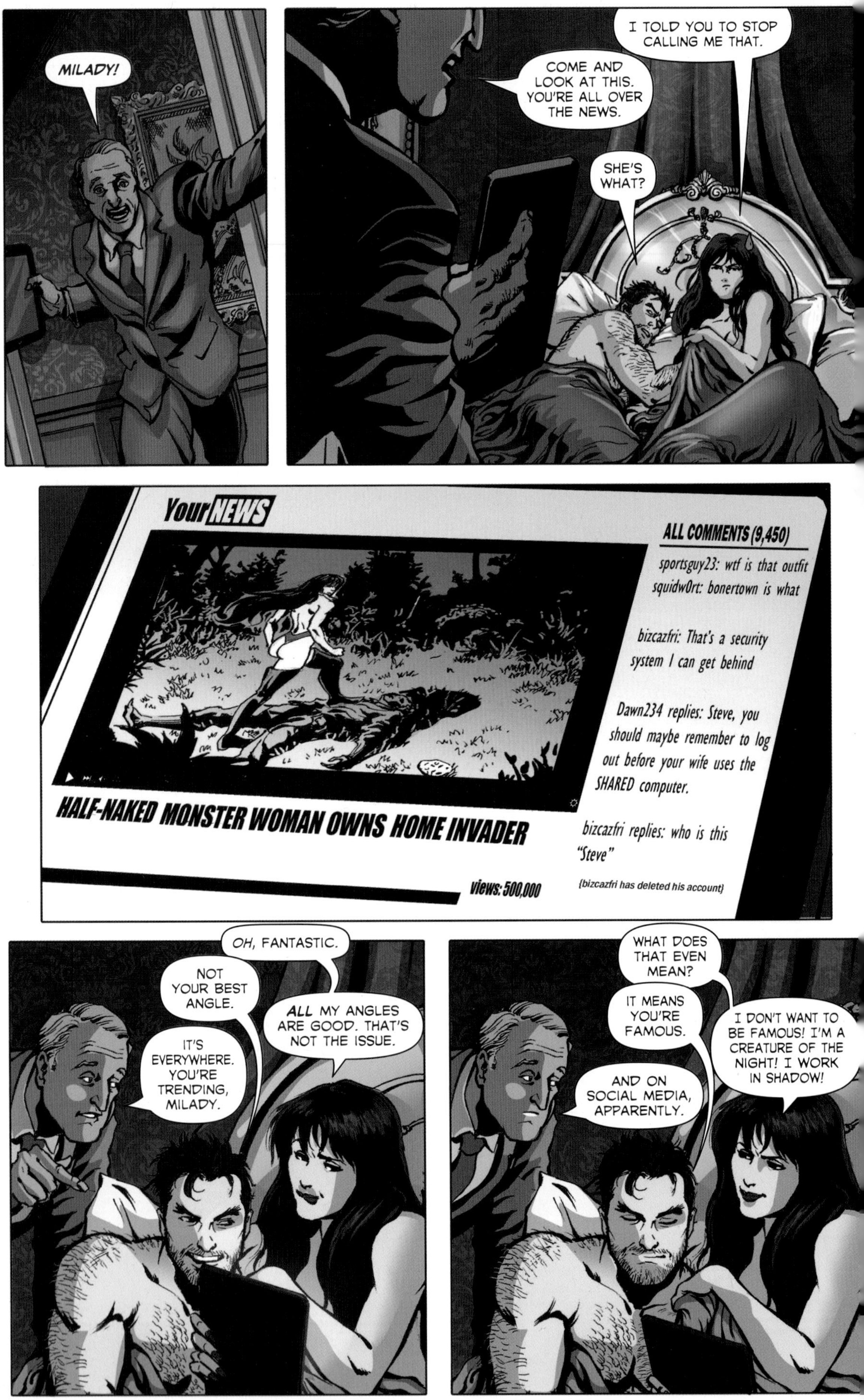
MILADY!
COME AND LOOK AT THIS. YOU'RE ALL OVER THE NEWS.
I TOLD YOU TO STOP CALLING ME THAT.
SHE'S WHAT?
Your NEWS
ALL COMMENTS (9,450)
sportsguy23: wtf is that outfit
squidw0rt: bonertown is what
bizcazfri: That's a security system I can get behind
Dawn234 replies: Steve, you should maybe remember to log out before your wife uses the SHARED computer.
bizcazfri replies: who is this "Steve"
{bizcazfri has deleted his account}
HALF-NAKED MONSTER WOMAN OWNS HOME INVADER
views: 500,000
IT'S EVERYWHERE. YOU'RE TRENDING, MILADY.
NOT YOUR BEST ANGLE.
OH, FANTASTIC.
ALL MY ANGLES ARE GOOD. THAT'S NOT THE ISSUE.
AND ON SOCIAL MEDIA, APPARENTLY.
WHAT DOES THAT EVEN MEAN?
IT MEANS YOU'RE FAMOUS.
I DON'T WANT TO BE FAMOUS! I'M A CREATURE OF THE NIGHT! I WORK IN SHADOW!

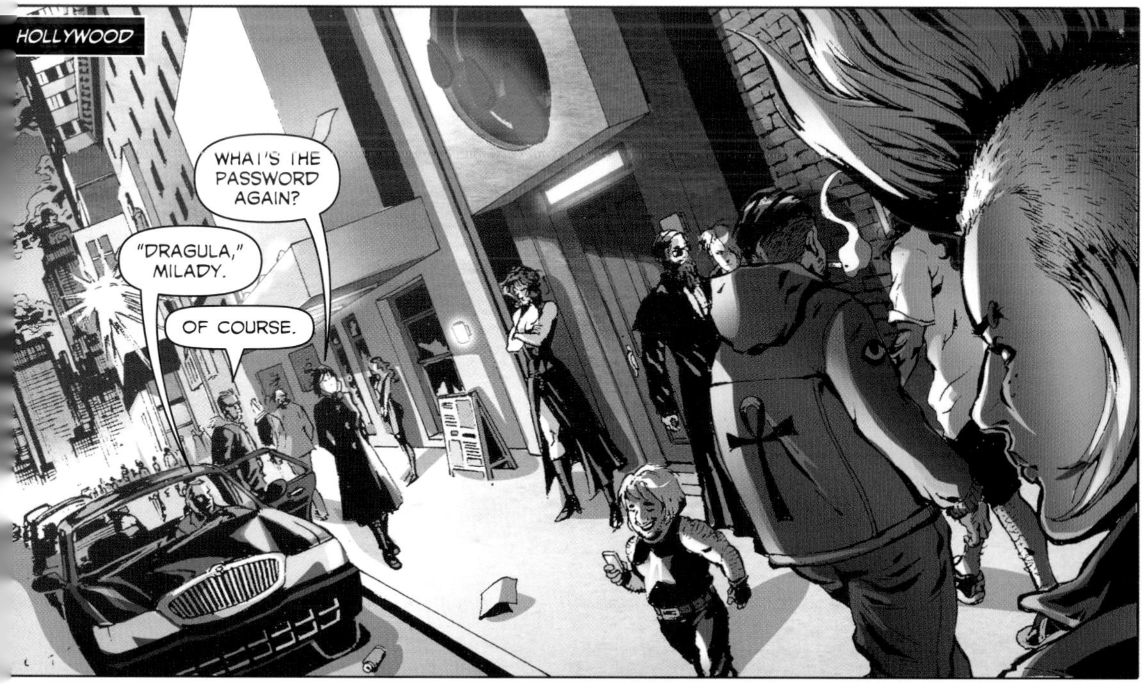
HOLLYWOOD
WHAT'S THE PASSWORD AGAIN?
"DRAGULA," MILADY.
OF COURSE.

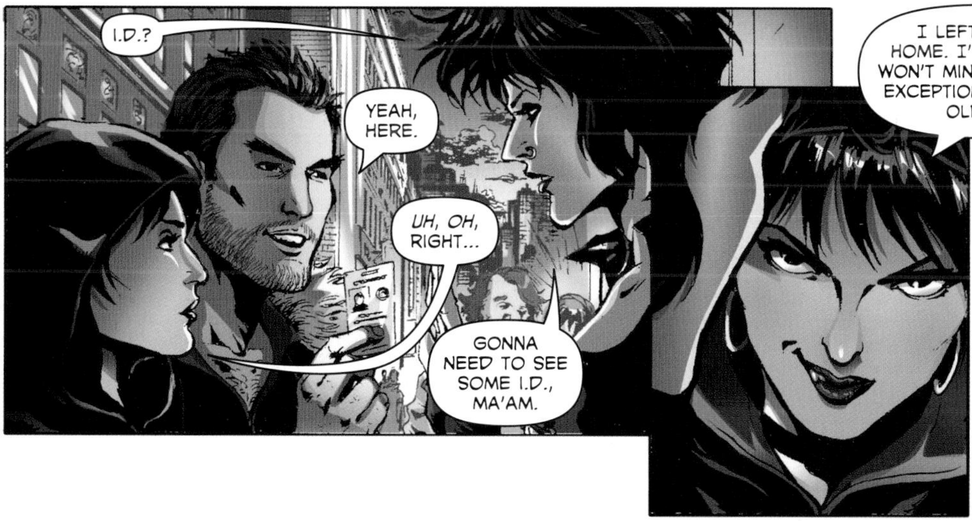
I.D.?
YEAH, HERE.
UH, OH, RIGHT...
GONNA NEED TO SEE SOME I.D., MA'AM.
I LEFT MINE AT HOME. I'M SURE YOU WON'T MIND MAKING AN EXCEPTION FOR LITTLE OLD ME?

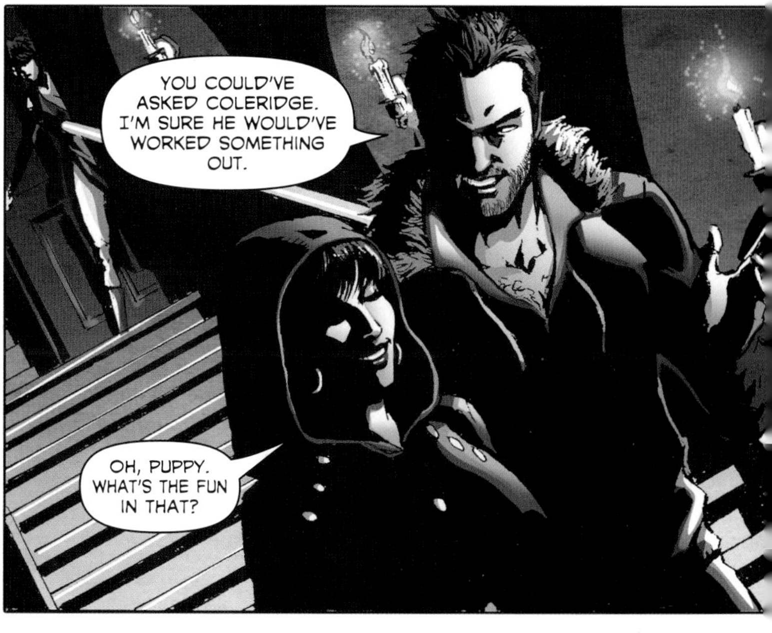
YOU COULD'VE ASKED COLERIDGE. I'M SURE HE WOULD'VE WORKED SOMETHING OUT.
OH, PUPPY. WHAT'S THE FUN IN THAT?

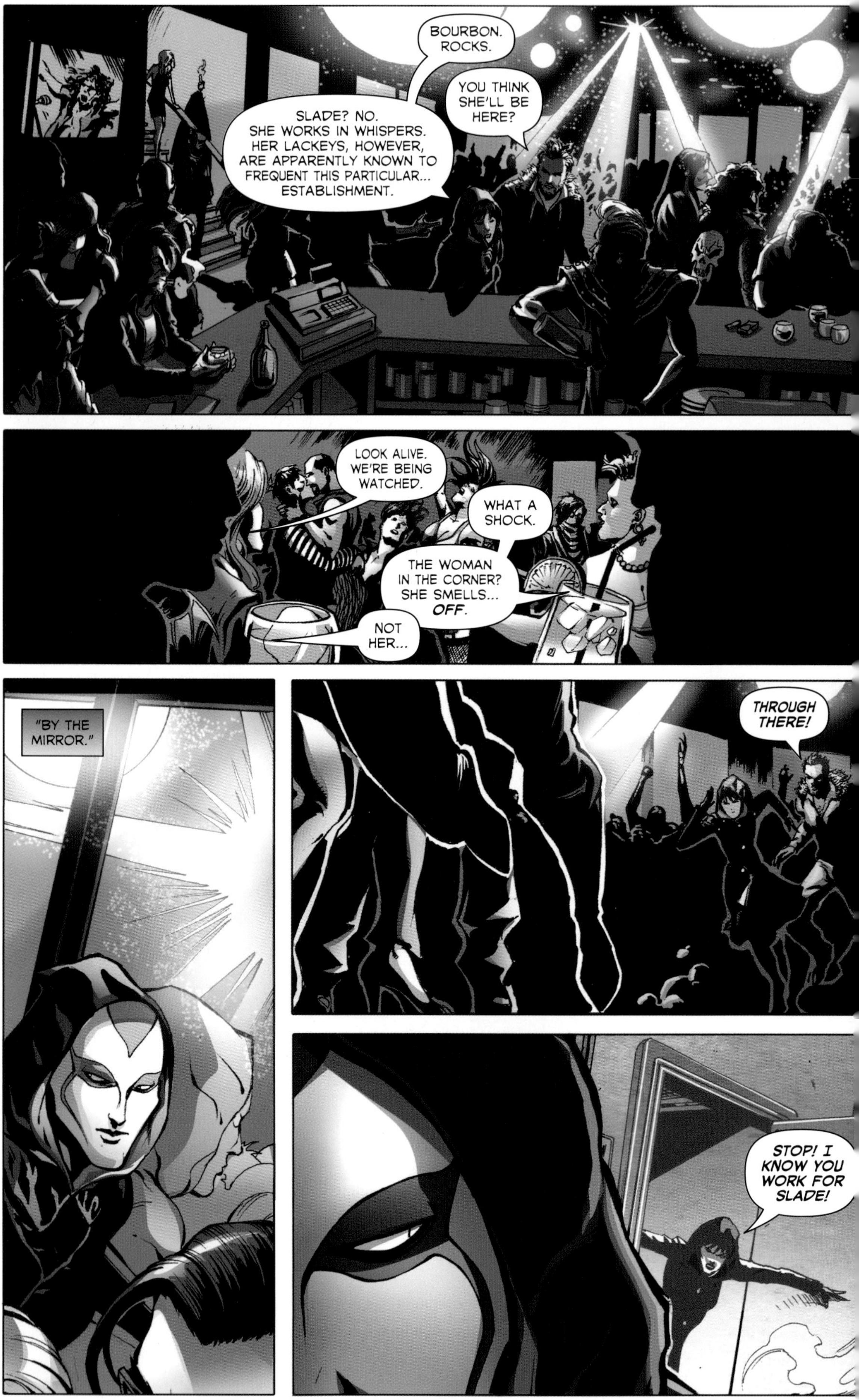
BOURBON. ROCKS.
SLADE? NO. SHE WORKS IN WHISPERS. HER LACKEYS, HOWEVER, ARE APPARENTLY KNOWN TO FREQUENT THIS PARTICULAR... ESTABLISHMENT.
YOU THINK SHE'LL BE HERE?
LOOK ALIVE. WE'RE BEING WATCHED.
WHAT A SHOCK.
THE WOMAN IN THE CORNER? SHE SMELLS... OFF.
NOT HER...
"BY THE MIRROR."
THROUGH THERE!
STOP! I KNOW YOU WORK FOR SLADE!

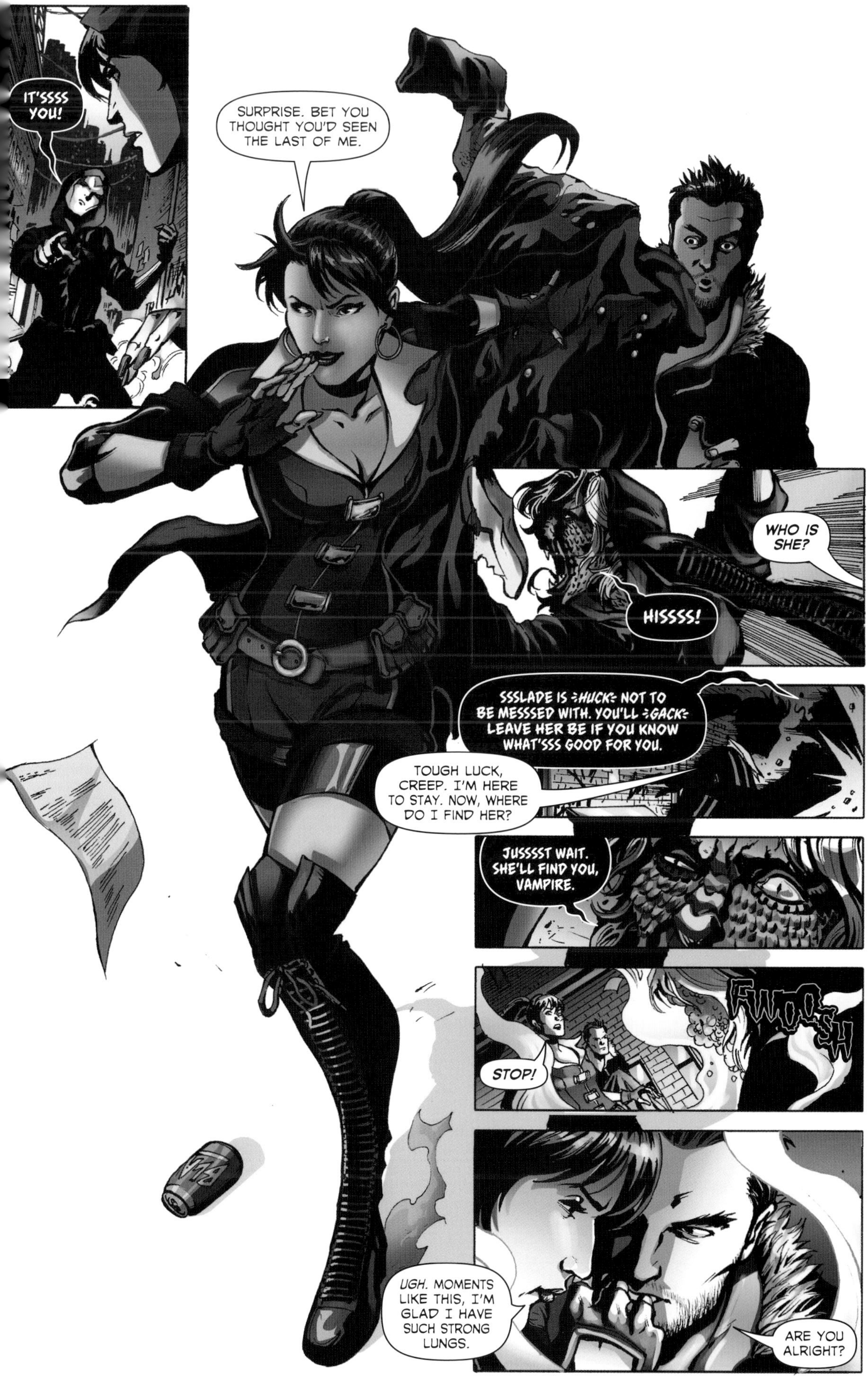
IT'SSSS YOU!
SURPRISE. BET YOU THOUGHT YOU'D SEEN THE LAST OF ME.
WHO IS SHE?
HISSSS!
SSSLADE IS =HUCK= NOT TO BE MESSSED WITH. YOU'LL =GACK= LEAVE HER BE IF YOU KNOW WHAT'SSS GOOD FOR YOU.
TOUGH LUCK, CREEP. I'M HERE TO STAY. NOW, WHERE DO I FIND HER?
JUSSSST WAIT. SHE'LL FIND YOU, VAMPIRE.
FWOOSH
STOP!
UGH. MOMENTS LIKE THIS, I'M GLAD I HAVE SUCH STRONG LUNGS.
ARE YOU ALRIGHT?

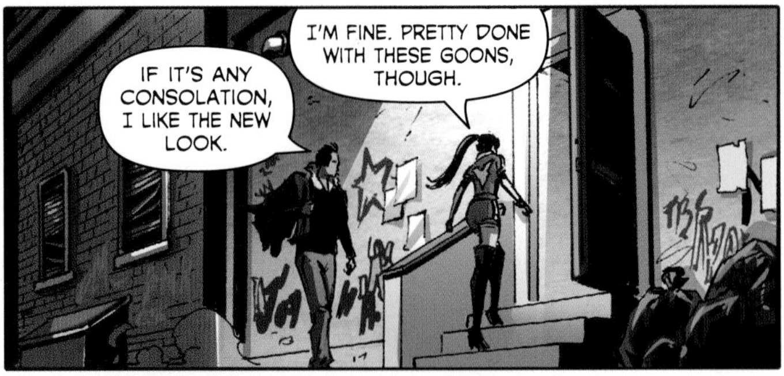
IF IT'S ANY CONSOLATION, I LIKE THE NEW LOOK.
I'M FINE. PRETTY DONE WITH THESE GOONS, THOUGH.

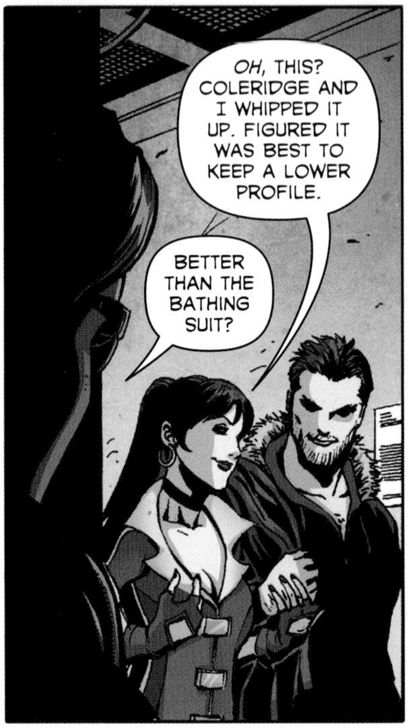
OH, THIS? COLERIDGE AND I WHIPPED IT UP. FIGURED IT WAS BEST TO KEEP A LOWER PROFILE.
BETTER THAN THE BATHING SUIT?

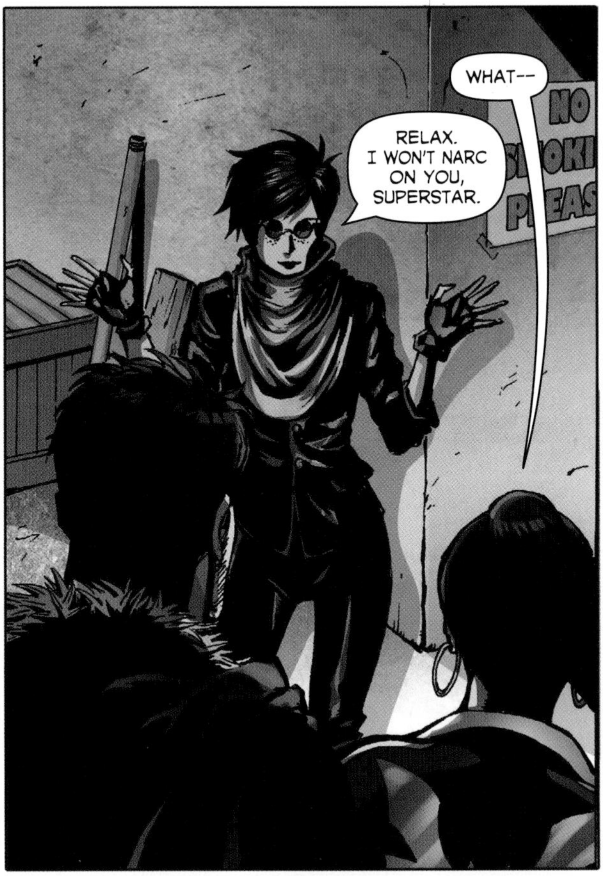
WHAT--
RELAX. I WON'T NARC ON YOU, SUPERSTAR.
NO

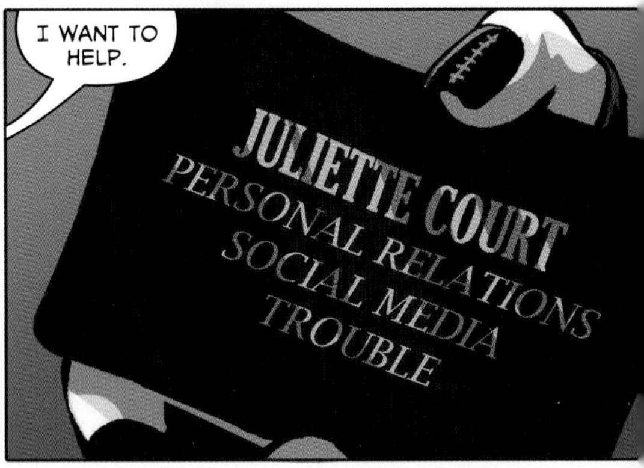
I WANT TO HELP.
JULIETTE COURT
PERSONAL RELATIONS
SOCIAL MEDIA
TROUBLE

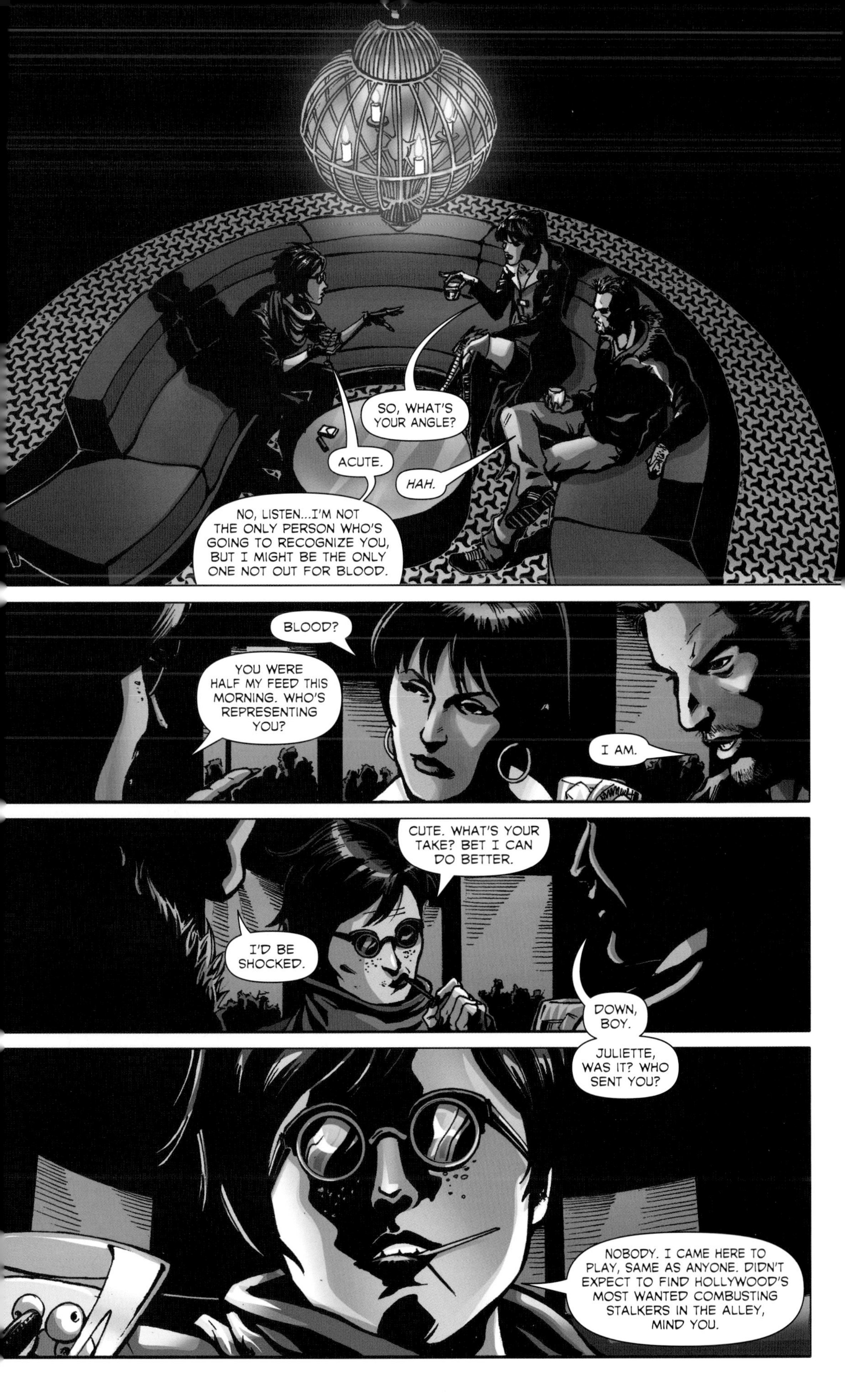
SO, WHAT'S YOUR ANGLE?
ACUTE.
HAH.
NO, LISTEN...I'M NOT THE ONLY PERSON WHO'S GOING TO RECOGNIZE YOU, BUT I MIGHT BE THE ONLY ONE NOT OUT FOR BLOOD.
BLOOD?
YOU WERE HALF MY FEED THIS MORNING. WHO'S REPRESENTING YOU?
I AM.
CUTE. WHAT'S YOUR TAKE? BET I CAN DO BETTER.
I'D BE SHOCKED.
DOWN, BOY.
JULIETTE, WAS IT? WHO SENT YOU?
NOBODY. I CAME HERE TO PLAY, SAME AS ANYONE. DIDN'T EXPECT TO FIND HOLLYWOOD'S MOST WANTED COMBUSTING STALKERS IN THE ALLEY, MIND YOU.

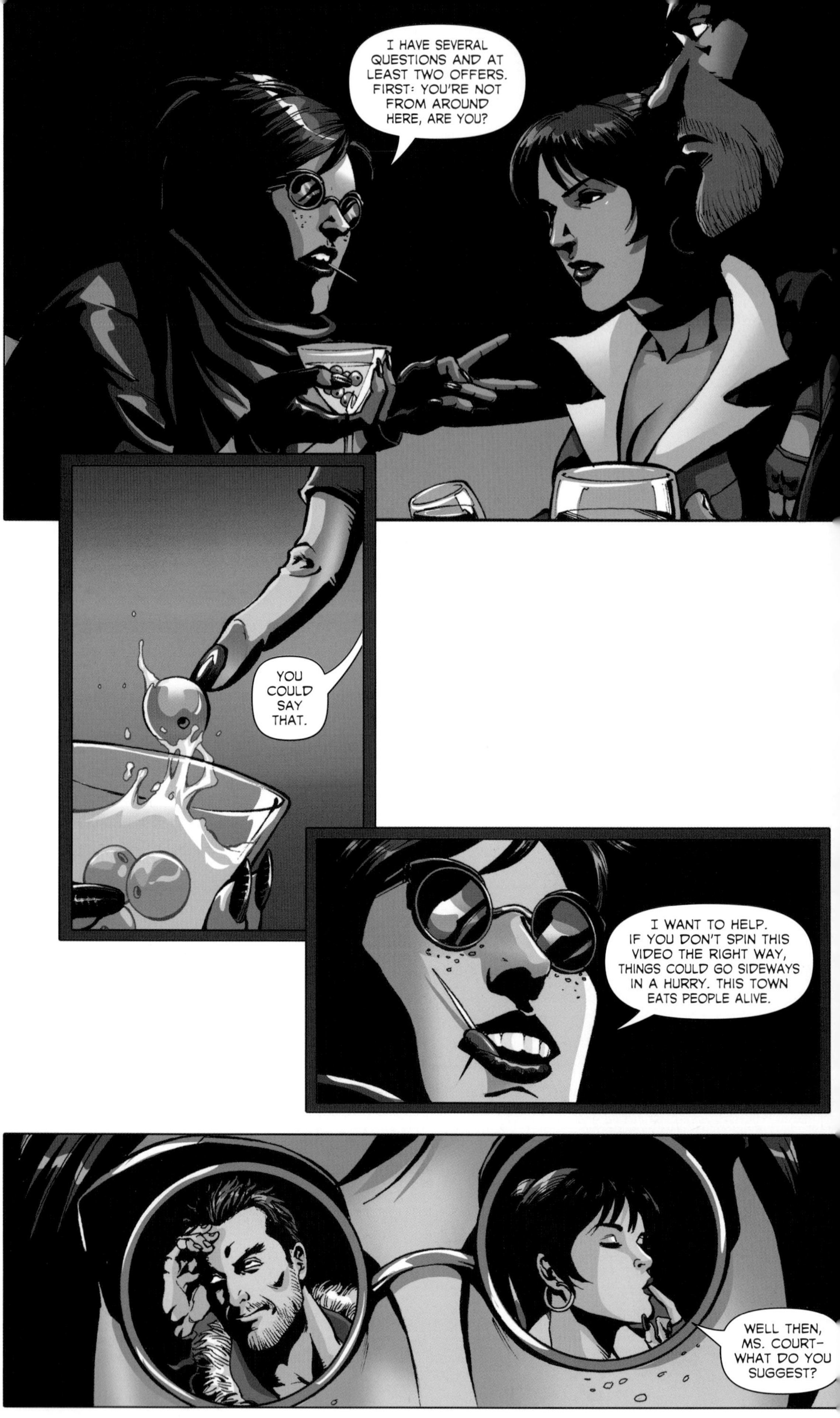
I HAVE SEVERAL QUESTIONS AND AT LEAST TWO OFFERS. FIRST: YOU'RE NOT FROM AROUND HERE, ARE YOU?
YOU COULD SAY THAT.
I WANT TO HELP. IF YOU DON'T SPIN THIS VIDEO THE RIGHT WAY, THINGS COULD GO SIDEWAYS IN A HURRY. THIS TOWN EATS PEOPLE ALIVE.
WELL THEN, MS. COURT– WHAT DO YOU SUGGEST?

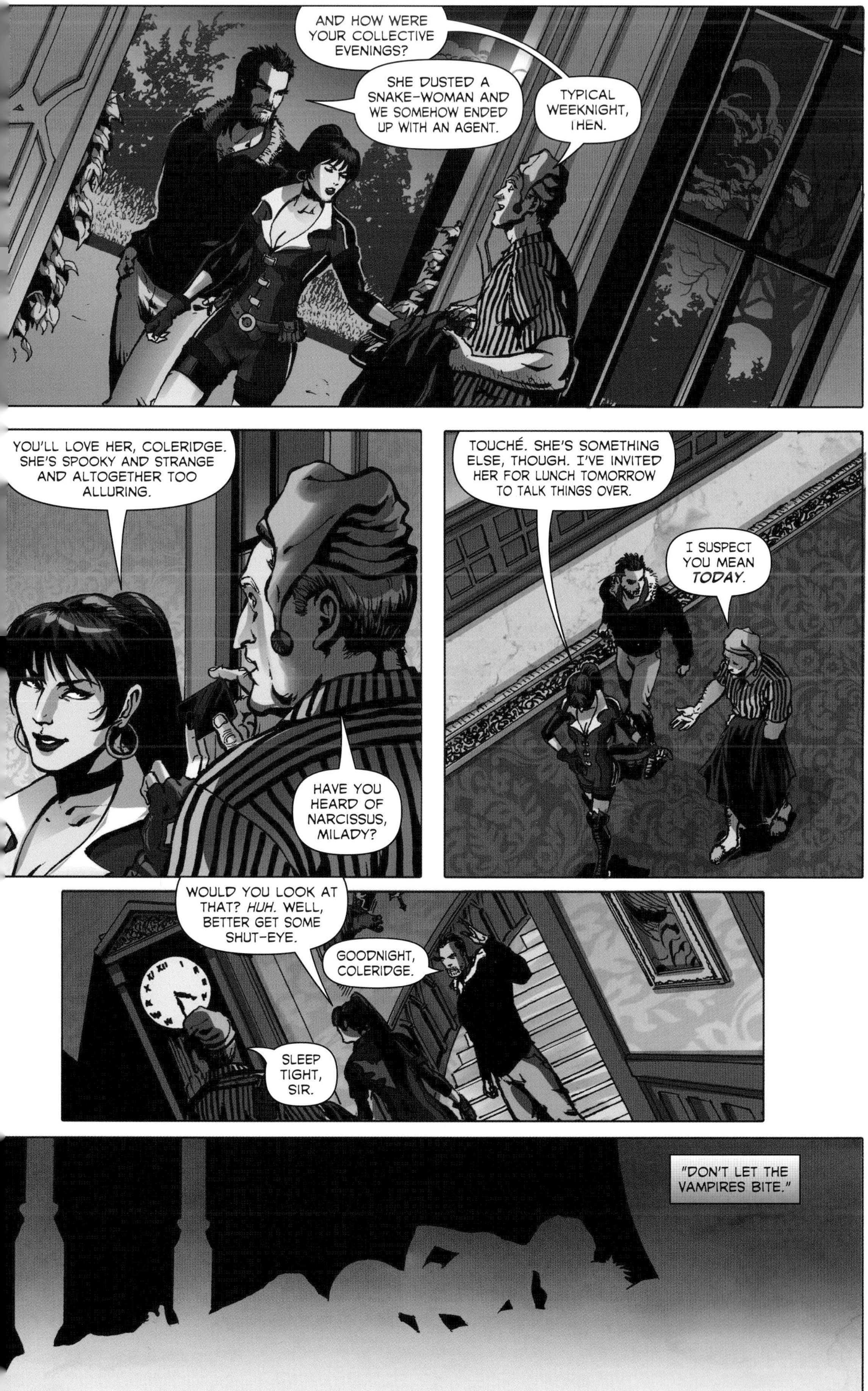
AND HOW WERE YOUR COLLECTIVE EVENINGS?
SHE DUSTED A SNAKE-WOMAN AND WE SOMEHOW ENDED UP WITH AN AGENT.
TYPICAL WEEKNIGHT, THEN.
YOU'LL LOVE HER, COLERIDGE. SHE'S SPOOKY AND STRANGE AND ALTOGETHER TOO ALLURING.
HAVE YOU HEARD OF NARCISSUS, MILADY?
TOUCHÉ. SHE'S SOMETHING ELSE, THOUGH. I'VE INVITED HER FOR LUNCH TOMORROW TO TALK THINGS OVER.
I SUSPECT YOU MEAN TODAY.
WOULD YOU LOOK AT THAT? HUH. WELL, BETTER GET SOME SHUT-EYE.
GOODNIGHT, COLERIDGE.
SLEEP TIGHT, SIR.
"DON'T LET THE VAMPIRES BITE."

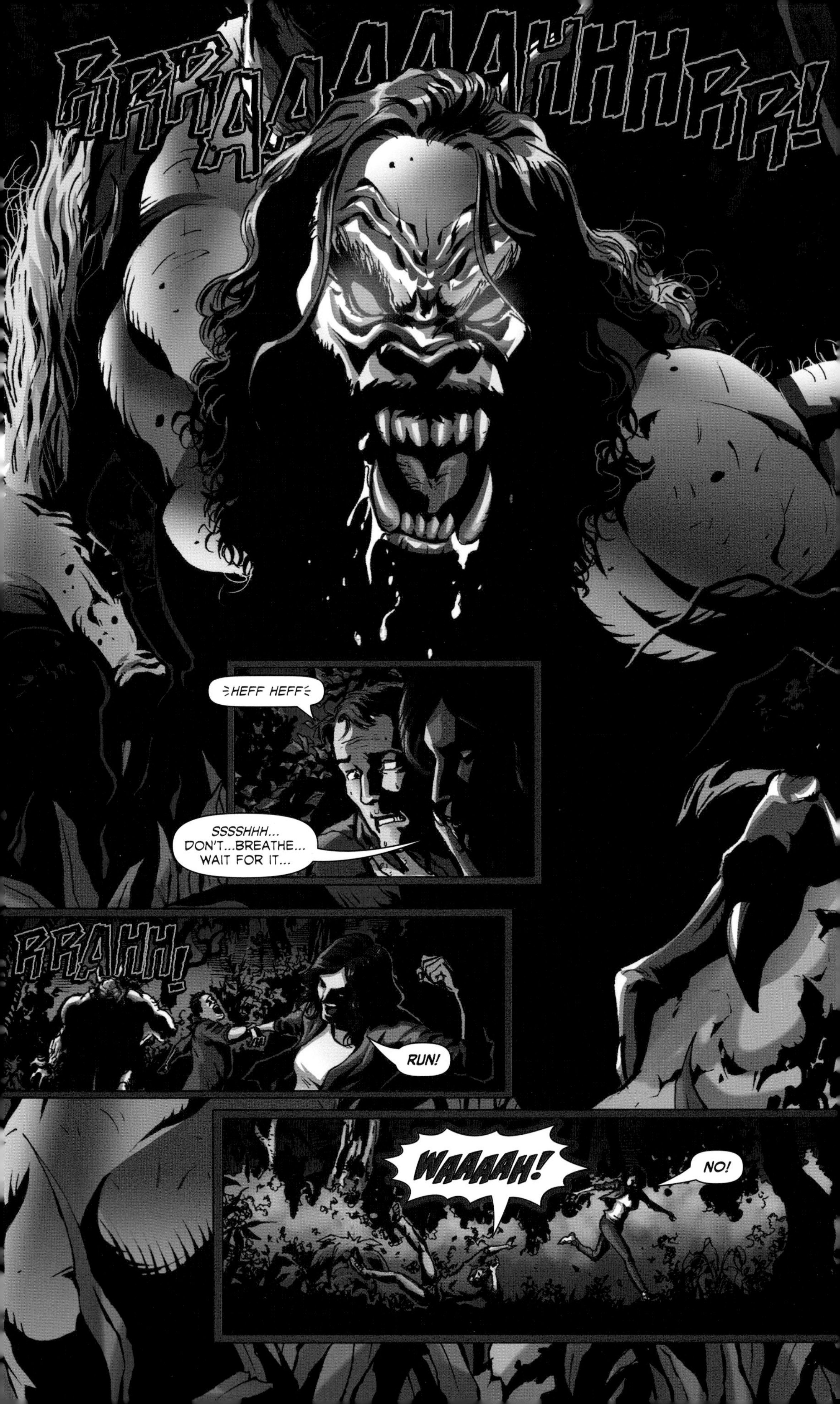
RRRAAAAAHHHRRR!
HEFF HEFF
SSSSHHH... DON'T...BREATHE... WAIT FOR IT...
RRAHH!
RUN!
WAAAAH!
NO!

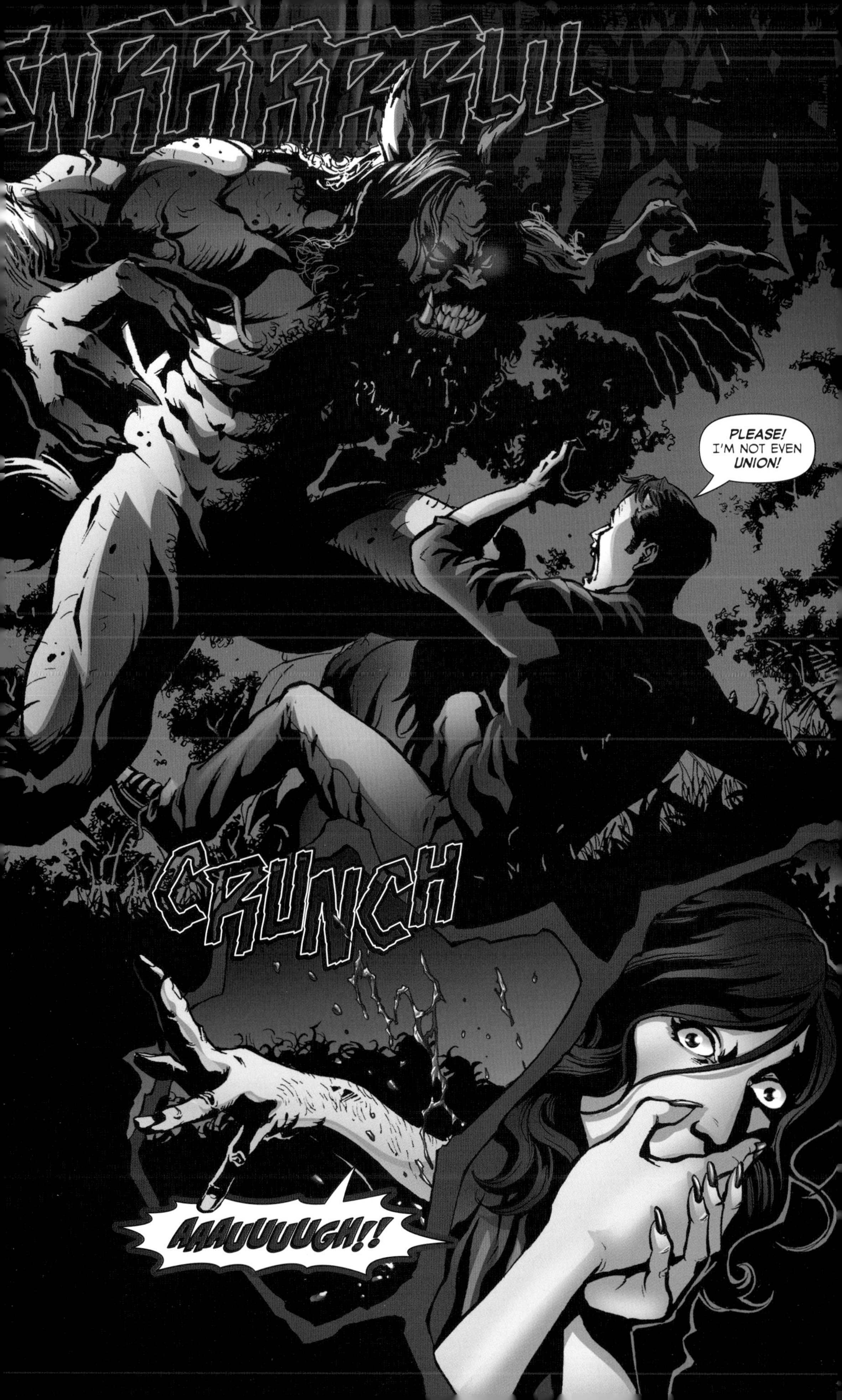
PLEASE! I'M NOT EVEN UNION!
CRUNCH
AAAUUUUUGH!!

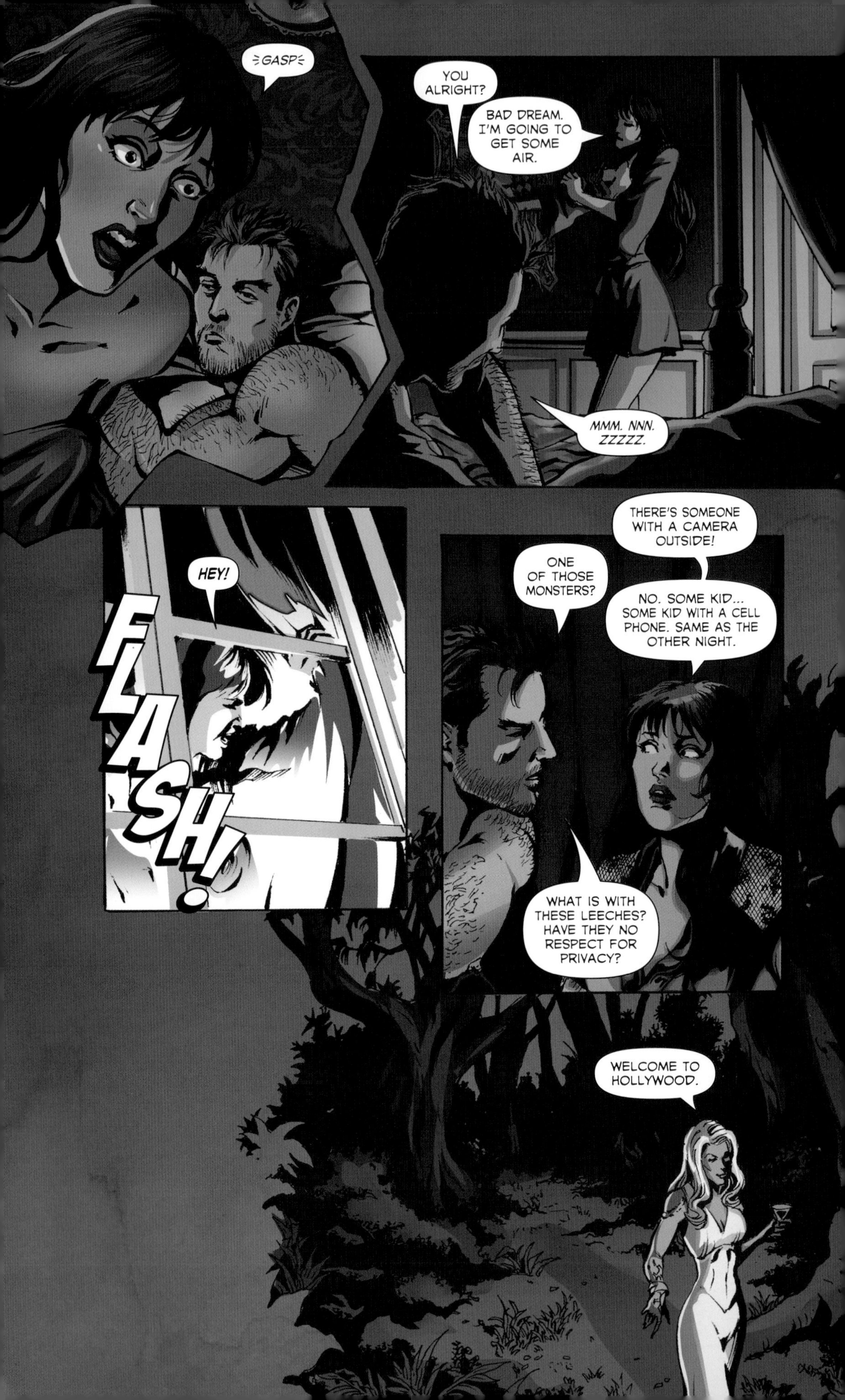

GASP
YOU ALRIGHT?
BAD DREAM. I'M GOING TO GET SOME AIR.
MMM. NNN. ZZZZZ.
HEY!
FLASH!
THERE'S SOMEONE WITH A CAMERA OUTSIDE!
ONE OF THOSE MONSTERS?
NO. SOME KID... SOME KID WITH A CELL PHONE. SAME AS THE OTHER NIGHT.
WHAT IS WITH THESE LEECHES? HAVE THEY NO RESPECT FOR PRIVACY?
WELCOME TO HOLLYWOOD.

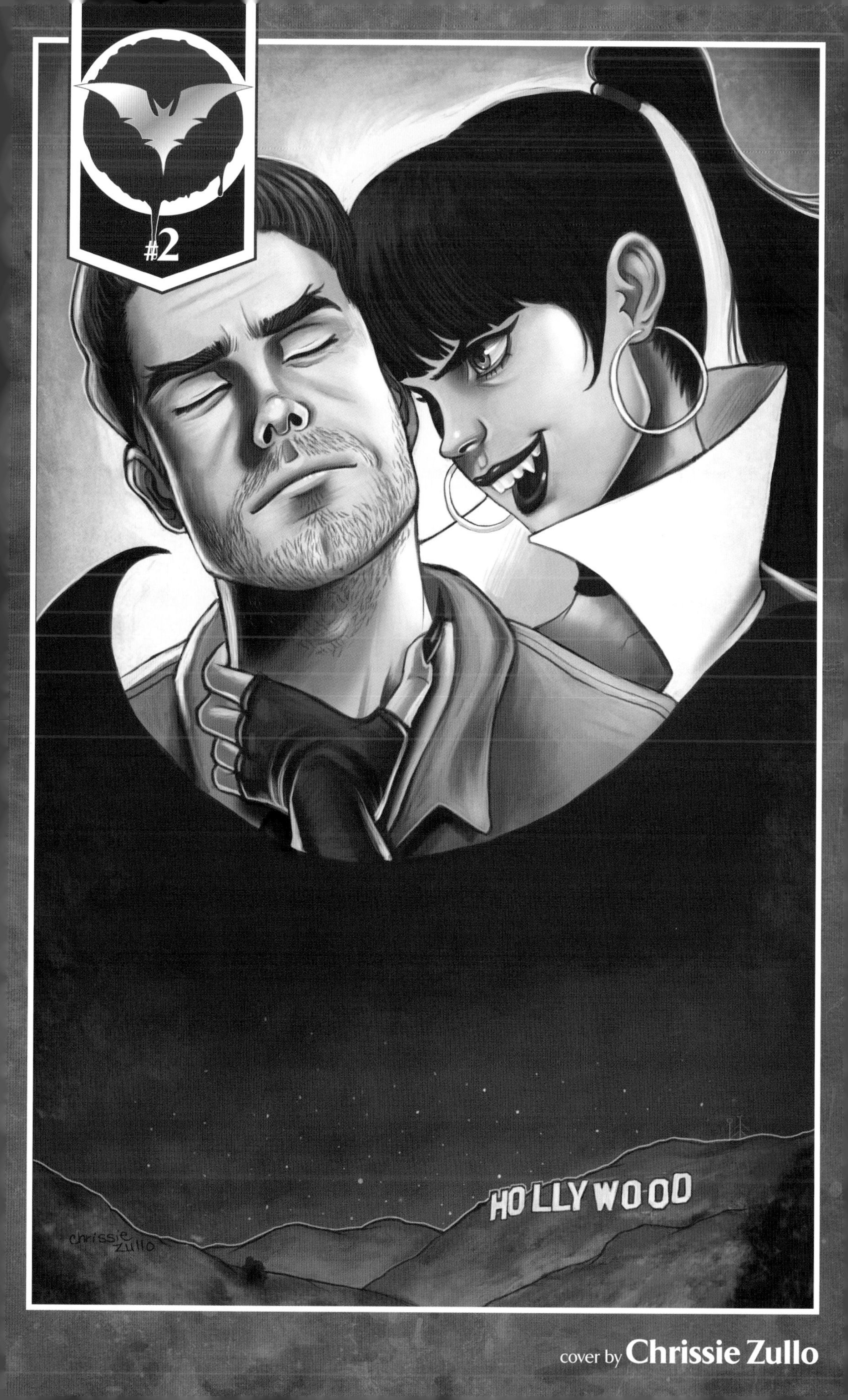
#2
HOLLYWOOD
chrissie zullo

cover by **Chrissie Zullo**

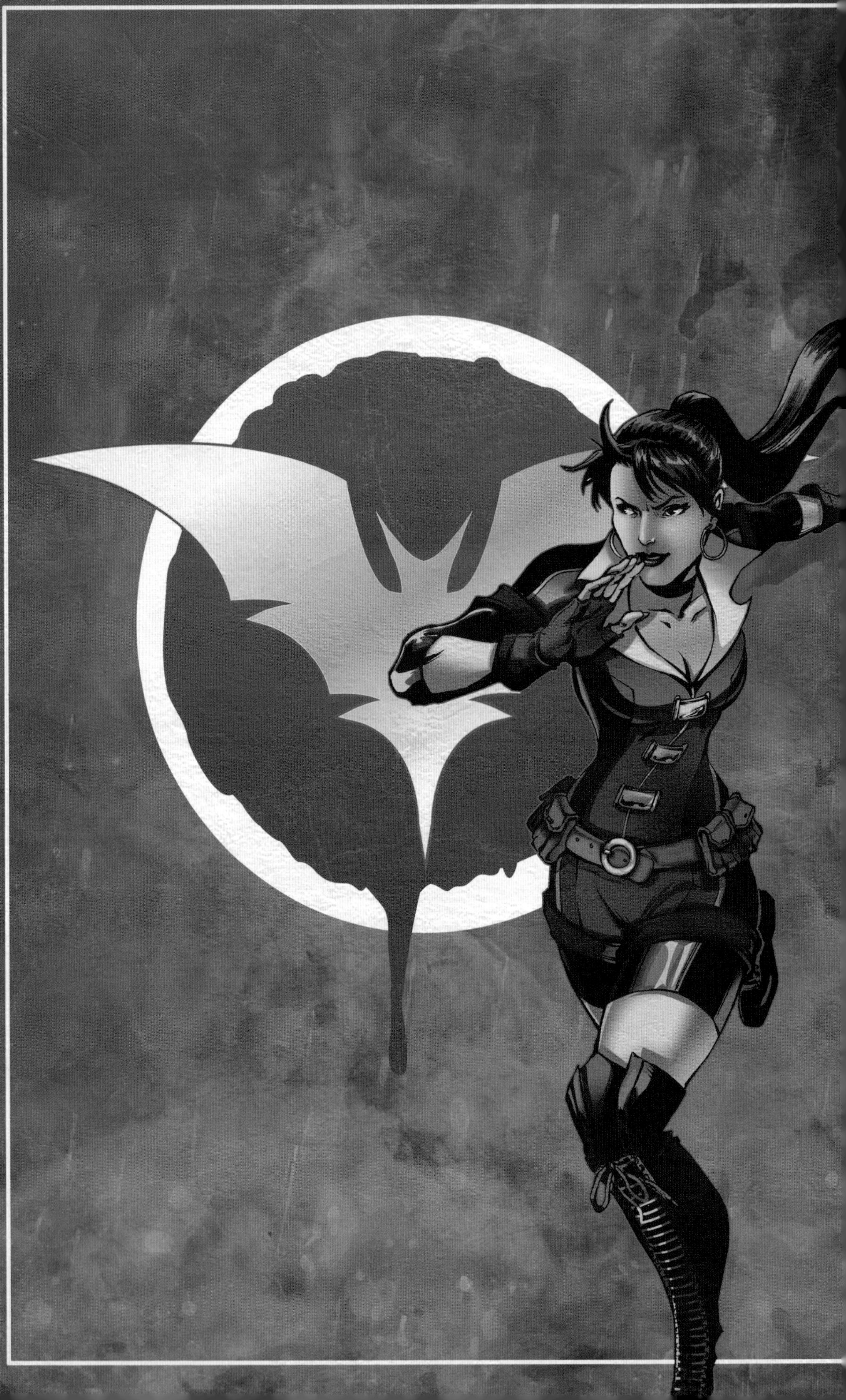

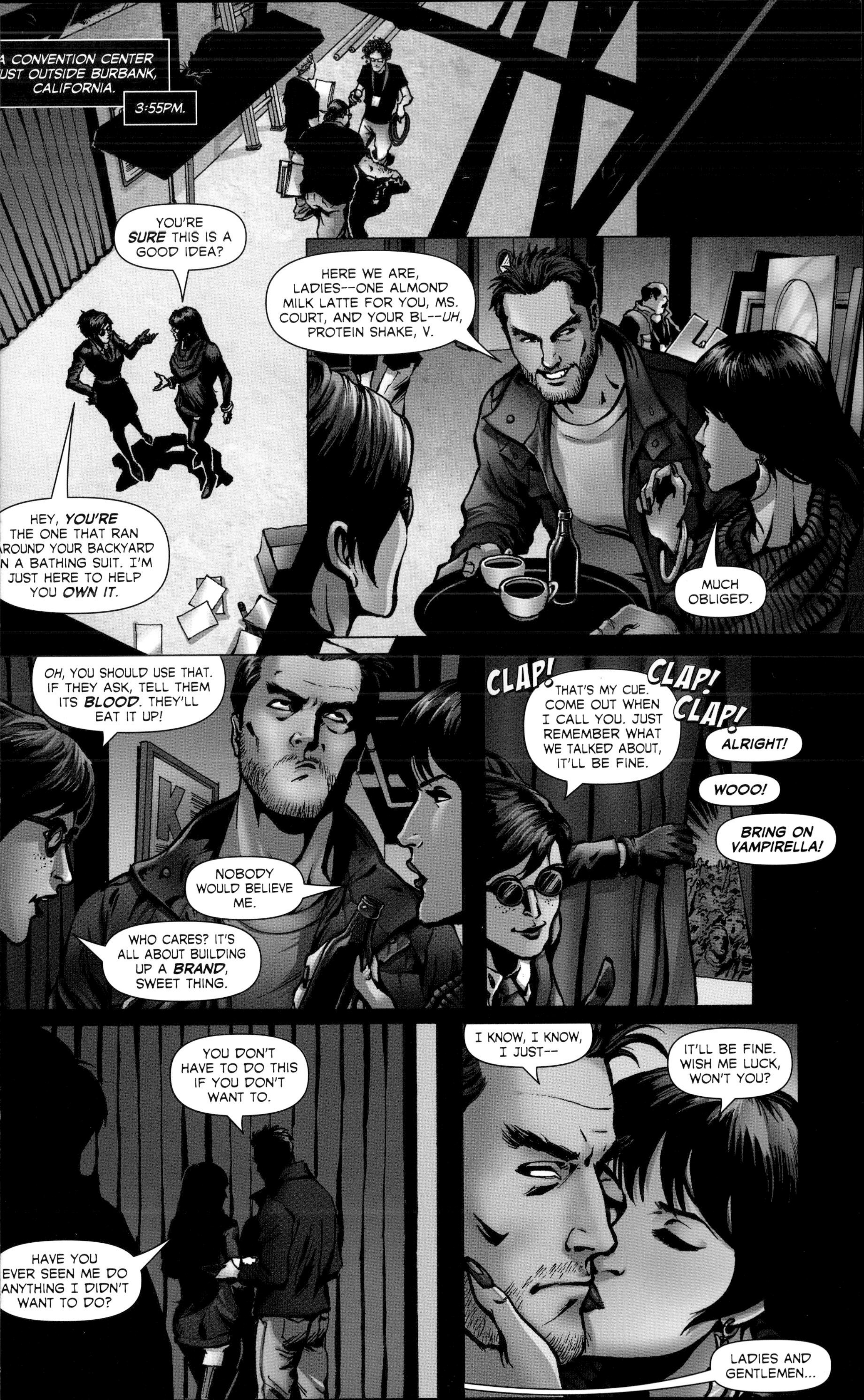
A CONVENTION CENTER
JUST OUTSIDE BURBANK, CALIFORNIA.
3:55PM.
YOU'RE SURE THIS IS A GOOD IDEA?
HEY, YOU'RE THE ONE THAT RAN AROUND YOUR BACKYARD IN A BATHING SUIT. I'M JUST HERE TO HELP YOU OWN IT.
HERE WE ARE, LADIES--ONE ALMOND MILK LATTE FOR YOU, MS. COURT, AND YOUR BL--UH, PROTEIN SHAKE, V.
MUCH OBLIGED.
OH, YOU SHOULD USE THAT. IF THEY ASK, TELL THEM ITS BLOOD. THEY'LL EAT IT UP!
NOBODY WOULD BELIEVE ME.
WHO CARES? IT'S ALL ABOUT BUILDING UP A BRAND, SWEET THING.
CLAP! CLAP! CLAP!
THAT'S MY CUE. COME OUT WHEN I CALL YOU. JUST REMEMBER WHAT WE TALKED ABOUT, IT'LL BE FINE.
ALRIGHT!
WOOO!
BRING ON VAMPIRELLA!
YOU DON'T HAVE TO DO THIS IF YOU DON'T WANT TO.
HAVE YOU EVER SEEN ME DO ANYTHING I DIDN'T WANT TO DO?
I KNOW, I KNOW, I JUST--
IT'LL BE FINE. WISH ME LUCK, WON'T YOU?
LADIES AND GENTLEMEN...

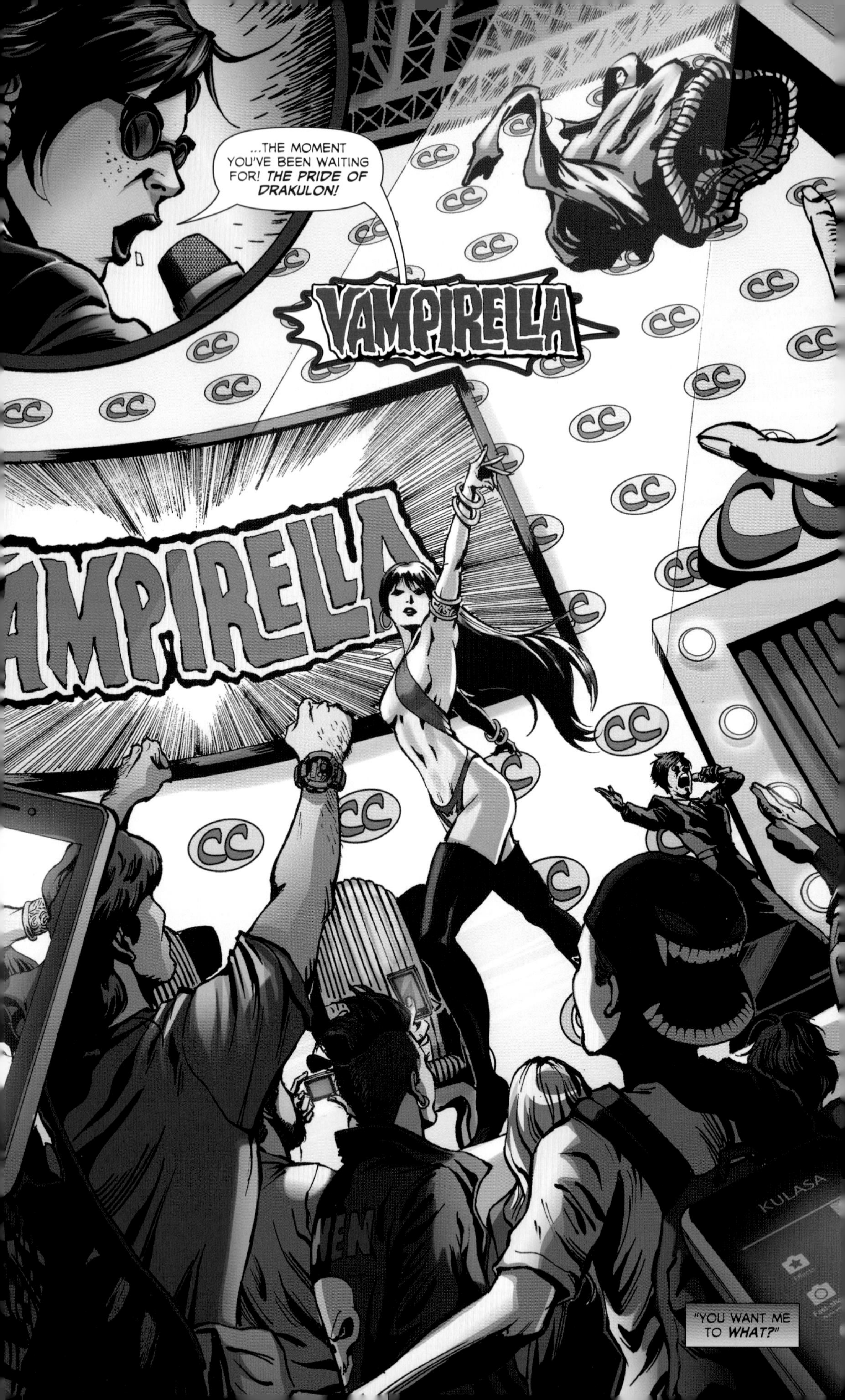
...THE MOMENT YOU'VE BEEN WAITING FOR! THE PRIDE OF DRAKULON!
VAMPIRELLA
VAMPIRELLA
KULASA
"YOU WANT ME TO WHAT?"

DO AN APPEARANCE. SHOW THE PEOPLE THAT YOU'RE REAL, TAKE A STAND BEFORE SOMEONE ON *DRAG RACE* DOES IT BETTER.

ONE CAN ONLY *DREAM*, MS. COURT.

COLERIDGE!

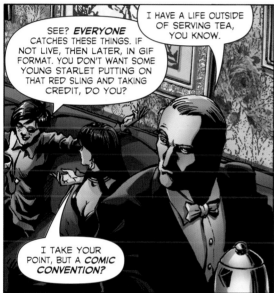

SEE? *EVERYONE* CATCHES THESE THINGS. IF NOT LIVE, THEN LATER, IN GIF FORMAT. YOU DON'T WANT SOME YOUNG STARLET PUTTING ON THAT RED SLING AND TAKING CREDIT, DO YOU?

I HAVE A LIFE OUTSIDE OF SERVING TEA, YOU KNOW.

I TAKE YOUR POINT, BUT A *COMIC CONVENTION?*

HAVE YOU BEEN TO ONE? COMICS ARE THE *LAST THING* THEY'RE ABOUT THESE DAYS. IT'S ALL MOVIES AND TV.

PLUS, IT'LL BE FULL OF NERDY FANBOYS, AND THEY'LL *ADORE* YOU.

NOT SURE HOW I FEEL ABOUT THAT.

YOU DON'T LIKE BEING ADORED?

I LIKE IT WHEN IT'S ON MY TERMS.

EXACTLY.

YOU GET OUT THERE AND TELL THE WORLD YOU'RE VAMPIRELLA, SIRED BY SOME UNHOLY BEAST--

DRAKULON.

YES! THAT'S FANTASTIC, SOME DARK DEMONIC CREATURE NAMED--

NO, THAT'S WHERE I'M FROM. *DRAKULON.*

PARDON?

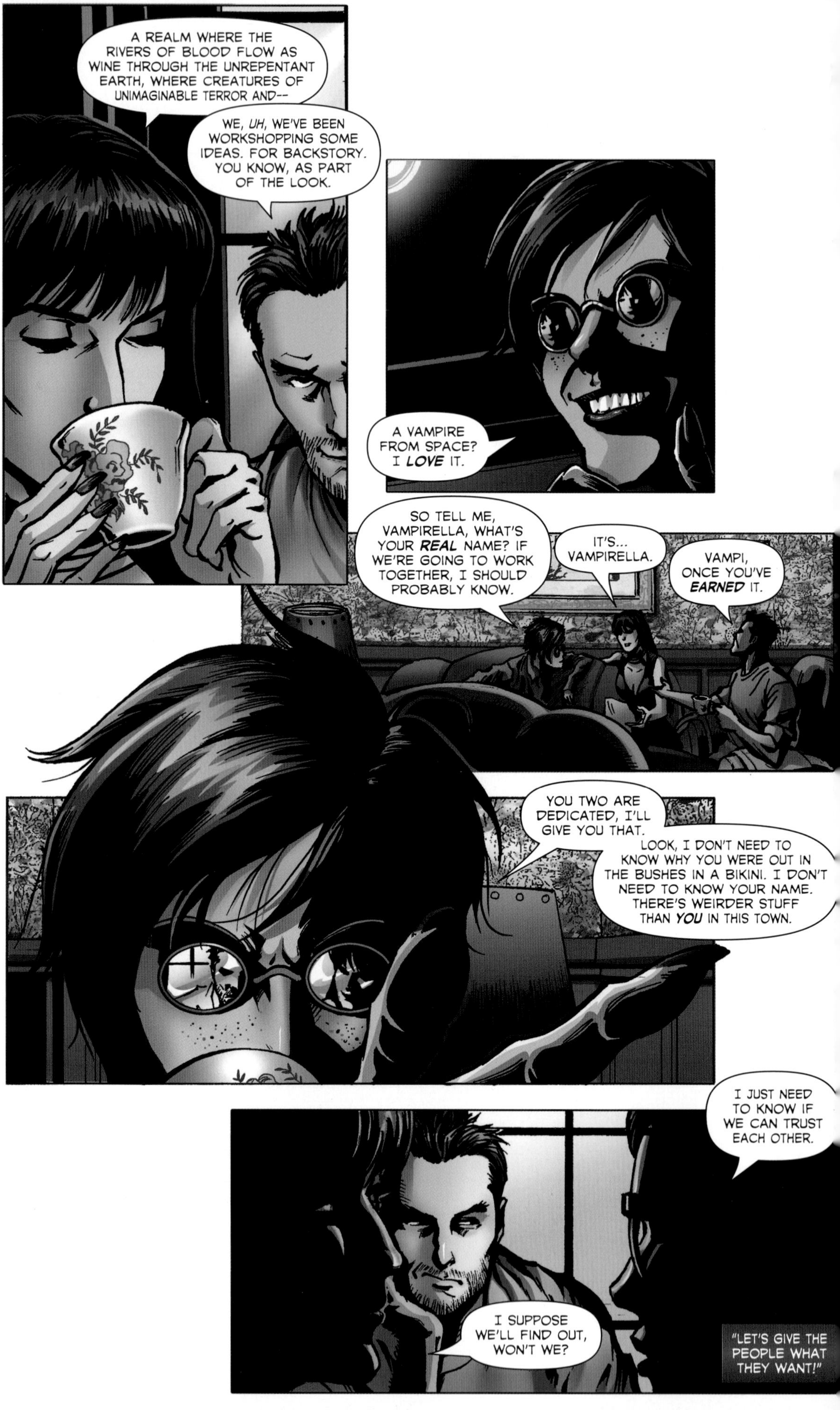
A REALM WHERE THE RIVERS OF BLOOD FLOW AS WINE THROUGH THE UNREPENTANT EARTH, WHERE CREATURES OF UNIMAGINABLE TERROR AND--
WE, *UH*, WE'VE BEEN WORKSHOPPING SOME IDEAS. FOR BACKSTORY. YOU KNOW, AS PART OF THE LOOK.
A VAMPIRE FROM SPACE? I ***LOVE*** IT.
SO TELL ME, VAMPIRELLA, WHAT'S YOUR ***REAL*** NAME? IF WE'RE GOING TO WORK TOGETHER, I SHOULD PROBABLY KNOW.
IT'S... VAMPIRELLA.
VAMPI, ONCE YOU'VE ***EARNED*** IT.
YOU TWO ARE DEDICATED, I'LL GIVE YOU THAT.
LOOK, I DON'T NEED TO KNOW WHY YOU WERE OUT IN THE BUSHES IN A BIKINI. I DON'T NEED TO KNOW YOUR NAME. THERE'S WEIRDER STUFF THAN ***YOU*** IN THIS TOWN.
I JUST NEED TO KNOW IF WE CAN TRUST EACH OTHER.
I SUPPOSE WE'LL FIND OUT, WON'T WE?
"LET'S GIVE THE PEOPLE WHAT THEY WANT!"

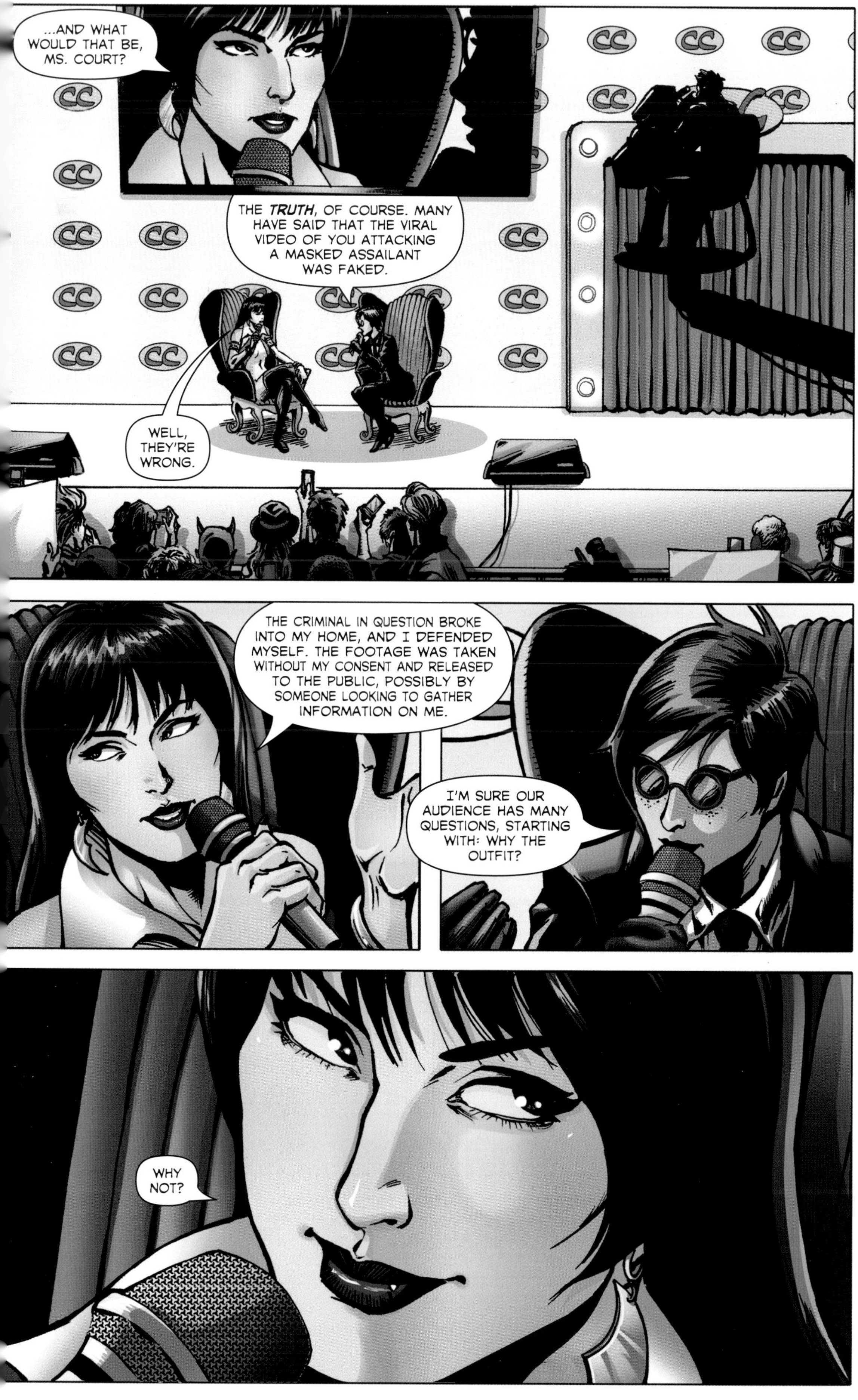
...AND WHAT WOULD THAT BE, MS. COURT?
THE TRUTH, OF COURSE. MANY HAVE SAID THAT THE VIRAL VIDEO OF YOU ATTACKING A MASKED ASSAILANT WAS FAKED.
WELL, THEY'RE WRONG.
THE CRIMINAL IN QUESTION BROKE INTO MY HOME, AND I DEFENDED MYSELF. THE FOOTAGE WAS TAKEN WITHOUT MY CONSENT AND RELEASED TO THE PUBLIC, POSSIBLY BY SOMEONE LOOKING TO GATHER INFORMATION ON ME.
I'M SURE OUR AUDIENCE HAS MANY QUESTIONS, STARTING WITH: WHY THE OUTFIT?
WHY NOT?

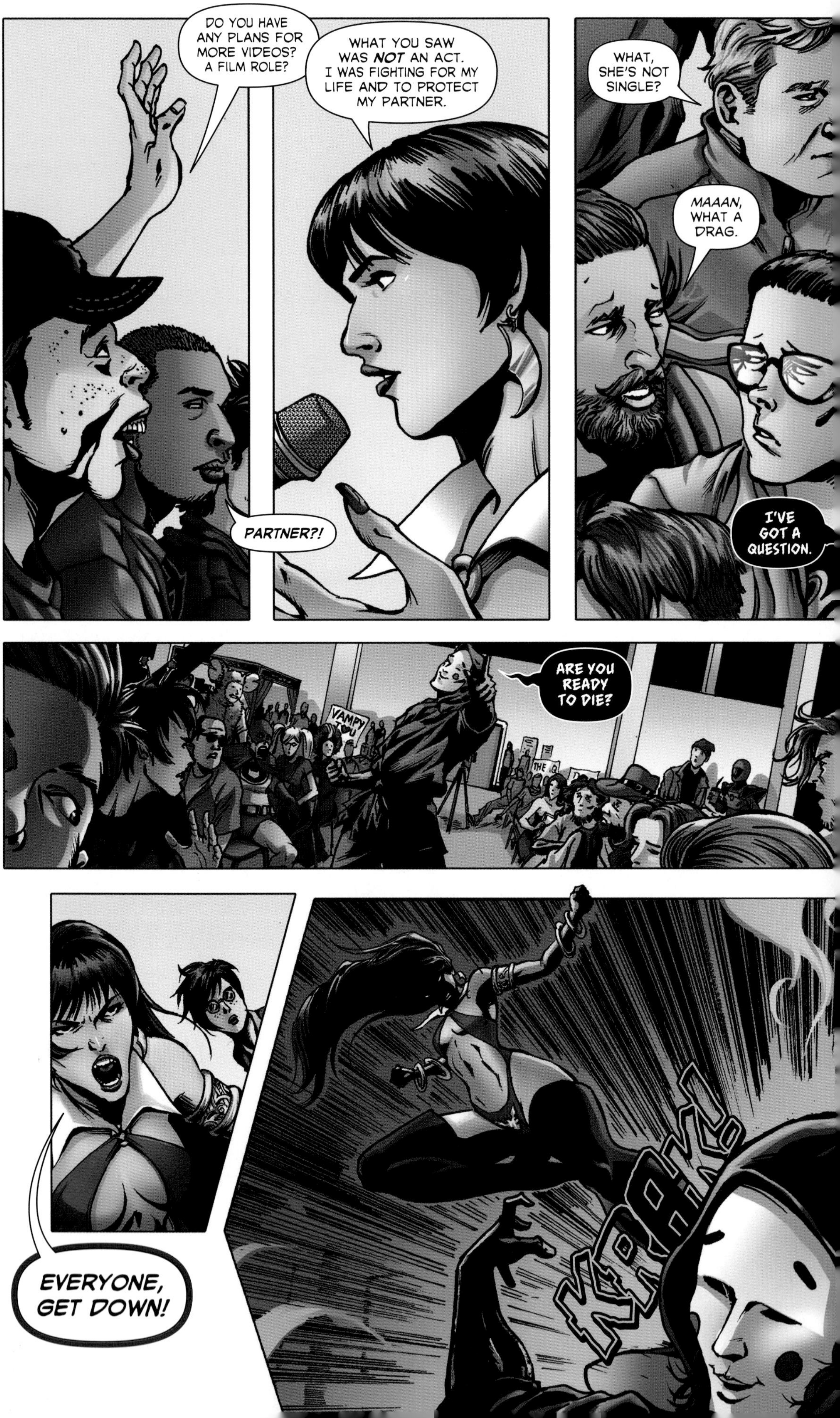
DO YOU HAVE ANY PLANS FOR MORE VIDEOS? A FILM ROLE?
WHAT YOU SAW WAS *NOT* AN ACT. I WAS FIGHTING FOR MY LIFE AND TO PROTECT MY PARTNER.
PARTNER?!
WHAT, SHE'S NOT SINGLE?
MAAAN, WHAT A DRAG.
I'VE GOT A QUESTION.
ARE YOU READY TO DIE?
VAMPY
THE
EVERYONE, GET DOWN!
KRAK

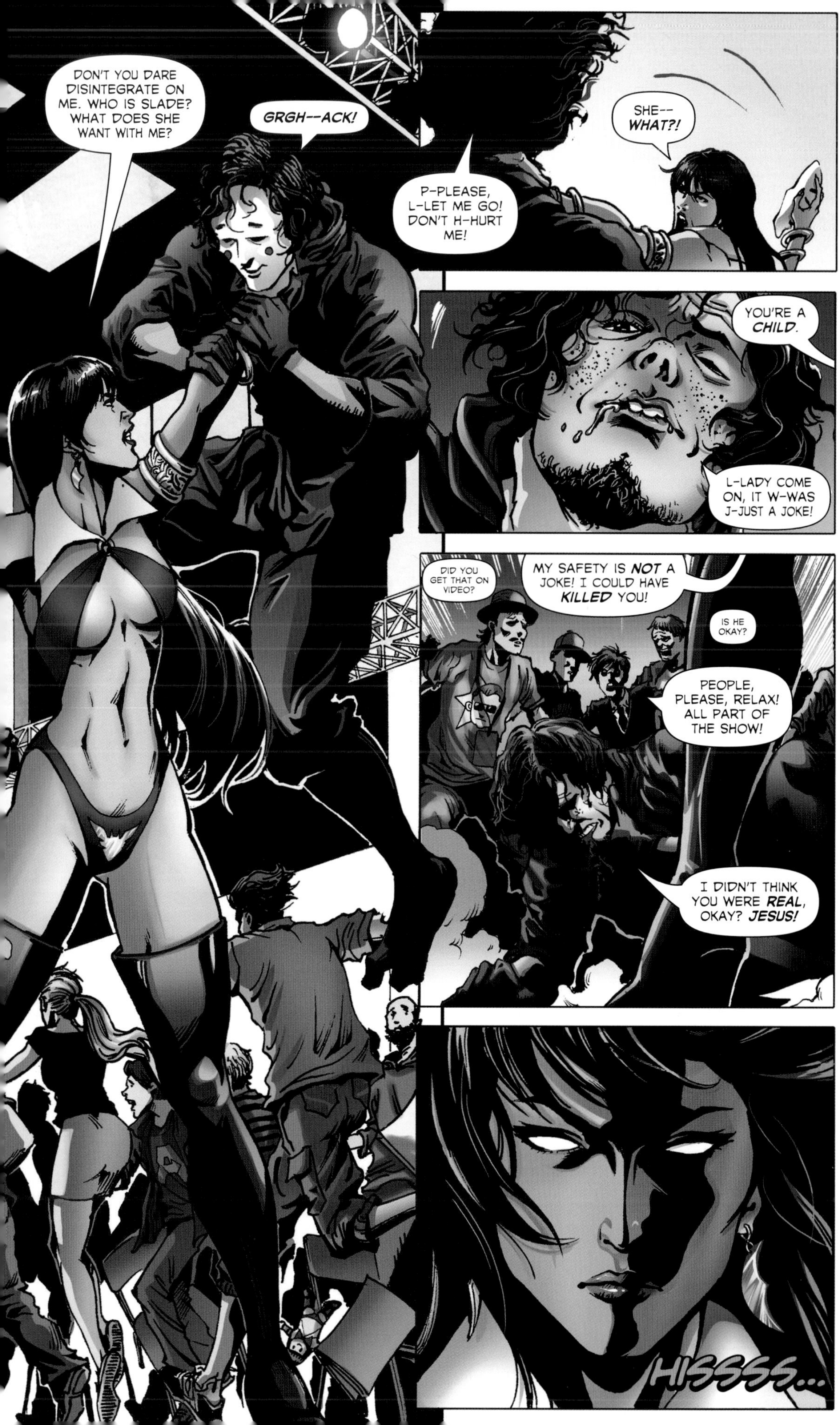
DON'T YOU DARE DISINTEGRATE ON ME. WHO IS SLADE? WHAT DOES SHE WANT WITH ME?
GRGH--ACK!
P-PLEASE, L-LET ME GO! DON'T H-HURT ME!
SHE-- WHAT?!
YOU'RE A CHILD.
L-LADY COME ON, IT W-WAS J-JUST A JOKE!
DID YOU GET THAT ON VIDEO?
MY SAFETY IS NOT A JOKE! I COULD HAVE KILLED YOU!
IS HE OKAY?
PEOPLE, PLEASE, RELAX! ALL PART OF THE SHOW!
I DIDN'T THINK YOU WERE REAL, OKAY? JESUS!
HISSSSS...

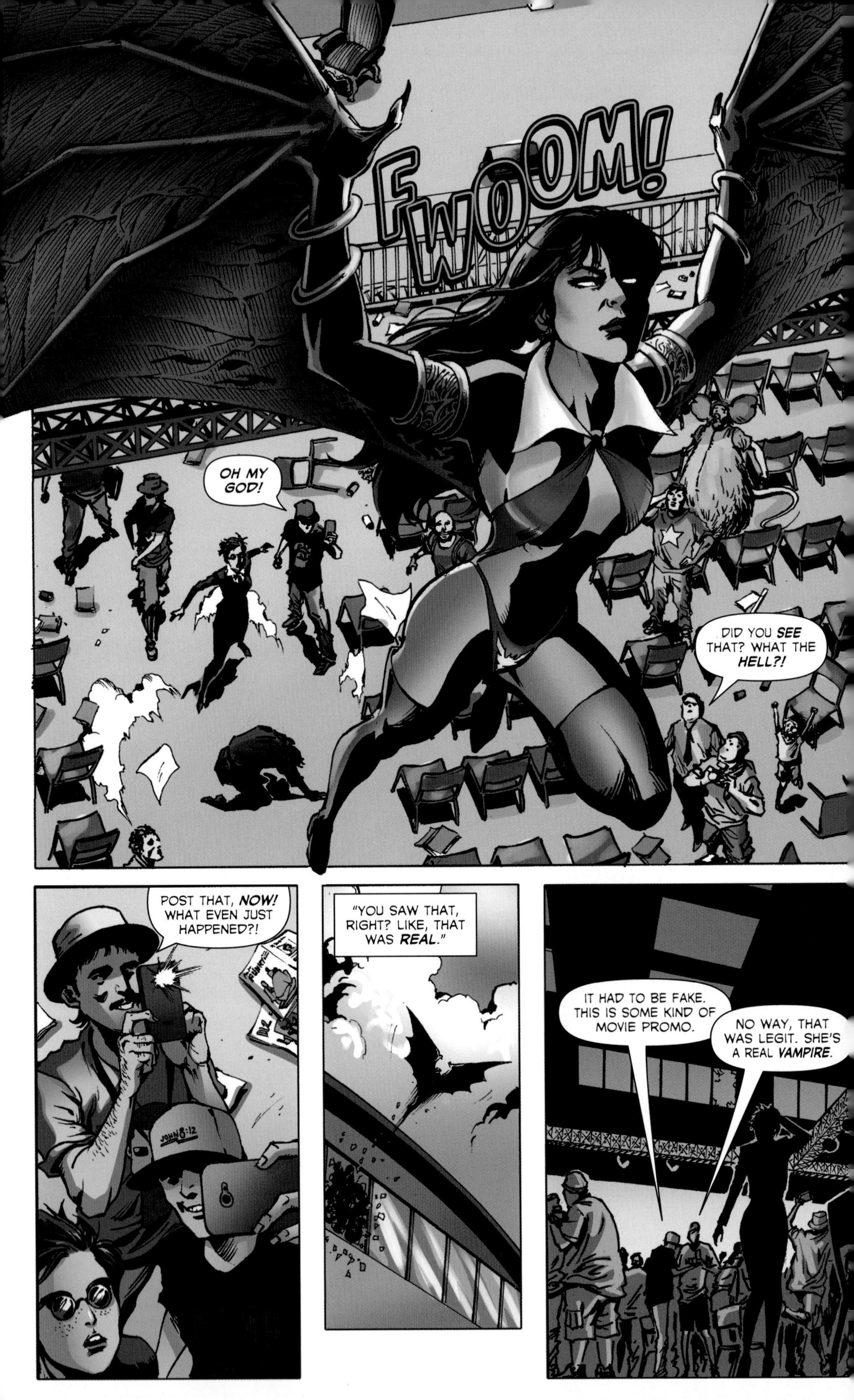
FWOOM!
OH MY GOD!
DID YOU SEE THAT? WHAT THE HELL?!
POST THAT, NOW! WHAT EVEN JUST HAPPENED?!
JOHN 8:12
"YOU SAW THAT, RIGHT? LIKE, THAT WAS REAL."
IT HAD TO BE FAKE. THIS IS SOME KIND OF MOVIE PROMO.
NO WAY, THAT WAS LEGIT. SHE'S A REAL VAMPIRE.

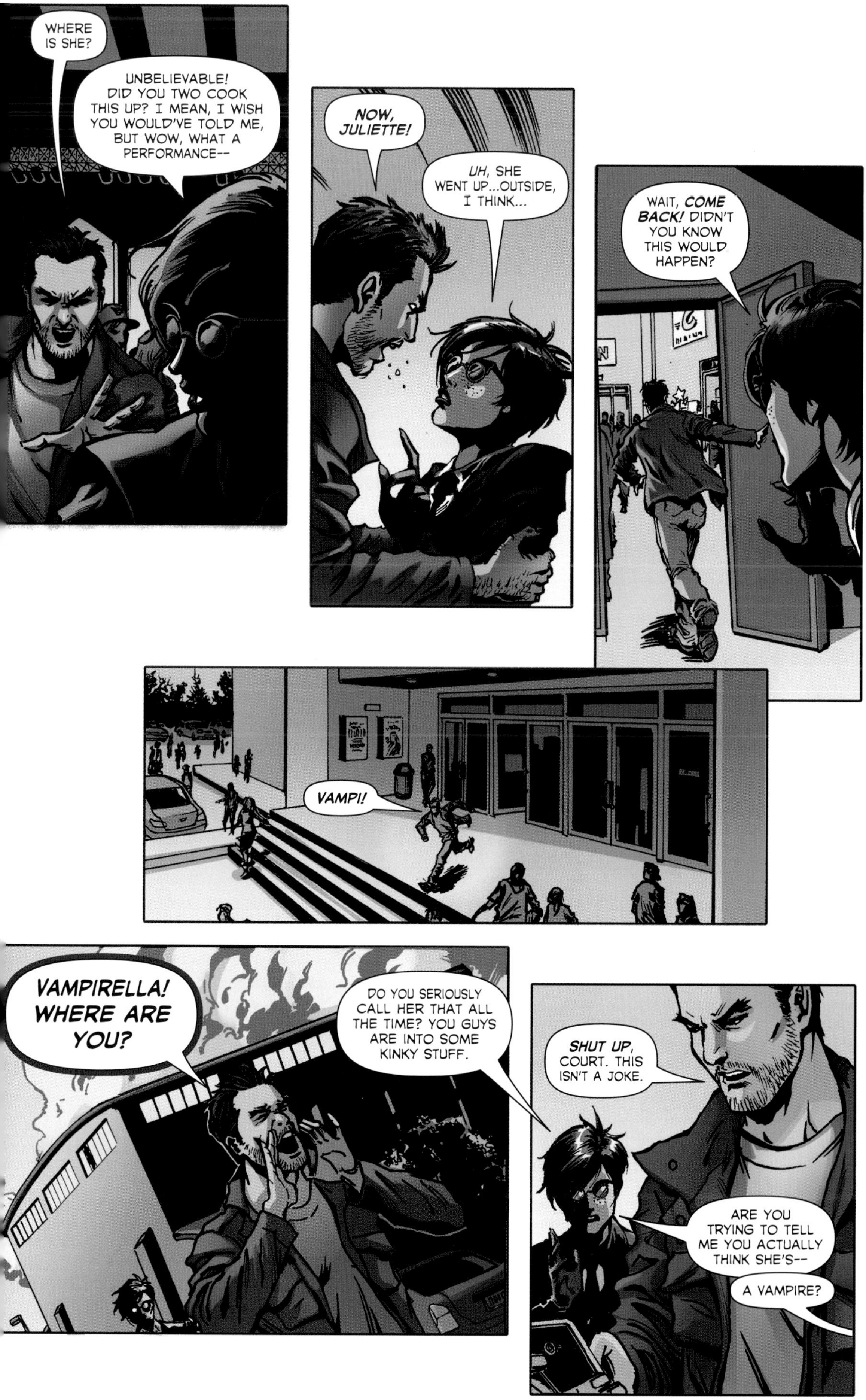
WHERE IS SHE?
UNBELIEVABLE! DID YOU TWO COOK THIS UP? I MEAN, I WISH YOU WOULD'VE TOLD ME, BUT WOW, WHAT A PERFORMANCE--
NOW, JULIETTE!
UH, SHE WENT UP...OUTSIDE, I THINK...
WAIT, COME BACK! DIDN'T YOU KNOW THIS WOULD HAPPEN?
VAMPI!
VAMPIRELLA! WHERE ARE YOU?
DO YOU SERIOUSLY CALL HER THAT ALL THE TIME? YOU GUYS ARE INTO SOME KINKY STUFF.
SHUT UP, COURT. THIS ISN'T A JOKE.
ARE YOU TRYING TO TELL ME YOU ACTUALLY THINK SHE'S--
A VAMPIRE?

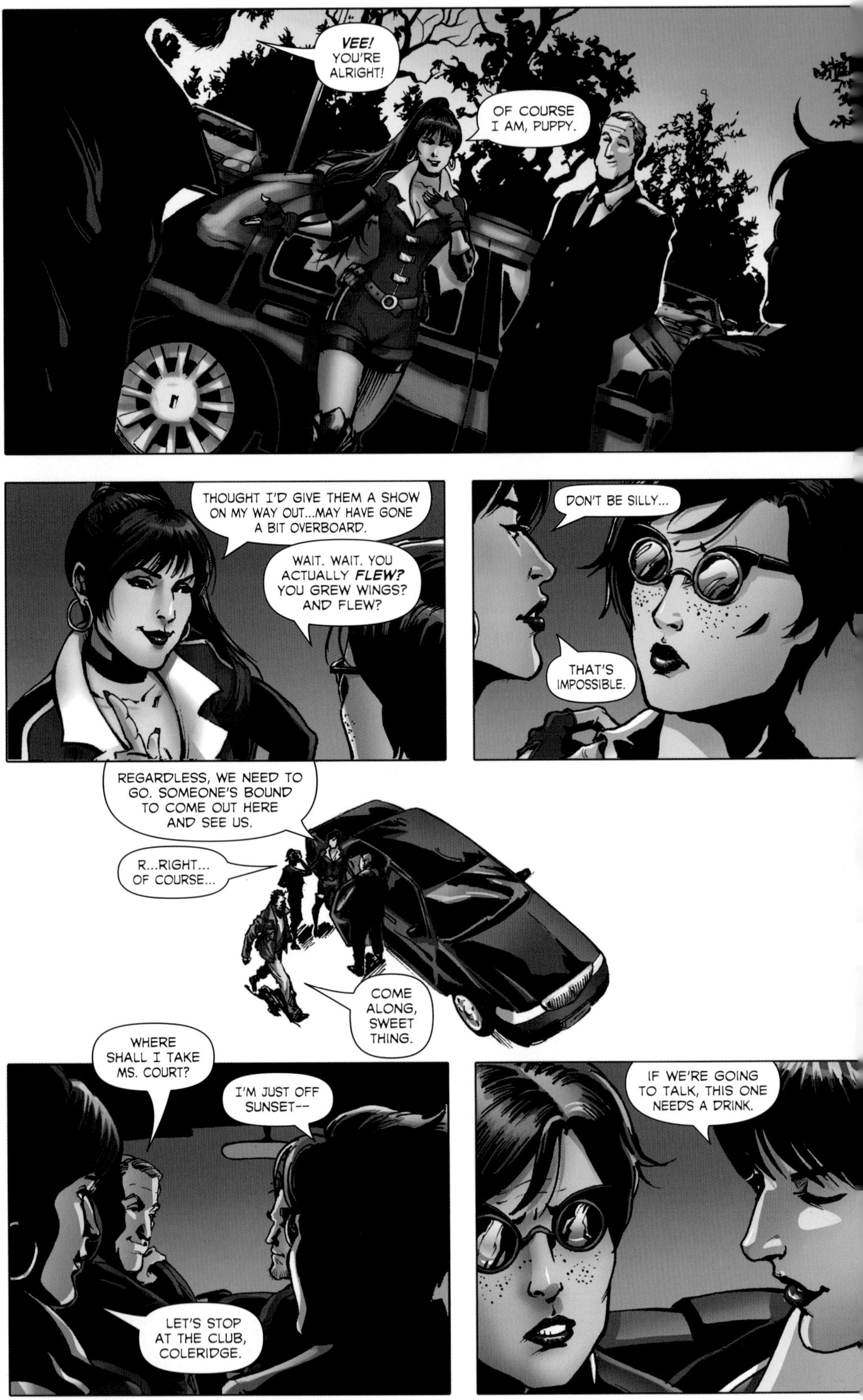
VEE! YOU'RE ALRIGHT!
OF COURSE I AM, PUPPY.
THOUGHT I'D GIVE THEM A SHOW ON MY WAY OUT...MAY HAVE GONE A BIT OVERBOARD.
WAIT. WAIT. YOU ACTUALLY FLEW? YOU GREW WINGS? AND FLEW?
DON'T BE SILLY...
THAT'S IMPOSSIBLE.
REGARDLESS, WE NEED TO GO. SOMEONE'S BOUND TO COME OUT HERE AND SEE US.
R...RIGHT... OF COURSE...
COME ALONG, SWEET THING.
WHERE SHALL I TAKE MS. COURT?
I'M JUST OFF SUNSET--
LET'S STOP AT THE CLUB, COLERIDGE.
IF WE'RE GOING TO TALK, THIS ONE NEEDS A DRINK.

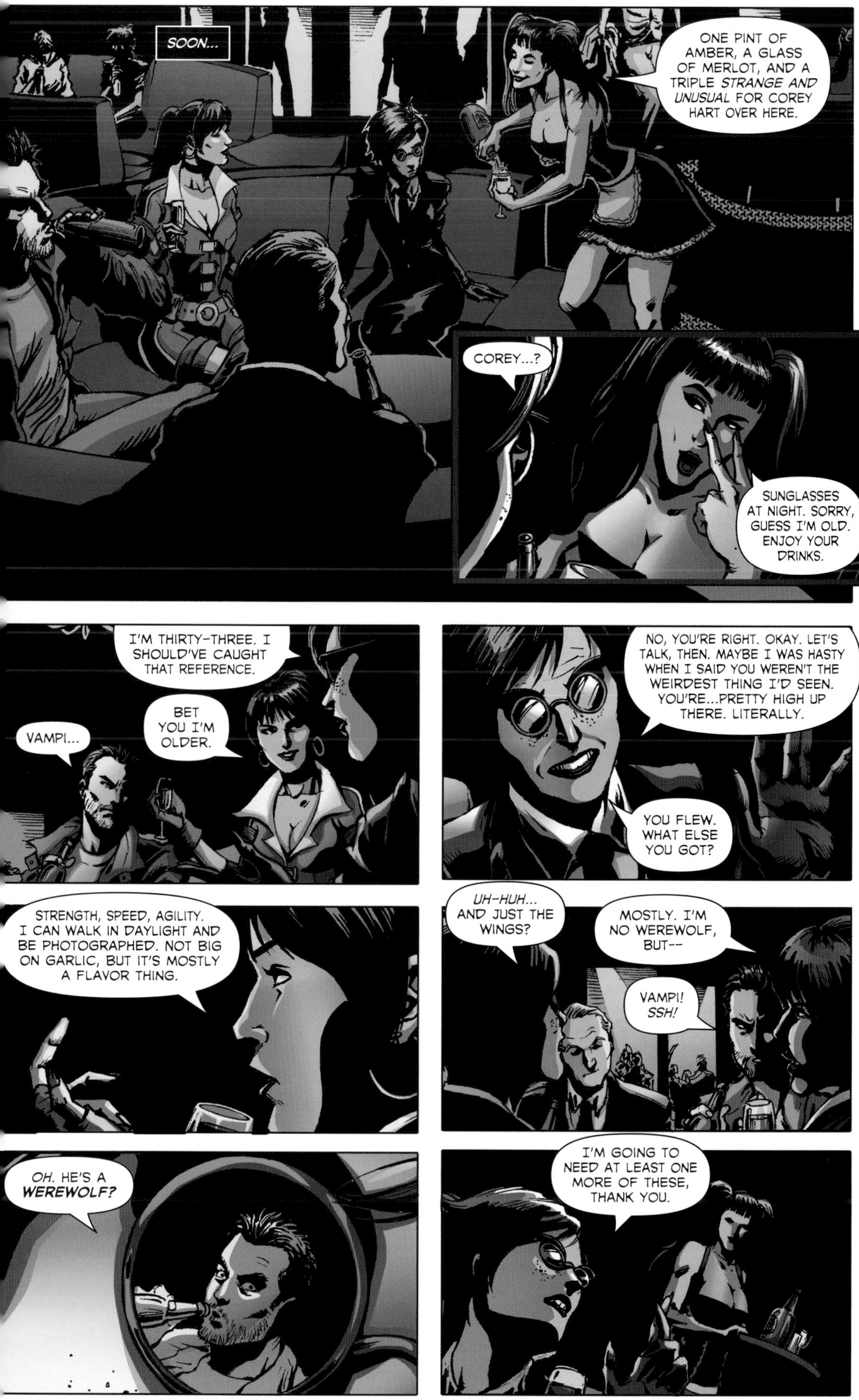
SOON...
ONE PINT OF AMBER, A GLASS OF MERLOT, AND A TRIPLE *STRANGE AND UNUSUAL* FOR COREY HART OVER HERE.
COREY...?
SUNGLASSES AT NIGHT. SORRY, GUESS I'M OLD. ENJOY YOUR DRINKS.
I'M THIRTY-THREE. I SHOULD'VE CAUGHT THAT REFERENCE.
VAMPI...
BET YOU I'M OLDER.
NO, YOU'RE RIGHT. OKAY. LET'S TALK, THEN. MAYBE I WAS HASTY WHEN I SAID YOU WEREN'T THE WEIRDEST THING I'D SEEN. YOU'RE...PRETTY HIGH UP THERE. LITERALLY.
YOU FLEW. WHAT ELSE YOU GOT?
STRENGTH, SPEED, AGILITY. I CAN WALK IN DAYLIGHT AND BE PHOTOGRAPHED. NOT BIG ON GARLIC, BUT IT'S MOSTLY A FLAVOR THING.
UH-HUH... AND JUST THE WINGS?
MOSTLY. I'M NO WEREWOLF, BUT--
VAMPI! *SSH!*
OH. HE'S A ***WEREWOLF?***
I'M GOING TO NEED AT LEAST ONE MORE OF THESE, THANK YOU.

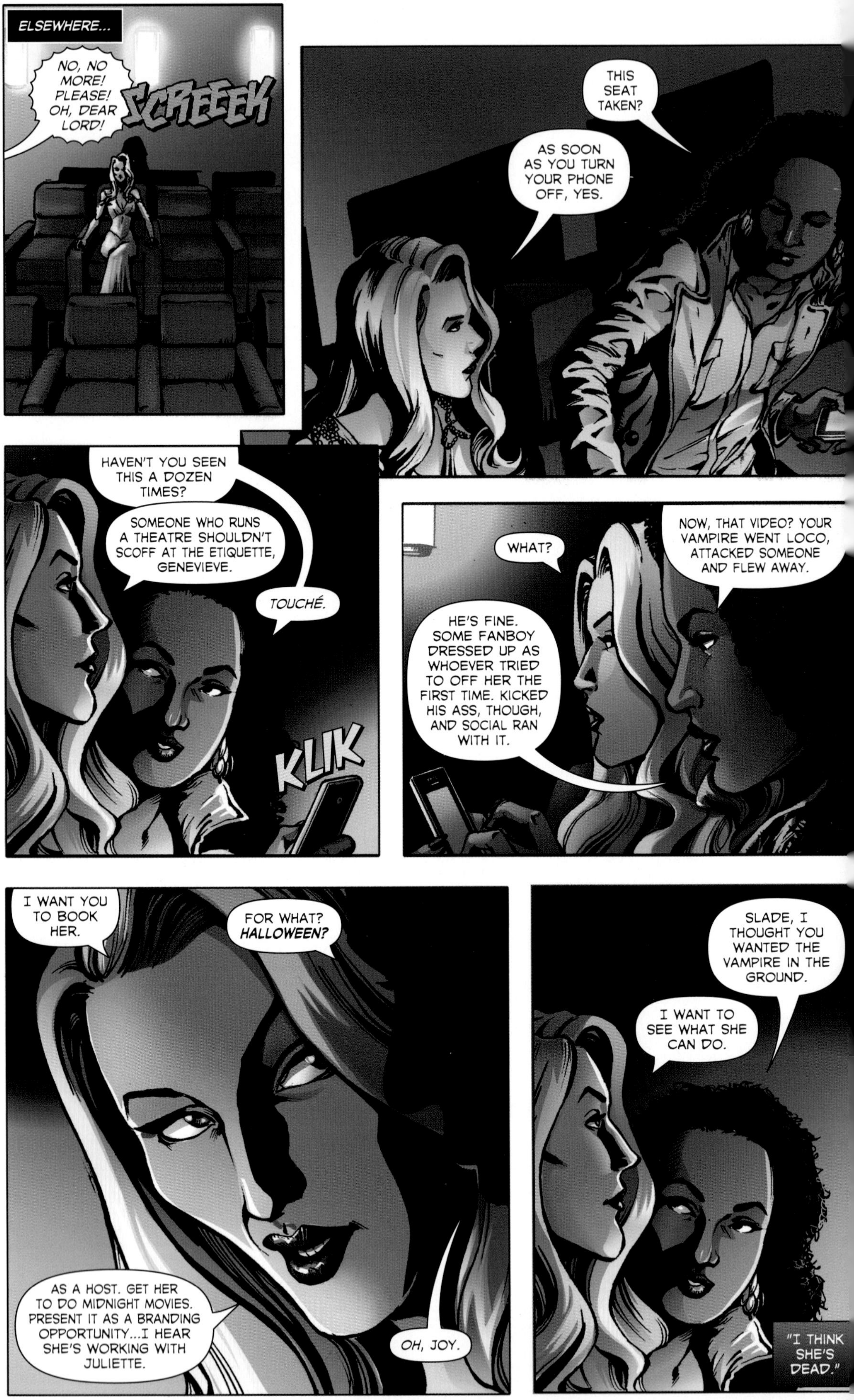
ELSEWHERE...
NO, NO MORE! PLEASE! OH, DEAR LORD!
SCREEEK
THIS SEAT TAKEN?
AS SOON AS YOU TURN YOUR PHONE OFF, YES.
HAVEN'T YOU SEEN THIS A DOZEN TIMES?
SOMEONE WHO RUNS A THEATRE SHOULDN'T SCOFF AT THE ETIQUETTE, GENEVIEVE.
TOUCHÉ.
KLIK
NOW, THAT VIDEO? YOUR VAMPIRE WENT LOCO, ATTACKED SOMEONE AND FLEW AWAY.
WHAT?
HE'S FINE. SOME FANBOY DRESSED UP AS WHOEVER TRIED TO OFF HER THE FIRST TIME. KICKED HIS ASS, THOUGH, AND SOCIAL RAN WITH IT.
I WANT YOU TO BOOK HER.
FOR WHAT? HALLOWEEN?
AS A HOST. GET HER TO DO MIDNIGHT MOVIES. PRESENT IT AS A BRANDING OPPORTUNITY...I HEAR SHE'S WORKING WITH JULIETTE.
OH, JOY.
SLADE, I THOUGHT YOU WANTED THE VAMPIRE IN THE GROUND.
I WANT TO SEE WHAT SHE CAN DO.
"I THINK SHE'S DEAD."

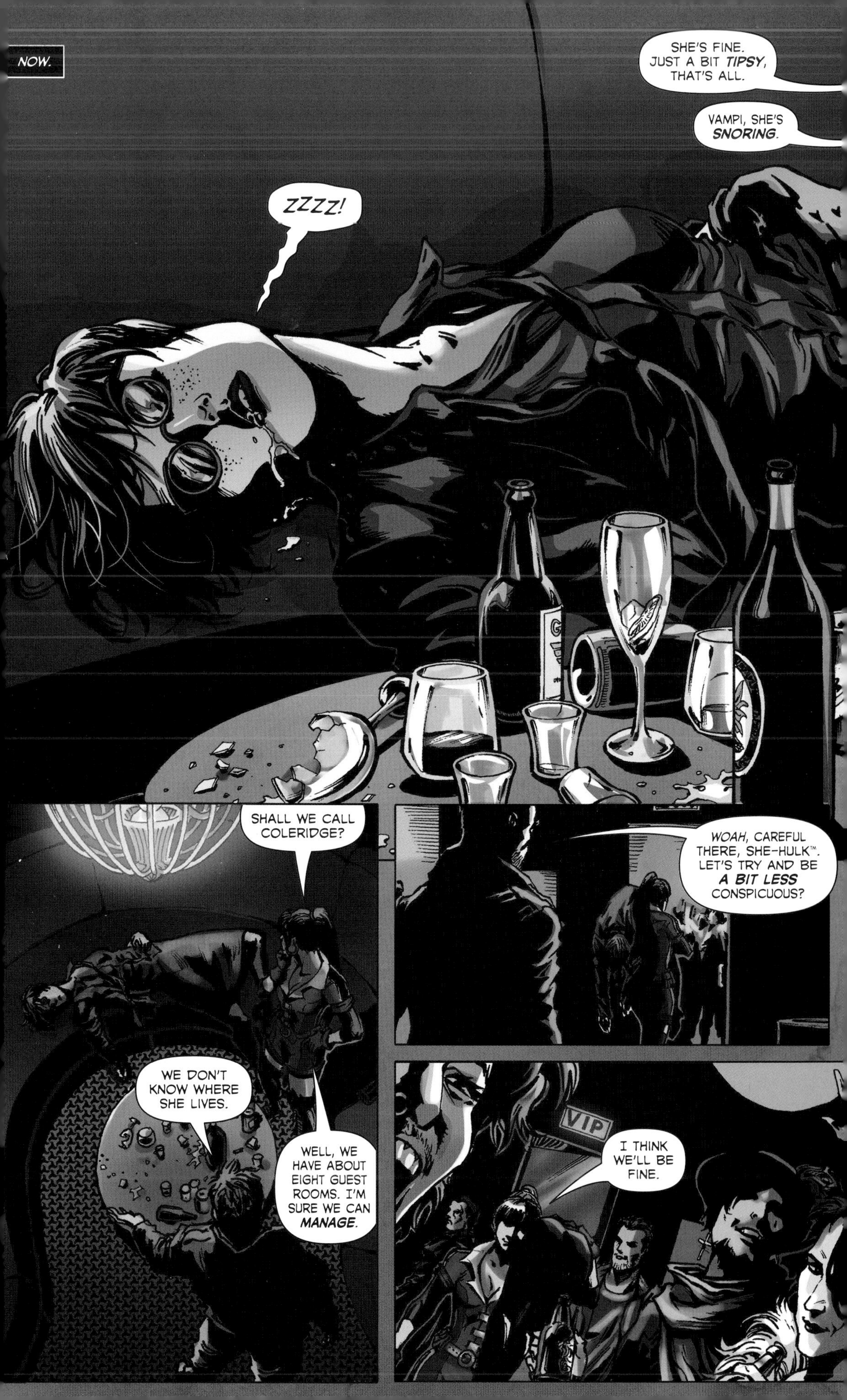
NOW.
SHE'S FINE. JUST A BIT *TIPSY*, THAT'S ALL.
VAMPI, SHE'S **SNORING**.
ZZZZ!
SHALL WE CALL COLERIDGE?
WE DON'T KNOW WHERE SHE LIVES.
WELL, WE HAVE ABOUT EIGHT GUEST ROOMS. I'M SURE WE CAN ***MANAGE***.
WOAH, CAREFUL THERE, SHE-HULK™. LET'S TRY AND BE ***A BIT LESS*** CONSPICUOUS?
VIP
I THINK WE'LL BE FINE.

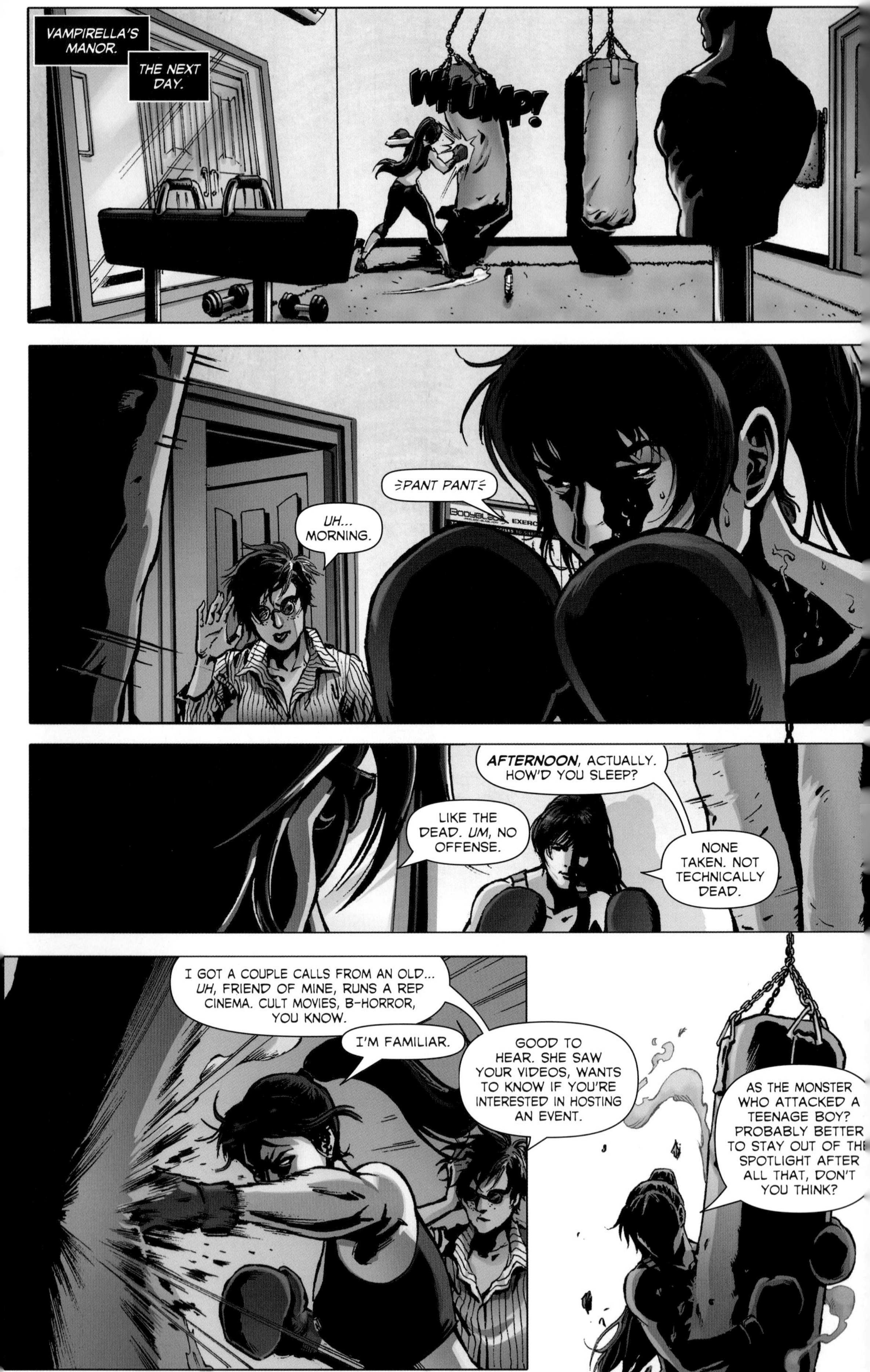

VAMPIRELLA'S MANOR.
THE NEXT DAY.
WHUMP!
UH... MORNING.
=PANT PANT=
AFTERNOON, ACTUALLY. HOW'D YOU SLEEP?
LIKE THE DEAD. UM, NO OFFENSE.
NONE TAKEN. NOT TECHNICALLY DEAD.
I GOT A COUPLE CALLS FROM AN OLD... UH, FRIEND OF MINE, RUNS A REP CINEMA. CULT MOVIES, B-HORROR, YOU KNOW.
I'M FAMILIAR.
GOOD TO HEAR. SHE SAW YOUR VIDEOS, WANTS TO KNOW IF YOU'RE INTERESTED IN HOSTING AN EVENT.
AS THE MONSTER WHO ATTACKED A TEENAGE BOY? PROBABLY BETTER TO STAY OUT OF THE SPOTLIGHT AFTER ALL THAT, DON'T YOU THINK?

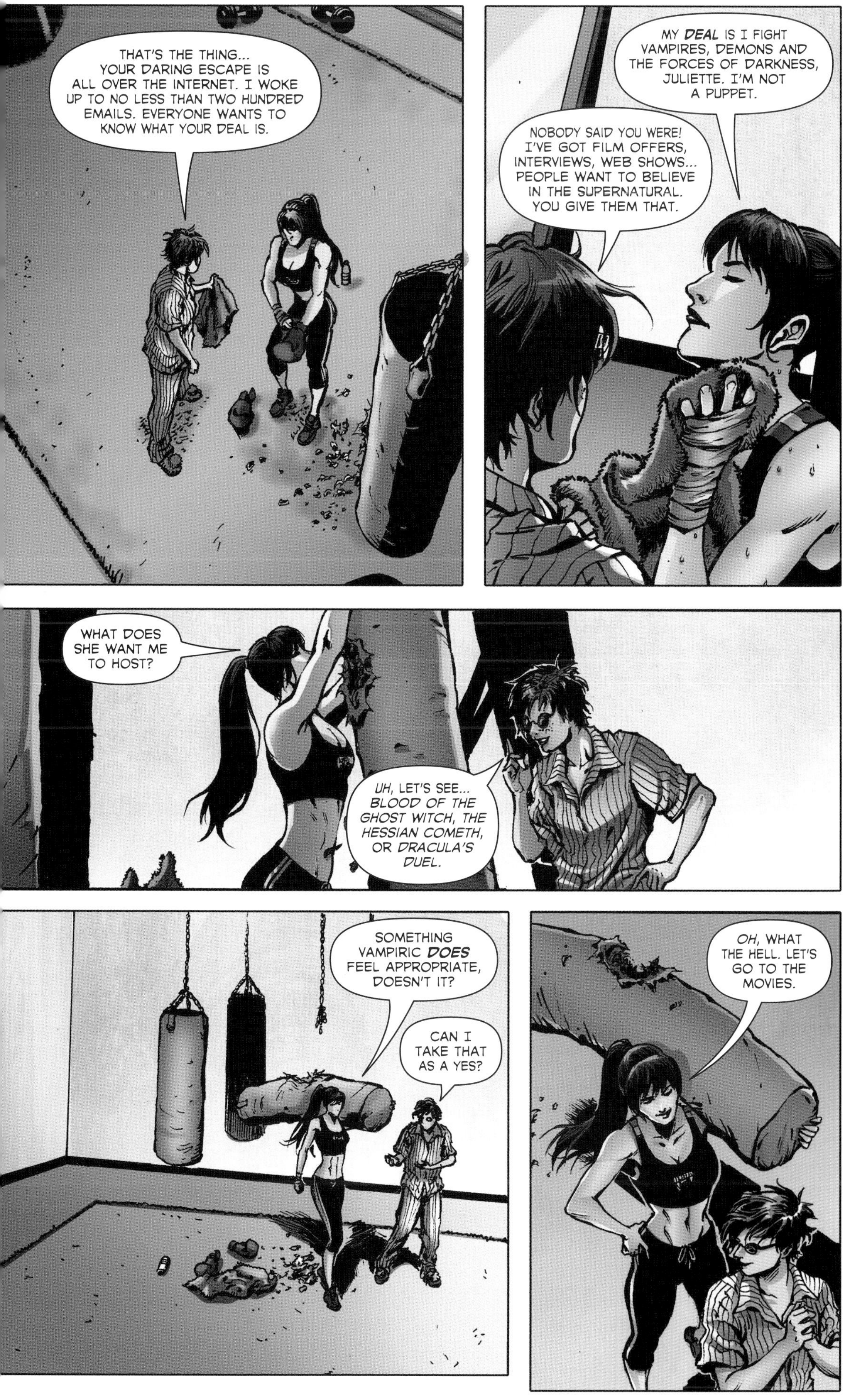
THAT'S THE THING... YOUR DARING ESCAPE IS ALL OVER THE INTERNET. I WOKE UP TO NO LESS THAN TWO HUNDRED EMAILS. EVERYONE WANTS TO KNOW WHAT YOUR DEAL IS.
MY *DEAL* IS I FIGHT VAMPIRES, DEMONS AND THE FORCES OF DARKNESS, JULIETTE. I'M NOT A PUPPET.
NOBODY SAID YOU WERE! I'VE GOT FILM OFFERS, INTERVIEWS, WEB SHOWS... PEOPLE WANT TO BELIEVE IN THE SUPERNATURAL. YOU GIVE THEM THAT.
WHAT DOES SHE WANT ME TO HOST?
UH, LET'S SEE... BLOOD OF THE GHOST WITCH, THE HESSIAN COMETH, OR DRACULA'S DUEL.
SOMETHING VAMPIRIC *DOES* FEEL APPROPRIATE, DOESN'T IT?
CAN I TAKE THAT AS A YES?
OH, WHAT THE HELL. LET'S GO TO THE MOVIES.

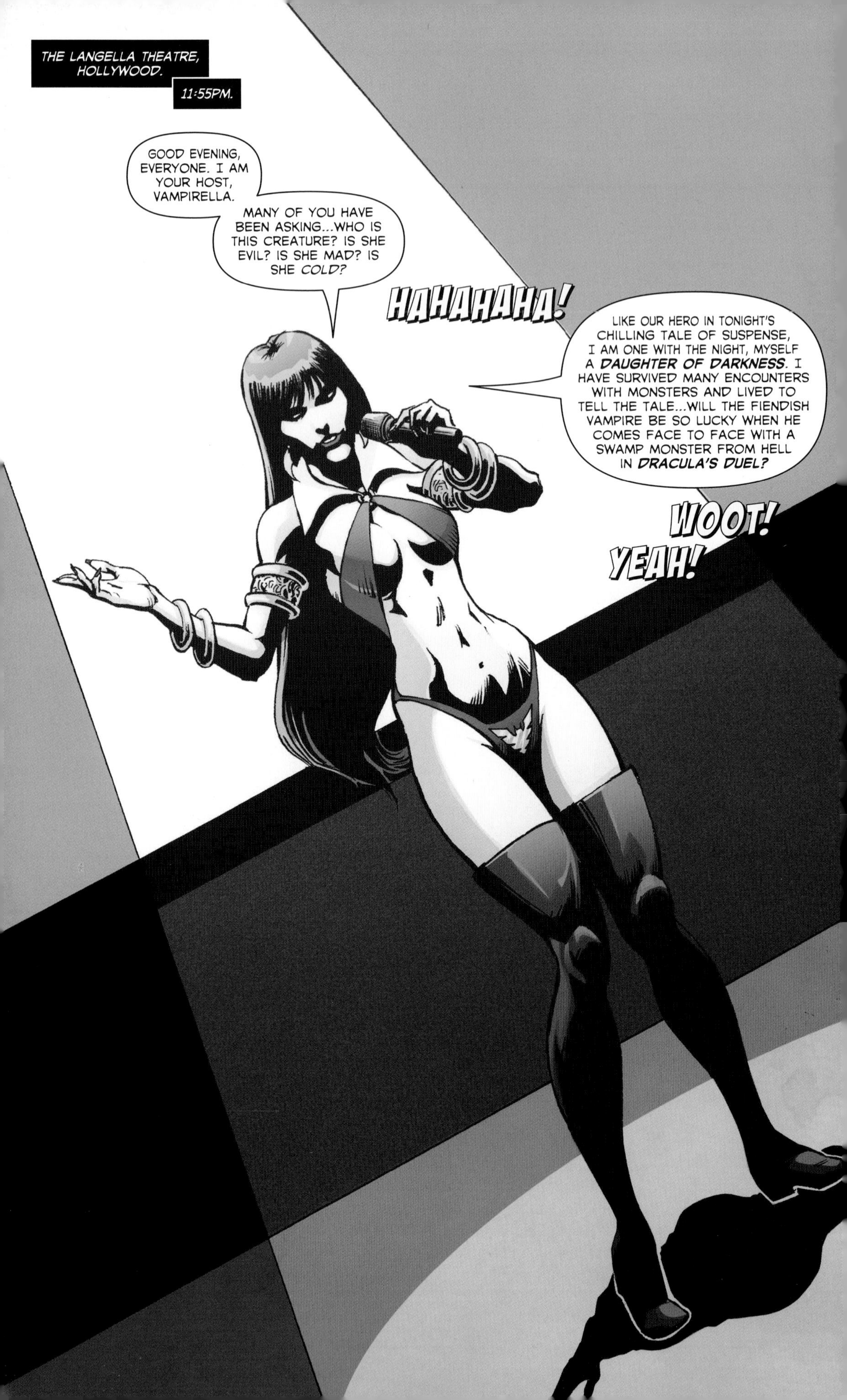
THE LANGELLA THEATRE, HOLLYWOOD.
11:55PM.
GOOD EVENING, EVERYONE. I AM YOUR HOST, VAMPIRELLA.
MANY OF YOU HAVE BEEN ASKING...WHO IS THIS CREATURE? IS SHE EVIL? IS SHE MAD? IS SHE *COLD?*
HAHAHAHA!
LIKE OUR HERO IN TONIGHT'S CHILLING TALE OF SUSPENSE, I AM ONE WITH THE NIGHT, MYSELF A ***DAUGHTER OF DARKNESS***. I HAVE SURVIVED MANY ENCOUNTERS WITH MONSTERS AND LIVED TO TELL THE TALE...WILL THE FIENDISH VAMPIRE BE SO LUCKY WHEN HE COMES FACE TO FACE WITH A SWAMP MONSTER FROM HELL IN ***DRACULA'S DUEL?***
WOOT!
YEAH!

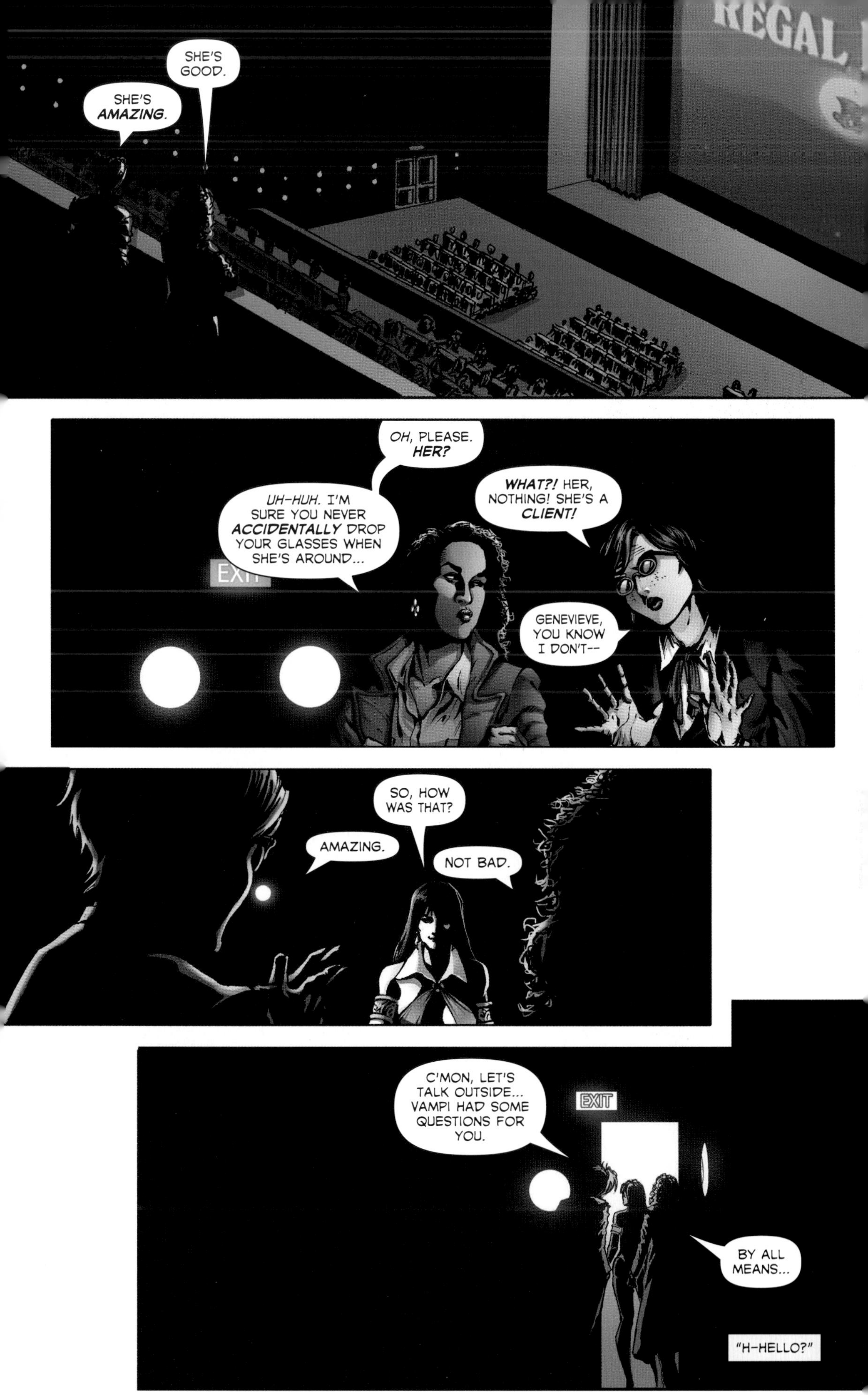
REGAL
SHE'S GOOD.
SHE'S *AMAZING.*
OH, PLEASE. ***HER?***
UH-HUH. I'M SURE YOU NEVER ***ACCIDENTALLY*** DROP YOUR GLASSES WHEN SHE'S AROUND...
EXIT
WHAT?! HER, NOTHING! SHE'S A ***CLIENT!***
GENEVIEVE, YOU KNOW I DON'T--
SO, HOW WAS THAT?
AMAZING.
NOT BAD.
EXIT
C'MON, LET'S TALK OUTSIDE... VAMPI HAD SOME QUESTIONS FOR YOU.
BY ALL MEANS...
"H-HELLO?"

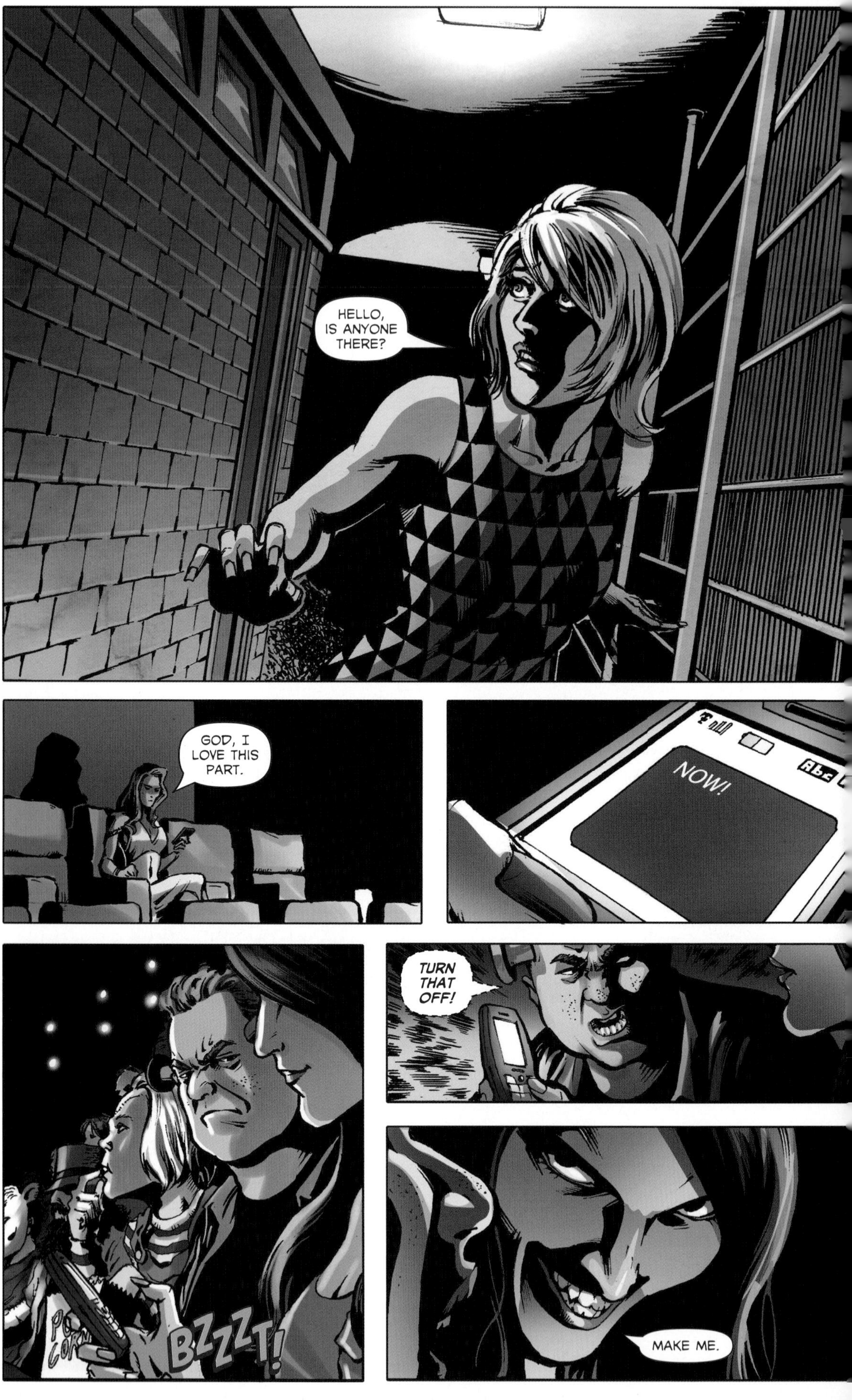
HELLO, IS ANYONE THERE?
GOD, I LOVE THIS PART.
NOW!
TURN THAT OFF!
BZZZT!
MAKE ME.

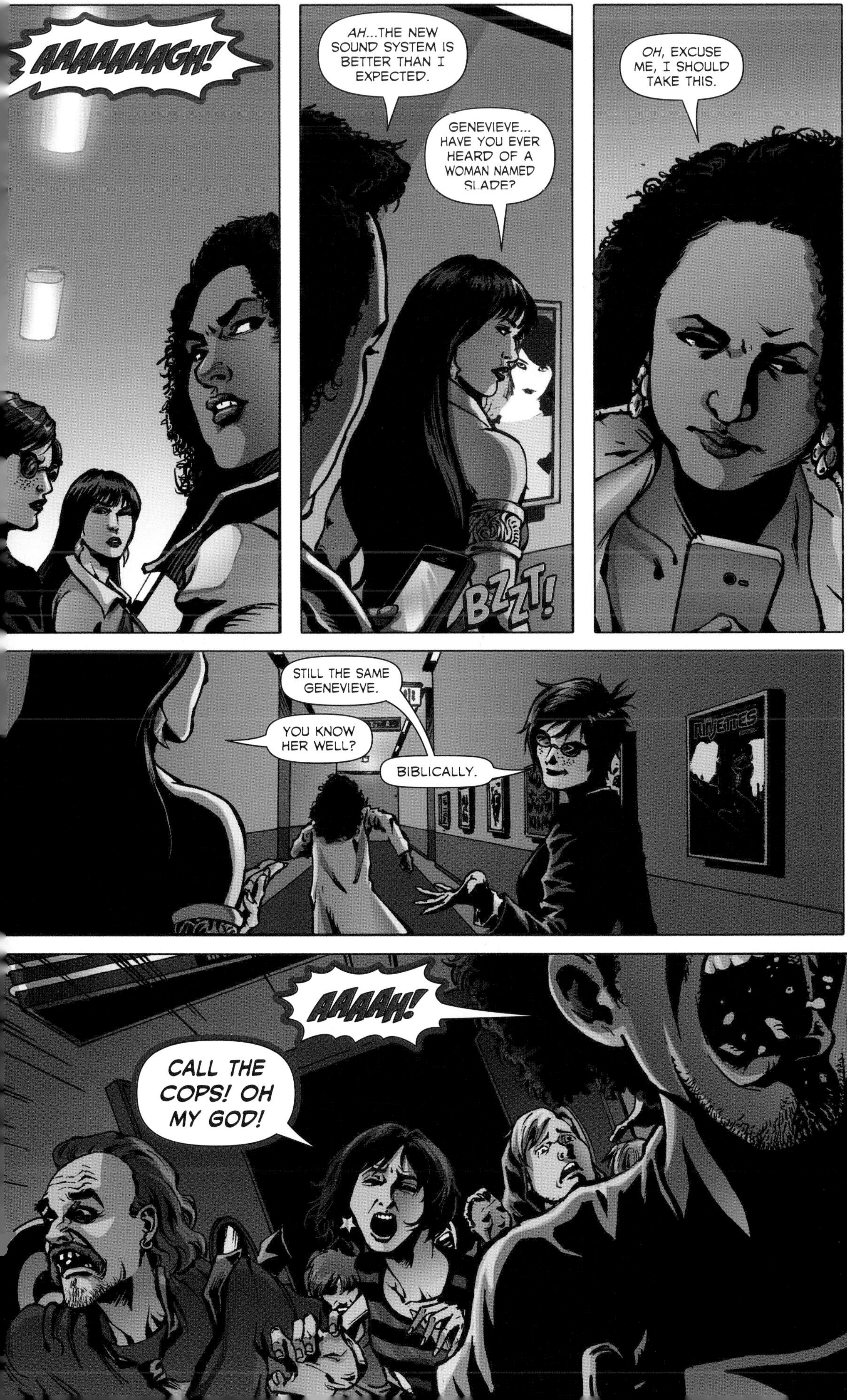
AAAAAAAGH!
AH...THE NEW SOUND SYSTEM IS BETTER THAN I EXPECTED.
GENEVIEVE... HAVE YOU EVER HEARD OF A WOMAN NAMED SLADE?
BZZT!
OH, EXCUSE ME, I SHOULD TAKE THIS.
STILL THE SAME GENEVIEVE.
YOU KNOW HER WELL?
BIBLICALLY.
AAAAH!
CALL THE COPS! OH MY GOD!

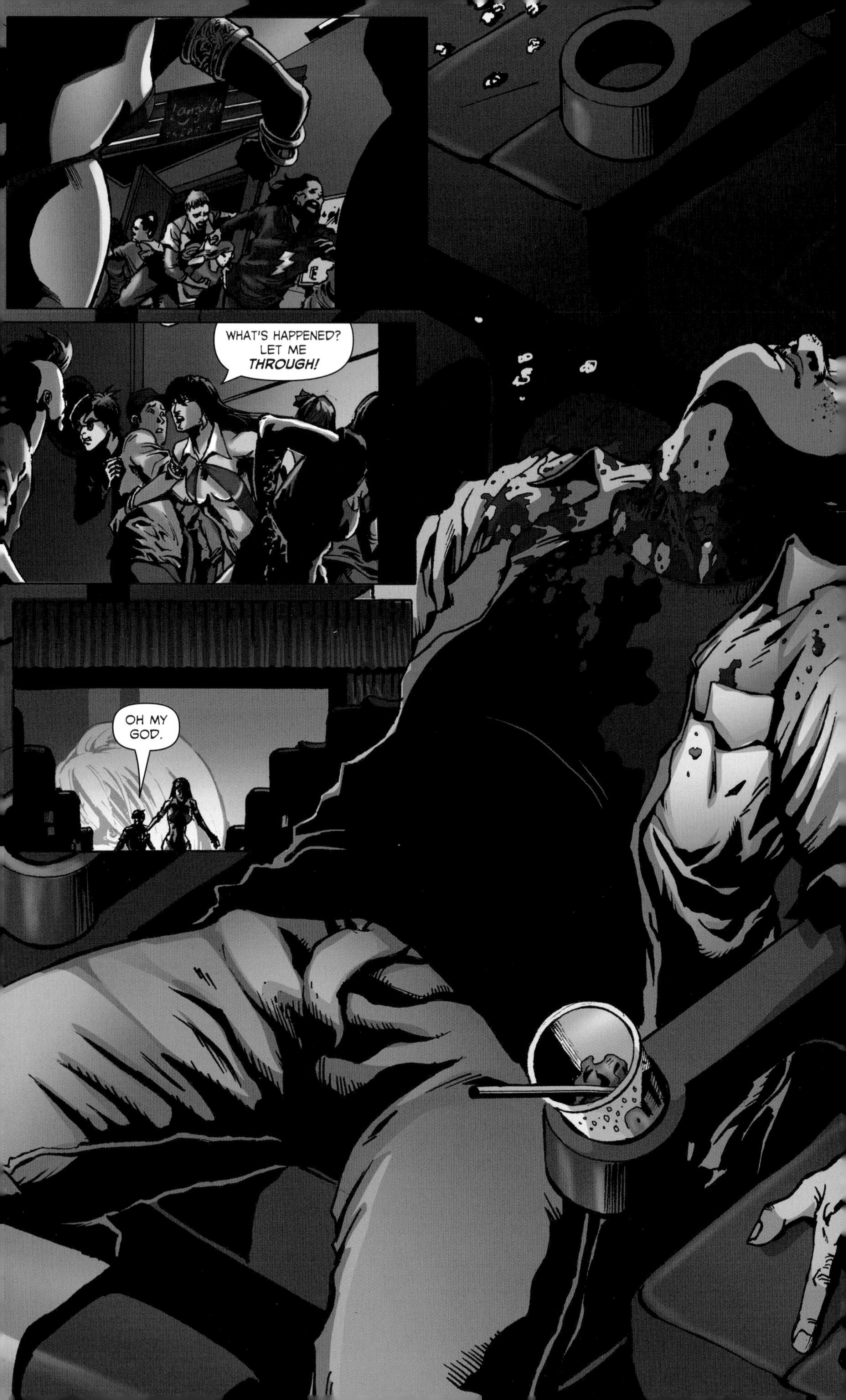
WHAT'S HAPPENED? LET ME *THROUGH!*
OH MY GOD.

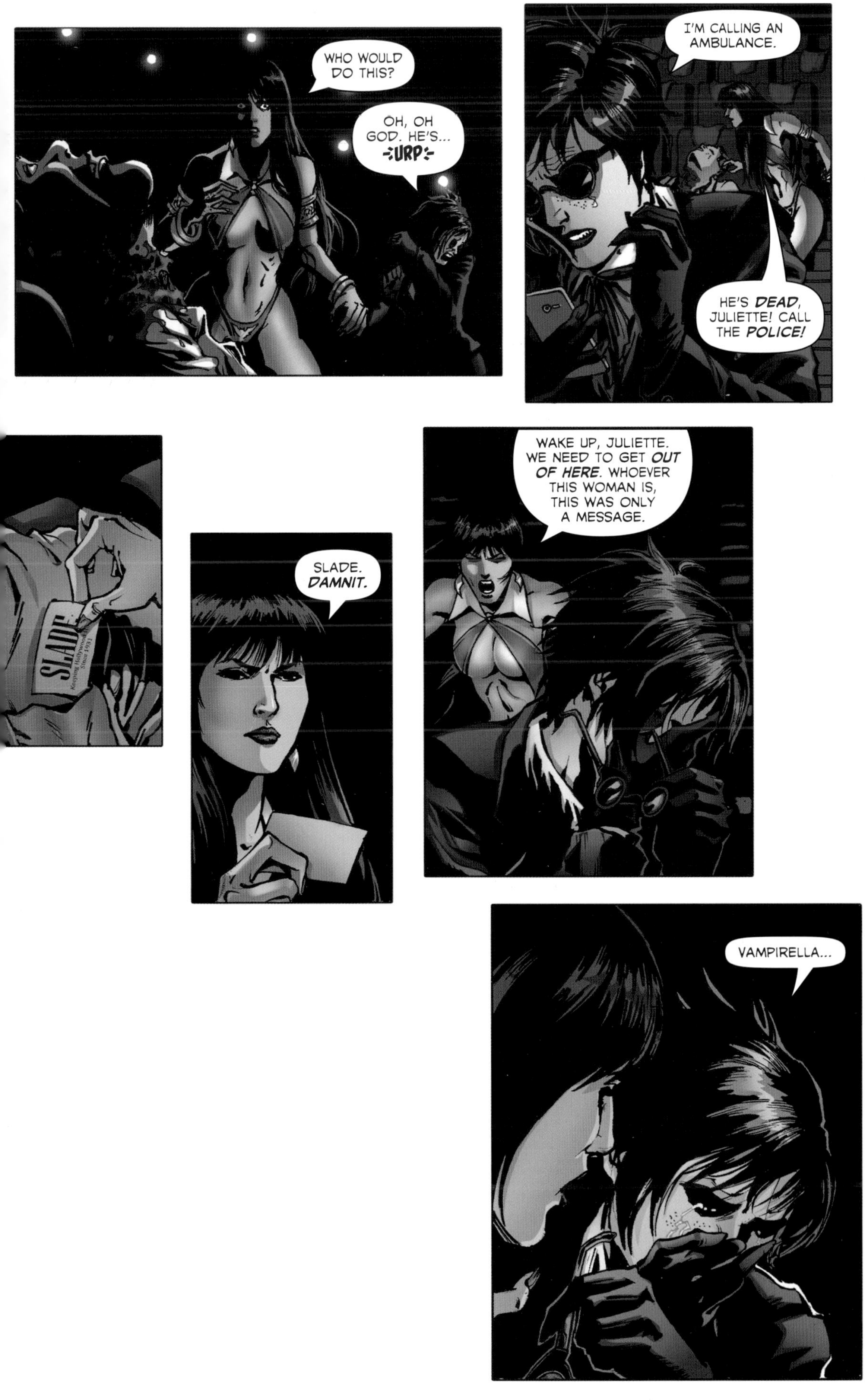

WHO WOULD DO THIS?
OH, OH GOD. HE'S... -URP-
I'M CALLING AN AMBULANCE.
HE'S *DEAD*, JULIETTE! CALL THE *POLICE!*
SLADE
SLADE. *DAMNIT.*
WAKE UP, JULIETTE. WE NEED TO GET *OUT OF HERE*. WHOEVER THIS WOMAN IS, THIS WAS ONLY A MESSAGE.
VAMPIRELLA...

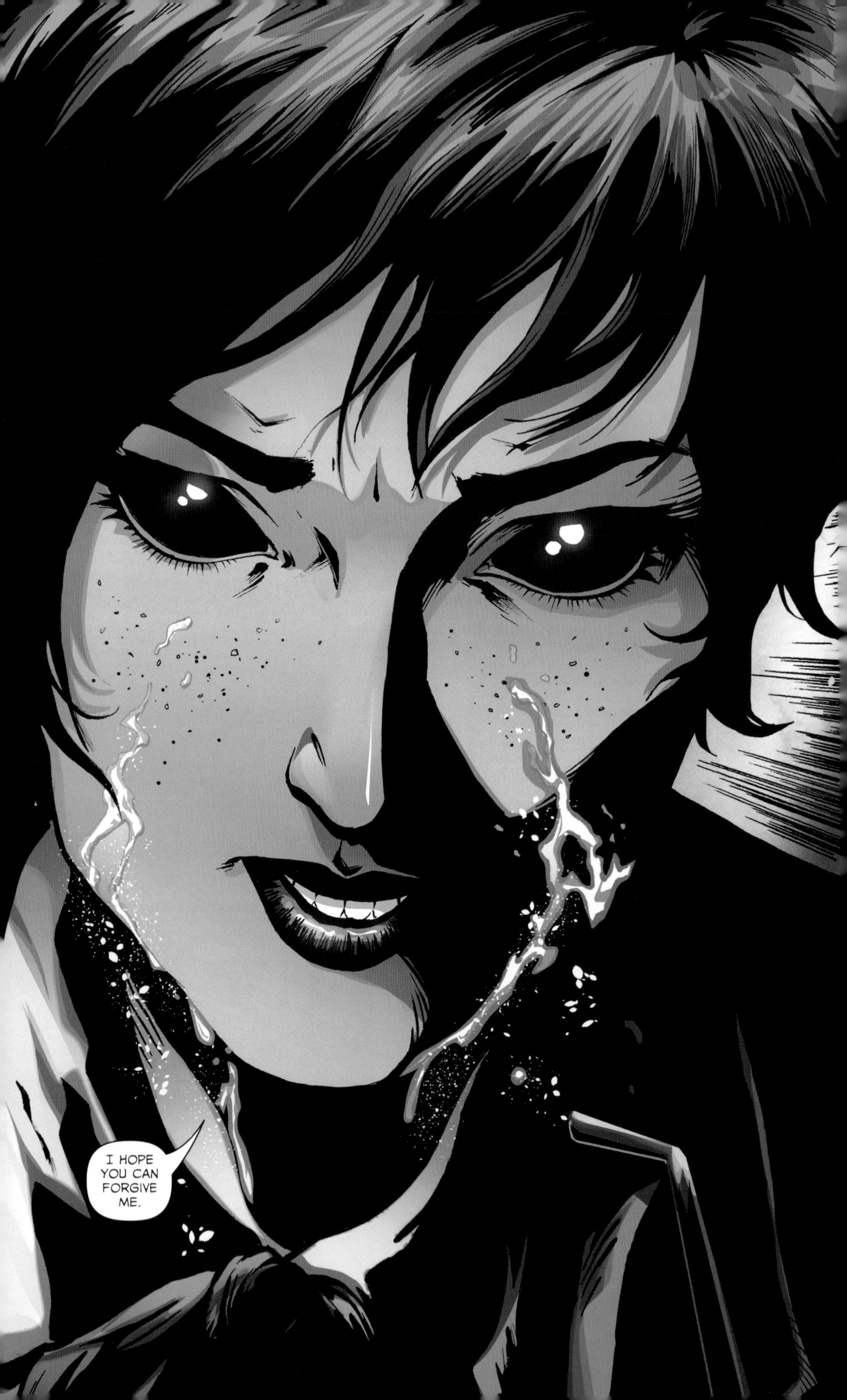
I HOPE YOU CAN FORGIVE ME.

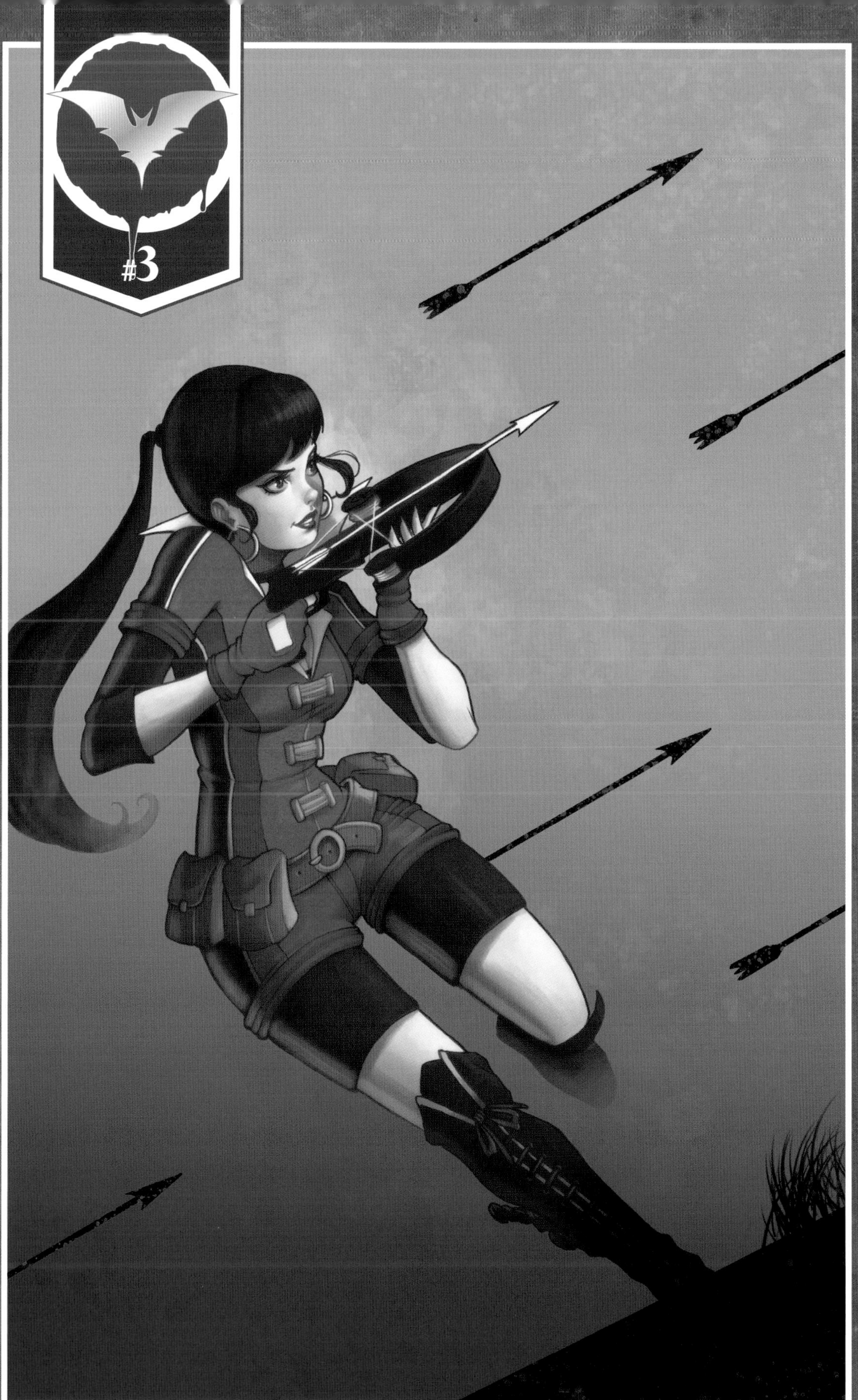
#3

cover by **Chrissie Zullo**

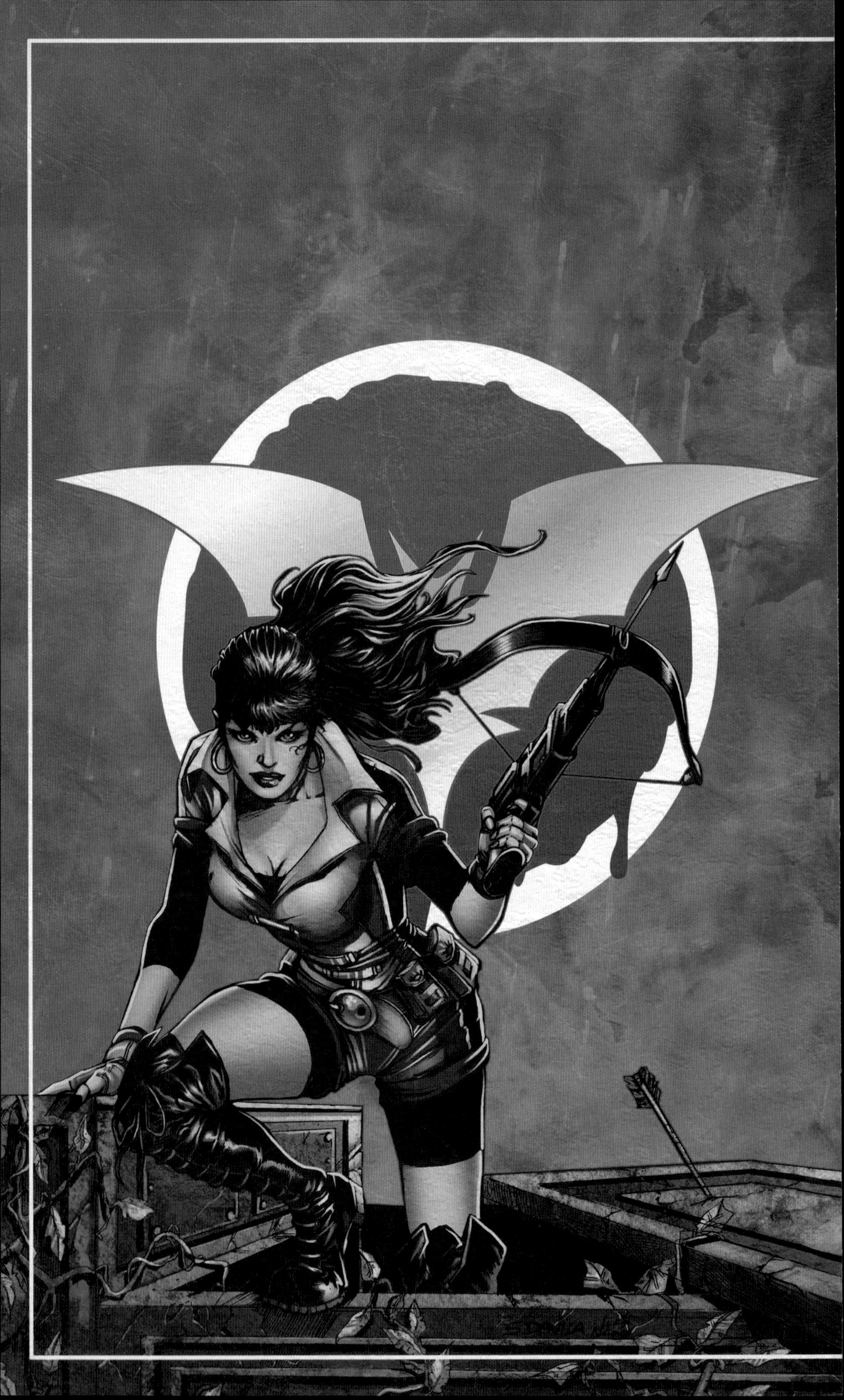

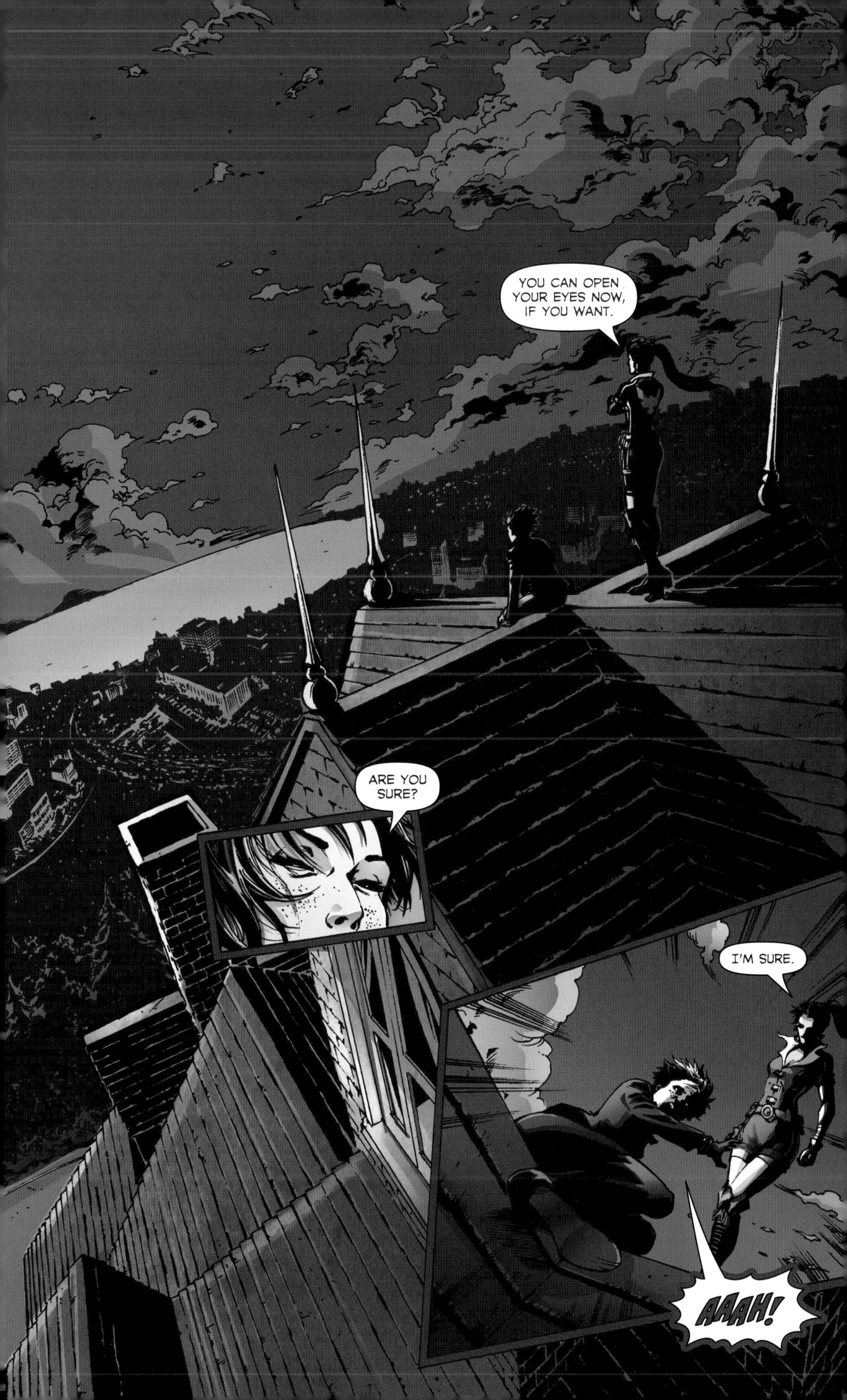
YOU CAN OPEN YOUR EYES NOW, IF YOU WANT.
ARE YOU SURE?
I'M SURE.
AAAH!

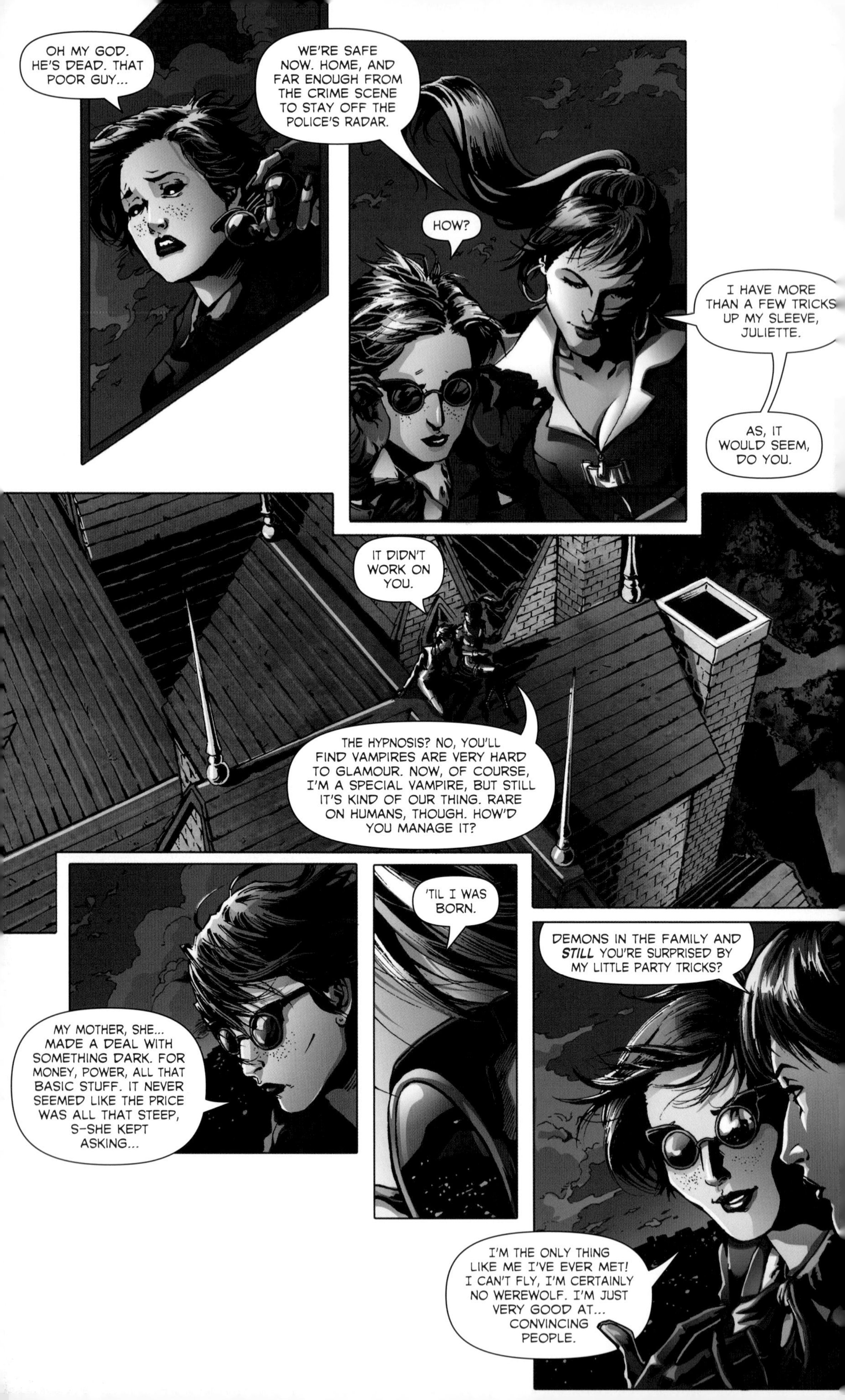
OH MY GOD. HE'S DEAD. THAT POOR GUY...
WE'RE SAFE NOW. HOME, AND FAR ENOUGH FROM THE CRIME SCENE TO STAY OFF THE POLICE'S RADAR.
HOW?
I HAVE MORE THAN A FEW TRICKS UP MY SLEEVE, JULIETTE.
AS, IT WOULD SEEM, DO YOU.
IT DIDN'T WORK ON YOU.
THE HYPNOSIS? NO, YOU'LL FIND VAMPIRES ARE VERY HARD TO GLAMOUR. NOW, OF COURSE, I'M A SPECIAL VAMPIRE, BUT STILL IT'S KIND OF OUR THING. RARE ON HUMANS, THOUGH. HOW'D YOU MANAGE IT?
MY MOTHER, SHE... MADE A DEAL WITH SOMETHING DARK. FOR MONEY, POWER, ALL THAT BASIC STUFF. IT NEVER SEEMED LIKE THE PRICE WAS ALL THAT STEEP, S-SHE KEPT ASKING...
'TIL I WAS BORN.
DEMONS IN THE FAMILY AND STILL YOU'RE SURPRISED BY MY LITTLE PARTY TRICKS?
I'M THE ONLY THING LIKE ME I'VE EVER MET! I CAN'T FLY, I'M CERTAINLY NO WEREWOLF. I'M JUST VERY GOOD AT... CONVINCING PEOPLE.

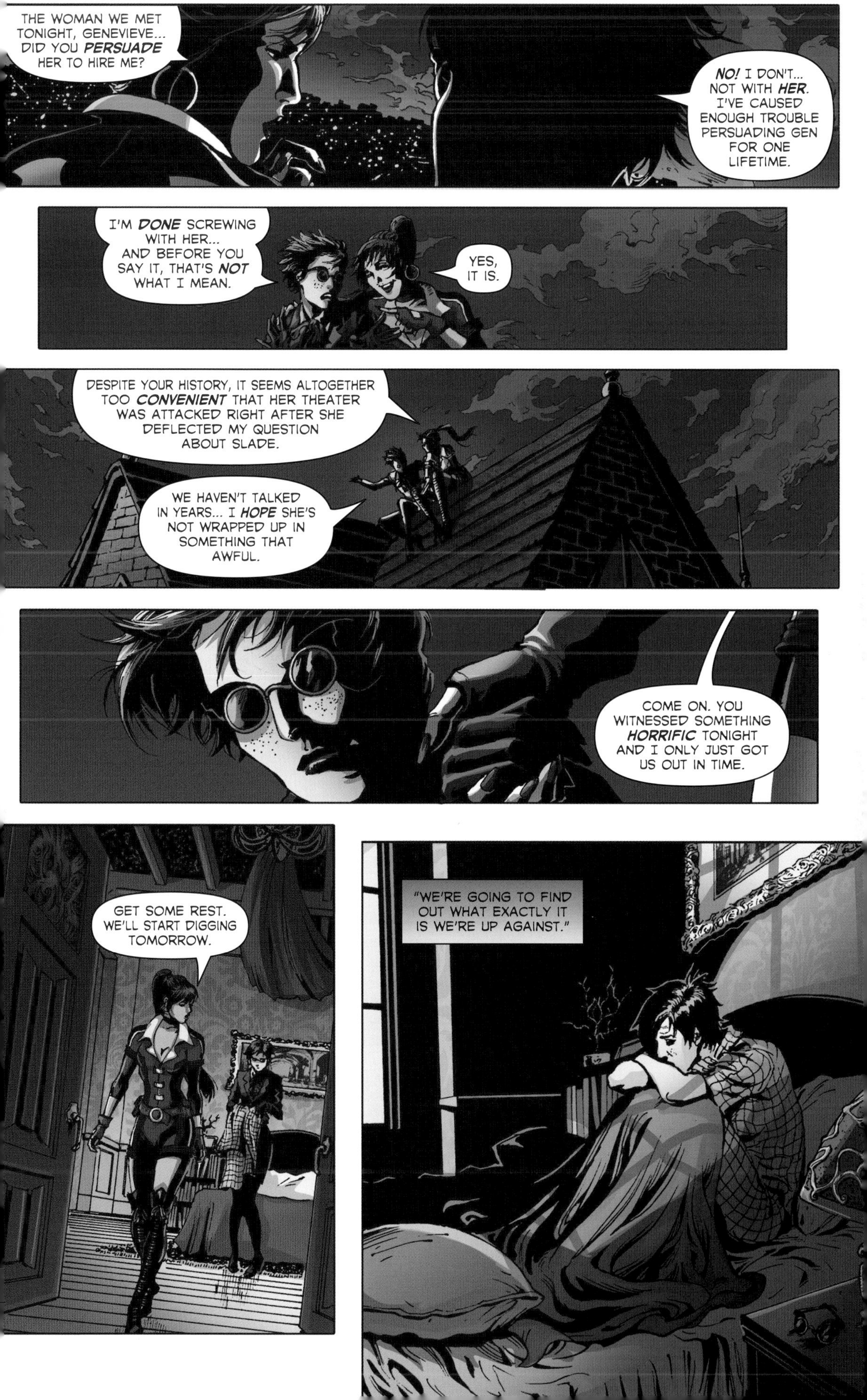
THE WOMAN WE MET TONIGHT, GENEVIEVE... DID YOU PERSUADE HER TO HIRE ME?
NO! I DON'T... NOT WITH HER. I'VE CAUSED ENOUGH TROUBLE PERSUADING GEN FOR ONE LIFETIME.
I'M DONE SCREWING WITH HER... AND BEFORE YOU SAY IT, THAT'S NOT WHAT I MEAN.
YES, IT IS.
DESPITE YOUR HISTORY, IT SEEMS ALTOGETHER TOO CONVENIENT THAT HER THEATER WAS ATTACKED RIGHT AFTER SHE DEFLECTED MY QUESTION ABOUT SLADE.
WE HAVEN'T TALKED IN YEARS... I HOPE SHE'S NOT WRAPPED UP IN SOMETHING THAT AWFUL.
COME ON. YOU WITNESSED SOMETHING HORRIFIC TONIGHT AND I ONLY JUST GOT US OUT IN TIME.
GET SOME REST. WE'LL START DIGGING TOMORROW.
"WE'RE GOING TO FIND OUT WHAT EXACTLY IT IS WE'RE UP AGAINST."

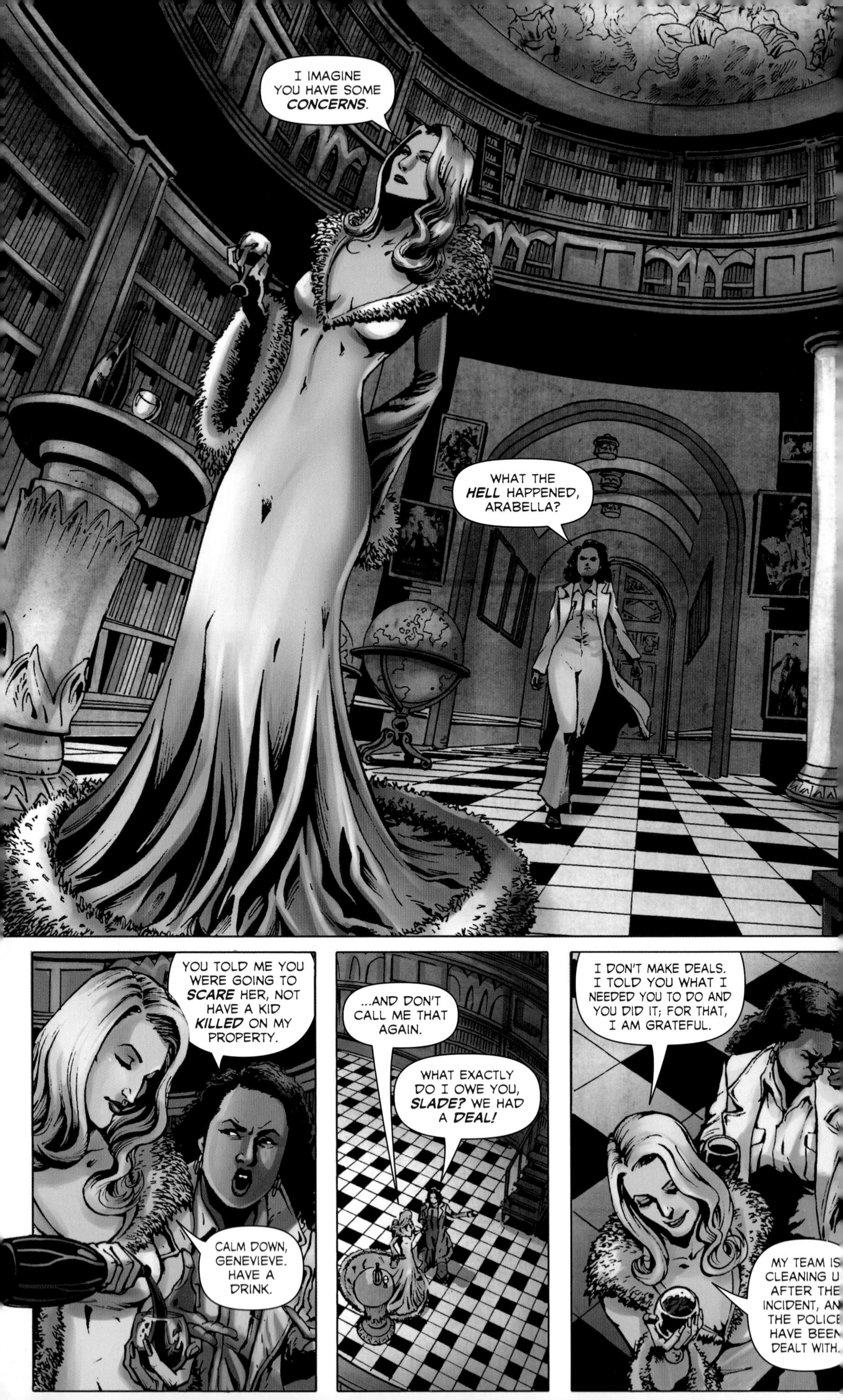
I IMAGINE YOU HAVE SOME CONCERNS.
WHAT THE HELL HAPPENED, ARABELLA?
YOU TOLD ME YOU WERE GOING TO SCARE HER, NOT HAVE A KID KILLED ON MY PROPERTY.
CALM DOWN, GENEVIEVE. HAVE A DRINK.
...AND DON'T CALL ME THAT AGAIN.
WHAT EXACTLY DO I OWE YOU, SLADE? WE HAD A DEAL!
I DON'T MAKE DEALS. I TOLD YOU WHAT I NEEDED YOU TO DO AND YOU DID IT; FOR THAT, I AM GRATEFUL.
MY TEAM IS CLEANING U AFTER THE INCIDENT, AN THE POLICE HAVE BEEN DEALT WITH.

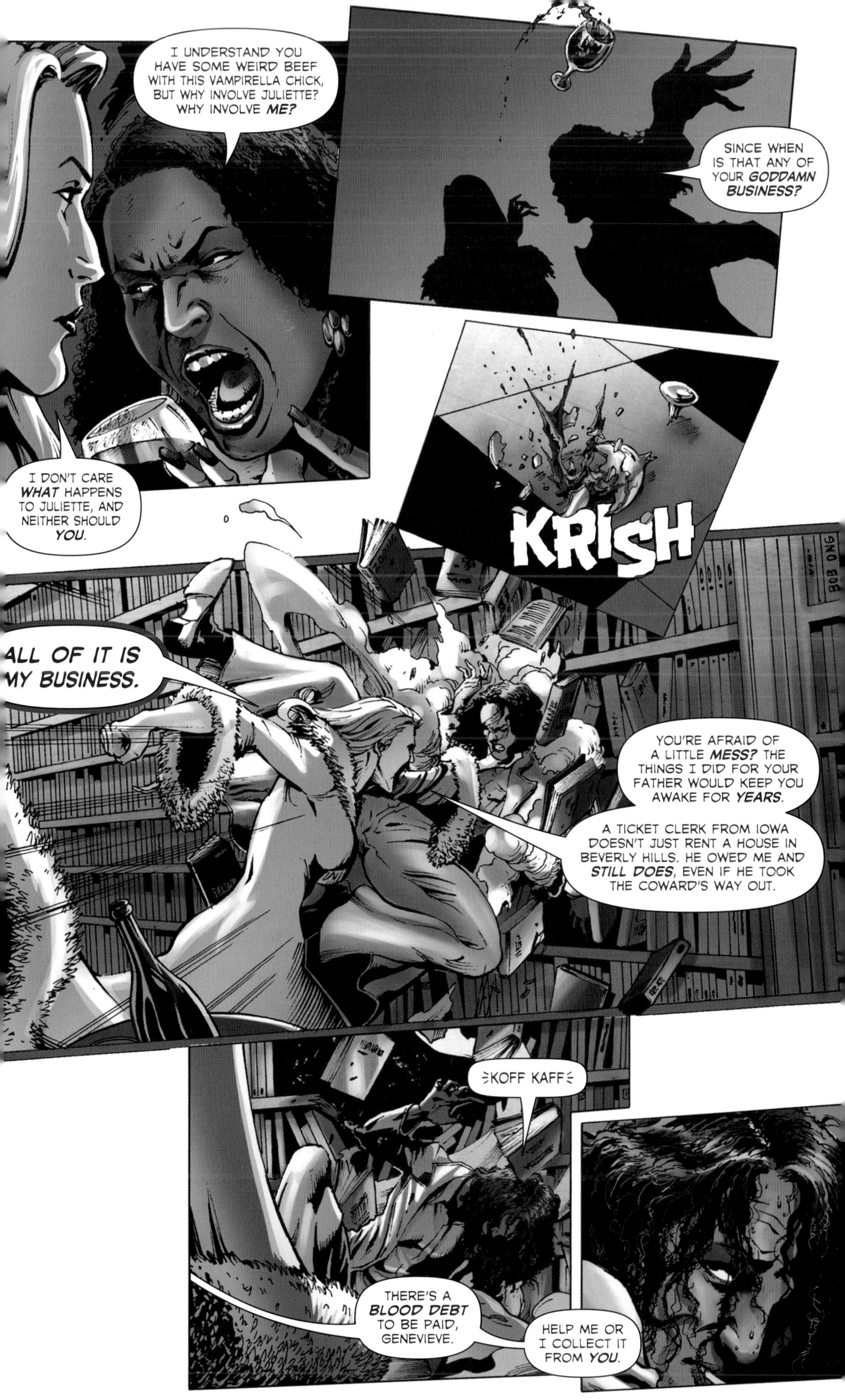
I UNDERSTAND YOU HAVE SOME WEIRD BEEF WITH THIS VAMPIRELLA CHICK, BUT WHY INVOLVE JULIETTE? WHY INVOLVE ME?
I DON'T CARE WHAT HAPPENS TO JULIETTE, AND NEITHER SHOULD YOU.
SINCE WHEN IS THAT ANY OF YOUR GODDAMN BUSINESS?
KRISH
ALL OF IT IS MY BUSINESS.
YOU'RE AFRAID OF A LITTLE MESS? THE THINGS I DID FOR YOUR FATHER WOULD KEEP YOU AWAKE FOR YEARS.
A TICKET CLERK FROM IOWA DOESN'T JUST RENT A HOUSE IN BEVERLY HILLS. HE OWED ME AND STILL DOES, EVEN IF HE TOOK THE COWARD'S WAY OUT.
BOB ONG
KOFF KAFF
THERE'S A BLOOD DEBT TO BE PAID, GENEVIEVE.
HELP ME OR I COLLECT IT FROM YOU.

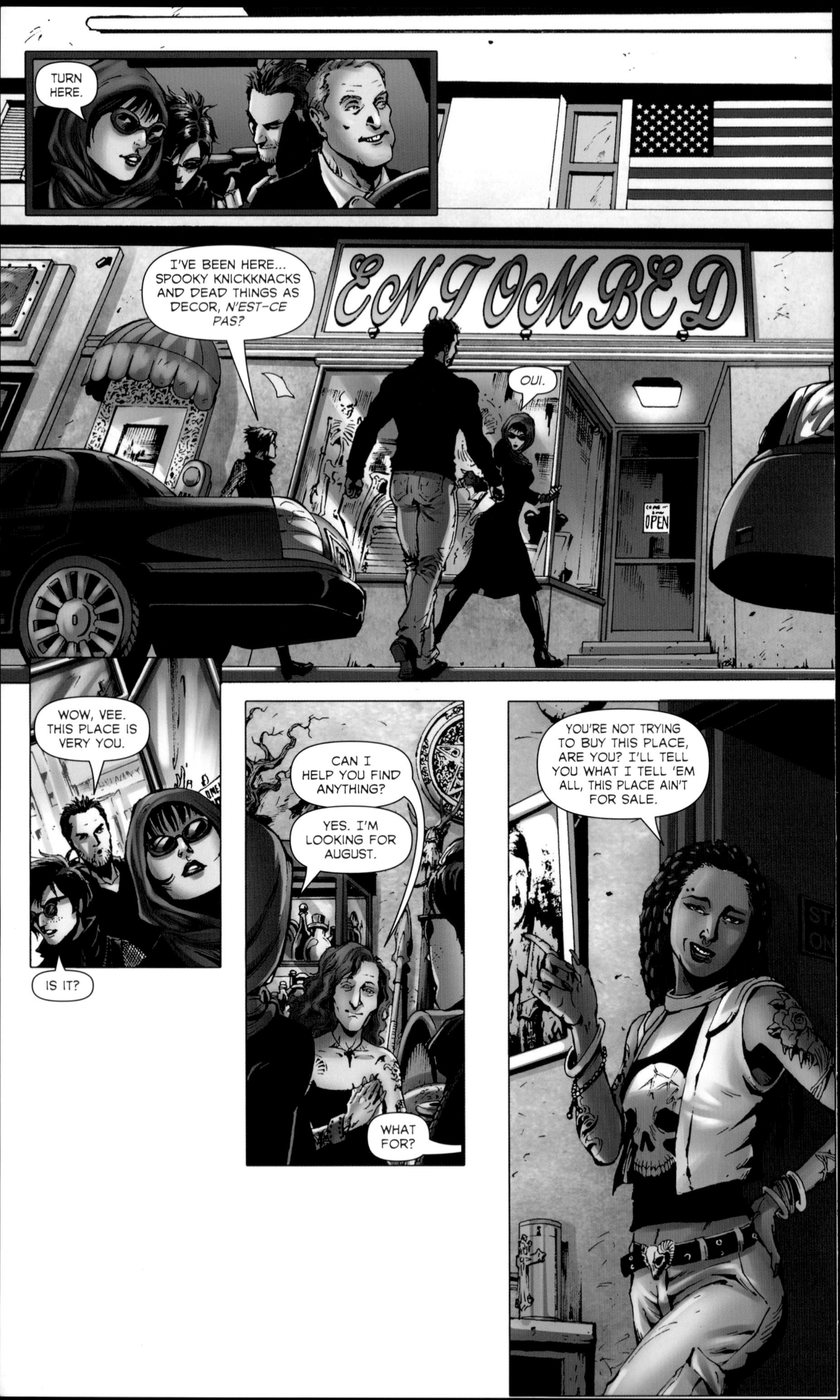
TURN HERE.
ENTOMBED
I'VE BEEN HERE... SPOOKY KNICKKNACKS AND DEAD THINGS AS DECOR, *N'EST-CE PAS?*
OUI.
OPEN
WOW, VEE. THIS PLACE IS VERY YOU.
IS IT?
CAN I HELP YOU FIND ANYTHING?
YES. I'M LOOKING FOR AUGUST.
WHAT FOR?
YOU'RE NOT TRYING TO BUY THIS PLACE, ARE YOU? I'LL TELL YOU WHAT I TELL 'EM ALL, THIS PLACE AIN'T FOR SALE.

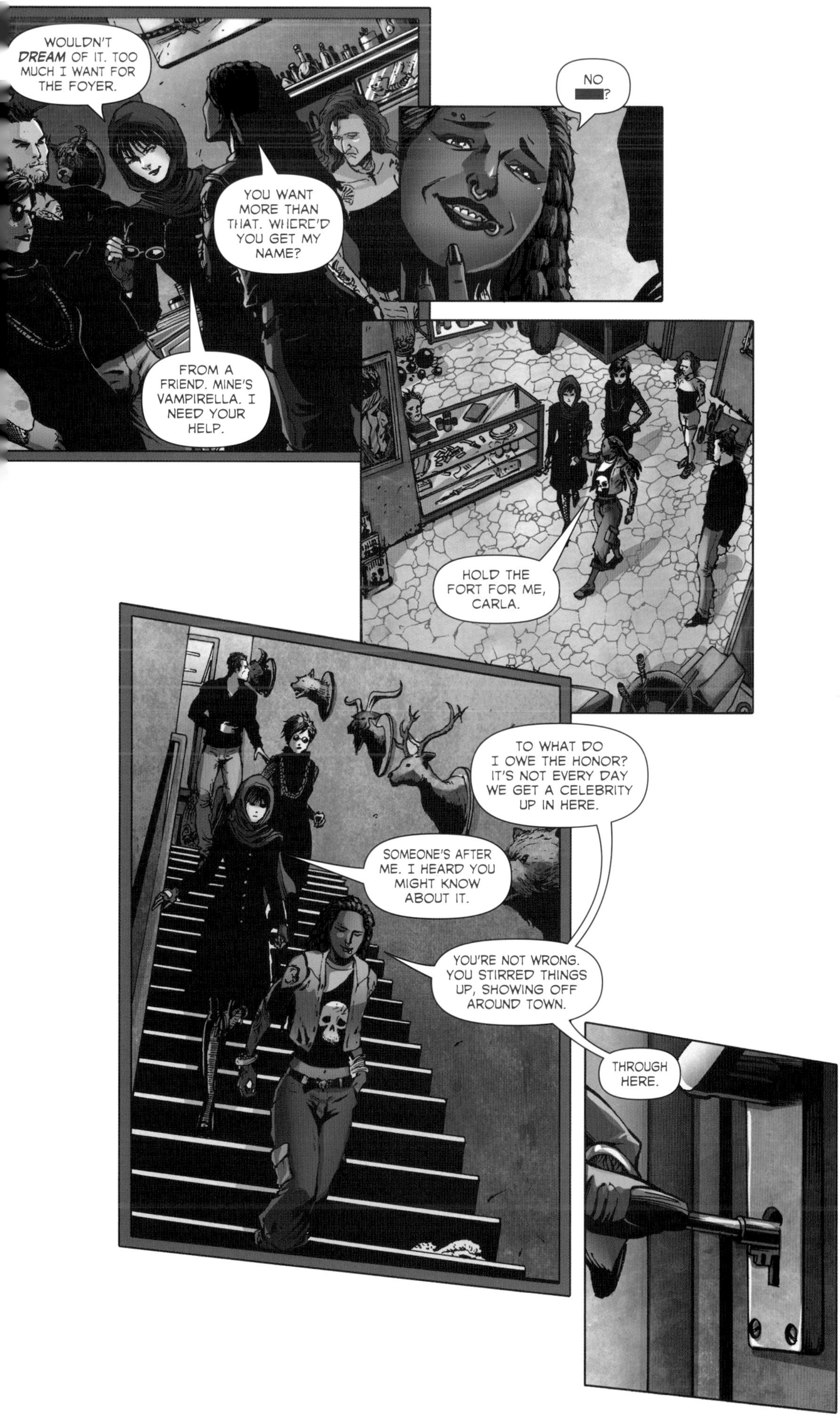

WOULDN'T *DREAM* OF IT. TOO MUCH I WANT FOR THE FOYER.
YOU WANT MORE THAN THAT. WHERE'D YOU GET MY NAME?
FROM A FRIEND. MINE'S VAMPIRELLA. I NEED YOUR HELP.
NO [redacted]?
HOLD THE FORT FOR ME, CARLA.
TO WHAT DO I OWE THE HONOR? IT'S NOT EVERY DAY WE GET A CELEBRITY UP IN HERE.
SOMEONE'S AFTER ME. I HEARD YOU MIGHT KNOW ABOUT IT.
YOU'RE NOT WRONG. YOU STIRRED THINGS UP, SHOWING OFF AROUND TOWN.
THROUGH HERE.

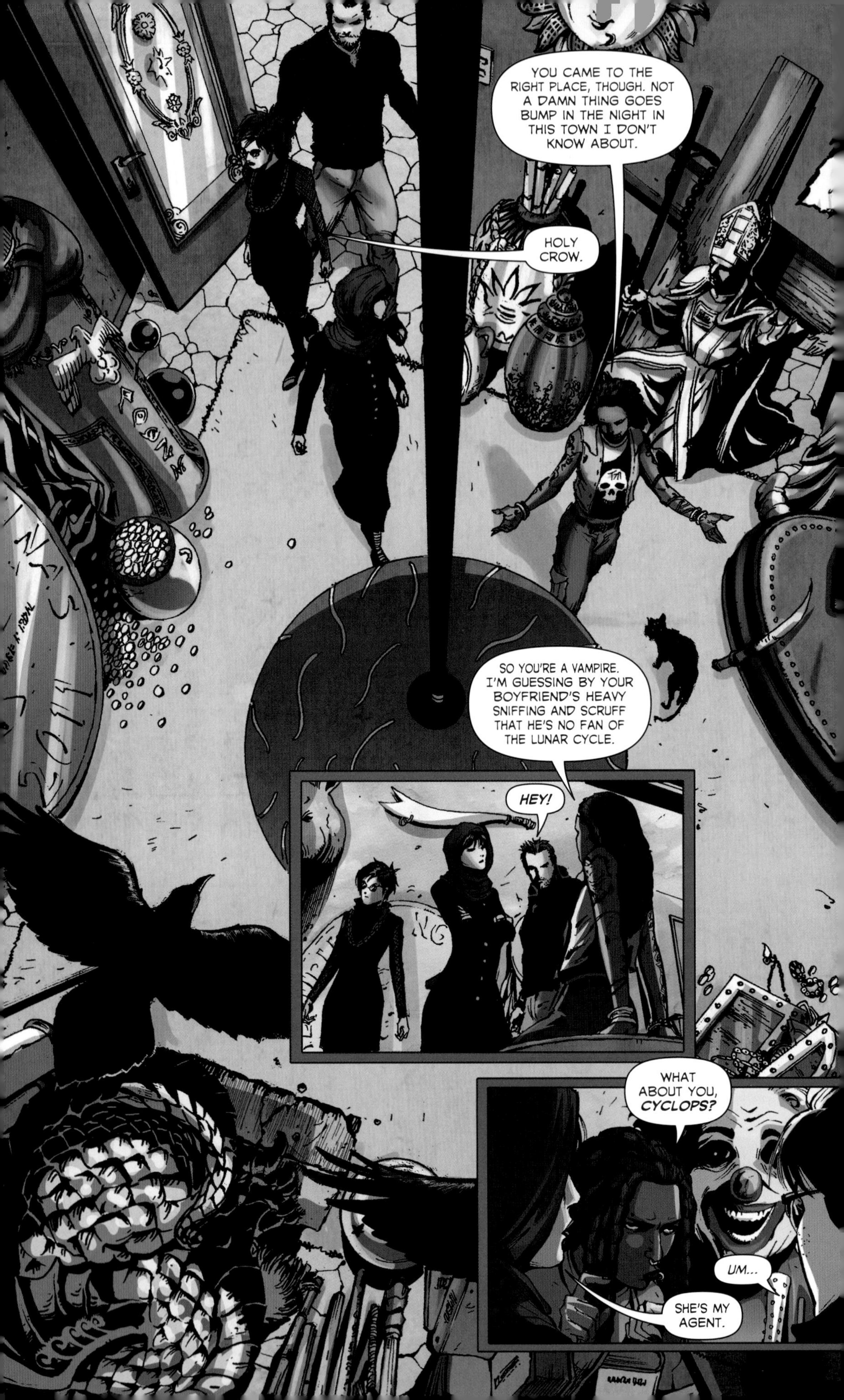

YOU CAME TO THE RIGHT PLACE, THOUGH. NOT A DAMN THING GOES BUMP IN THE NIGHT IN THIS TOWN I DON'T KNOW ABOUT.
HOLY CROW.
SO YOU'RE A VAMPIRE. I'M GUESSING BY YOUR BOYFRIEND'S HEAVY SNIFFING AND SCRUFF THAT HE'S NO FAN OF THE LUNAR CYCLE.
HEY!
WHAT ABOUT YOU, *CYCLOPS?*
UM...
SHE'S MY AGENT.

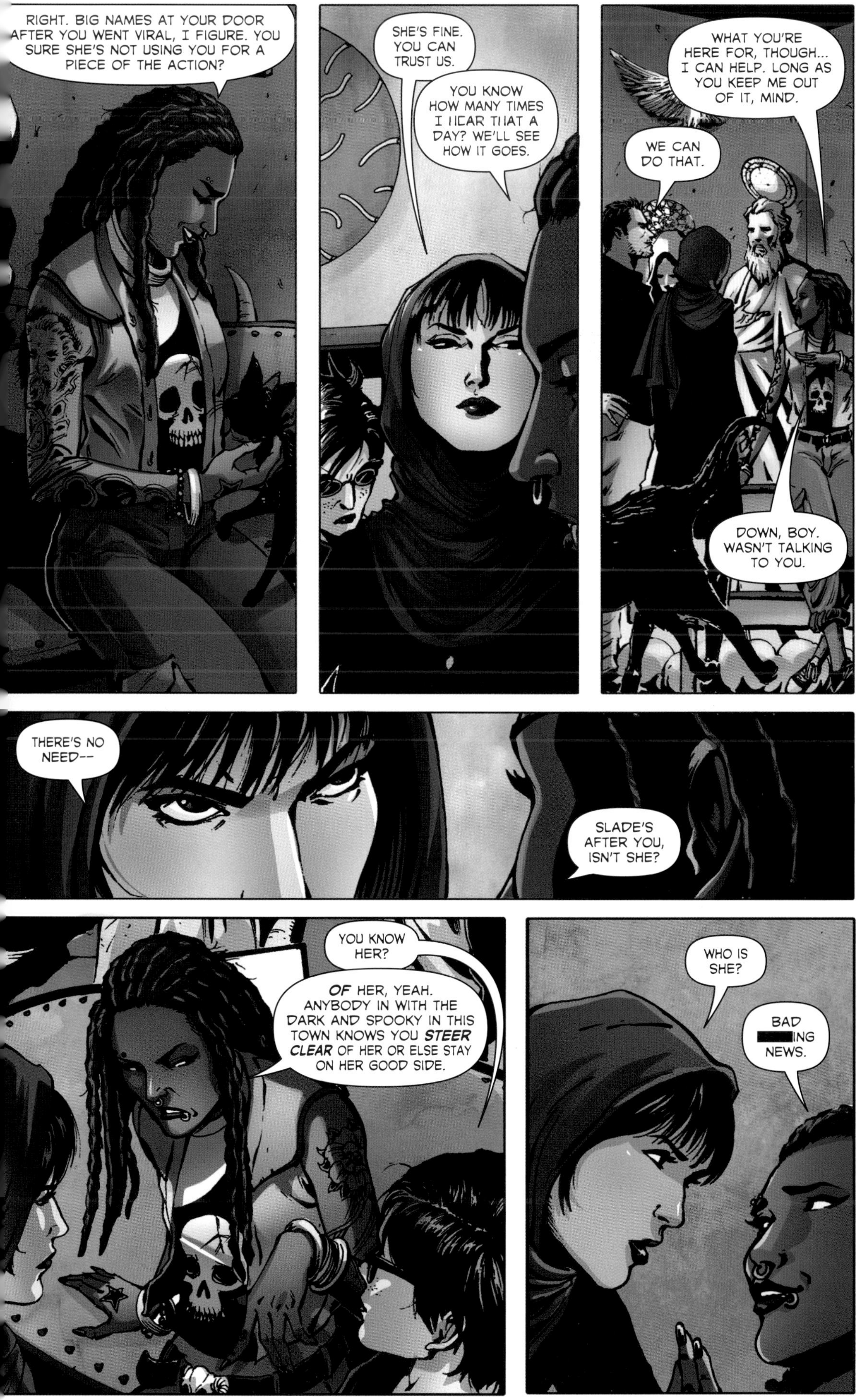
RIGHT. BIG NAMES AT YOUR DOOR AFTER YOU WENT VIRAL, I FIGURE. YOU SURE SHE'S NOT USING YOU FOR A PIECE OF THE ACTION?
SHE'S FINE. YOU CAN TRUST US.
YOU KNOW HOW MANY TIMES I HEAR THAT A DAY? WE'LL SEE HOW IT GOES.
WHAT YOU'RE HERE FOR, THOUGH... I CAN HELP. LONG AS YOU KEEP ME OUT OF IT, MIND.
WE CAN DO THAT.
DOWN, BOY. WASN'T TALKING TO YOU.
THERE'S NO NEED--
SLADE'S AFTER YOU, ISN'T SHE?
YOU KNOW HER?
OF HER, YEAH. ANYBODY IN WITH THE DARK AND SPOOKY IN THIS TOWN KNOWS YOU ***STEER CLEAR*** OF HER OR ELSE STAY ON HER GOOD SIDE.
WHO IS SHE?
BAD [redacted]ING NEWS.

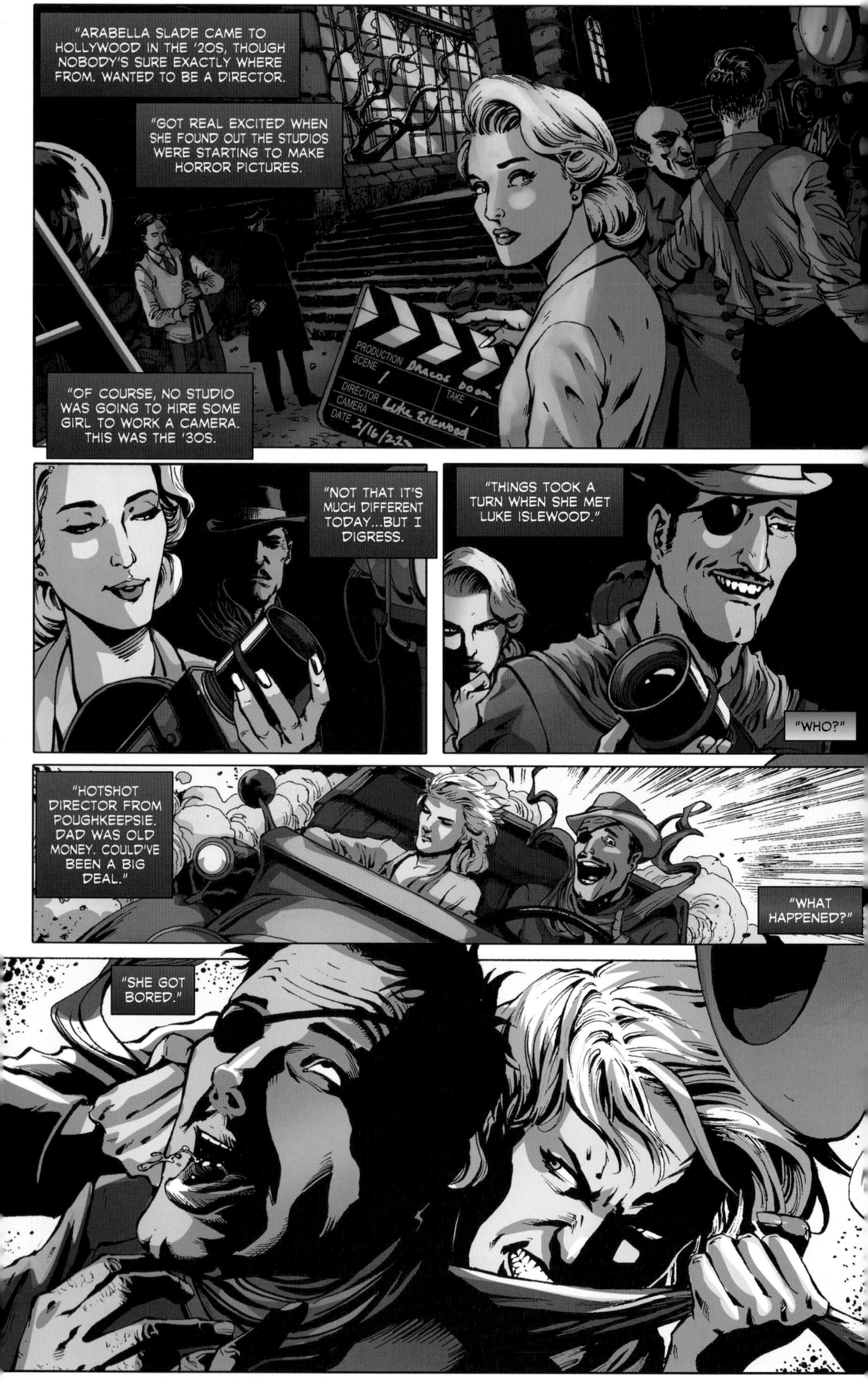
"ARABELLA SLADE CAME TO HOLLYWOOD IN THE '20S, THOUGH NOBODY'S SURE EXACTLY WHERE FROM. WANTED TO BE A DIRECTOR.
"GOT REAL EXCITED WHEN SHE FOUND OUT THE STUDIOS WERE STARTING TO MAKE HORROR PICTURES.
PRODUCTION
SCENE
DIRECTOR
CAMERA
DATE
TAKE
"OF COURSE, NO STUDIO WAS GOING TO HIRE SOME GIRL TO WORK A CAMERA. THIS WAS THE '30S.
"NOT THAT IT'S MUCH DIFFERENT TODAY...BUT I DIGRESS.
"THINGS TOOK A TURN WHEN SHE MET LUKE ISLEWOOD."
"WHO?"
"HOTSHOT DIRECTOR FROM POUGHKEEPSIE. DAD WAS OLD MONEY. COULD'VE BEEN A BIG DEAL."
"WHAT HAPPENED?"
"SHE GOT BORED."

OH MY GOD.

SHE KILLED HIM?

OH YEAH. CUT HIM UP, TOO. RITUAL-STYLE. COPS COULD NEVER PROVE IT WAS HER, SOMEHOW...

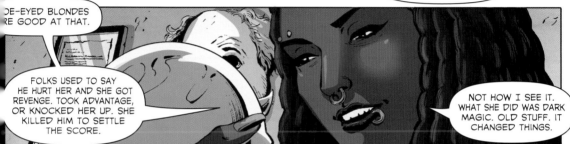

DE-EYED BLONDES RE GOOD AT THAT.

FOLKS USED TO SAY HE HURT HER AND SHE GOT REVENGE. TOOK ADVANTAGE, OR KNOCKED HER UP. SHE KILLED HIM TO SETTLE THE SCORE.

NOT HOW I SEE IT. WHAT SHE DID WAS DARK MAGIC. OLD STUFF. IT CHANGED THINGS.

BEFORE LONG SHE WAS RUNNING THE SHOW HERE IN TOWN. NOT A CREATURE FEATURE GOT MADE WITHOUT HER CLAWS DUG INTO IT. THEN, FOLKS STARTED TO GO MISSING ON SET. BACKGROUND GUYS, DRIVERS.

SERIAL KILLERS GO AFTER SEX WORKERS BECAUSE THEY DON'T SEE THEM AS *PEOPLE*, YEAH? SLADE'S LIKE THAT, BUT WITH *EXTRAS*.

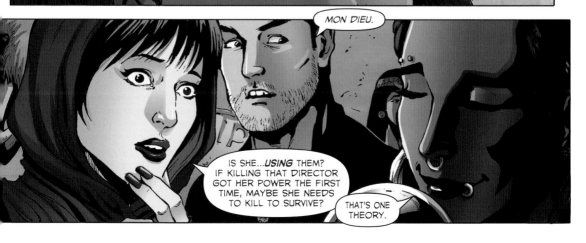

MON DIEU.

IS SHE...*USING* THEM? IF KILLING THAT DIRECTOR GOT HER POWER THE FIRST TIME, MAYBE SHE NEEDS TO KILL TO SURVIVE?

THAT'S ONE THEORY.

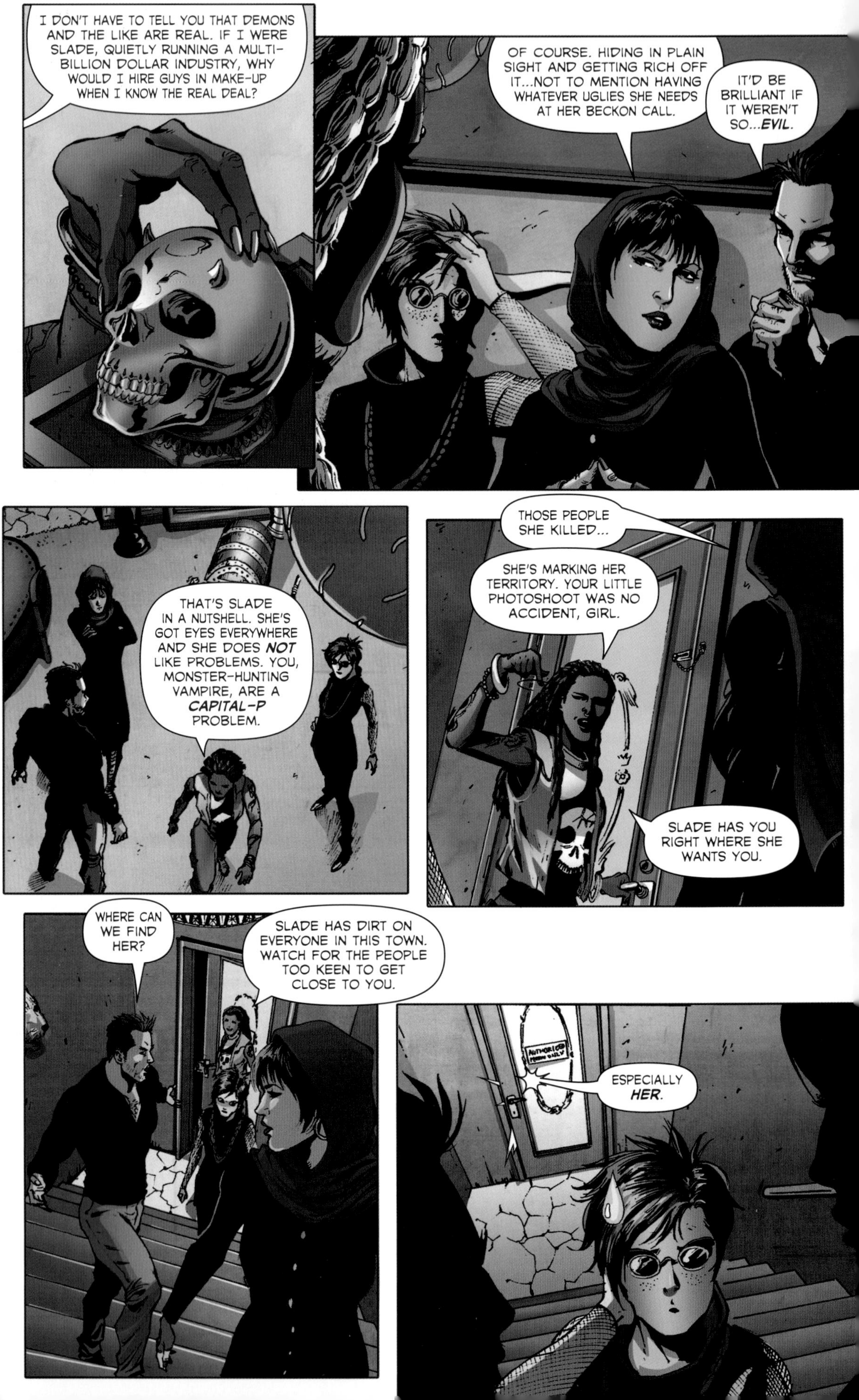
I DON'T HAVE TO TELL YOU THAT DEMONS AND THE LIKE ARE REAL. IF I WERE SLADE, QUIETLY RUNNING A MULTI-BILLION DOLLAR INDUSTRY, WHY WOULD I HIRE GUYS IN MAKE-UP WHEN I KNOW THE REAL DEAL?
OF COURSE. HIDING IN PLAIN SIGHT AND GETTING RICH OFF IT...NOT TO MENTION HAVING WHATEVER UGLIES SHE NEEDS AT HER BECKON CALL.
IT'D BE BRILLIANT IF IT WEREN'T SO...*EVIL*.
THAT'S SLADE IN A NUTSHELL. SHE'S GOT EYES EVERYWHERE AND SHE DOES *NOT* LIKE PROBLEMS. YOU, MONSTER-HUNTING VAMPIRE, ARE A *CAPITAL-P* PROBLEM.
THOSE PEOPLE SHE KILLED...
SHE'S MARKING HER TERRITORY. YOUR LITTLE PHOTOSHOOT WAS NO ACCIDENT, GIRL.
SLADE HAS YOU RIGHT WHERE SHE WANTS YOU.
WHERE CAN WE FIND HER?
SLADE HAS DIRT ON EVERYONE IN THIS TOWN. WATCH FOR THE PEOPLE TOO KEEN TO GET CLOSE TO YOU.
ESPECIALLY *HER*.

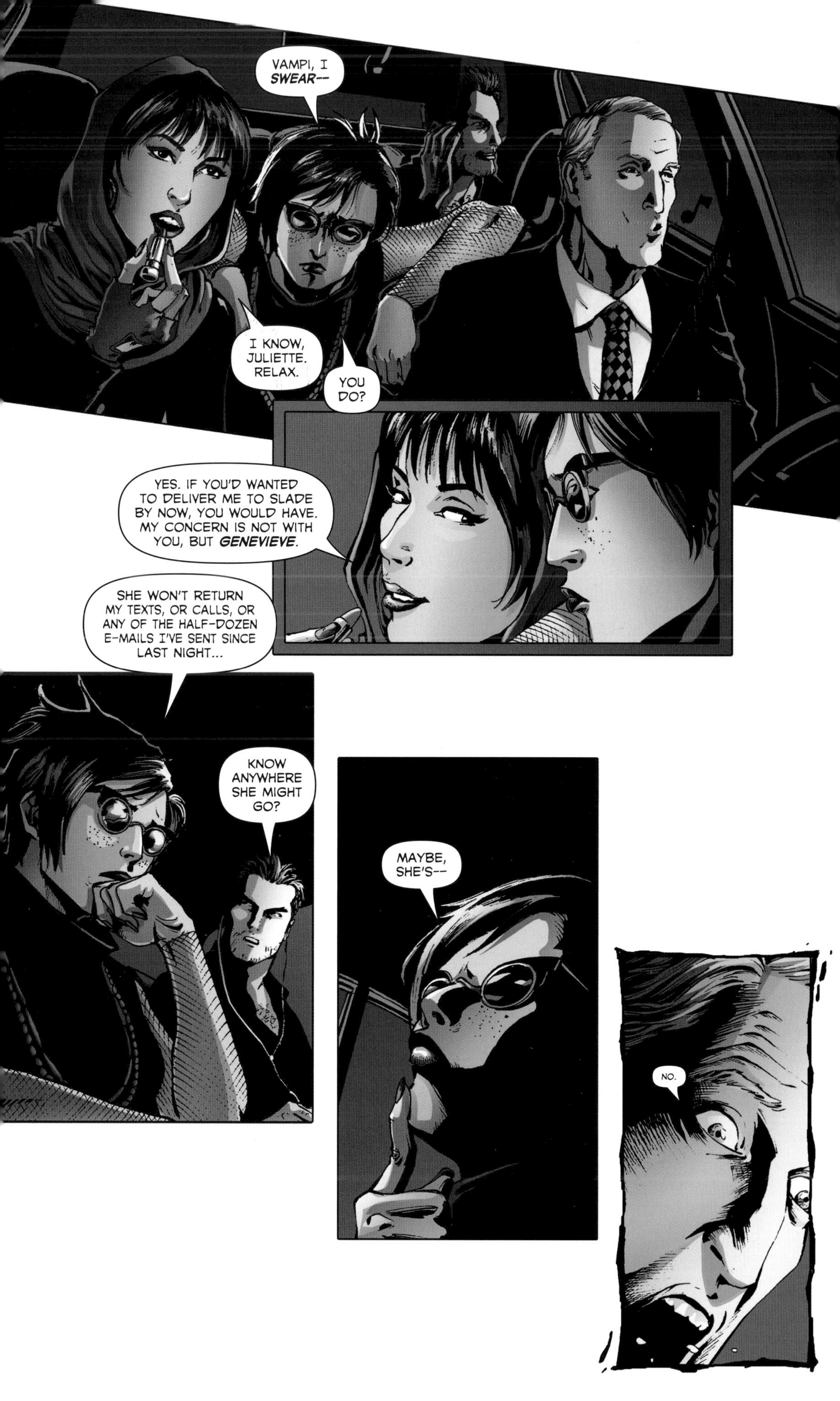
VAMPI, I *SWEAR--*
I KNOW, JULIETTE. RELAX.
YOU DO?
YES. IF YOU'D WANTED TO DELIVER ME TO SLADE BY NOW, YOU WOULD HAVE. MY CONCERN IS NOT WITH YOU, BUT *GENEVIEVE*.
SHE WON'T RETURN MY TEXTS, OR CALLS, OR ANY OF THE HALF-DOZEN E-MAILS I'VE SENT SINCE LAST NIGHT...
KNOW ANYWHERE SHE MIGHT GO?
MAYBE, SHE'S--
NO.

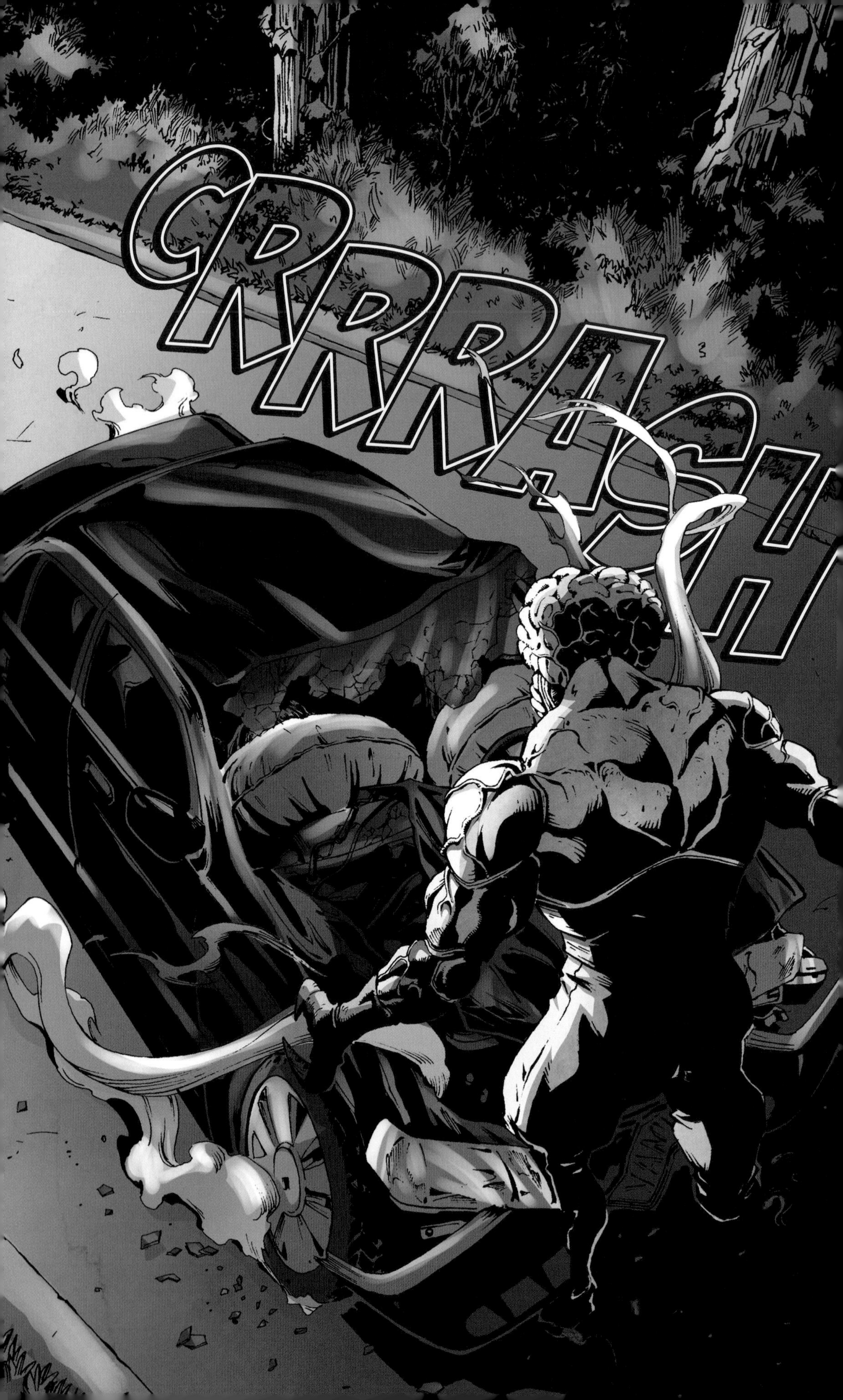
CRRRASH

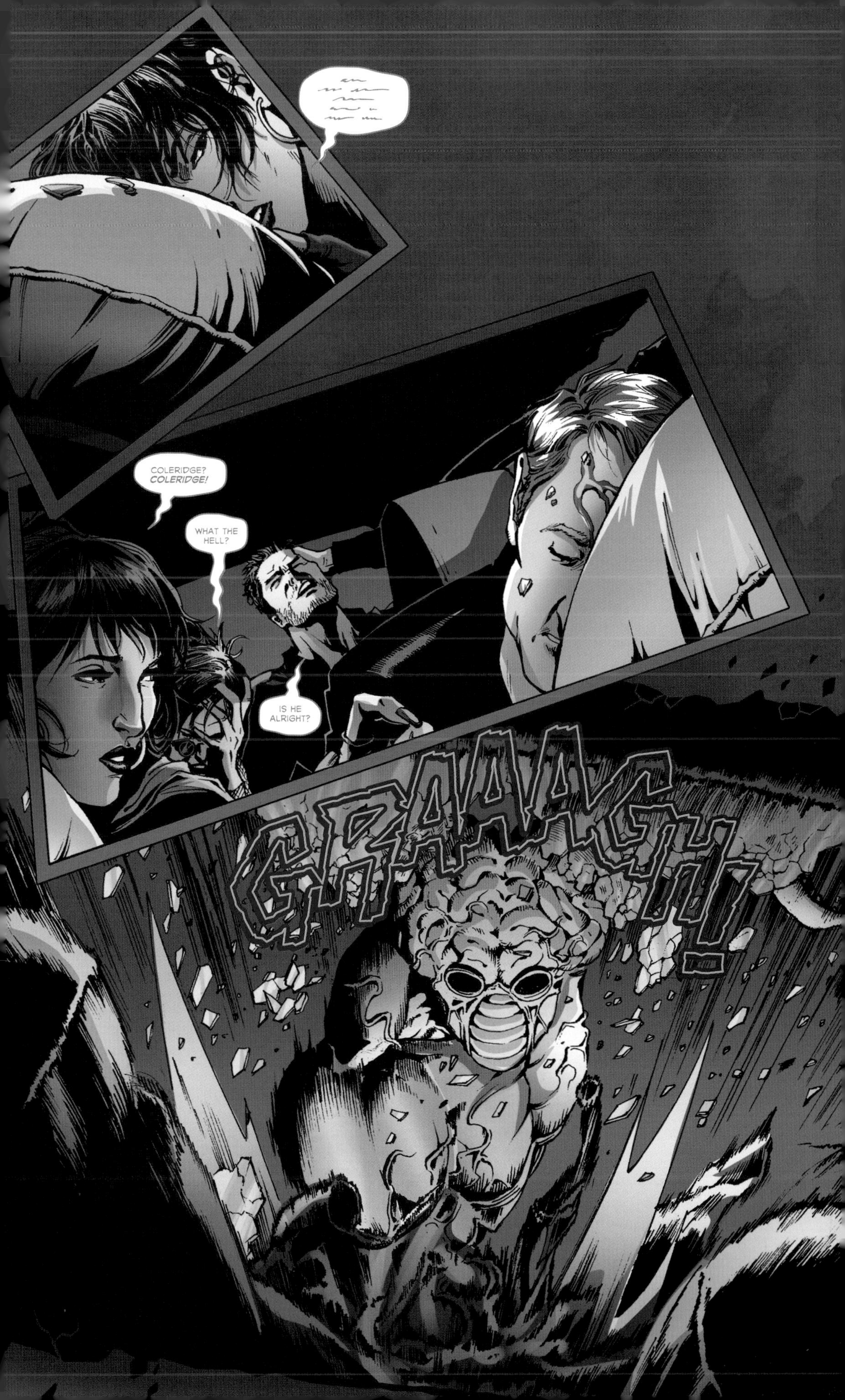
COLERIDGE? COLERIDGE!
WHAT THE HELL?
IS HE ALRIGHT?
GRAAAGH!

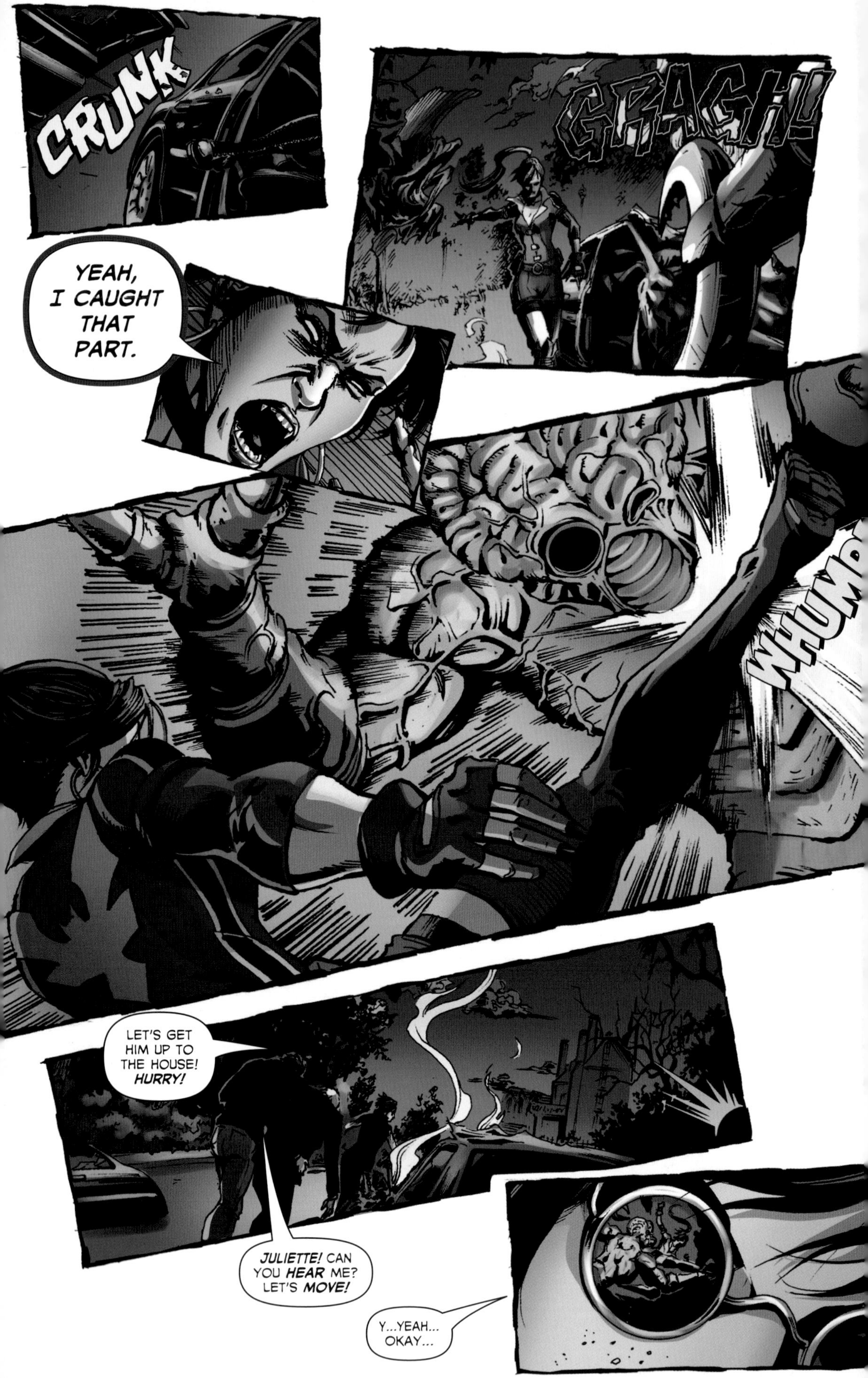
CRUNK
GRAGH!
YEAH, I CAUGHT THAT PART.
WHUMP
LET'S GET HIM UP TO THE HOUSE! HURRY!
JULIETTE! CAN YOU HEAR ME? LET'S MOVE!
Y...YEAH... OKAY...

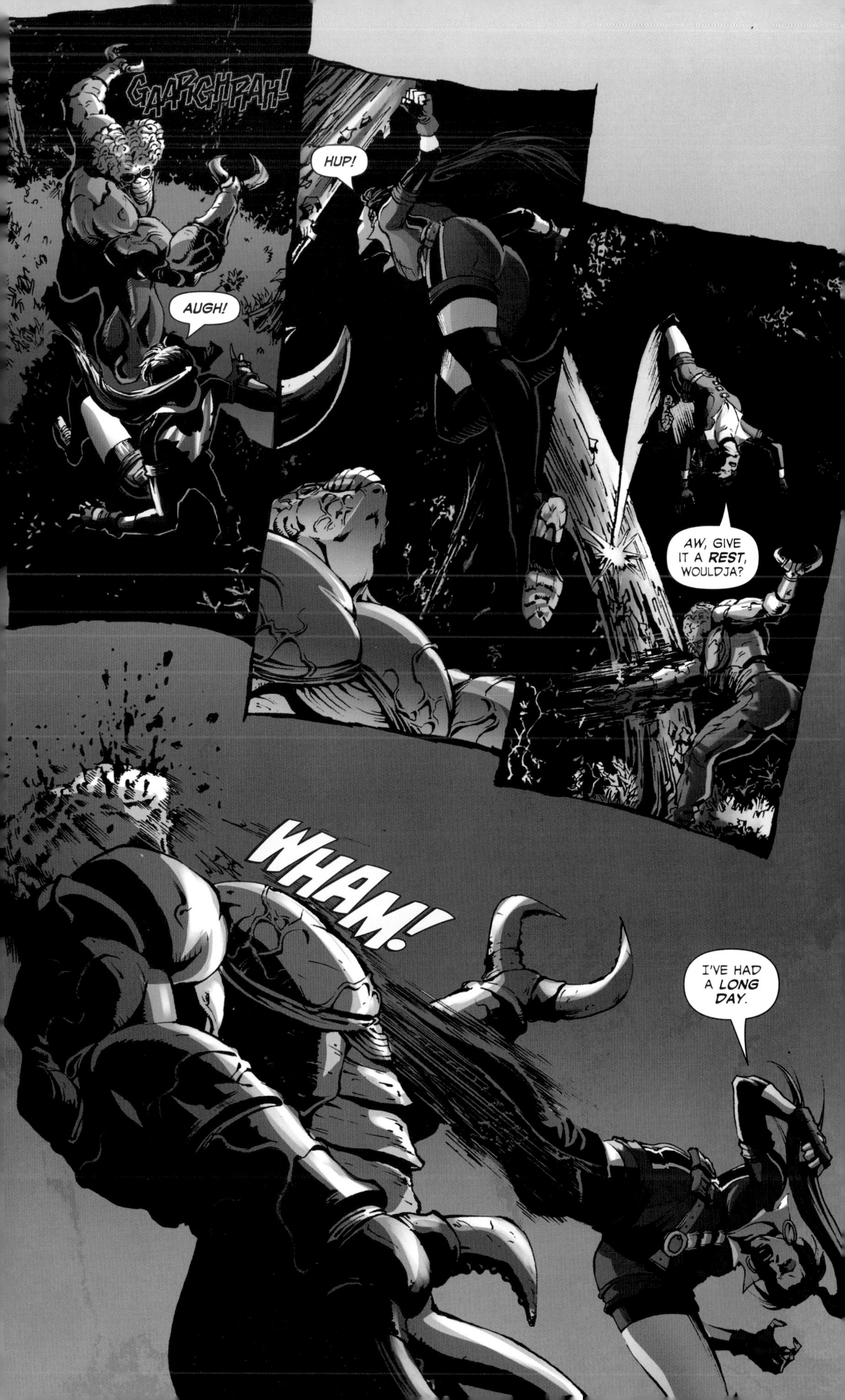
GAARGHRAH!
HUP!
AUGH!
AW, GIVE IT A REST, WOULDJA?
WHAM!
I'VE HAD A LONG DAY.

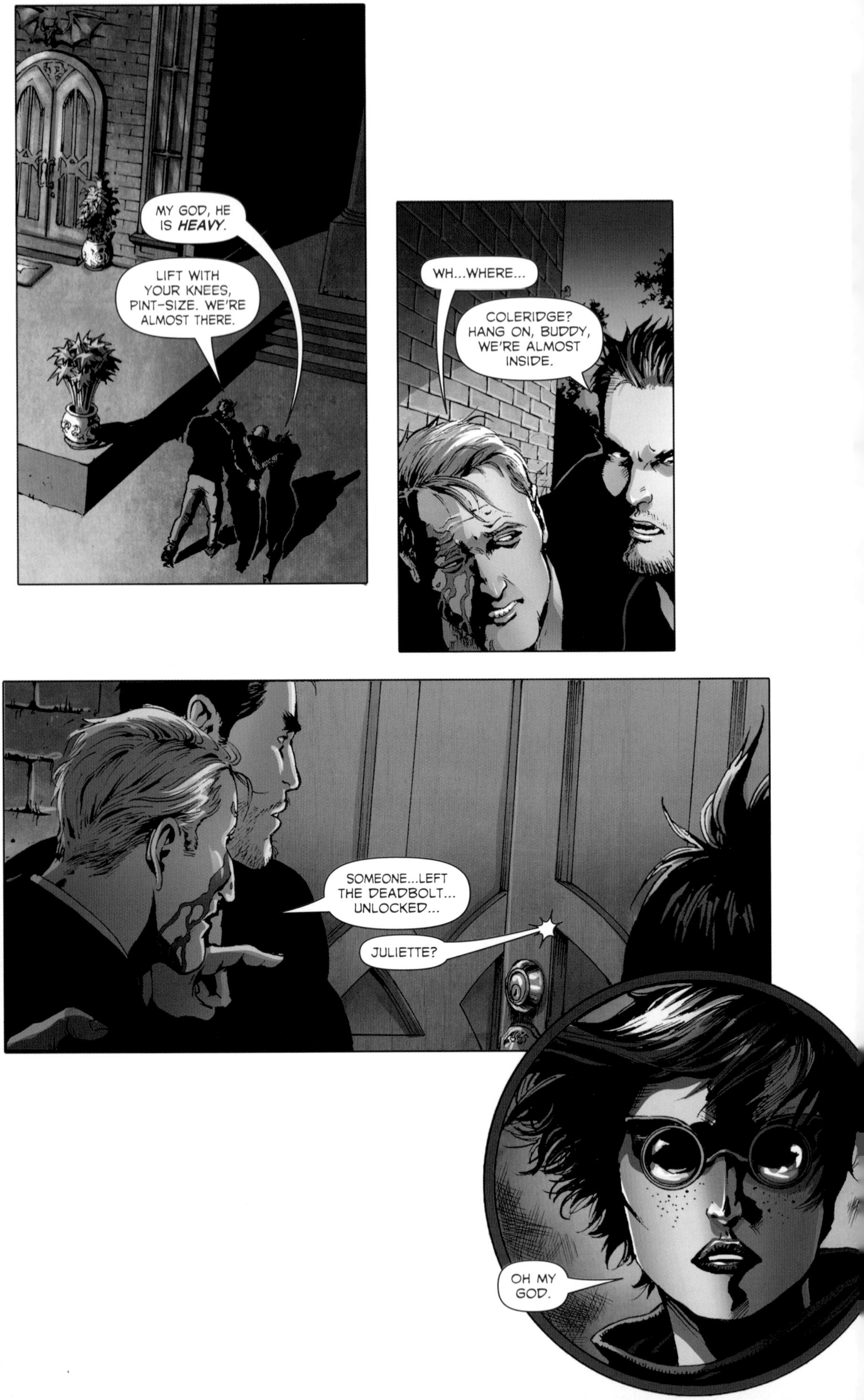
MY GOD, HE IS *HEAVY*.
LIFT WITH YOUR KNEES, PINT-SIZE. WE'RE ALMOST THERE.
WH...WHERE...
COLERIDGE? HANG ON, BUDDY, WE'RE ALMOST INSIDE.
SOMEONE...LEFT THE DEADBOLT... UNLOCKED...
JULIETTE?
OH MY GOD.

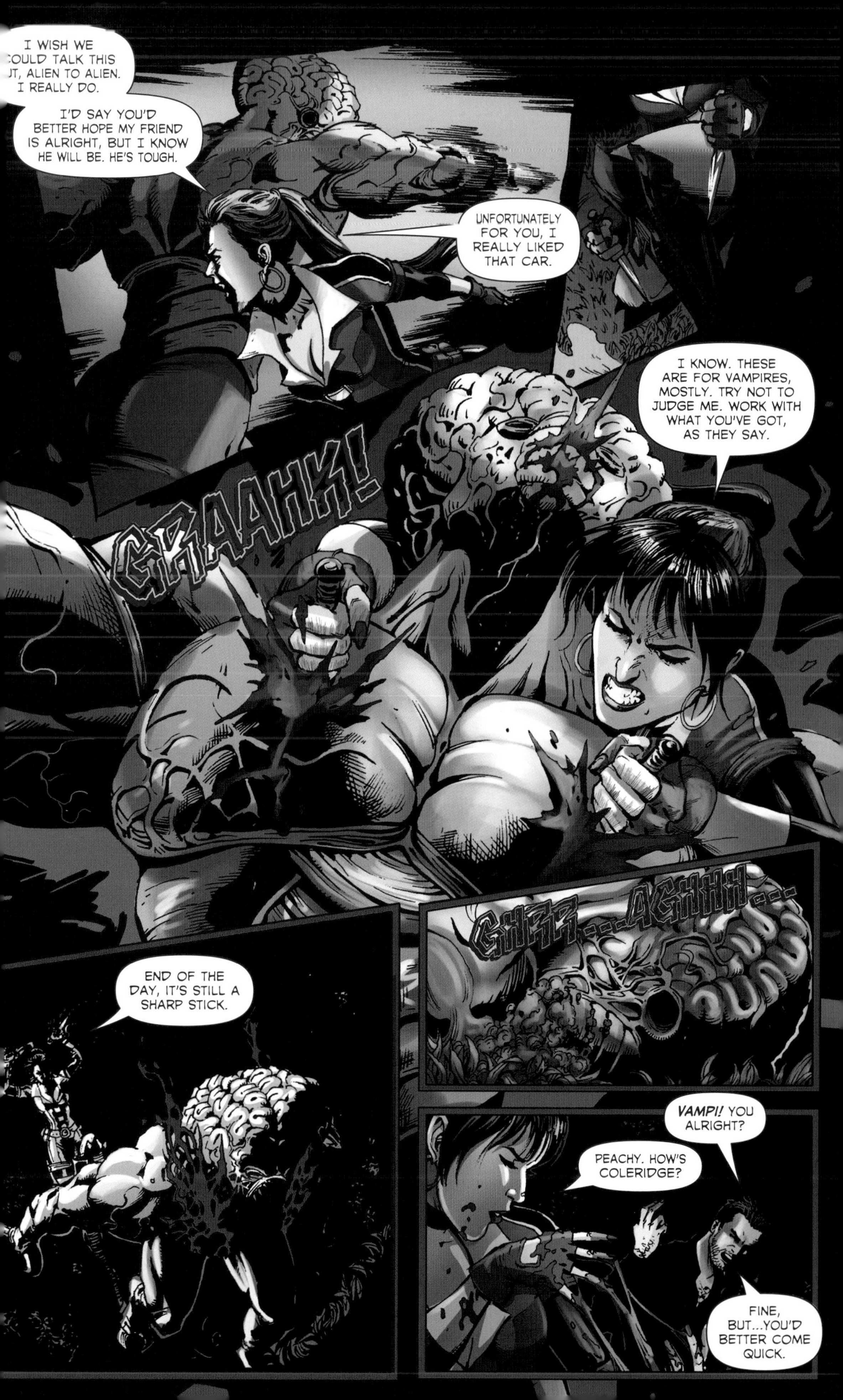
I WISH WE
COULD TALK THIS
UT, ALIEN TO ALIEN.
I REALLY DO.
I'D SAY YOU'D BETTER HOPE MY FRIEND IS ALRIGHT, BUT I KNOW HE WILL BE. HE'S TOUGH.
UNFORTUNATELY FOR YOU, I REALLY LIKED THAT CAR.
I KNOW. THESE ARE FOR VAMPIRES, MOSTLY. TRY NOT TO JUDGE ME. WORK WITH WHAT YOU'VE GOT, AS THEY SAY.
GRAAHK!
GHZZ...AGHHH...
END OF THE DAY, IT'S STILL A SHARP STICK.
VAMPI! YOU ALRIGHT?
PEACHY. HOW'S COLERIDGE?
FINE, BUT...YOU'D BETTER COME QUICK.

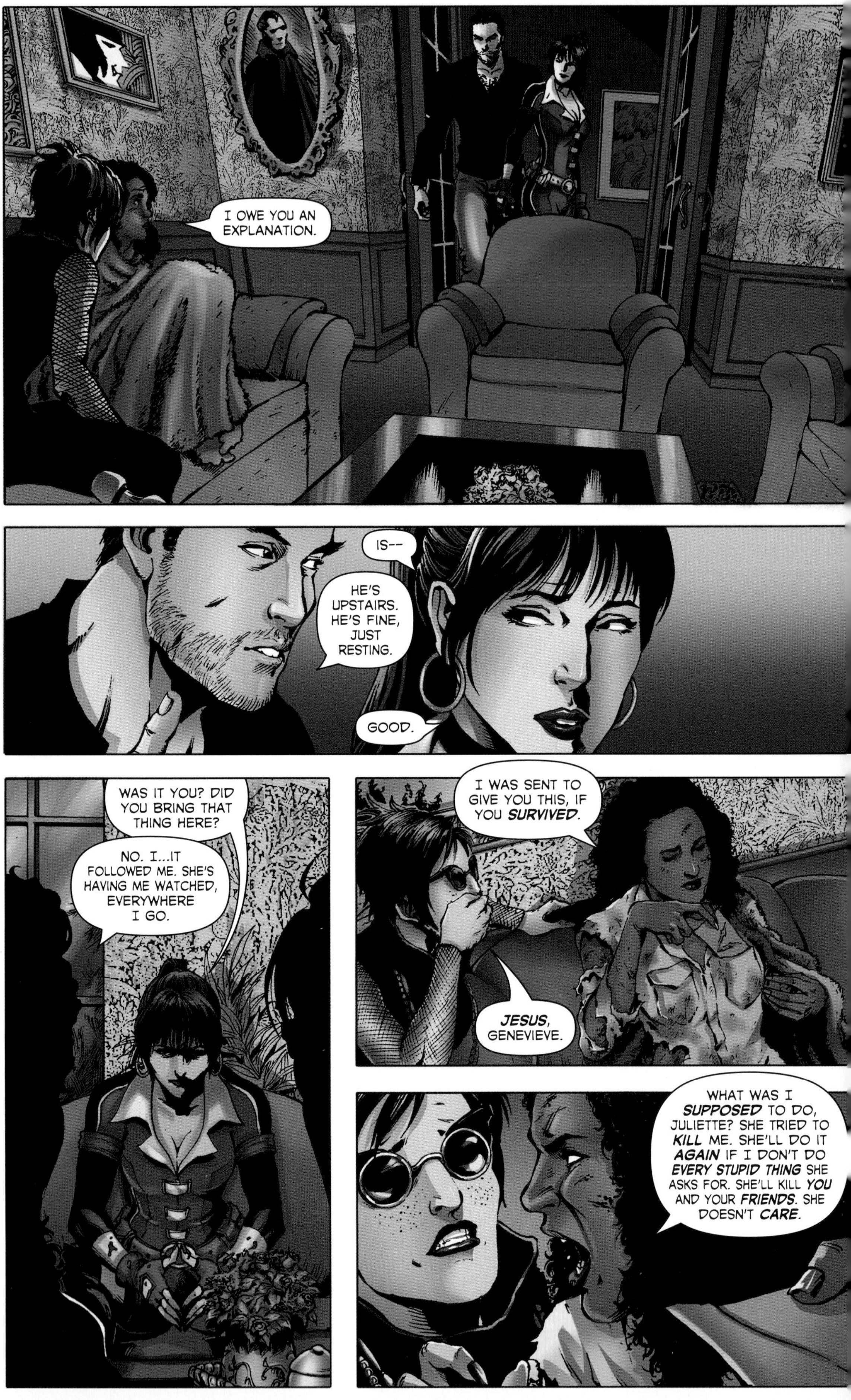
I OWE YOU AN EXPLANATION.
IS--
HE'S UPSTAIRS. HE'S FINE, JUST RESTING.
GOOD.
WAS IT YOU? DID YOU BRING THAT THING HERE?
NO. I...IT FOLLOWED ME. SHE'S HAVING ME WATCHED, EVERYWHERE I GO.
I WAS SENT TO GIVE YOU THIS, IF YOU *SURVIVED*.
JESUS, GENEVIEVE.
WHAT WAS I *SUPPOSED* TO DO, JULIETTE? SHE TRIED TO *KILL* ME. SHE'LL DO IT *AGAIN* IF I DON'T DO *EVERY STUPID THING* SHE ASKS FOR. SHE'LL KILL *YOU* AND YOUR *FRIENDS*. SHE DOESN'T *CARE*.

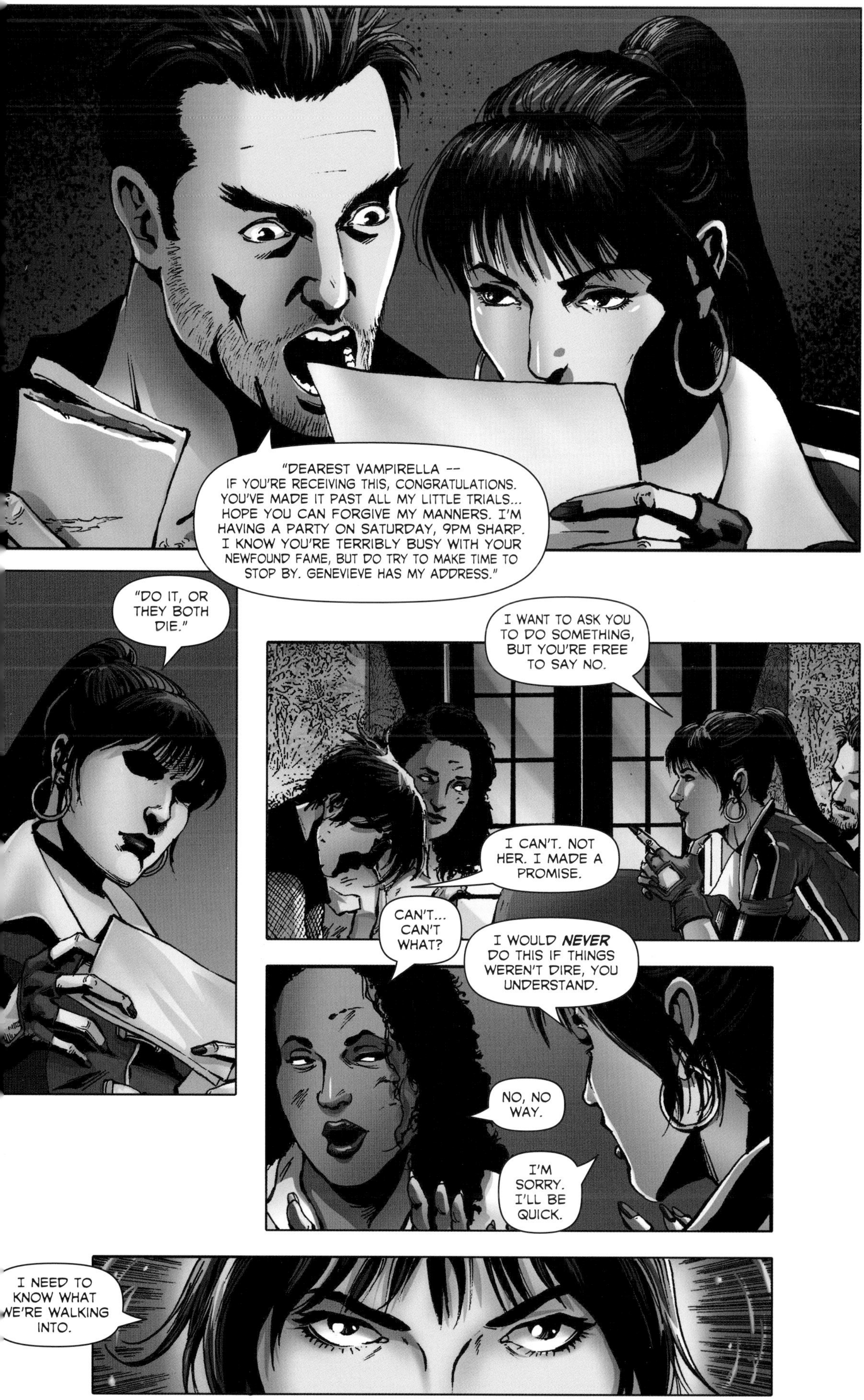
"DEAREST VAMPIRELLA --
IF YOU'RE RECEIVING THIS, CONGRATULATIONS. YOU'VE MADE IT PAST ALL MY LITTLE TRIALS... HOPE YOU CAN FORGIVE MY MANNERS. I'M HAVING A PARTY ON SATURDAY, 9PM SHARP. I KNOW YOU'RE TERRIBLY BUSY WITH YOUR NEWFOUND FAME, BUT DO TRY TO MAKE TIME TO STOP BY. GENEVIEVE HAS MY ADDRESS."
"DO IT, OR THEY BOTH DIE."
I WANT TO ASK YOU TO DO SOMETHING, BUT YOU'RE FREE TO SAY NO.
I CAN'T. NOT HER. I MADE A PROMISE.
CAN'T... CAN'T WHAT?
I WOULD **NEVER** DO THIS IF THINGS WEREN'T DIRE, YOU UNDERSTAND.
NO, NO WAY.
I'M SORRY. I'LL BE QUICK.
I NEED TO KNOW WHAT WE'RE WALKING INTO.

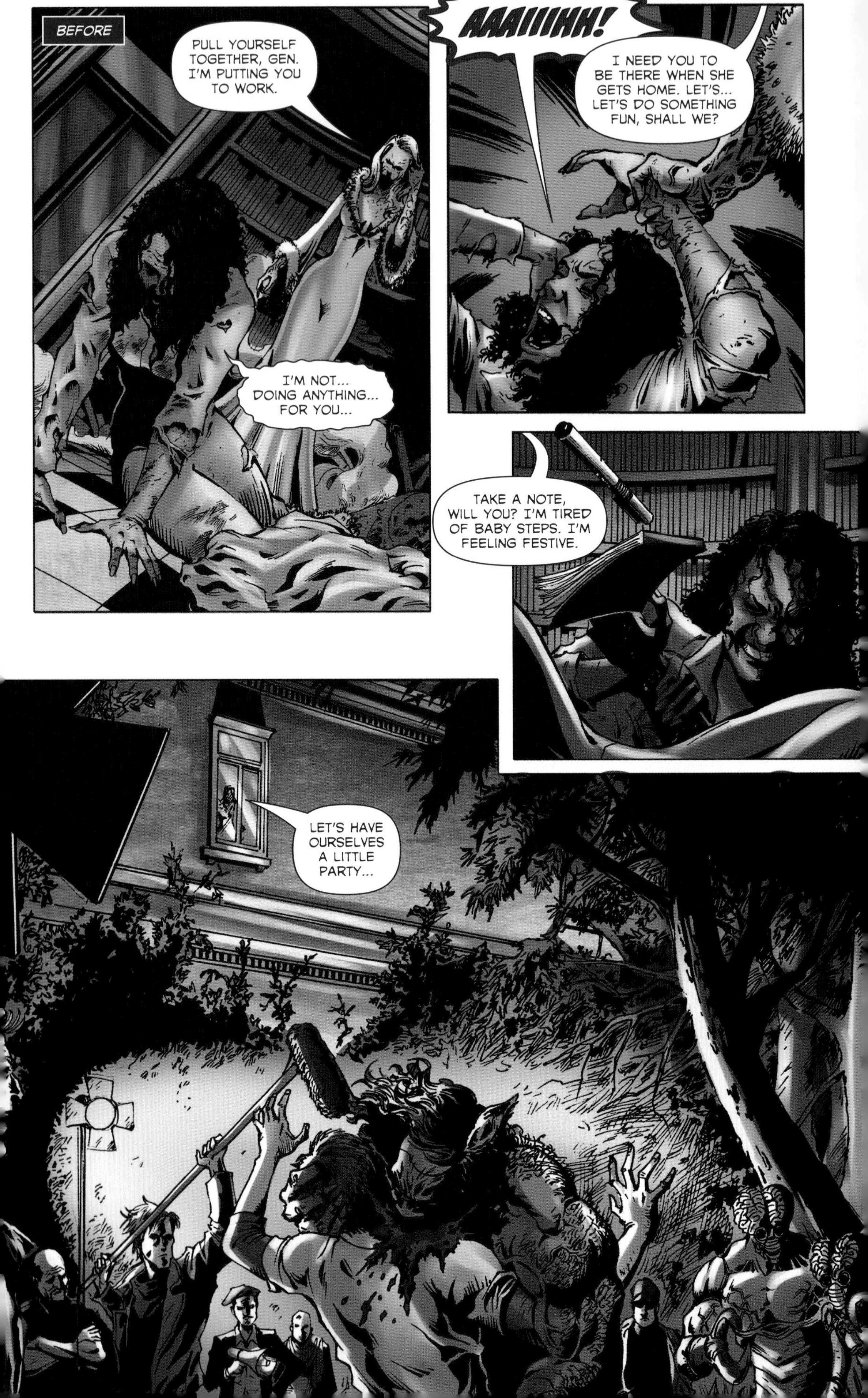
BEFORE
PULL YOURSELF TOGETHER, GEN. I'M PUTTING YOU TO WORK.
I'M NOT... DOING ANYTHING... FOR YOU...
AAAIIIHH!
I NEED YOU TO BE THERE WHEN SHE GETS HOME. LET'S... LET'S DO SOMETHING FUN, SHALL WE?
TAKE A NOTE, WILL YOU? I'M TIRED OF BABY STEPS. I'M FEELING FESTIVE.
LET'S HAVE OURSELVES A LITTLE PARTY...

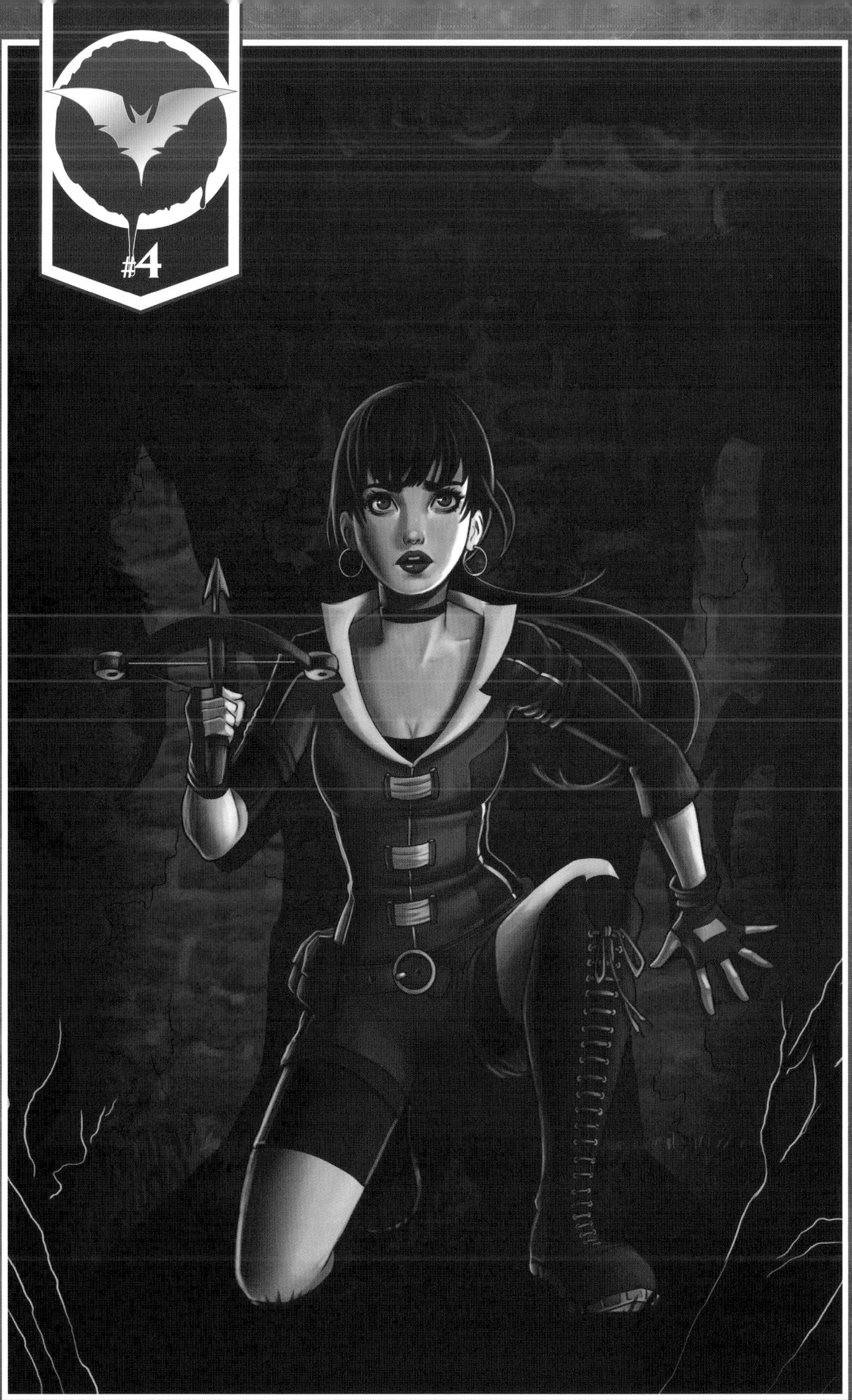
#4

cover by **Chrissie Zullo**

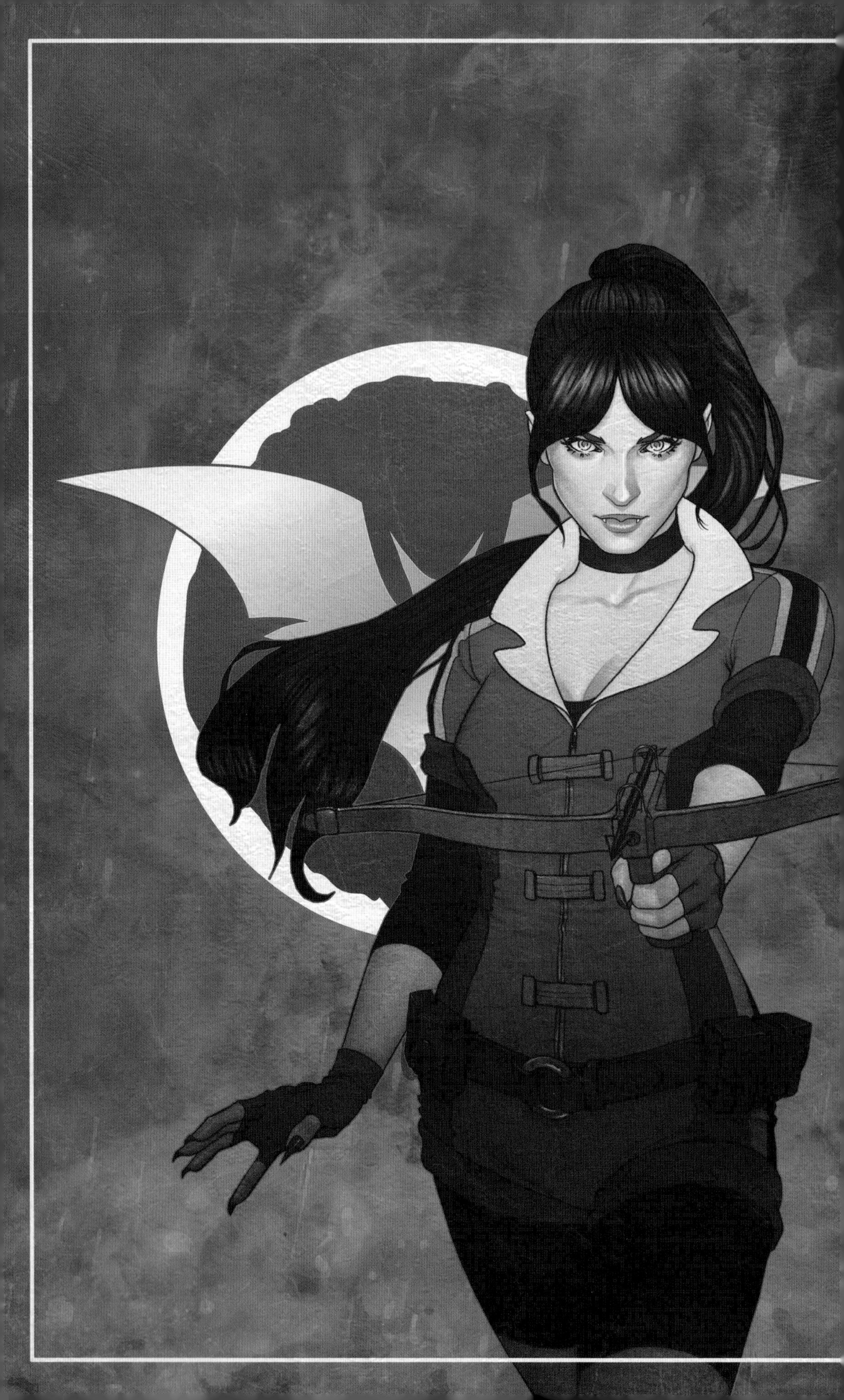

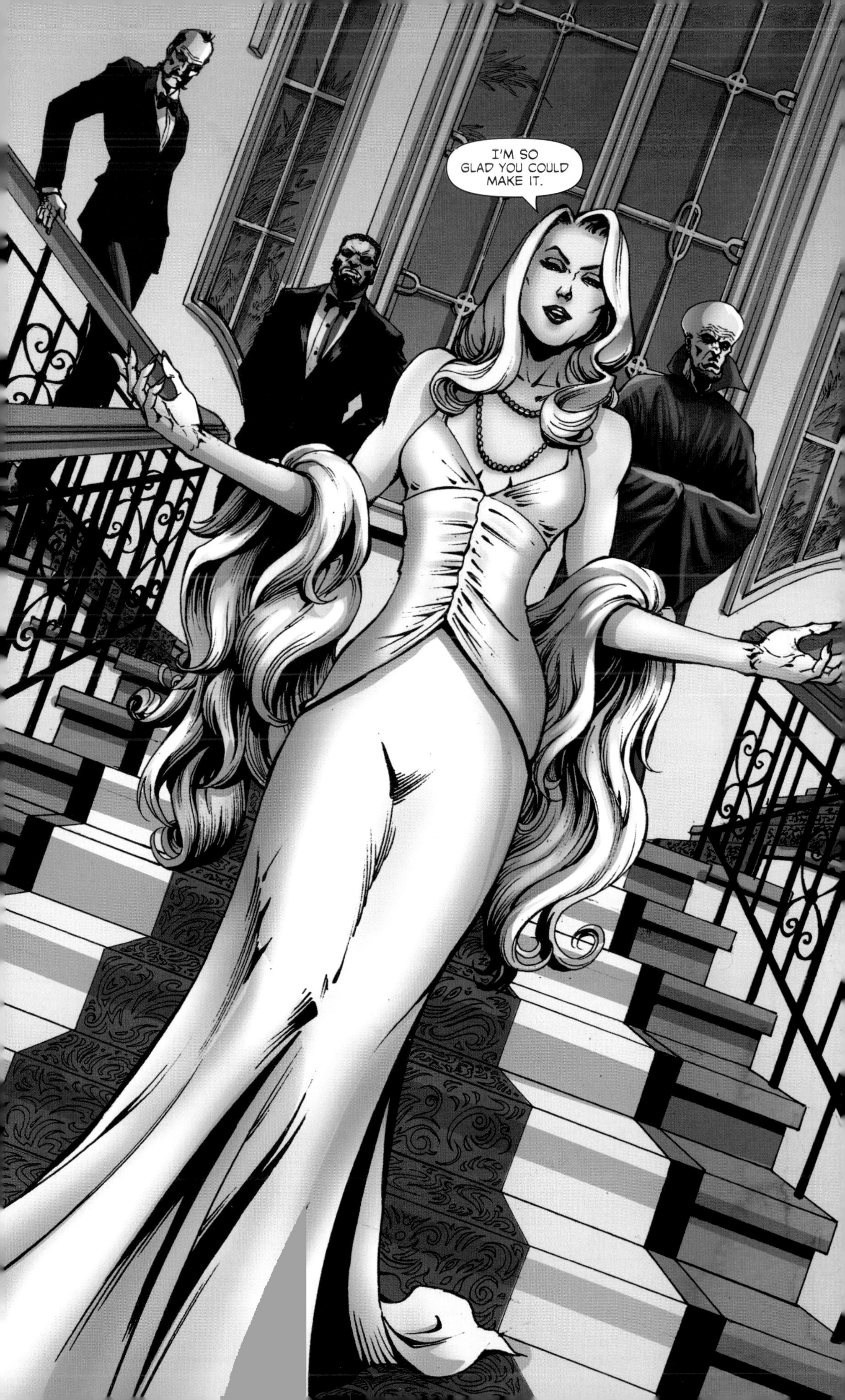
I'M SO GLAD YOU COULD MAKE IT.

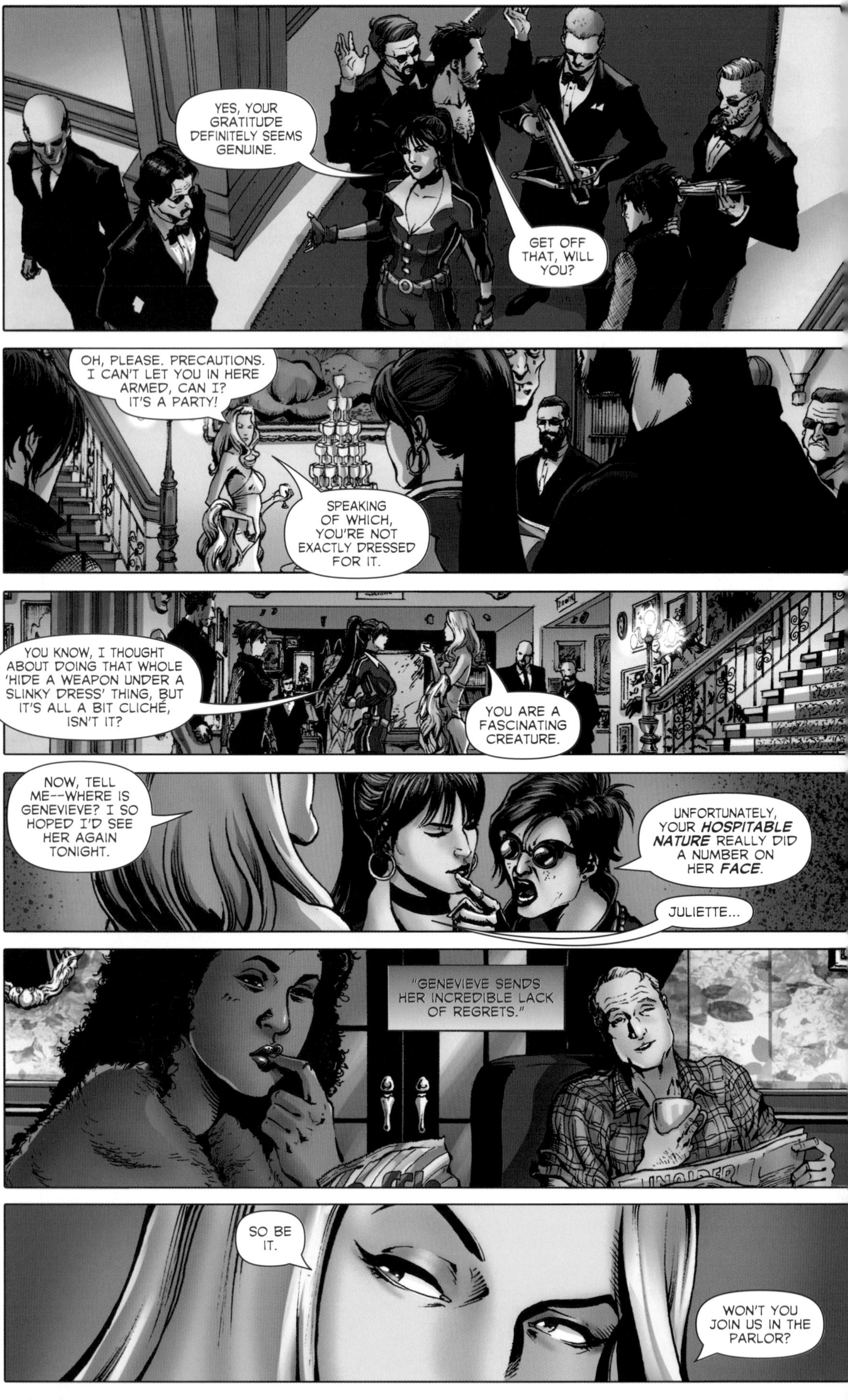
YES, YOUR GRATITUDE DEFINITELY SEEMS GENUINE.
GET OFF THAT, WILL YOU?
OH, PLEASE. PRECAUTIONS. I CAN'T LET YOU IN HERE ARMED, CAN I? IT'S A PARTY!
SPEAKING OF WHICH, YOU'RE NOT EXACTLY DRESSED FOR IT.
YOU KNOW, I THOUGHT ABOUT DOING THAT WHOLE 'HIDE A WEAPON UNDER A SLINKY DRESS' THING, BUT IT'S ALL A BIT CLICHÉ, ISN'T IT?
YOU ARE A FASCINATING CREATURE.
NOW, TELL ME--WHERE IS GENEVIEVE? I SO HOPED I'D SEE HER AGAIN TONIGHT.
UNFORTUNATELY, YOUR ***HOSPITABLE NATURE*** REALLY DID A NUMBER ON HER ***FACE***.
JULIETTE...
"GENEVIEVE SENDS HER INCREDIBLE LACK OF REGRETS."
SO BE IT.
WON'T YOU JOIN US IN THE PARLOR?

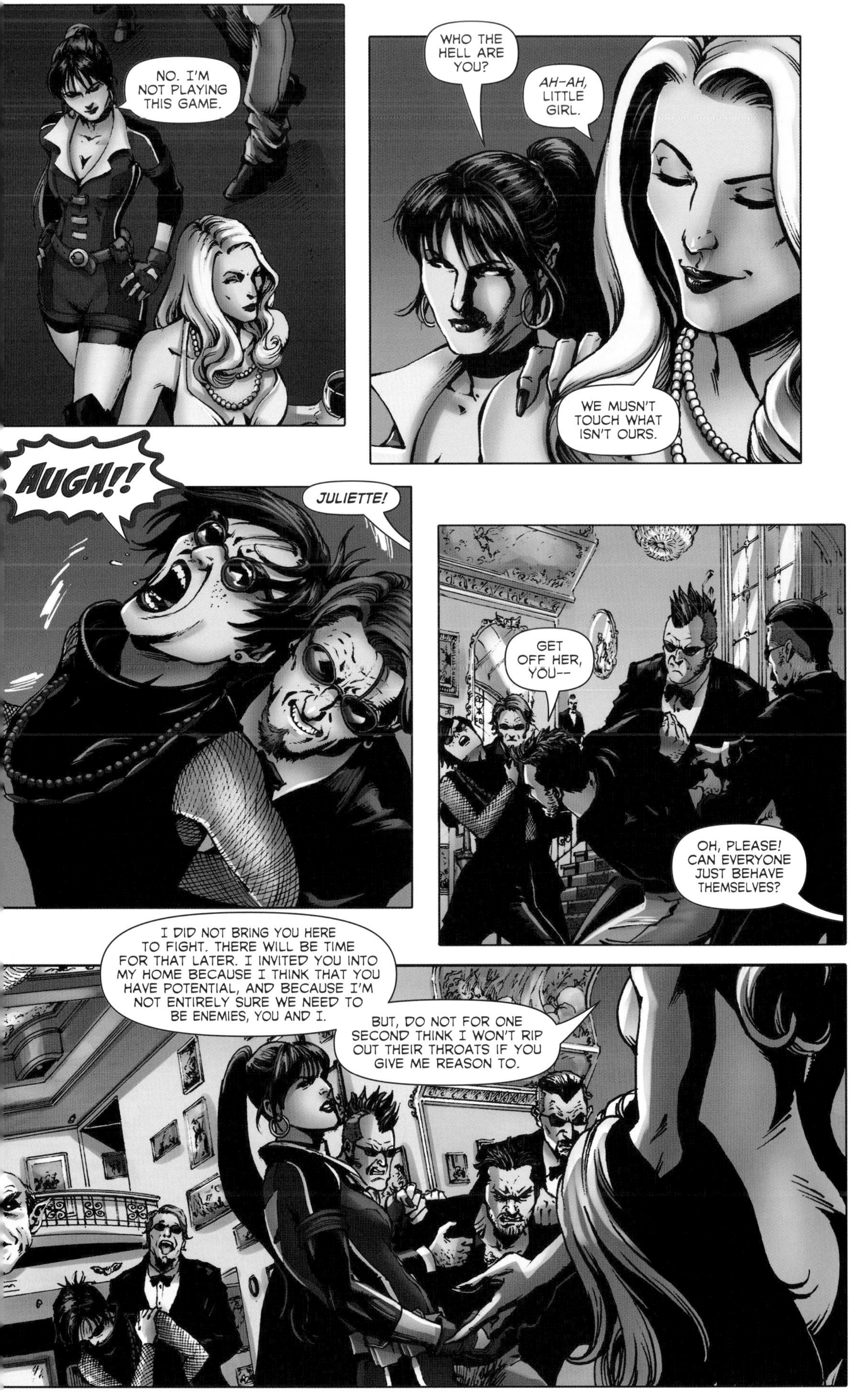
NO. I'M NOT PLAYING THIS GAME.
WHO THE HELL ARE YOU?
AH-AH, LITTLE GIRL.
WE MUSN'T TOUCH WHAT ISN'T OURS.
AUGH!!
JULIETTE!
GET OFF HER, YOU--
OH, PLEASE! CAN EVERYONE JUST BEHAVE THEMSELVES?
I DID NOT BRING YOU HERE TO FIGHT. THERE WILL BE TIME FOR THAT LATER. I INVITED YOU INTO MY HOME BECAUSE I THINK THAT YOU HAVE POTENTIAL, AND BECAUSE I'M NOT ENTIRELY SURE WE NEED TO BE ENEMIES, YOU AND I.
BUT, DO NOT FOR ONE SECOND THINK I WON'T RIP OUT THEIR THROATS IF YOU GIVE ME REASON TO.

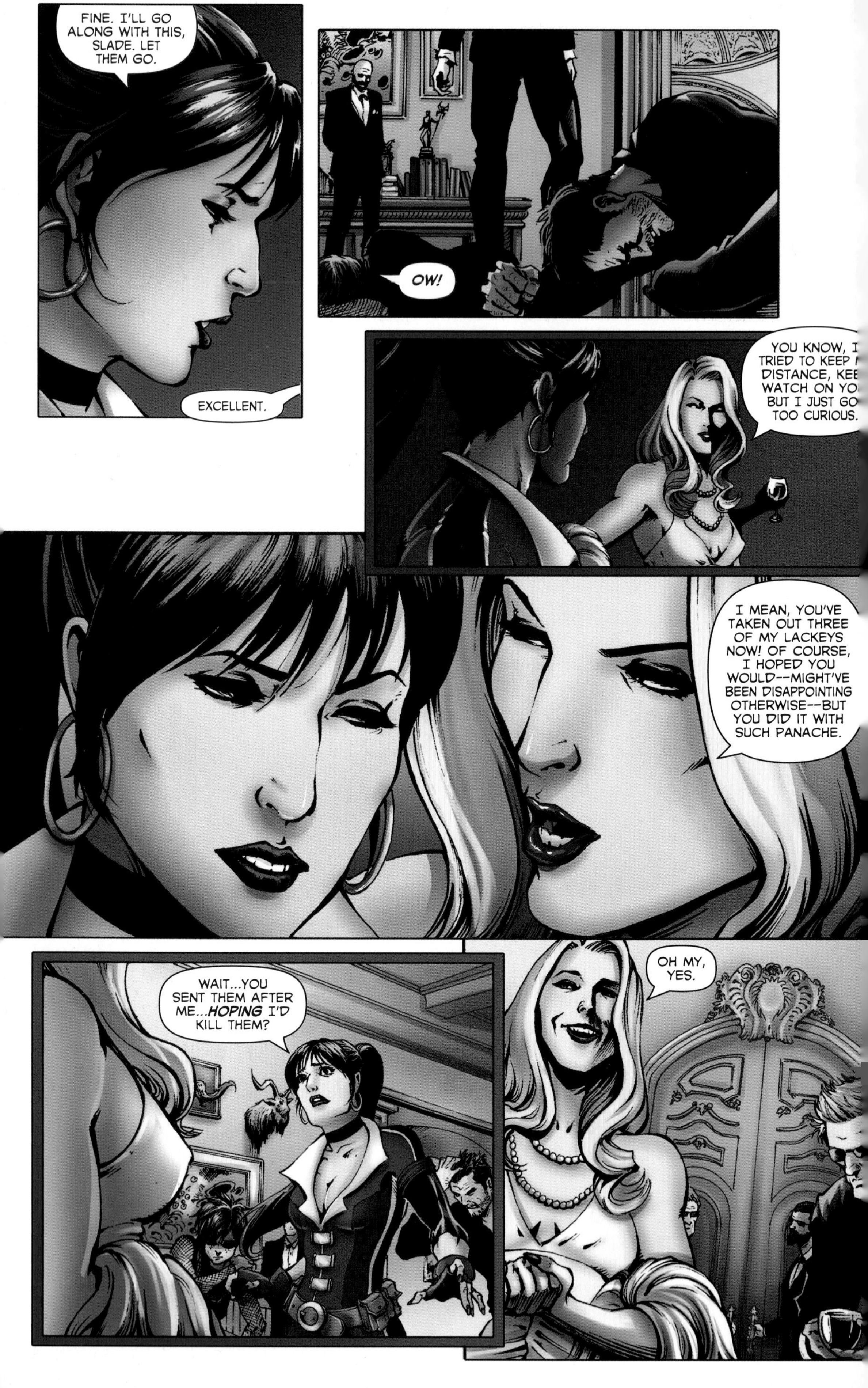
FINE. I'LL GO ALONG WITH THIS, SLADE. LET THEM GO.
EXCELLENT.
OW!
YOU KNOW, I TRIED TO KEEP DISTANCE, KEE WATCH ON YO BUT I JUST GO TOO CURIOUS.
I MEAN, YOU'VE TAKEN OUT THREE OF MY LACKEYS NOW! OF COURSE, I HOPED YOU WOULD--MIGHT'VE BEEN DISAPPOINTING OTHERWISE--BUT YOU DID IT WITH SUCH PANACHE.
WAIT...YOU SENT THEM AFTER ME...HOPING I'D KILL THEM?
OH MY, YES.

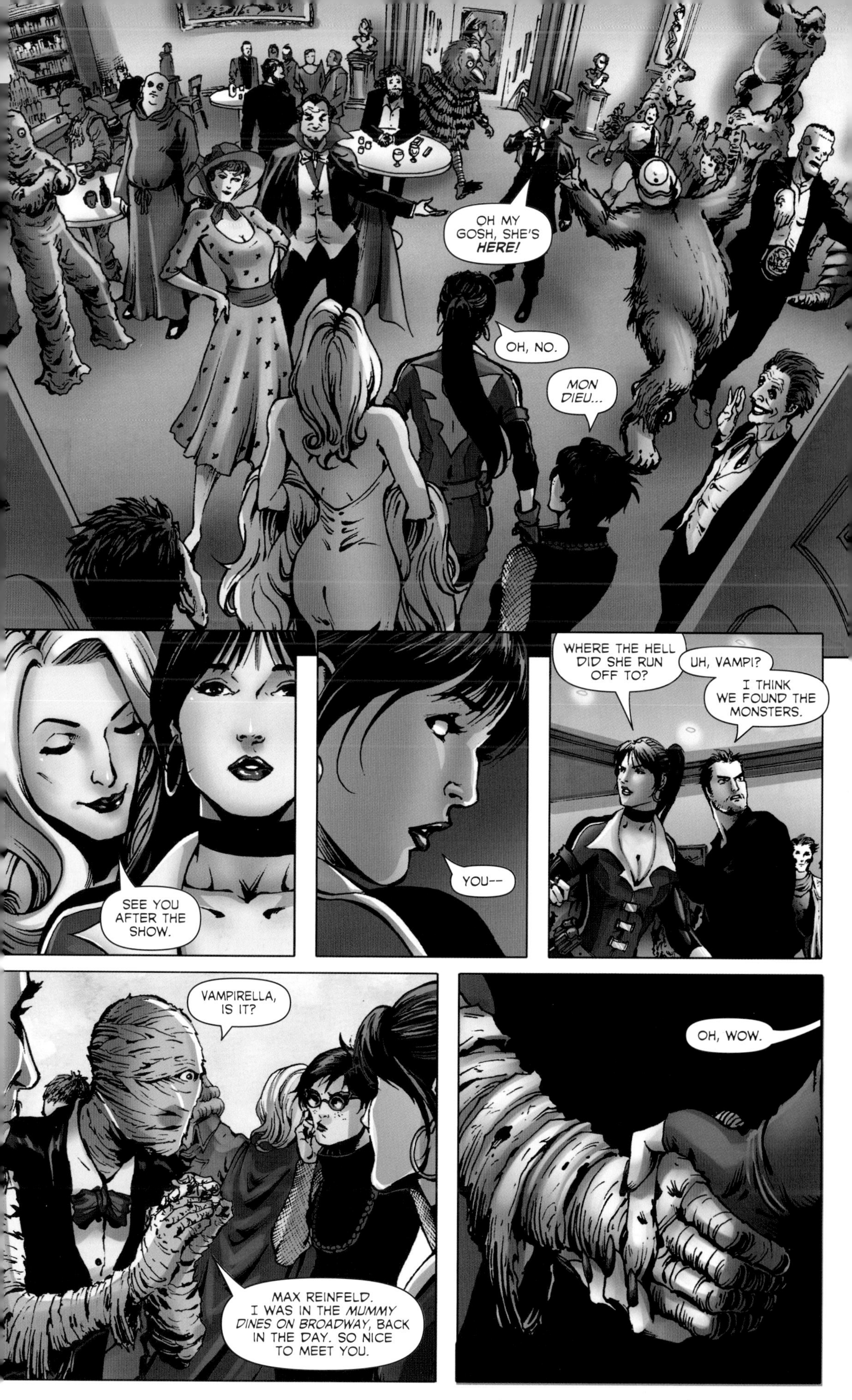
OH MY GOSH, SHE'S *HERE!*
OH, NO.
MON DIEU...
SEE YOU AFTER THE SHOW.
YOU--
WHERE THE HELL DID SHE RUN OFF TO?
UH, VAMPI?
I THINK WE FOUND THE MONSTERS.
VAMPIRELLA, IS IT?
MAX REINFELD. I WAS IN THE *MUMMY DINES ON BROADWAY*, BACK IN THE DAY. SO NICE TO MEET YOU.
OH, WOW.

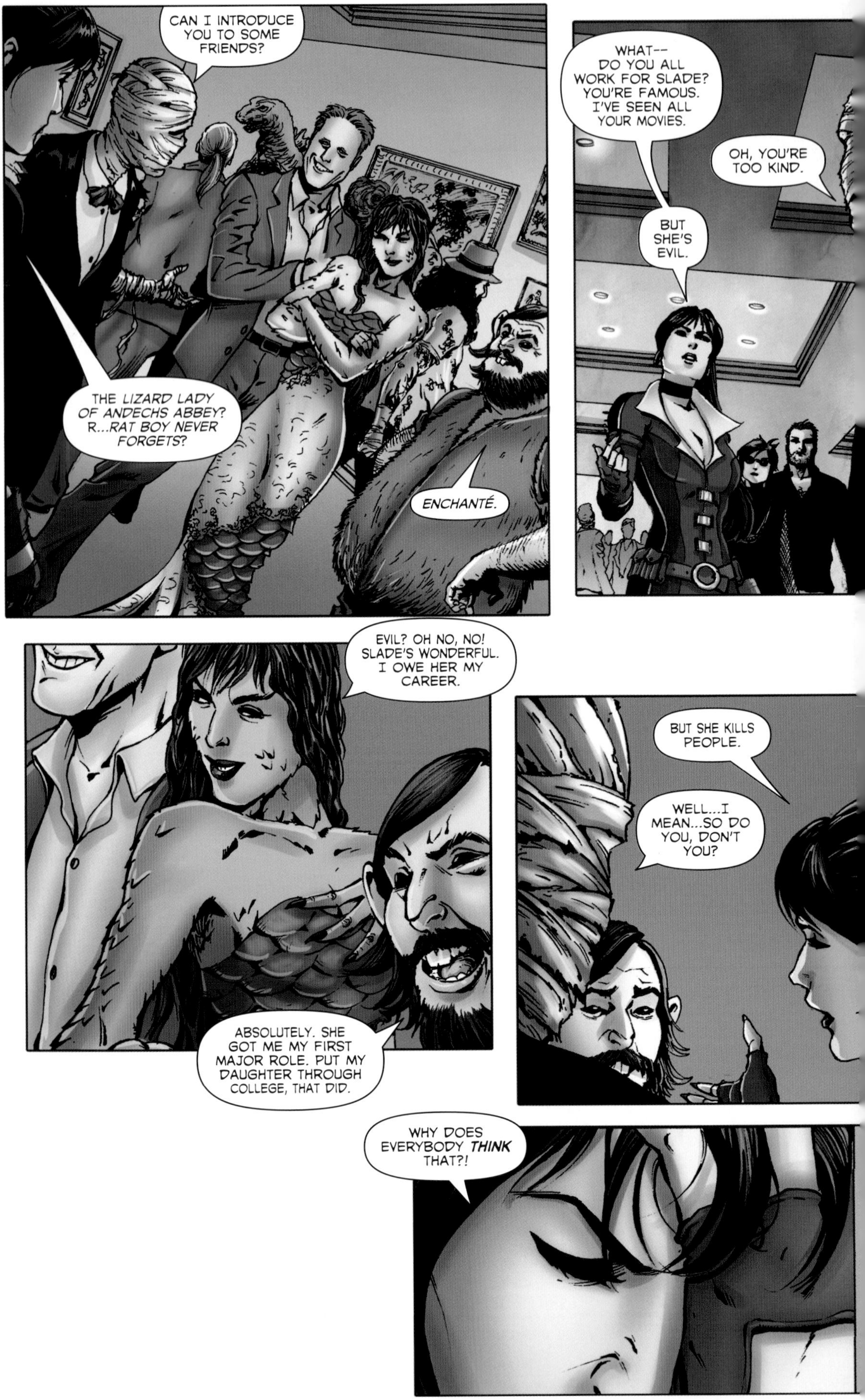
CAN I INTRODUCE YOU TO SOME FRIENDS?
THE *LIZARD LADY OF ANDECHS ABBEY?* R...*RAT BOY NEVER FORGETS?*
ENCHANTÉ.
WHAT-- DO YOU ALL WORK FOR SLADE? YOU'RE FAMOUS. I'VE SEEN ALL YOUR MOVIES.
OH, YOU'RE TOO KIND.
BUT SHE'S EVIL.
EVIL? OH NO, NO! SLADE'S WONDERFUL. I OWE HER MY CAREER.
ABSOLUTELY. SHE GOT ME MY FIRST MAJOR ROLE. PUT MY DAUGHTER THROUGH COLLEGE, THAT DID.
BUT SHE KILLS PEOPLE.
WELL...I MEAN...SO DO YOU, DON'T YOU?
WHY DOES EVERYBODY ***THINK*** THAT?!

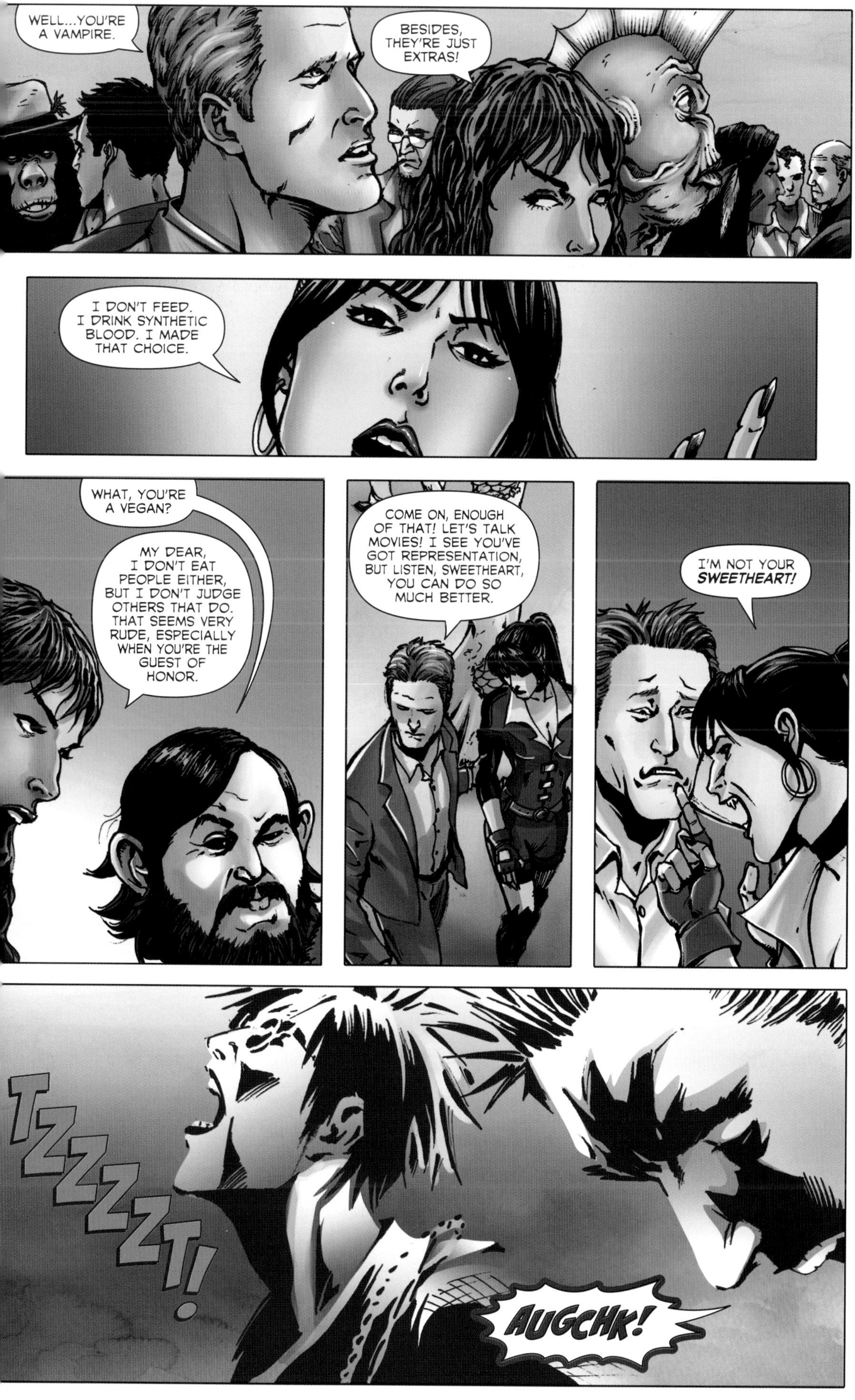
WELL...YOU'RE A VAMPIRE.
BESIDES, THEY'RE JUST EXTRAS!
I DON'T FEED. I DRINK SYNTHETIC BLOOD. I MADE THAT CHOICE.
WHAT, YOU'RE A VEGAN?
MY DEAR, I DON'T EAT PEOPLE EITHER, BUT I DON'T JUDGE OTHERS THAT DO. THAT SEEMS VERY RUDE, ESPECIALLY WHEN YOU'RE THE GUEST OF HONOR.
COME ON, ENOUGH OF THAT! LET'S TALK MOVIES! I SEE YOU'VE GOT REPRESENTATION, BUT LISTEN, SWEETHEART, YOU CAN DO SO MUCH BETTER.
I'M NOT YOUR SWEETHEART!
TZZZZT!
AUGCHK!

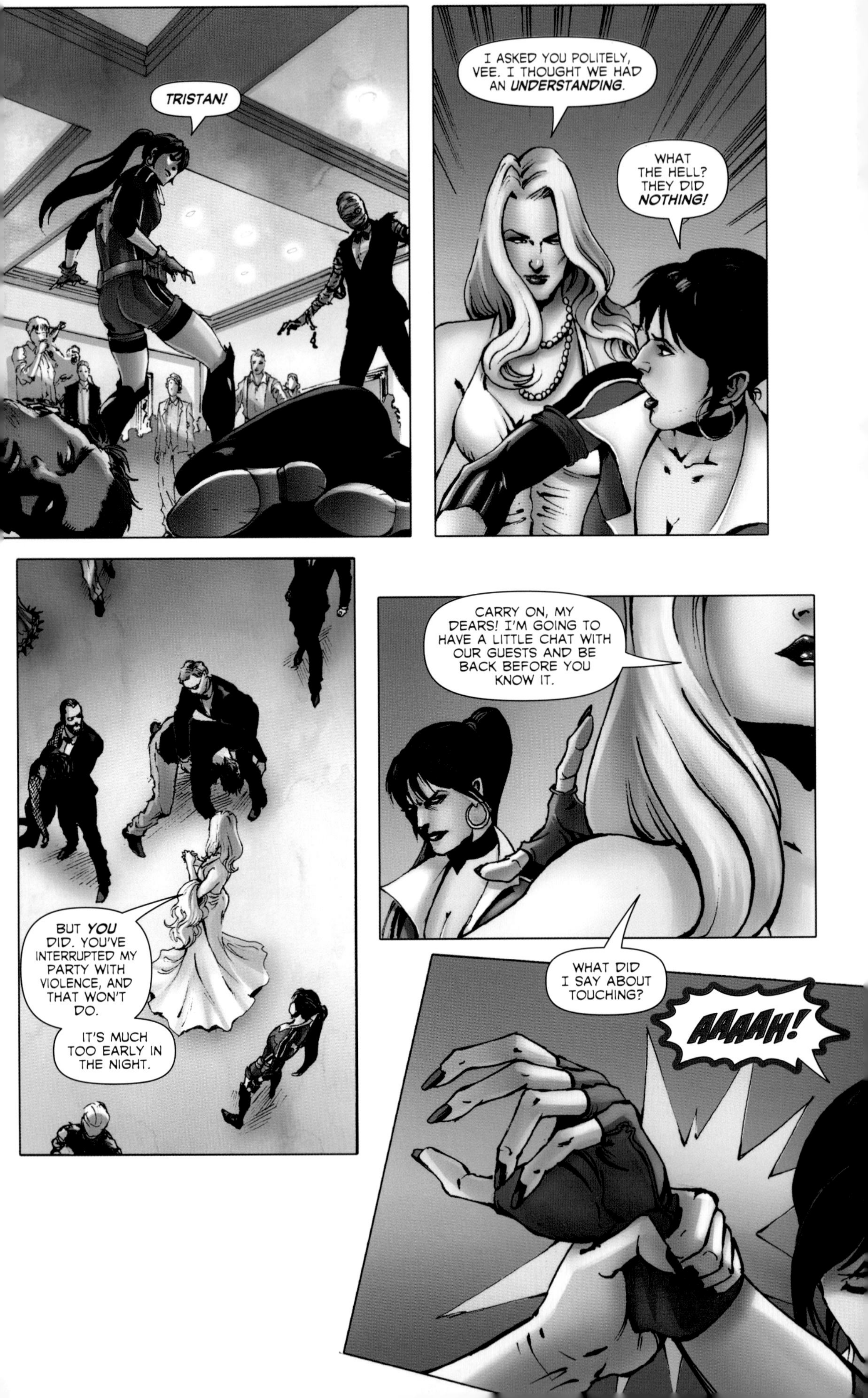

TRISTAN!
I ASKED YOU POLITELY, VEE. I THOUGHT WE HAD AN *UNDERSTANDING*.
WHAT THE HELL? THEY DID *NOTHING!*
BUT *YOU* DID. YOU'VE INTERRUPTED MY PARTY WITH VIOLENCE, AND THAT WON'T DO.
IT'S MUCH TOO EARLY IN THE NIGHT.
CARRY ON, MY DEARS! I'M GOING TO HAVE A LITTLE CHAT WITH OUR GUESTS AND BE BACK BEFORE YOU KNOW IT.
WHAT DID I SAY ABOUT TOUCHING?
AAAAH!

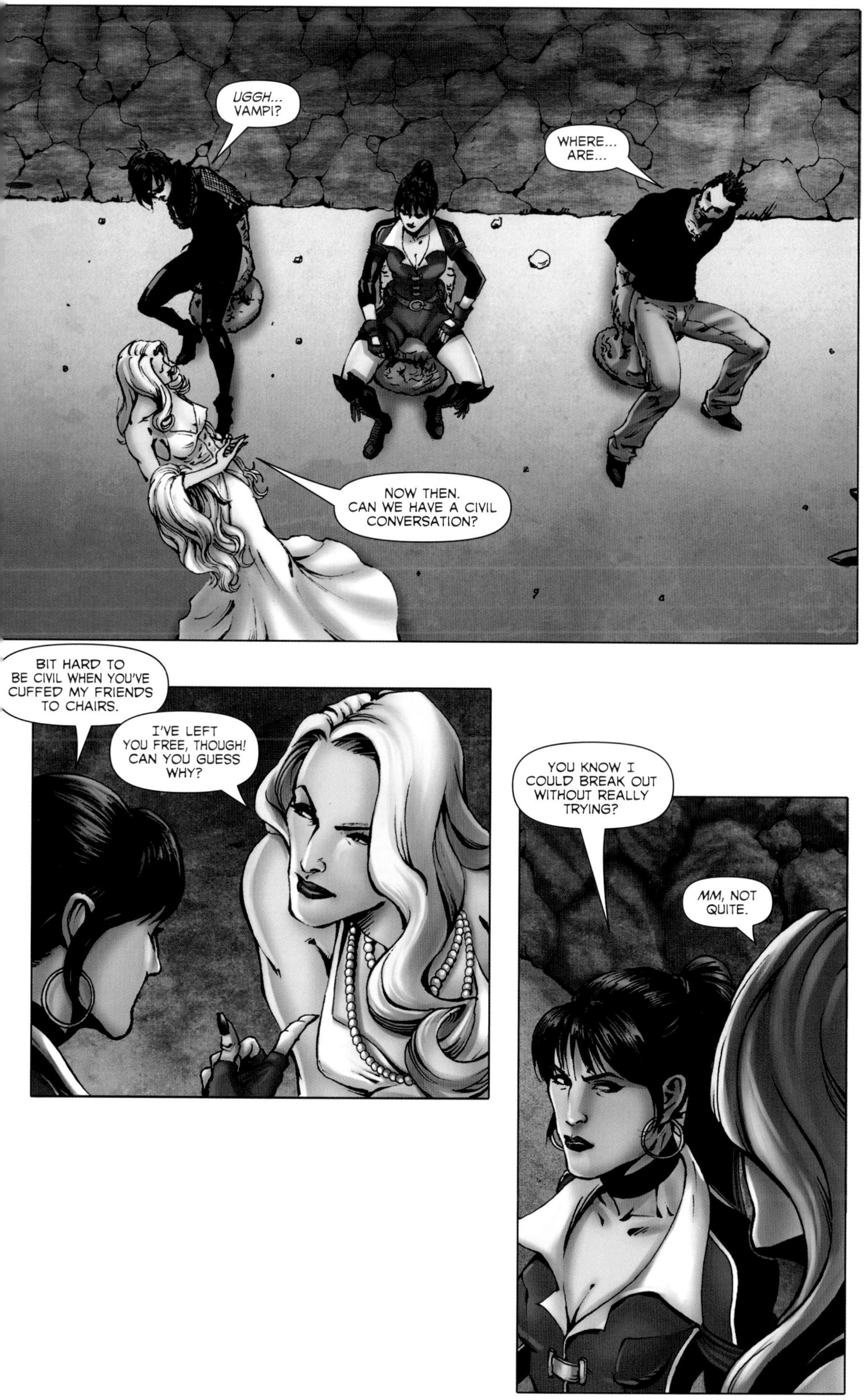
UGGH... VAMPI?
WHERE... ARE...
NOW THEN. CAN WE HAVE A CIVIL CONVERSATION?
BIT HARD TO BE CIVIL WHEN YOU'VE CUFFED MY FRIENDS TO CHAIRS.
I'VE LEFT YOU FREE, THOUGH! CAN YOU GUESS WHY?
YOU KNOW I COULD BREAK OUT WITHOUT REALLY TRYING?
MM, NOT QUITE.

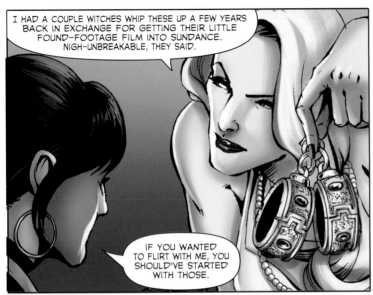

I HAD A COUPLE WITCHES WHIP THESE UP A FEW YEARS BACK IN EXCHANGE FOR GETTING THEIR LITTLE FOUND-FOOTAGE FILM INTO SUNDANCE. NIGH-UNBREAKABLE, THEY SAID.

IF YOU WANTED TO FLIRT WITH ME, YOU SHOULD'VE STARTED WITH THOSE.

HAH! YOU'RE FUNNY, YOU ARE.

THAT'S WHY I WANT YOU.

HEY!

I HEARD YOU PAID A VISIT TO MY OLD FRIEND, AUGUST, AT HER SHOP DOWNTOWN.

YOU'RE AWFUL *BONY* FOR A PSYCHOPATH.

I SWEAR, IF YOU HURT HER...

"AUGIE? NO, I WOULD NEVER.

"BESIDES, HER LITTLE SHOPKEEP TOLD ME EVERYTHING BEFORE I'D EVEN FINISHED BREAKING ALL THE FINGERS ON HER LEFT HAND."

CAN YOU IMAGINE? WHAT A WUSS!

AUGH!

LISTEN. YOU'RE A CREATURE OF THE NIGHT TRYING TO MAKE A LIVING IN THE CITY OF ANGELS. I WANT TO HELP YOU. I UNDERSTAND!

LET ME GET AHEAD OF YOU AND SAY "NO THANKS."

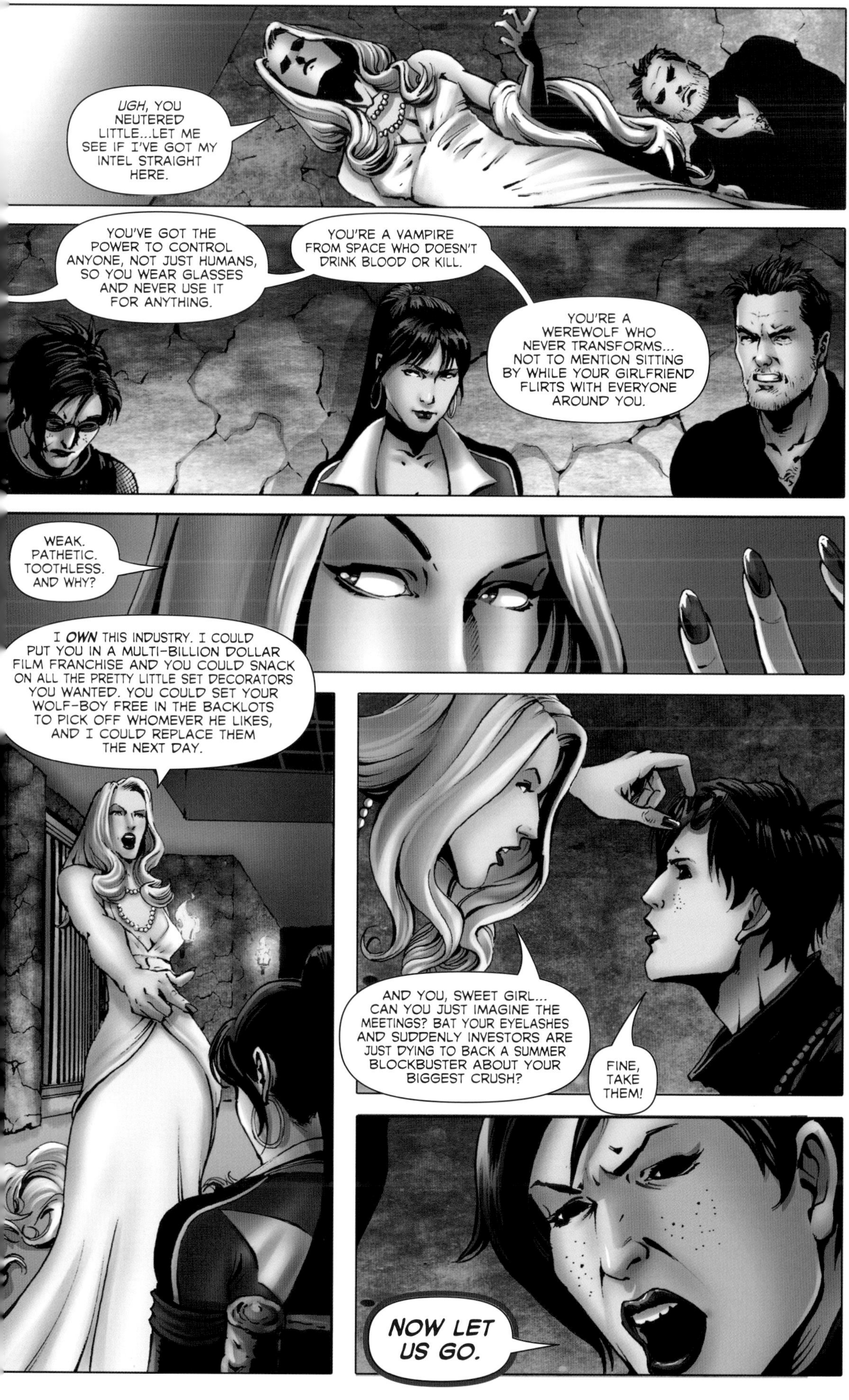
UGH, YOU NEUTERED LITTLE...LET ME SEE IF I'VE GOT MY INTEL STRAIGHT HERE.
YOU'VE GOT THE POWER TO CONTROL ANYONE, NOT JUST HUMANS, SO YOU WEAR GLASSES AND NEVER USE IT FOR ANYTHING.
YOU'RE A VAMPIRE FROM SPACE WHO DOESN'T DRINK BLOOD OR KILL.
YOU'RE A WEREWOLF WHO NEVER TRANSFORMS... NOT TO MENTION SITTING BY WHILE YOUR GIRLFRIEND FLIRTS WITH EVERYONE AROUND YOU.
WEAK. PATHETIC. TOOTHLESS. AND WHY?
I OWN THIS INDUSTRY. I COULD PUT YOU IN A MULTI-BILLION DOLLAR FILM FRANCHISE AND YOU COULD SNACK ON ALL THE PRETTY LITTLE SET DECORATORS YOU WANTED. YOU COULD SET YOUR WOLF-BOY FREE IN THE BACKLOTS TO PICK OFF WHOMEVER HE LIKES, AND I COULD REPLACE THEM THE NEXT DAY.
AND YOU, SWEET GIRL... CAN YOU JUST IMAGINE THE MEETINGS? BAT YOUR EYELASHES AND SUDDENLY INVESTORS ARE JUST DYING TO BACK A SUMMER BLOCKBUSTER ABOUT YOUR BIGGEST CRUSH?
FINE, TAKE THEM!
NOW LET US GO.

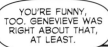
YOU'RE FUNNY, TOO. GENEVIEVE WAS RIGHT ABOUT THAT, AT LEAST.

GET THEM UP. I'M DONE MONOLOGUING. TIME TO HAVE SOME FUN.

BETTER KEEP THOSE ON, *HMM?*

VAMPIRELLA, KILL HER! I DON'T CARE WHAT HAPPENS TO ME!

WE'LL GET OUT OF HERE! IT'S OKAY!

YOU'LL COME AROUND. I KNOW YOU WILL. I'M REALLY RATHER GOOD AT THIS.

HEY, GET OFF! VAMPI, KNOCK THEM--

"IT'S SO MUCH BETTER TO BE FRIENDS."

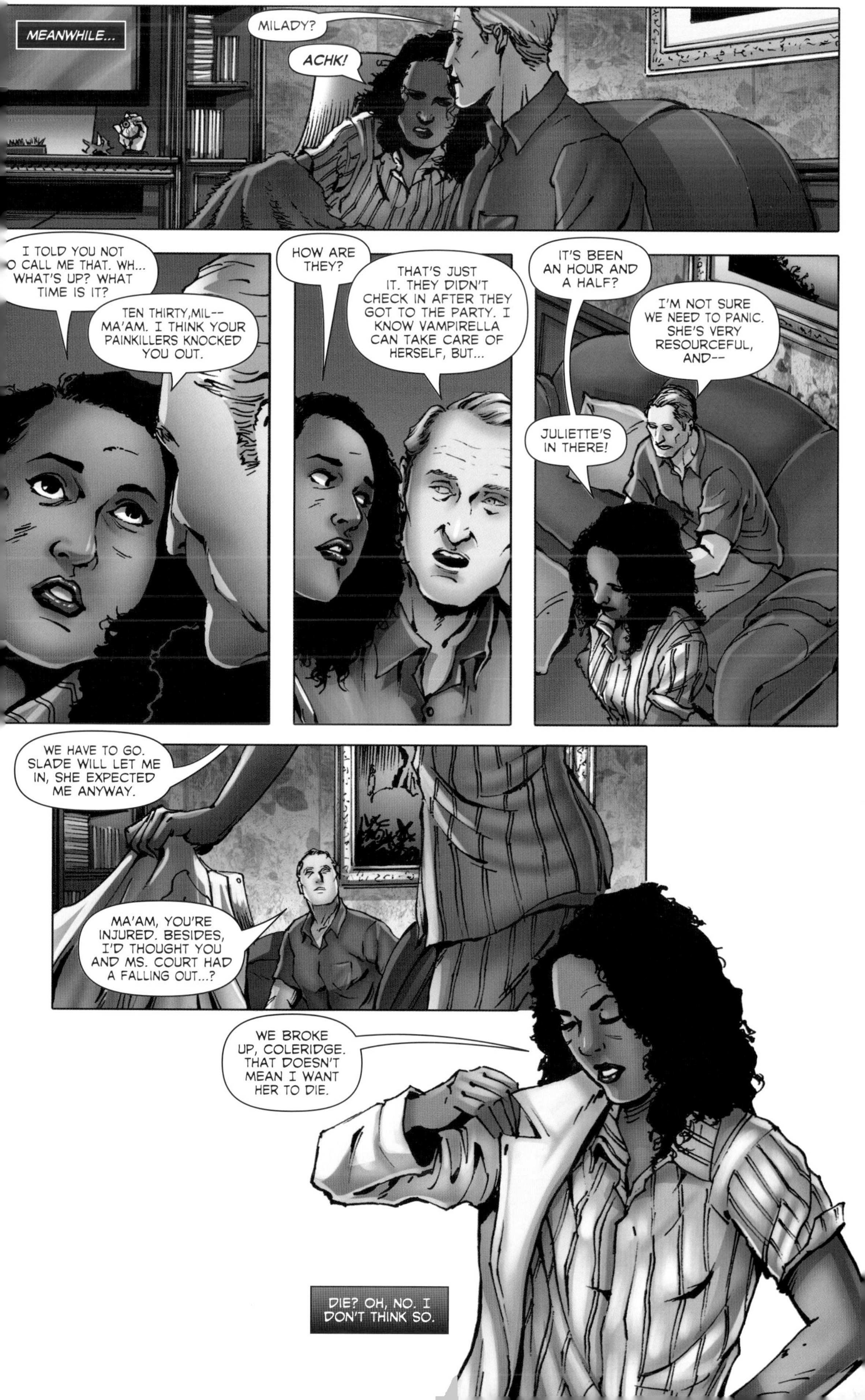
MEANWHILE...
MILADY?
ACHK!
I TOLD YOU NOT TO CALL ME THAT. WH... WHAT'S UP? WHAT TIME IS IT?
TEN THIRTY, MIL-- MA'AM. I THINK YOUR PAINKILLERS KNOCKED YOU OUT.
HOW ARE THEY?
THAT'S JUST IT. THEY DIDN'T CHECK IN AFTER THEY GOT TO THE PARTY. I KNOW VAMPIRELLA CAN TAKE CARE OF HERSELF, BUT...
IT'S BEEN AN HOUR AND A HALF?
I'M NOT SURE WE NEED TO PANIC. SHE'S VERY RESOURCEFUL, AND--
JULIETTE'S IN THERE!
WE HAVE TO GO. SLADE WILL LET ME IN, SHE EXPECTED ME ANYWAY.
MA'AM, YOU'RE INJURED. BESIDES, I'D THOUGHT YOU AND MS. COURT HAD A FALLING OUT...?
WE BROKE UP, COLERIDGE. THAT DOESN'T MEAN I WANT HER TO DIE.
DIE? OH, NO. I DON'T THINK SO.

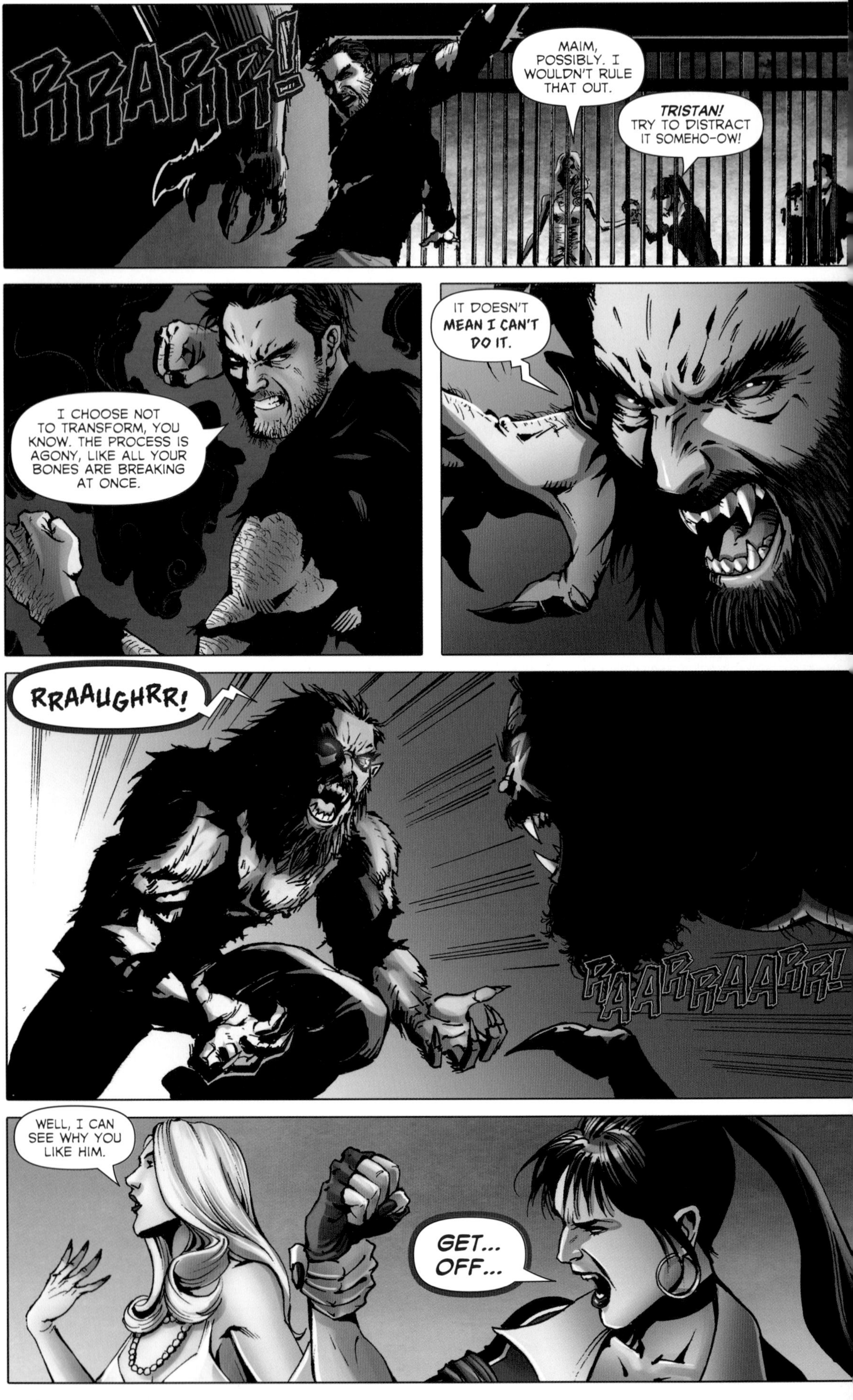
RRARR!
MAIM, POSSIBLY. I WOULDN'T RULE THAT OUT.
TRISTAN! TRY TO DISTRACT IT SOMEHO-OW!
I CHOOSE NOT TO TRANSFORM, YOU KNOW. THE PROCESS IS AGONY, LIKE ALL YOUR BONES ARE BREAKING AT ONCE.
IT DOESN'T MEAN I CAN'T DO IT.
RRAAUGHRR!
RAARRAARR!
WELL, I CAN SEE WHY YOU LIKE HIM.
GET... OFF...

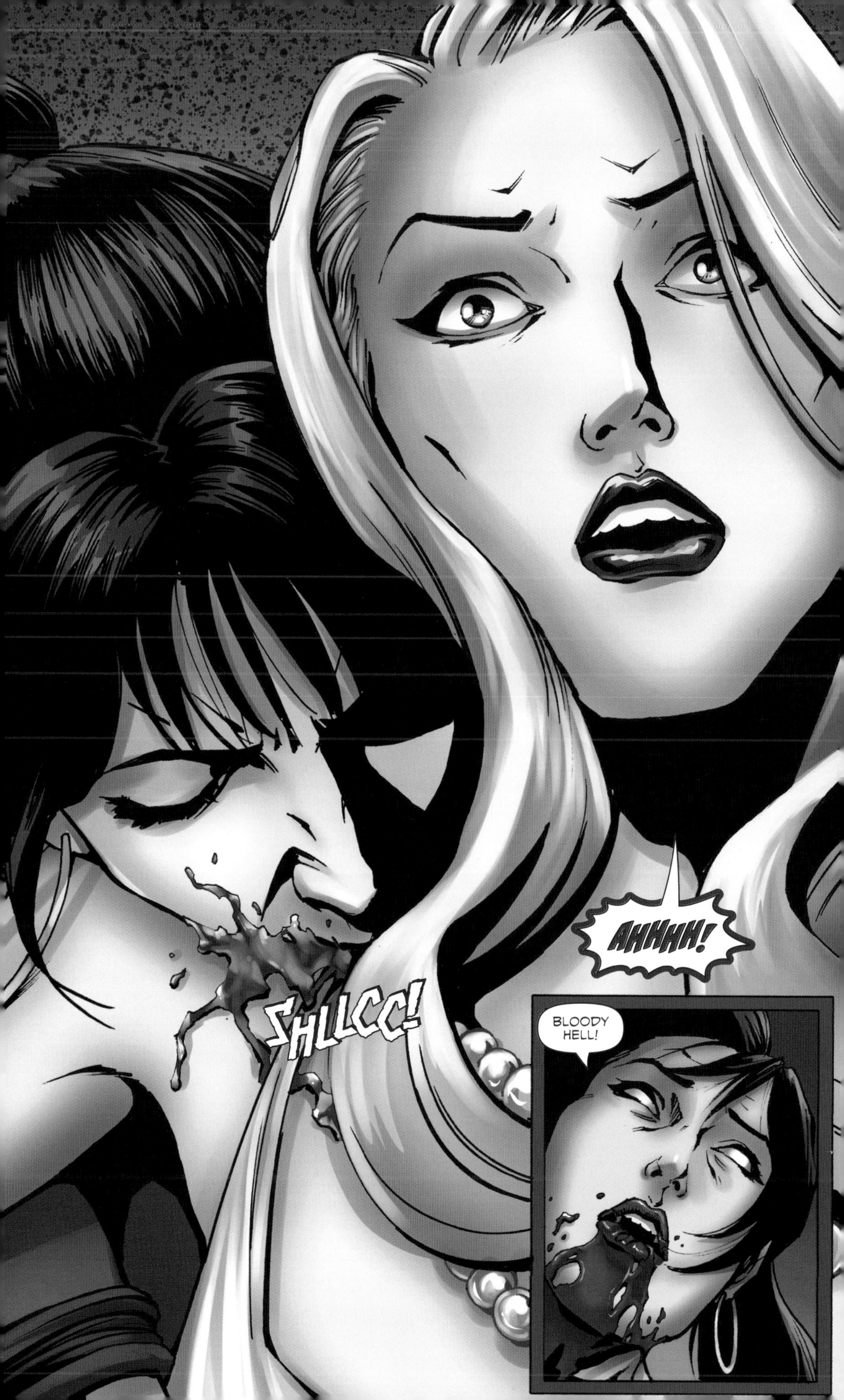
AHHHH!
SHLLCC!
BLOODY HELL!

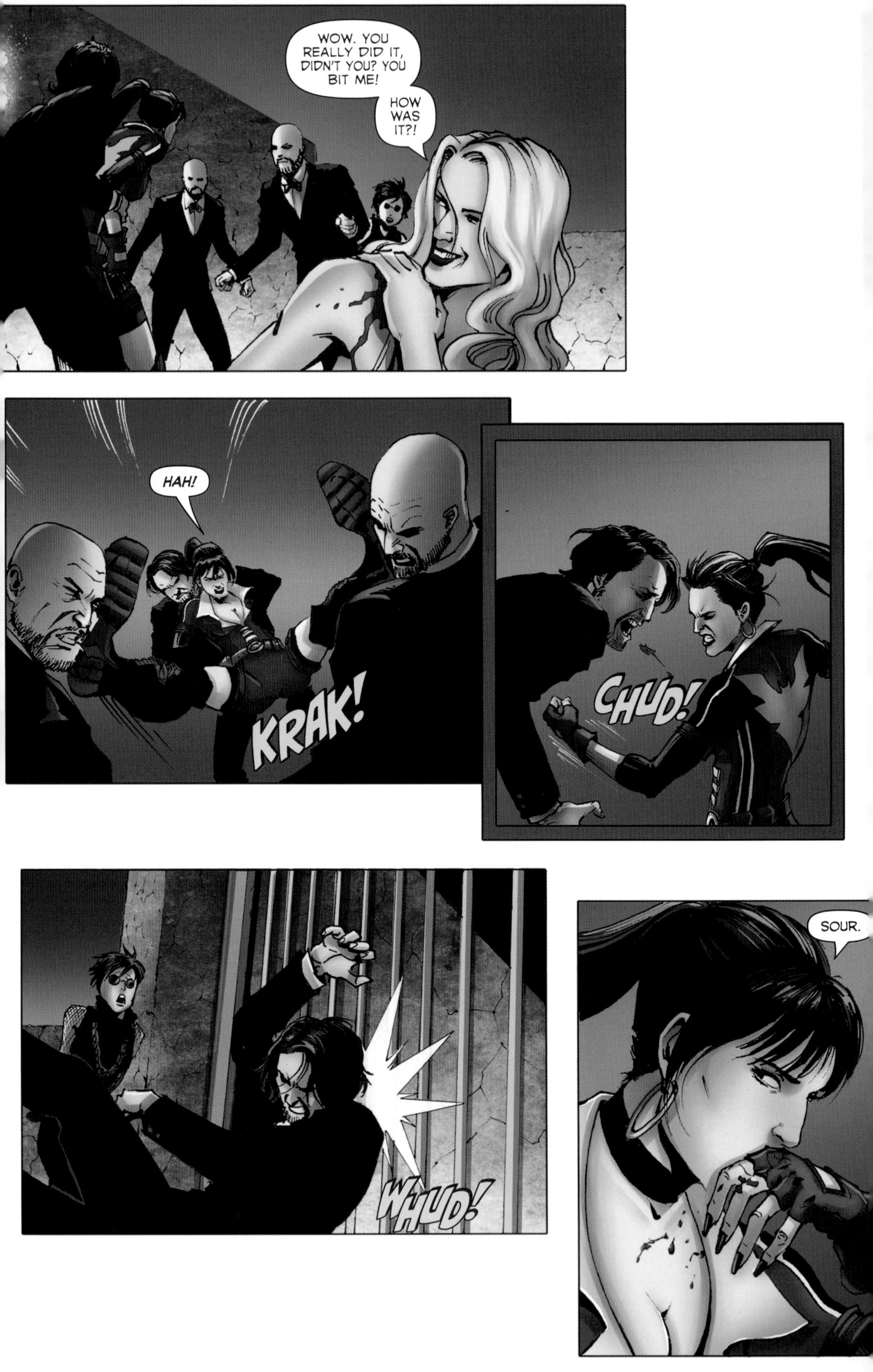
WOW. YOU REALLY DID IT, DIDN'T YOU? YOU BIT ME!
HOW WAS IT?!
HAH!
KRAK!
CHUD!
WHUD!
SOUR.

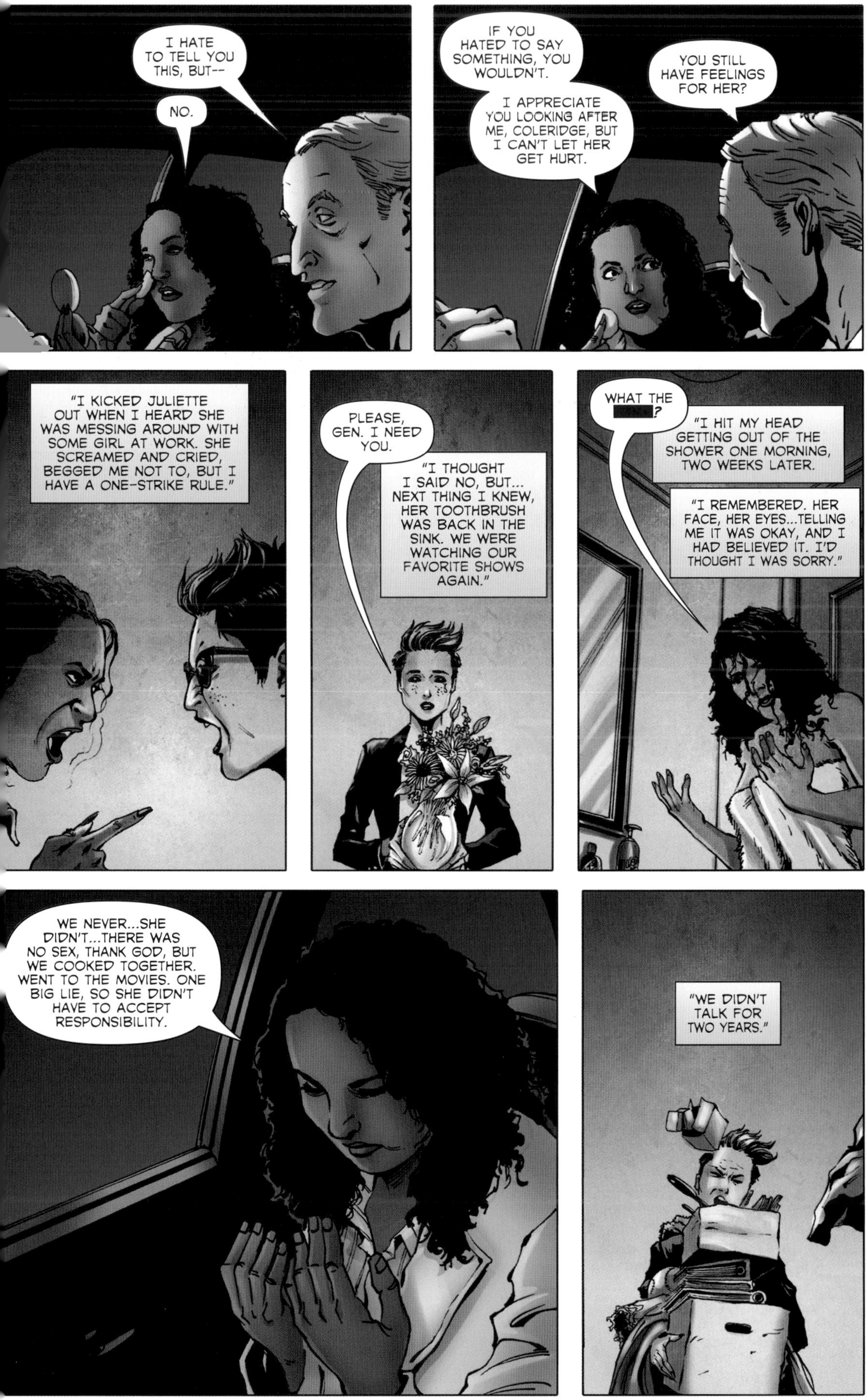

I HATE TO TELL YOU THIS, BUT--
NO.
IF YOU HATED TO SAY SOMETHING, YOU WOULDN'T.
I APPRECIATE YOU LOOKING AFTER ME, COLERIDGE, BUT I CAN'T LET HER GET HURT.
YOU STILL HAVE FEELINGS FOR HER?
"I KICKED JULIETTE OUT WHEN I HEARD SHE WAS MESSING AROUND WITH SOME GIRL AT WORK. SHE SCREAMED AND CRIED, BEGGED ME NOT TO, BUT I HAVE A ONE-STRIKE RULE."
PLEASE, GEN. I NEED YOU.
"I THOUGHT I SAID NO, BUT... NEXT THING I KNEW, HER TOOTHBRUSH WAS BACK IN THE SINK. WE WERE WATCHING OUR FAVORITE SHOWS AGAIN."
WHAT THE [redacted]?
"I HIT MY HEAD GETTING OUT OF THE SHOWER ONE MORNING, TWO WEEKS LATER.
"I REMEMBERED. HER FACE, HER EYES...TELLING ME IT WAS OKAY, AND I HAD BELIEVED IT. I'D THOUGHT I WAS SORRY."
WE NEVER...SHE DIDN'T...THERE WAS NO SEX, THANK GOD, BUT WE COOKED TOGETHER. WENT TO THE MOVIES. ONE BIG LIE, SO SHE DIDN'T HAVE TO ACCEPT RESPONSIBILITY.
"WE DIDN'T TALK FOR TWO YEARS."

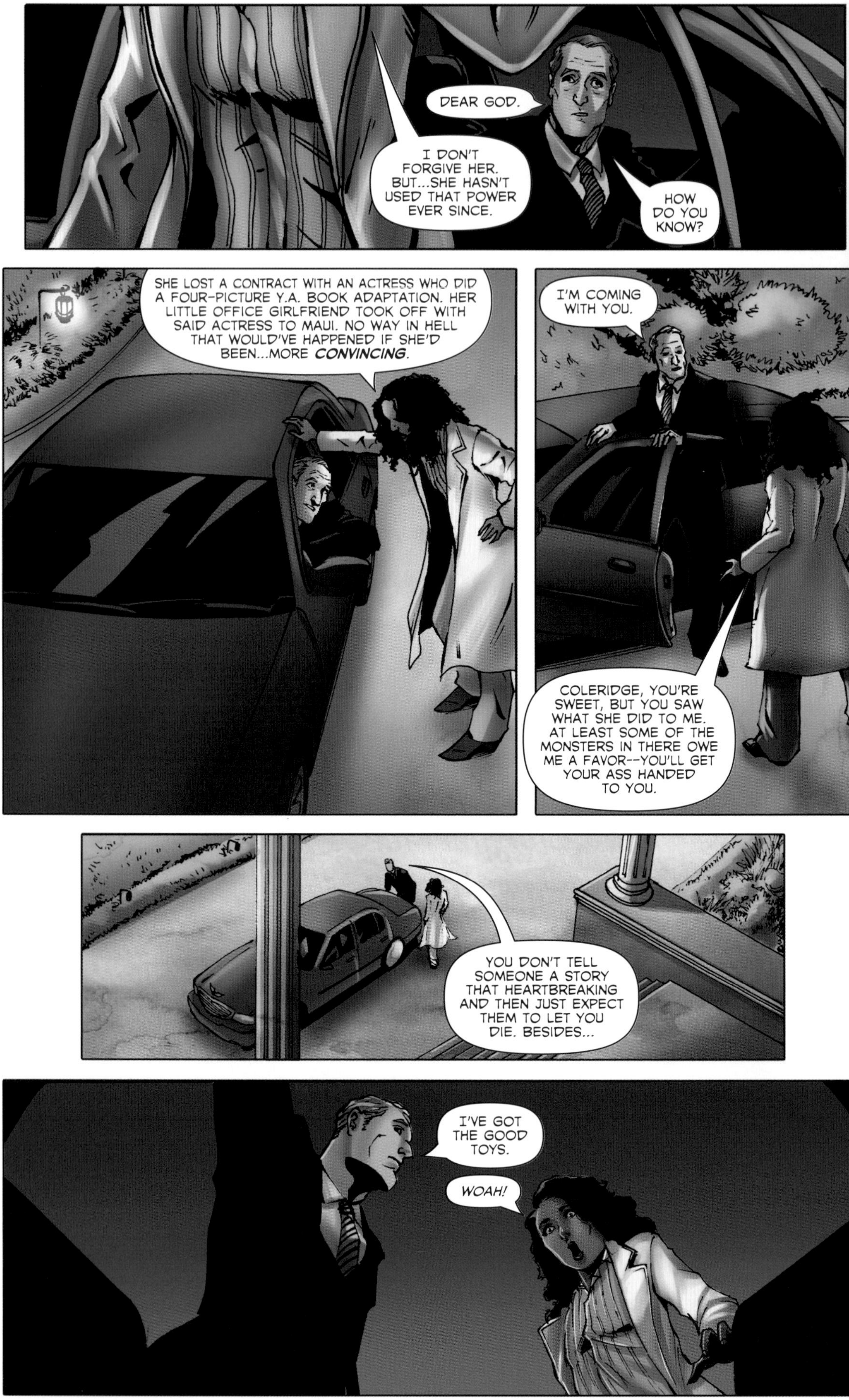
DEAR GOD.
I DON'T FORGIVE HER. BUT...SHE HASN'T USED THAT POWER EVER SINCE.
HOW DO YOU KNOW?
SHE LOST A CONTRACT WITH AN ACTRESS WHO DID A FOUR-PICTURE Y.A. BOOK ADAPTATION. HER LITTLE OFFICE GIRLFRIEND TOOK OFF WITH SAID ACTRESS TO MAUI. NO WAY IN HELL THAT WOULD'VE HAPPENED IF SHE'D BEEN...MORE *CONVINCING*.
I'M COMING WITH YOU.
COLERIDGE, YOU'RE SWEET, BUT YOU SAW WHAT SHE DID TO ME. AT LEAST SOME OF THE MONSTERS IN THERE OWE ME A FAVOR--YOU'LL GET YOUR ASS HANDED TO YOU.
YOU DON'T TELL SOMEONE A STORY THAT HEARTBREAKING AND THEN JUST EXPECT THEM TO LET YOU DIE. BESIDES...
I'VE GOT THE GOOD TOYS.
WOAH!

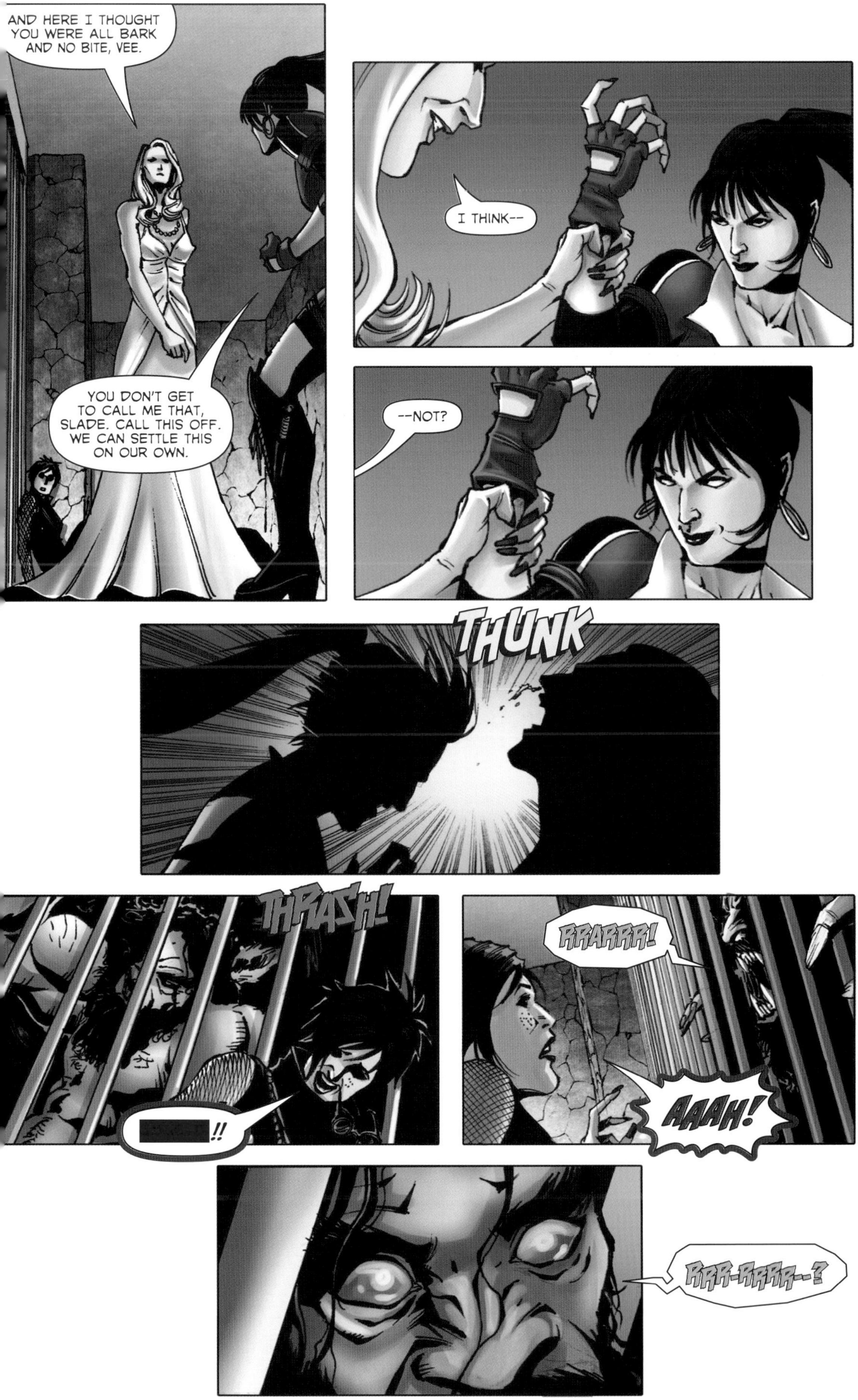
AND HERE I THOUGHT YOU WERE ALL BARK AND NO BITE, VEE.
YOU DON'T GET TO CALL ME THAT, SLADE. CALL THIS OFF. WE CAN SETTLE THIS ON OUR OWN.
I THINK--
--NOT?
THUNK
THRASH!
[redacted]!!
RRARRR!
AAAH!
RRR-RRRR--?

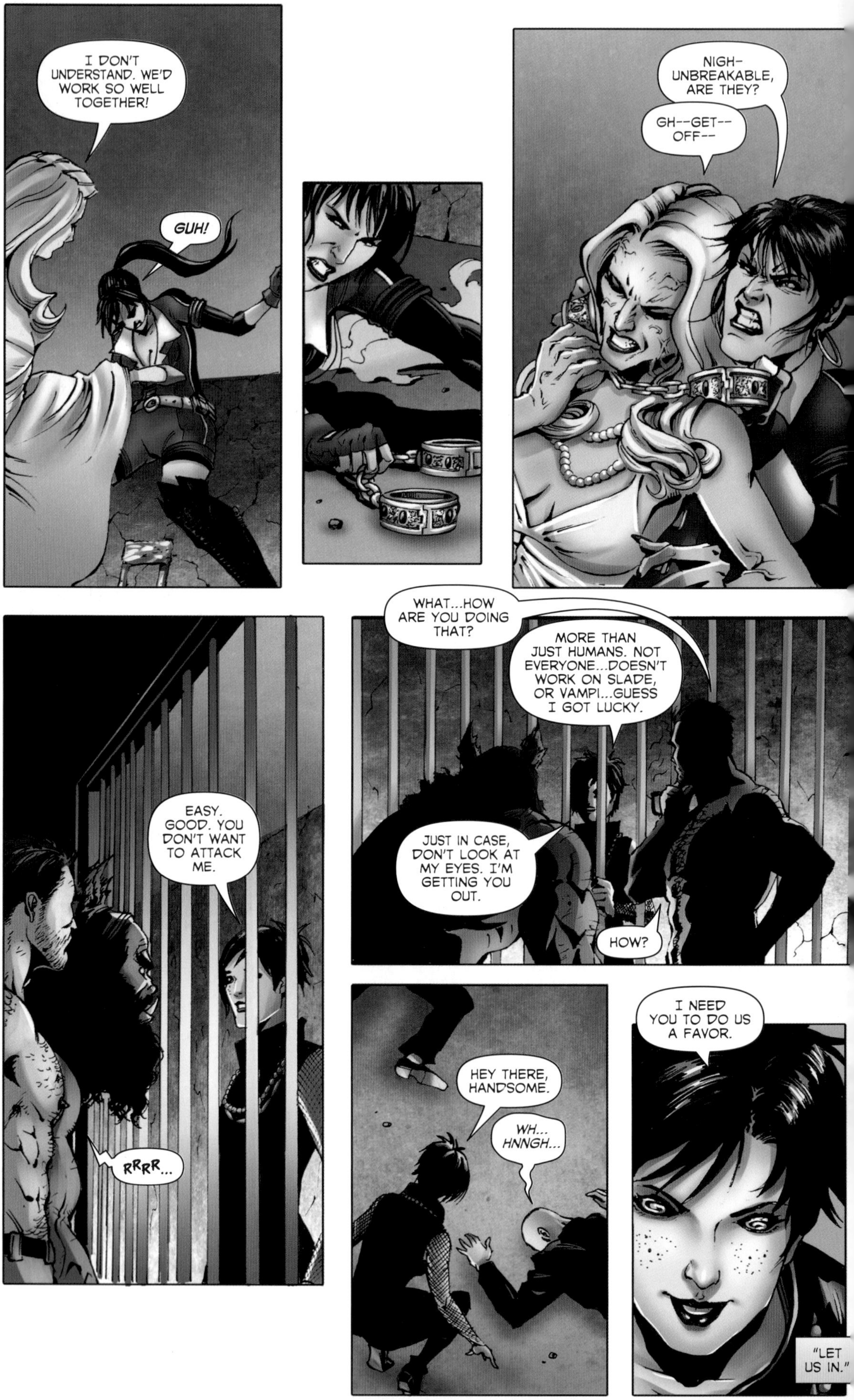
I DON'T UNDERSTAND. WE'D WORK SO WELL TOGETHER!
GUH!
NIGH-UNBREAKABLE, ARE THEY?
GH--GET--OFF--
EASY. GOOD. YOU DON'T WANT TO ATTACK ME.
RRRR...
WHAT...HOW ARE YOU DOING THAT?
MORE THAN JUST HUMANS. NOT EVERYONE...DOESN'T WORK ON SLADE, OR VAMPI...GUESS I GOT LUCKY.
JUST IN CASE, DON'T LOOK AT MY EYES. I'M GETTING YOU OUT.
HOW?
HEY THERE, HANDSOME.
WH... HNNGH...
I NEED YOU TO DO US A FAVOR.
"LET US IN."

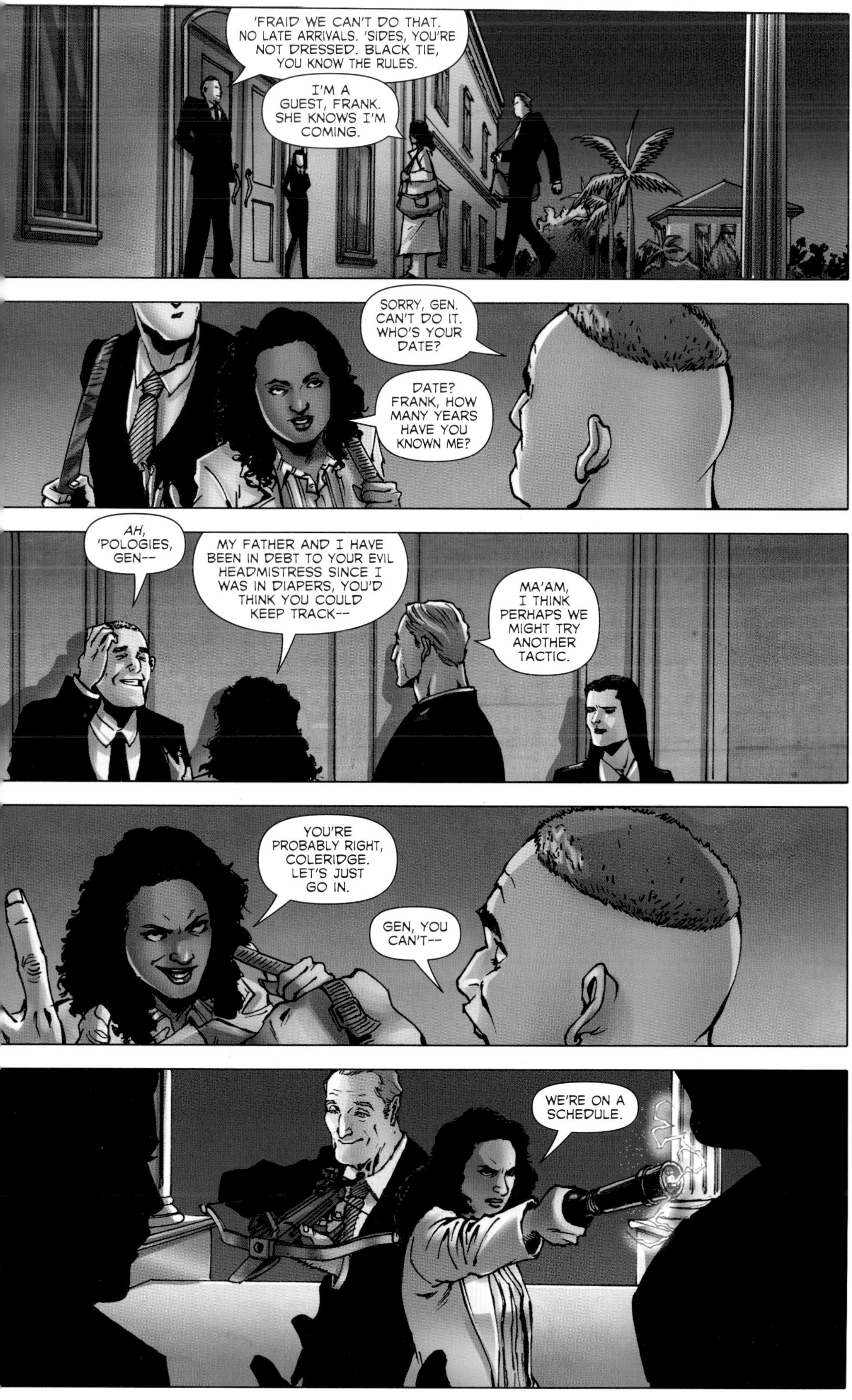
'FRAID WE CAN'T DO THAT. NO LATE ARRIVALS. 'SIDES, YOU'RE NOT DRESSED. BLACK TIE, YOU KNOW THE RULES.
I'M A GUEST, FRANK. SHE KNOWS I'M COMING.
SORRY, GEN. CAN'T DO IT. WHO'S YOUR DATE?
DATE? FRANK, HOW MANY YEARS HAVE YOU KNOWN ME?
AH, 'POLOGIES, GEN--
MY FATHER AND I HAVE BEEN IN DEBT TO YOUR EVIL HEADMISTRESS SINCE I WAS IN DIAPERS, YOU'D THINK YOU COULD KEEP TRACK--
MA'AM, I THINK PERHAPS WE MIGHT TRY ANOTHER TACTIC.
YOU'RE PROBABLY RIGHT, COLERIDGE. LET'S JUST GO IN.
GEN, YOU CAN'T--
WE'RE ON A SCHEDULE.

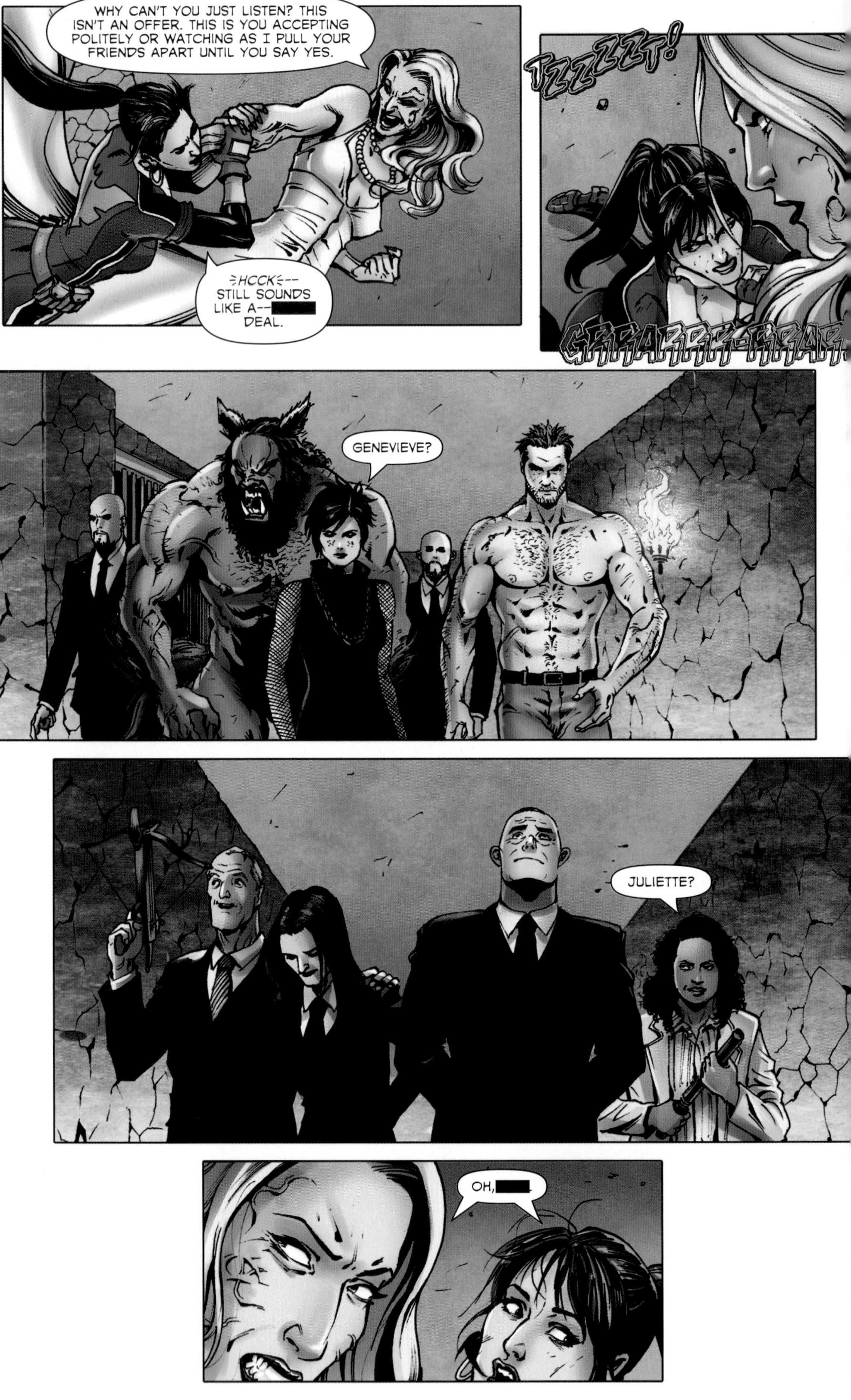
WHY CAN'T YOU JUST LISTEN? THIS ISN'T AN OFFER. THIS IS YOU ACCEPTING POLITELY OR WATCHING AS I PULL YOUR FRIENDS APART UNTIL YOU SAY YES.
HCCK-- STILL SOUNDS LIKE A--[redacted] DEAL.
GENEVIEVE?
JULIETTE?
OH, [redacted].

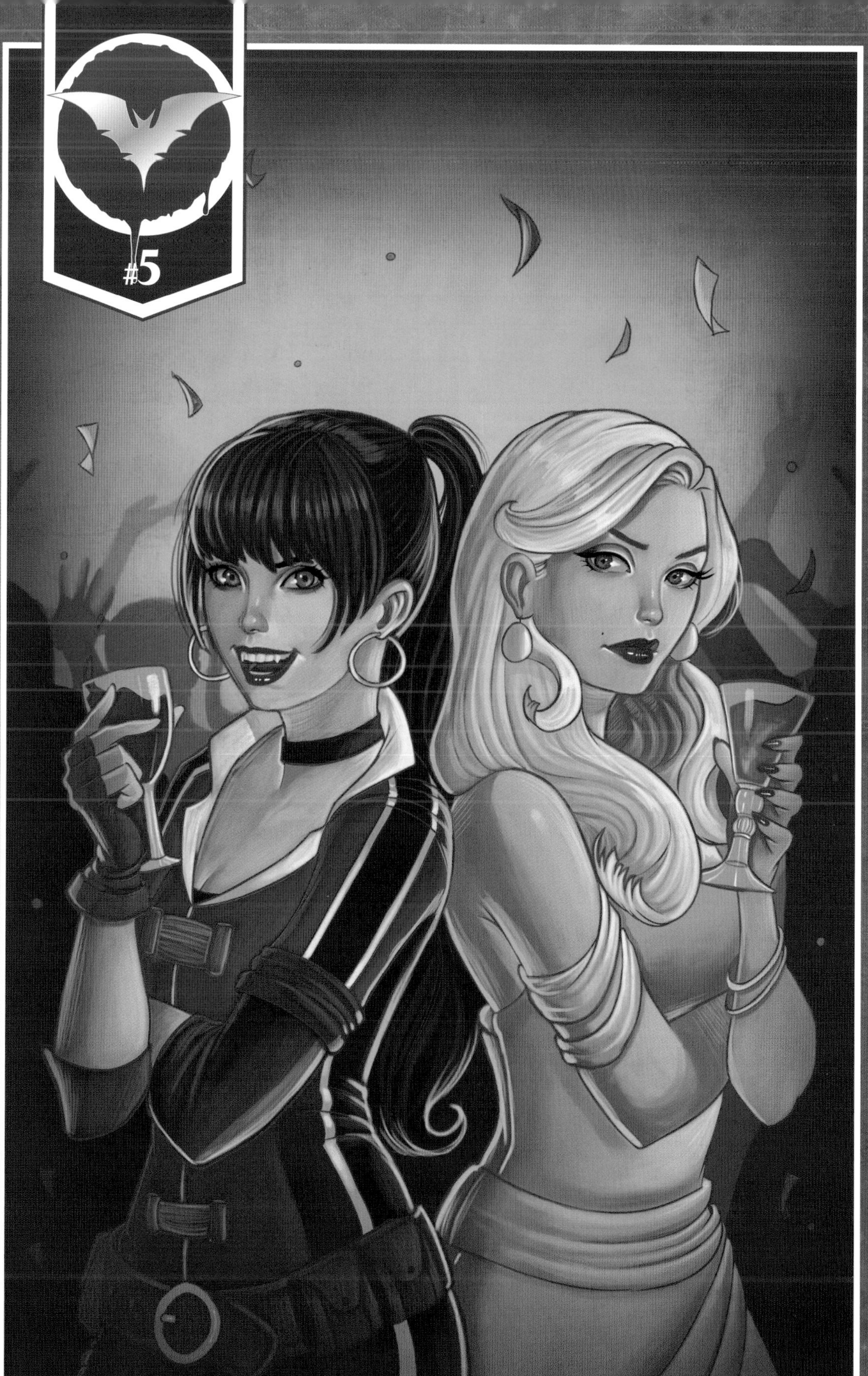
#5

cover by **Chrissie Zullo**

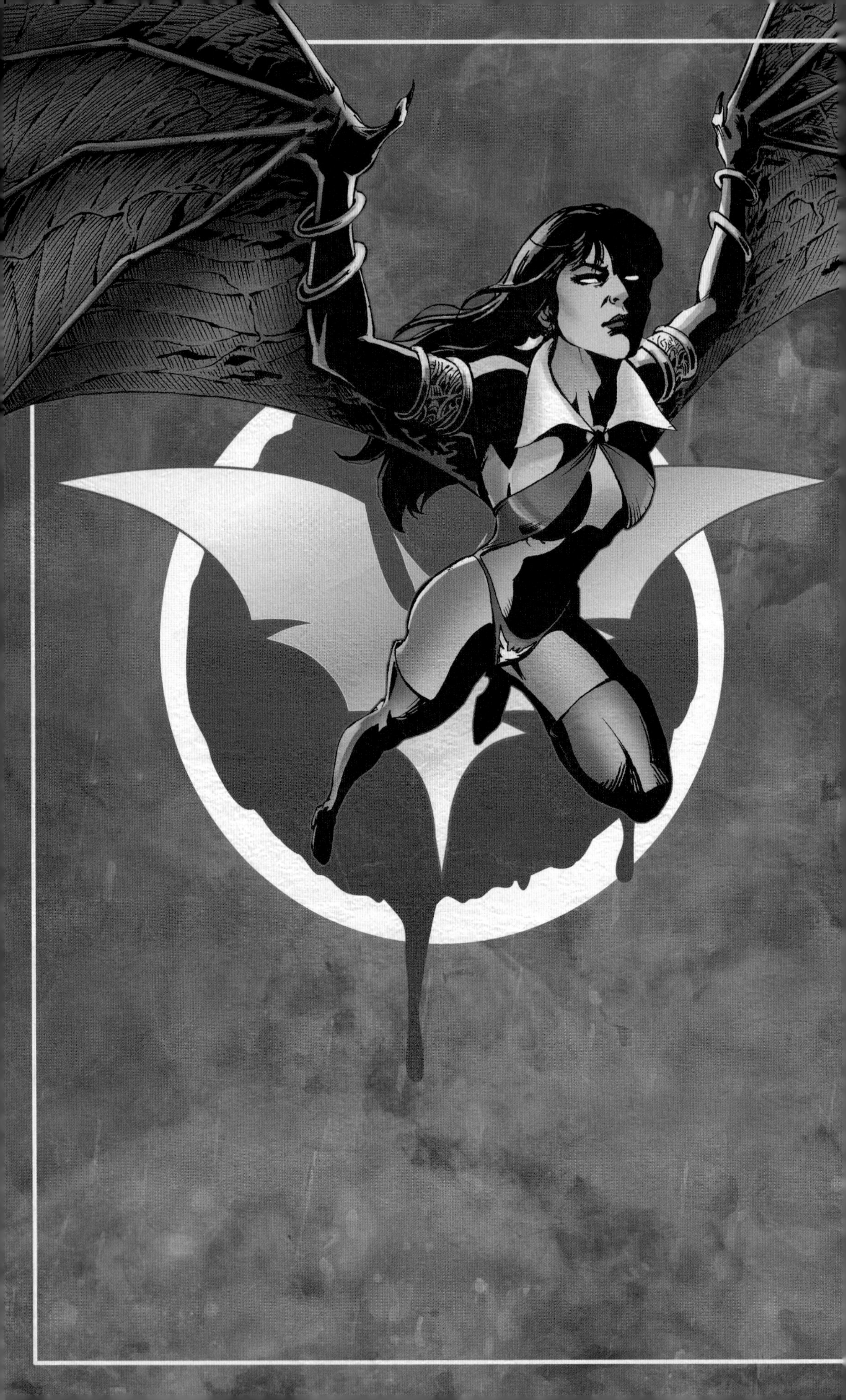

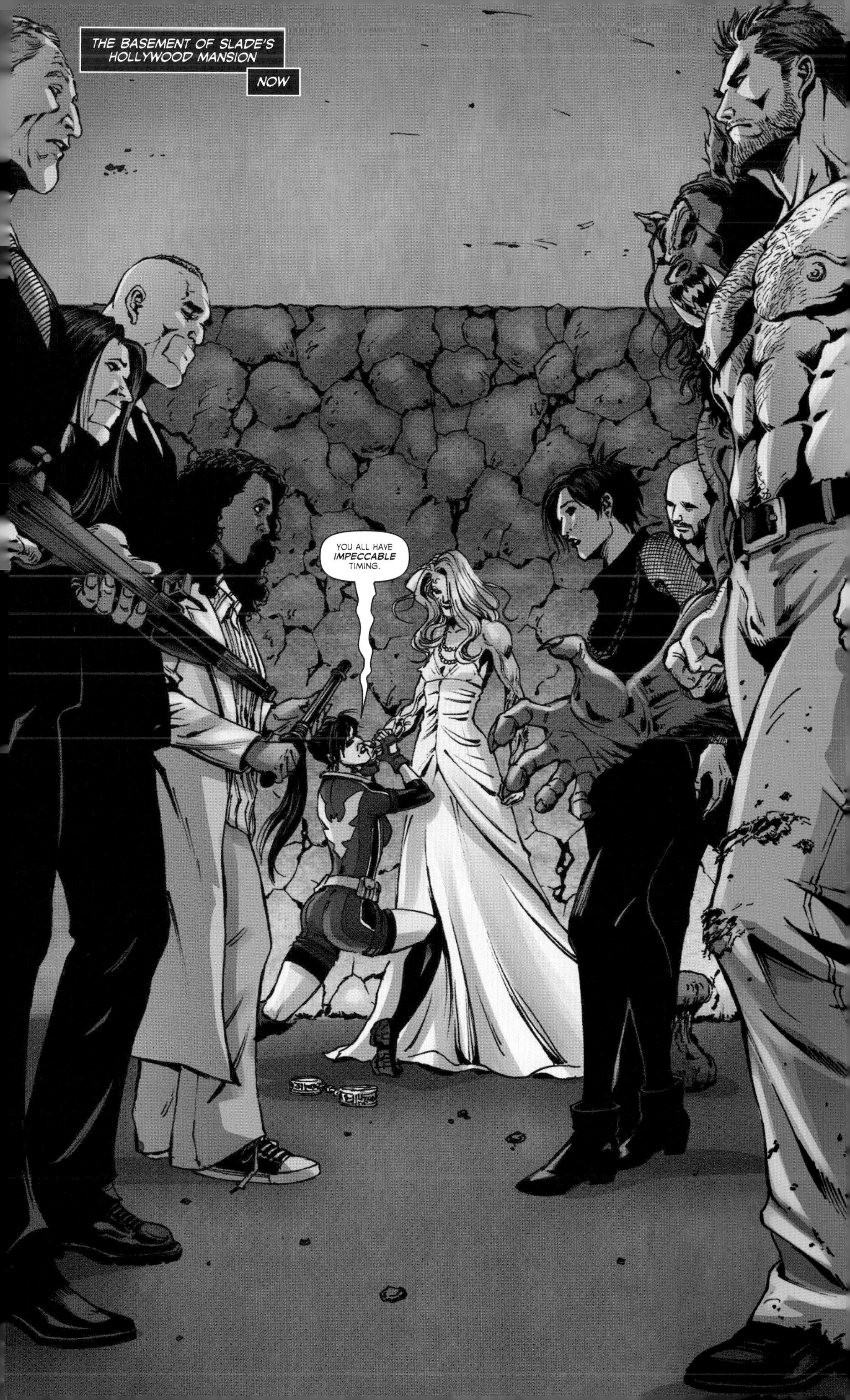
THE BASEMENT OF SLADE'S HOLLYWOOD MANSION
NOW
YOU ALL HAVE *IMPECCABLE* TIMING.

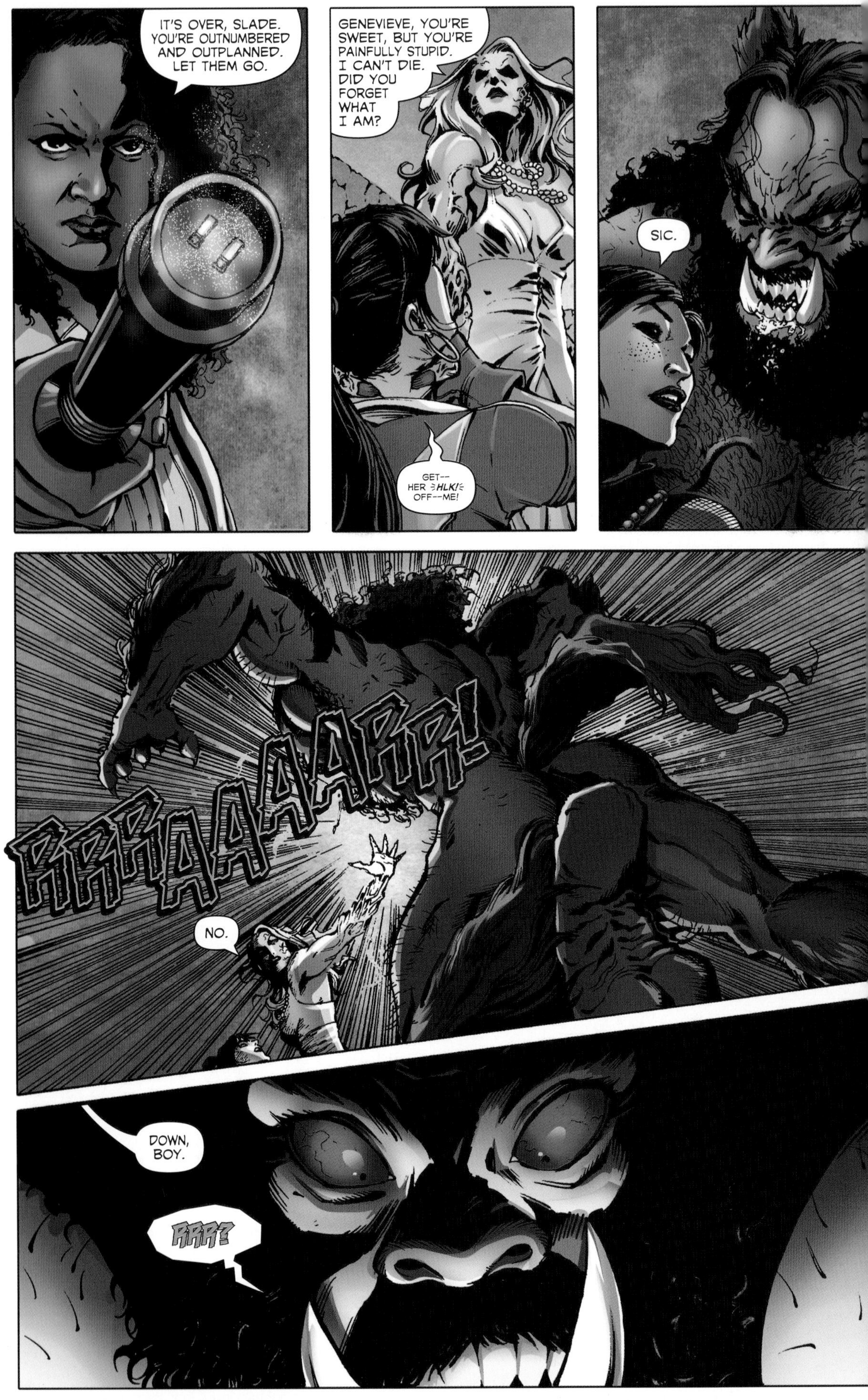
IT'S OVER, SLADE. YOU'RE OUTNUMBERED AND OUTPLANNED. LET THEM GO.
GENEVIEVE, YOU'RE SWEET, BUT YOU'RE PAINFULLY STUPID. I CAN'T DIE. DID YOU FORGET WHAT I AM?
GET-- HER *HLK!* OFF--ME!
SIC.
RRRAAAARR!
NO.
DOWN, BOY.
RRR?

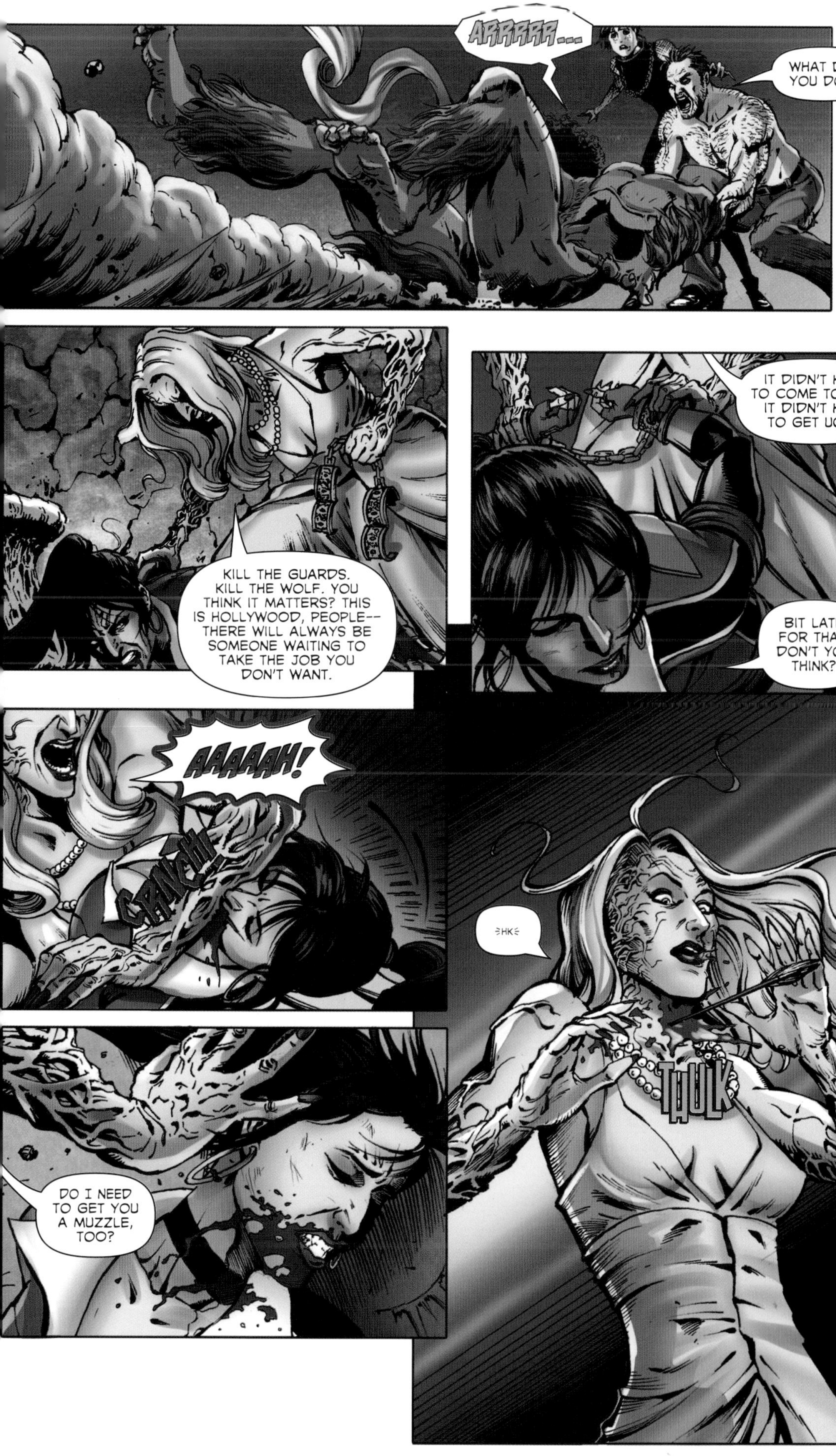
ARRRRR...
WHAT DID YOU DO?!
KILL THE GUARDS. KILL THE WOLF. YOU THINK IT MATTERS? THIS IS HOLLYWOOD, PEOPLE-- THERE WILL ALWAYS BE SOMEONE WAITING TO TAKE THE JOB YOU DON'T WANT.
IT DIDN'T HAVE TO COME TO THIS. IT DIDN'T HAVE TO GET UGLY.
BIT LATE FOR THAT, DON'T YOU THINK?
AAAAAH!
CRNCH!
DO I NEED TO GET YOU A MUZZLE, TOO?
HK
THULK

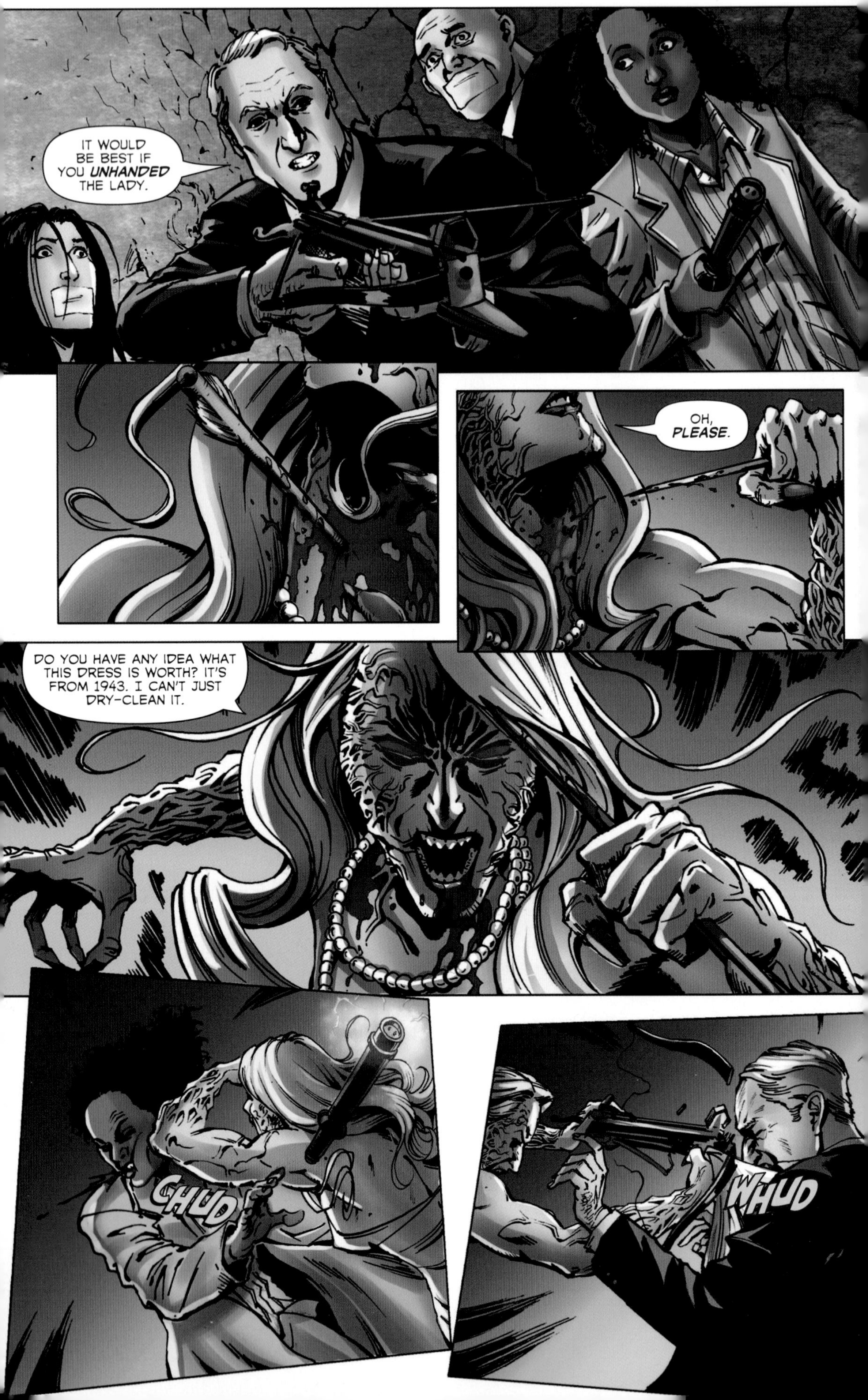
IT WOULD BE BEST IF YOU *UNHANDED* THE LADY.
OH, *PLEASE*.
DO YOU HAVE ANY IDEA WHAT THIS DRESS IS WORTH? IT'S FROM 1943. I CAN'T JUST DRY-CLEAN IT.
CHUD
WHUD

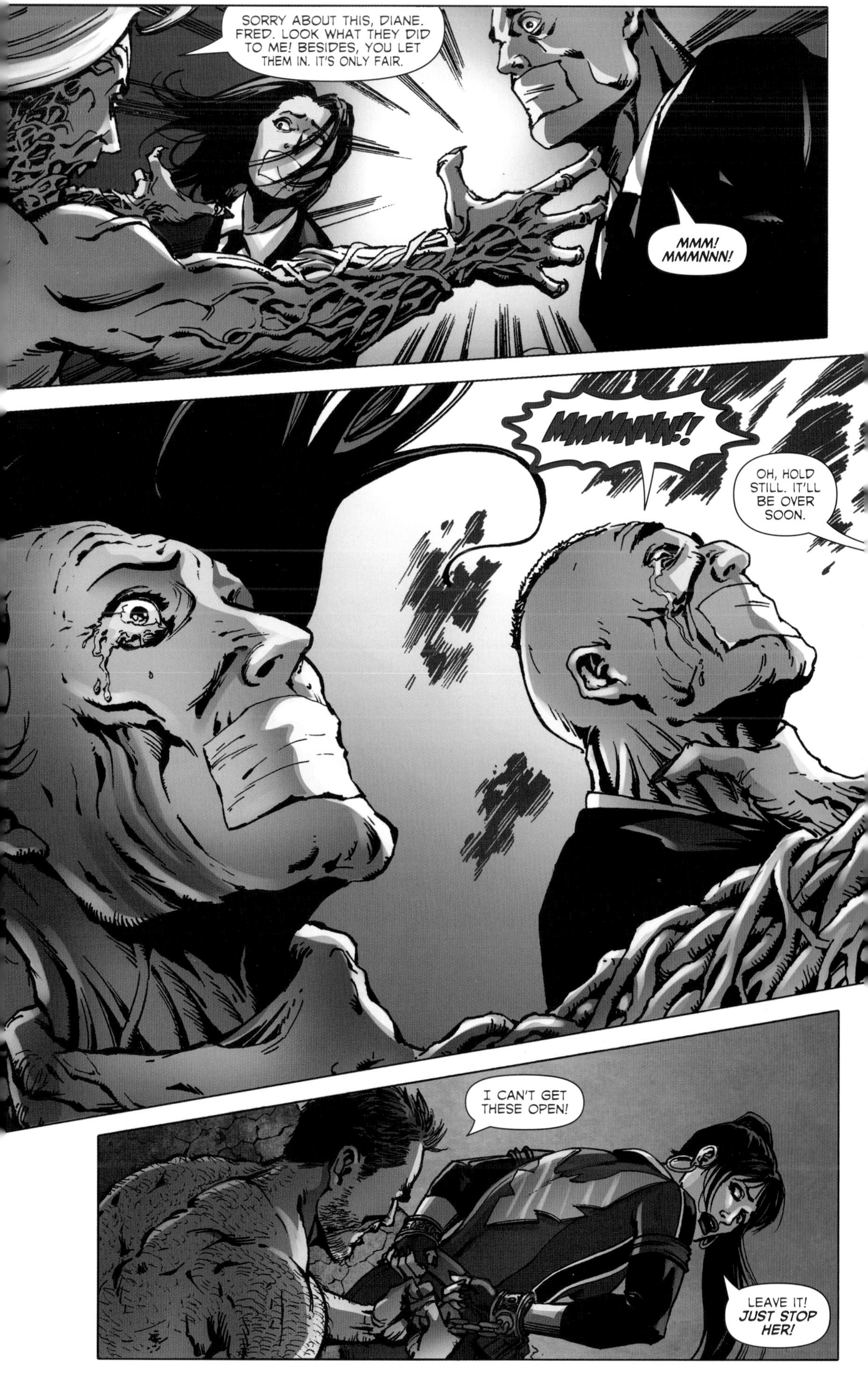
SORRY ABOUT THIS, DIANE. FRED. LOOK WHAT THEY DID TO ME! BESIDES, YOU LET THEM IN. IT'S ONLY FAIR.
MMM! MMMNNN!
MMMNNN!!
OH, HOLD STILL. IT'LL BE OVER SOON.
I CAN'T GET THESE OPEN!
LEAVE IT! JUST STOP HER!

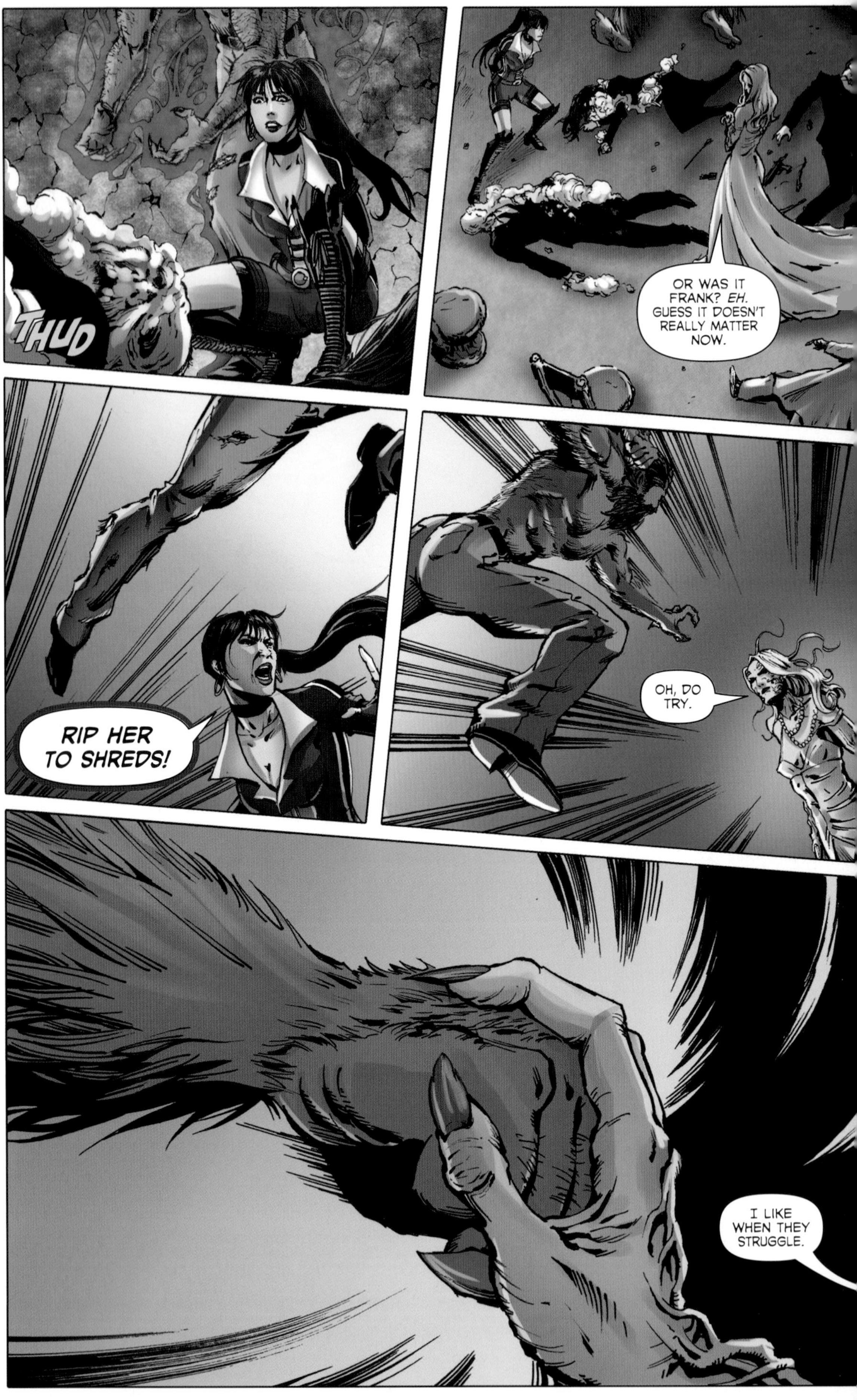
THUD
OR WAS IT FRANK? EH. GUESS IT DOESN'T REALLY MATTER NOW.
RIP HER TO SHREDS!
OH, DO TRY.
I LIKE WHEN THEY STRUGGLE.

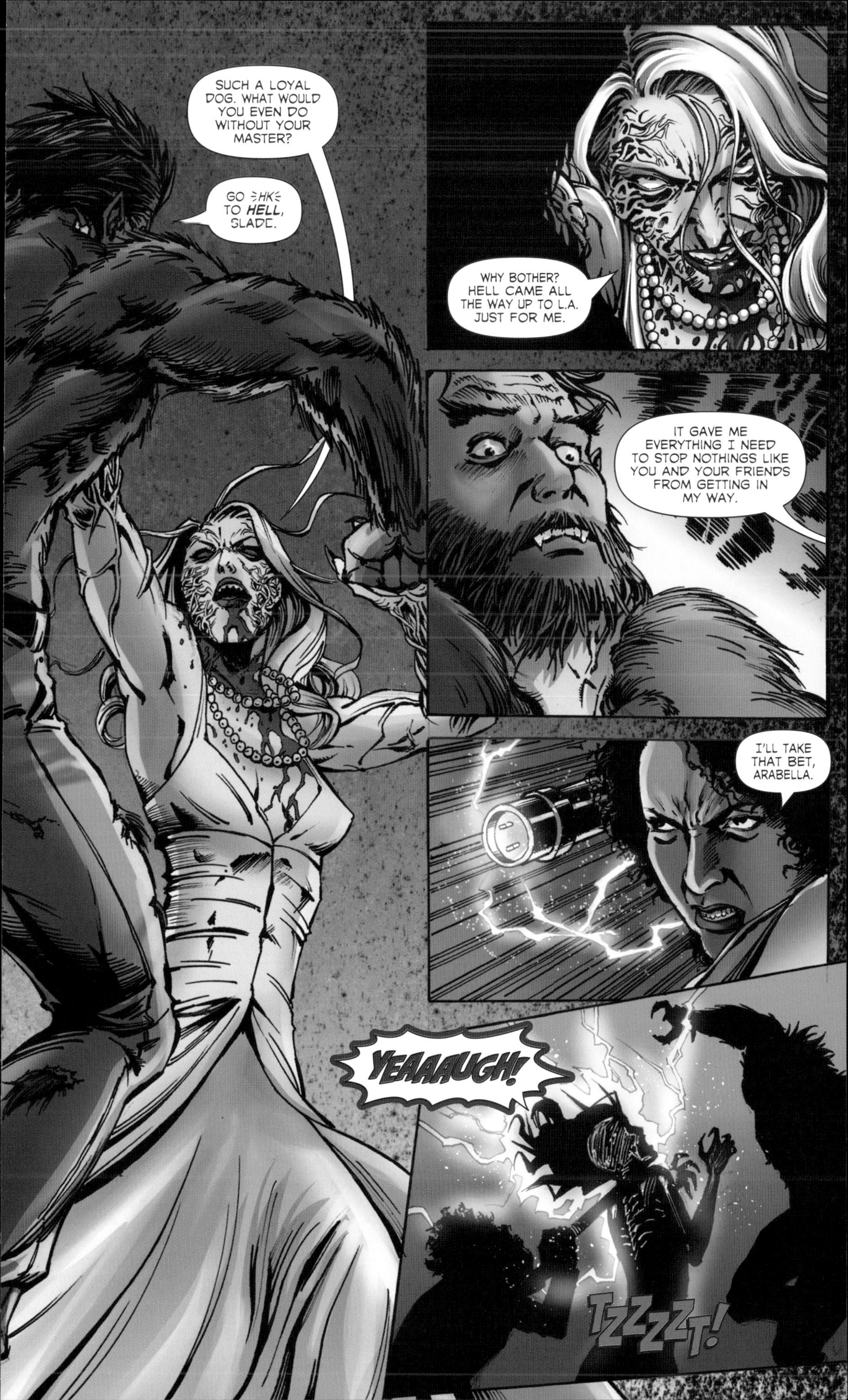
SUCH A LOYAL DOG. WHAT WOULD YOU EVEN DO WITHOUT YOUR MASTER?
GO =HK= TO **HELL**, SLADE.
WHY BOTHER? HELL CAME ALL THE WAY UP TO L.A. JUST FOR ME.
IT GAVE ME EVERYTHING I NEED TO STOP NOTHINGS LIKE YOU AND YOUR FRIENDS FROM GETTING IN MY WAY.
I'LL TAKE THAT BET, ARABELLA.
YEAAAUGH!
TZZZZT!

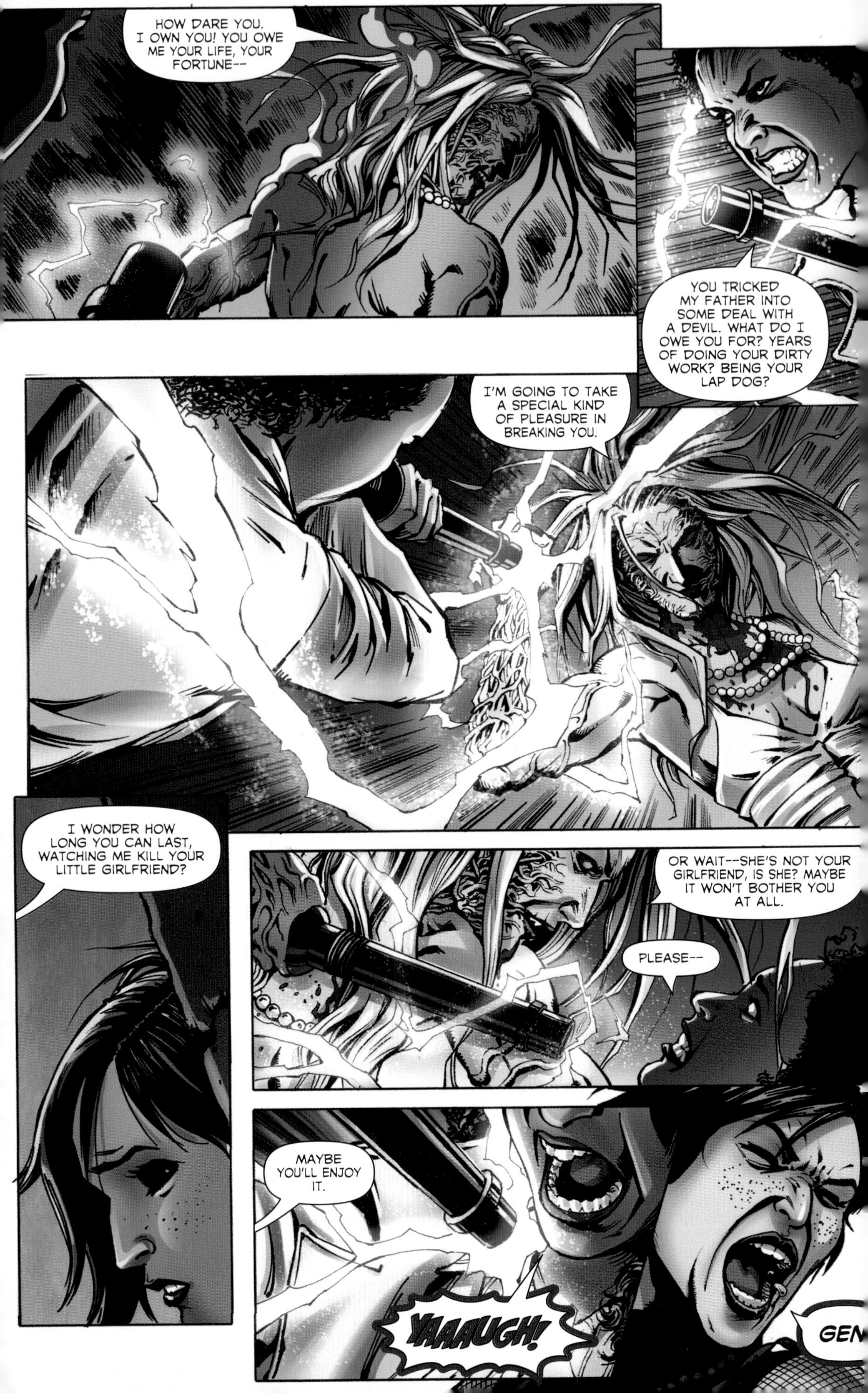
HOW DARE YOU. I OWN YOU! YOU OWE ME YOUR LIFE, YOUR FORTUNE--
YOU TRICKED MY FATHER INTO SOME DEAL WITH A DEVIL. WHAT DO I OWE YOU FOR? YEARS OF DOING YOUR DIRTY WORK? BEING YOUR LAP DOG?
I'M GOING TO TAKE A SPECIAL KIND OF PLEASURE IN BREAKING YOU.
I WONDER HOW LONG YOU CAN LAST, WATCHING ME KILL YOUR LITTLE GIRLFRIEND?
OR WAIT--SHE'S NOT YOUR GIRLFRIEND, IS SHE? MAYBE IT WON'T BOTHER YOU AT ALL.
PLEASE--
MAYBE YOU'LL ENJOY IT.
YAAAUGH!
GEN

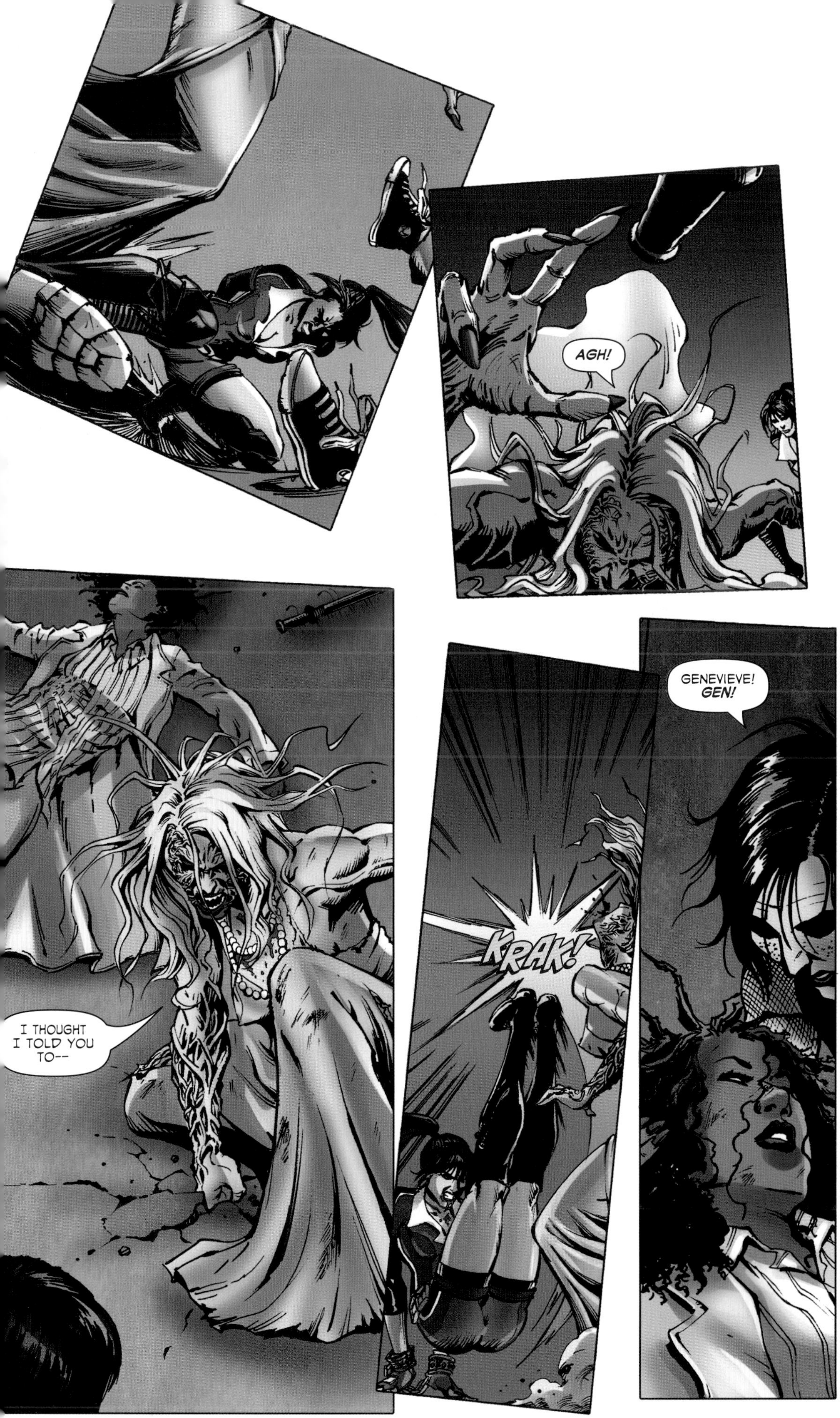
AGH!
I THOUGHT I TOLD YOU TO--
KRAK!
GENEVIEVE! GEN!

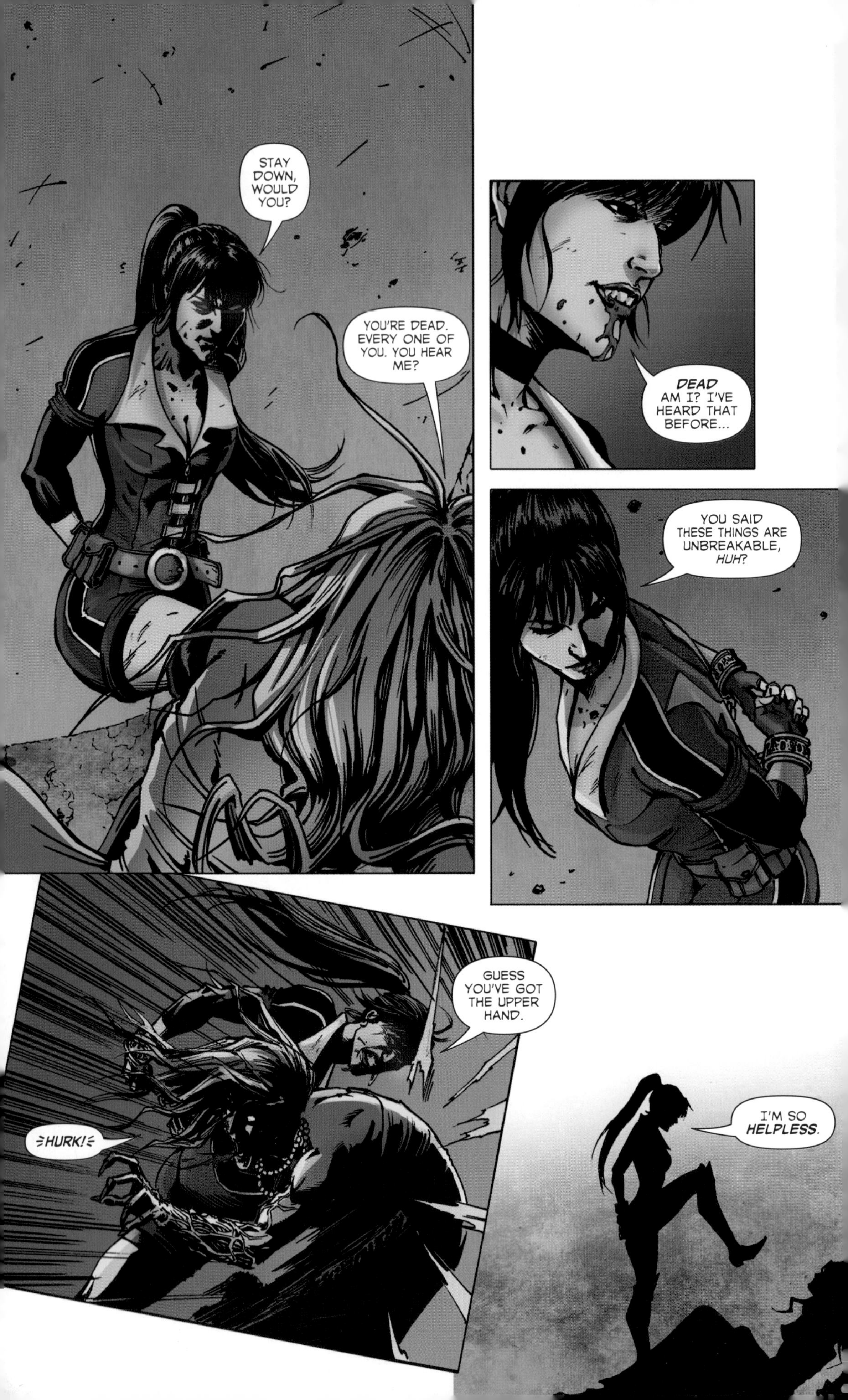
STAY DOWN, WOULD YOU?
YOU'RE DEAD. EVERY ONE OF YOU. YOU HEAR ME?
DEAD AM I? I'VE HEARD THAT BEFORE...
YOU SAID THESE THINGS ARE UNBREAKABLE, HUH?
GUESS YOU'VE GOT THE UPPER HAND.
HURK!
I'M SO HELPLESS.

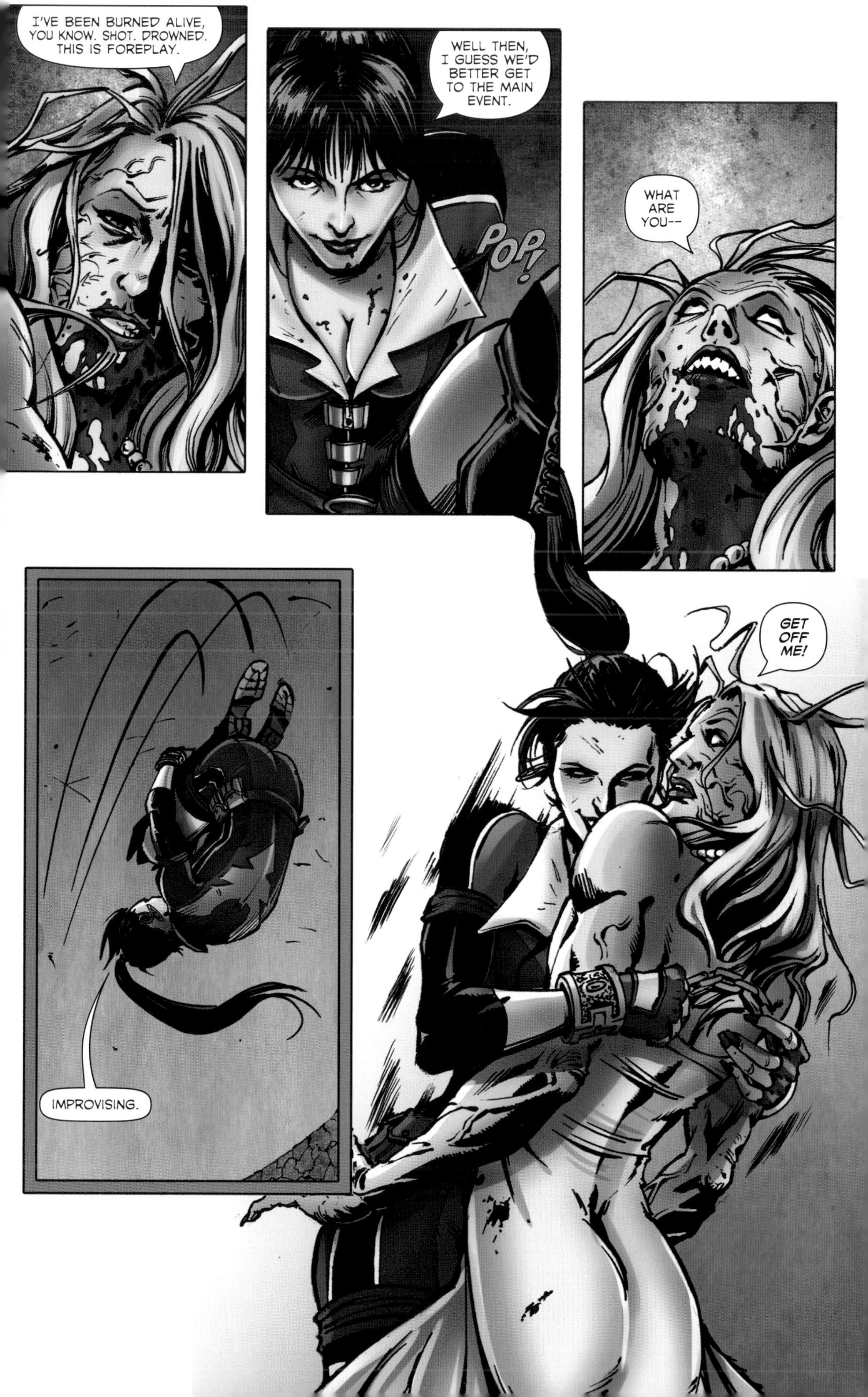
I'VE BEEN BURNED ALIVE, YOU KNOW. SHOT. DROWNED. THIS IS FOREPLAY.
WELL THEN, I GUESS WE'D BETTER GET TO THE MAIN EVENT.
POP!
WHAT ARE YOU--
GET OFF ME!
IMPROVISING.

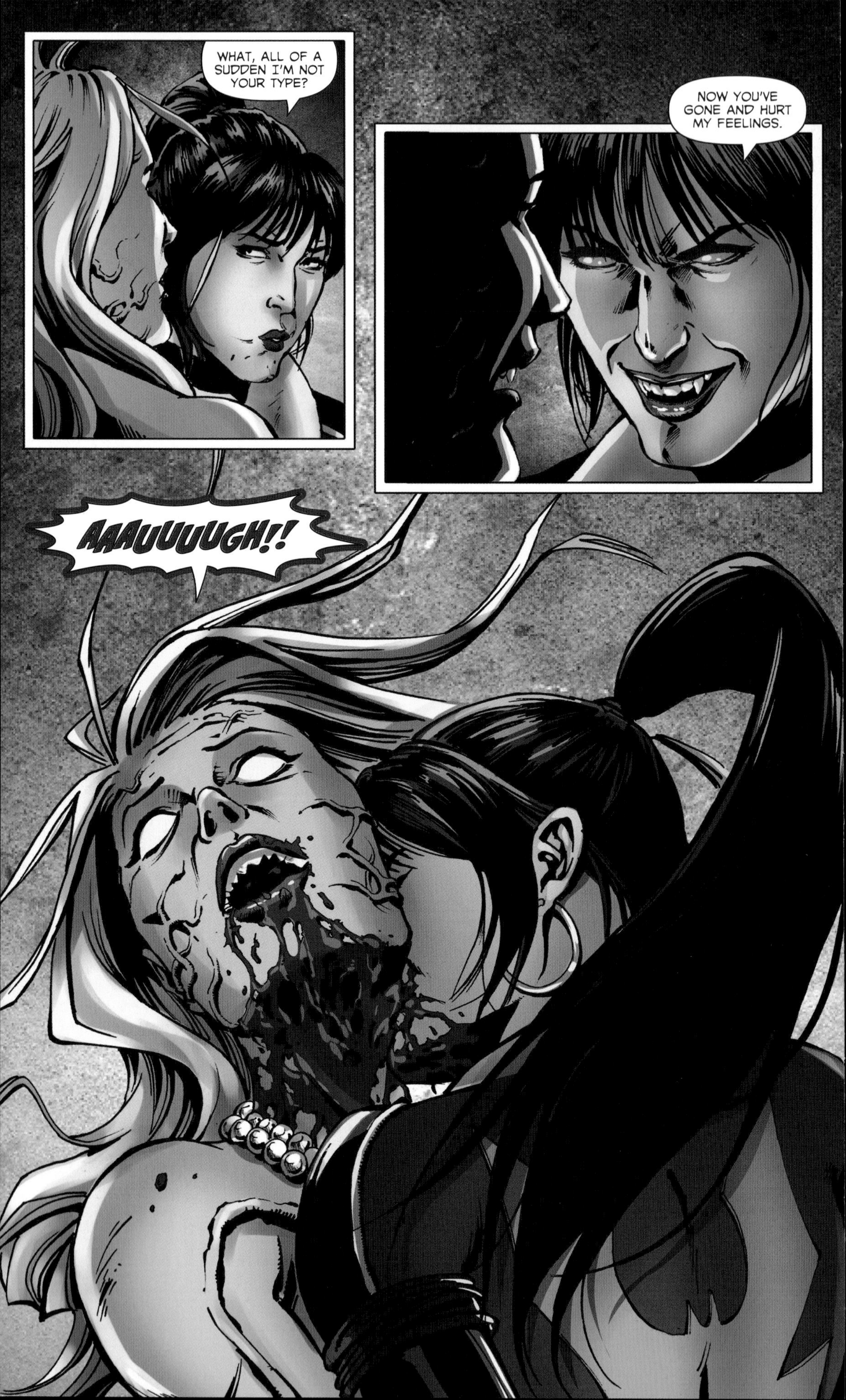
WHAT, ALL OF A SUDDEN I'M NOT YOUR TYPE?
NOW YOU'VE GONE AND HURT MY FEELINGS.
AAAUUUUGH!!

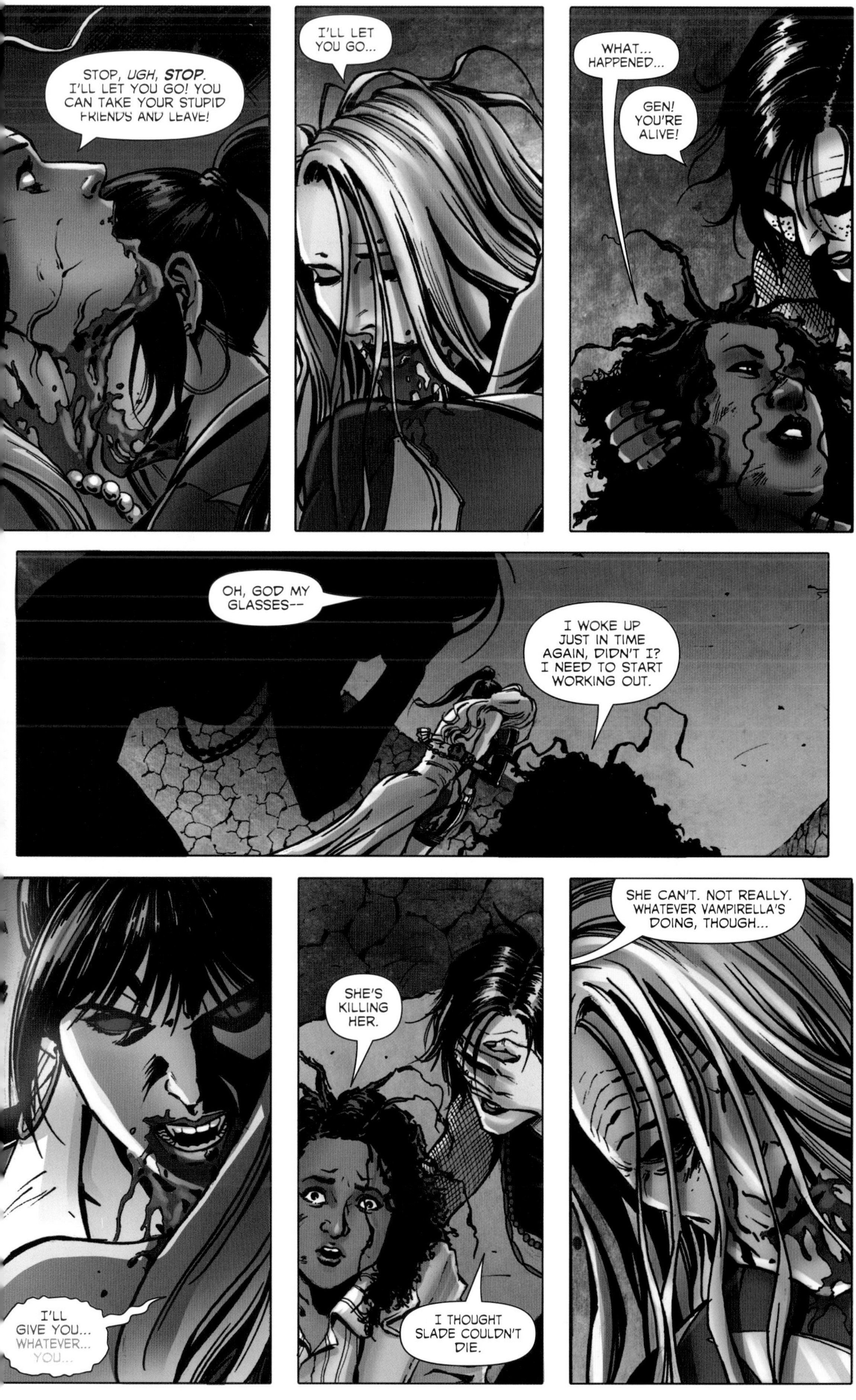
STOP, *UGH*, **STOP**. I'LL LET YOU GO! YOU CAN TAKE YOUR STUPID FRIENDS AND LEAVE!
I'LL LET YOU GO...
WHAT... HAPPENED...
GEN! YOU'RE ALIVE!
OH, GOD MY GLASSES--
I WOKE UP JUST IN TIME AGAIN, DIDN'T I? I NEED TO START WORKING OUT.
I'LL GIVE YOU... WHATEVER... YOU...
SHE'S KILLING HER.
I THOUGHT SLADE COULDN'T DIE.
SHE CAN'T. NOT REALLY. WHATEVER VAMPIRELLA'S DOING, THOUGH...

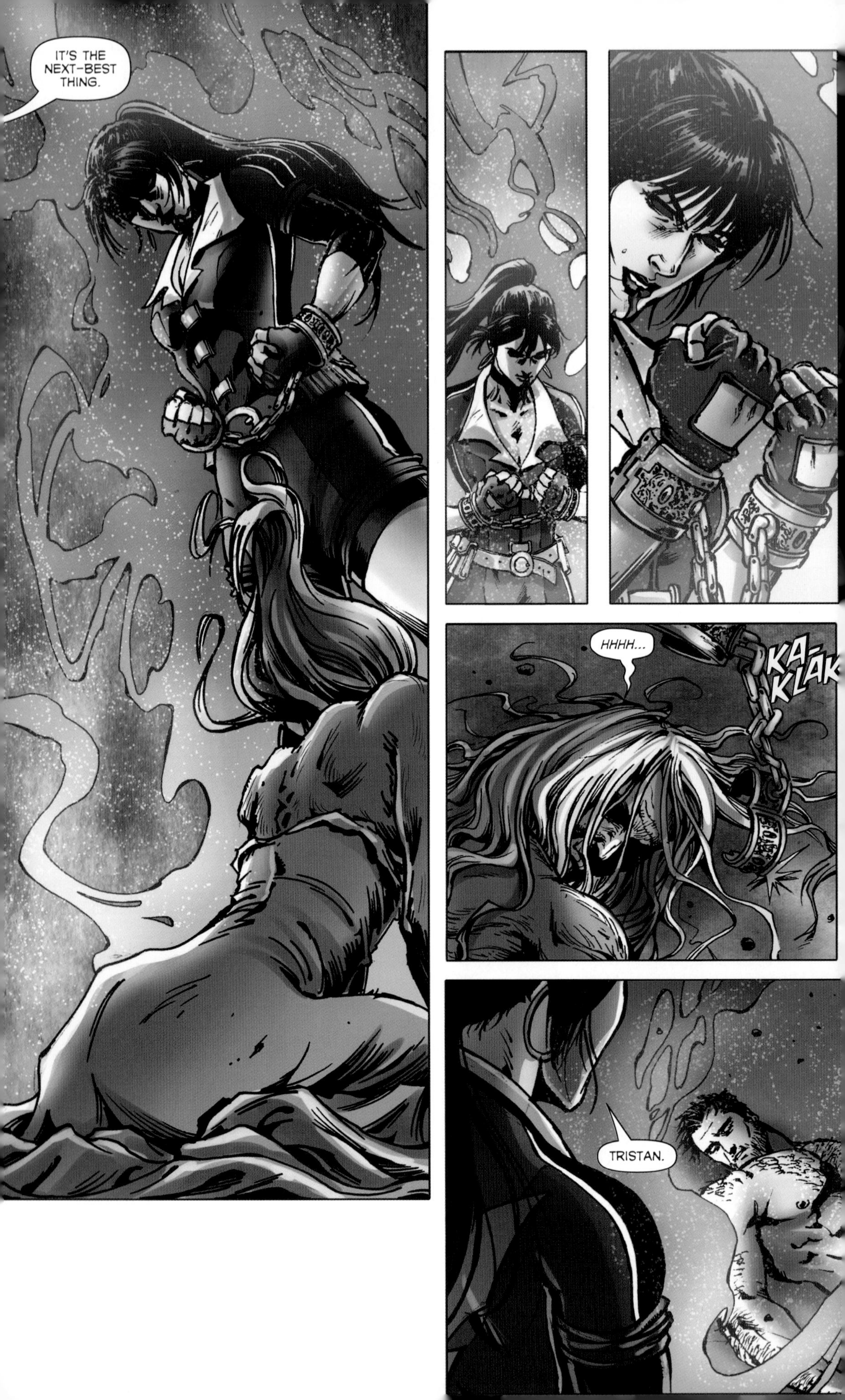
IT'S THE NEXT-BEST THING.
HHHH...
KA-KLAK
TRISTAN.

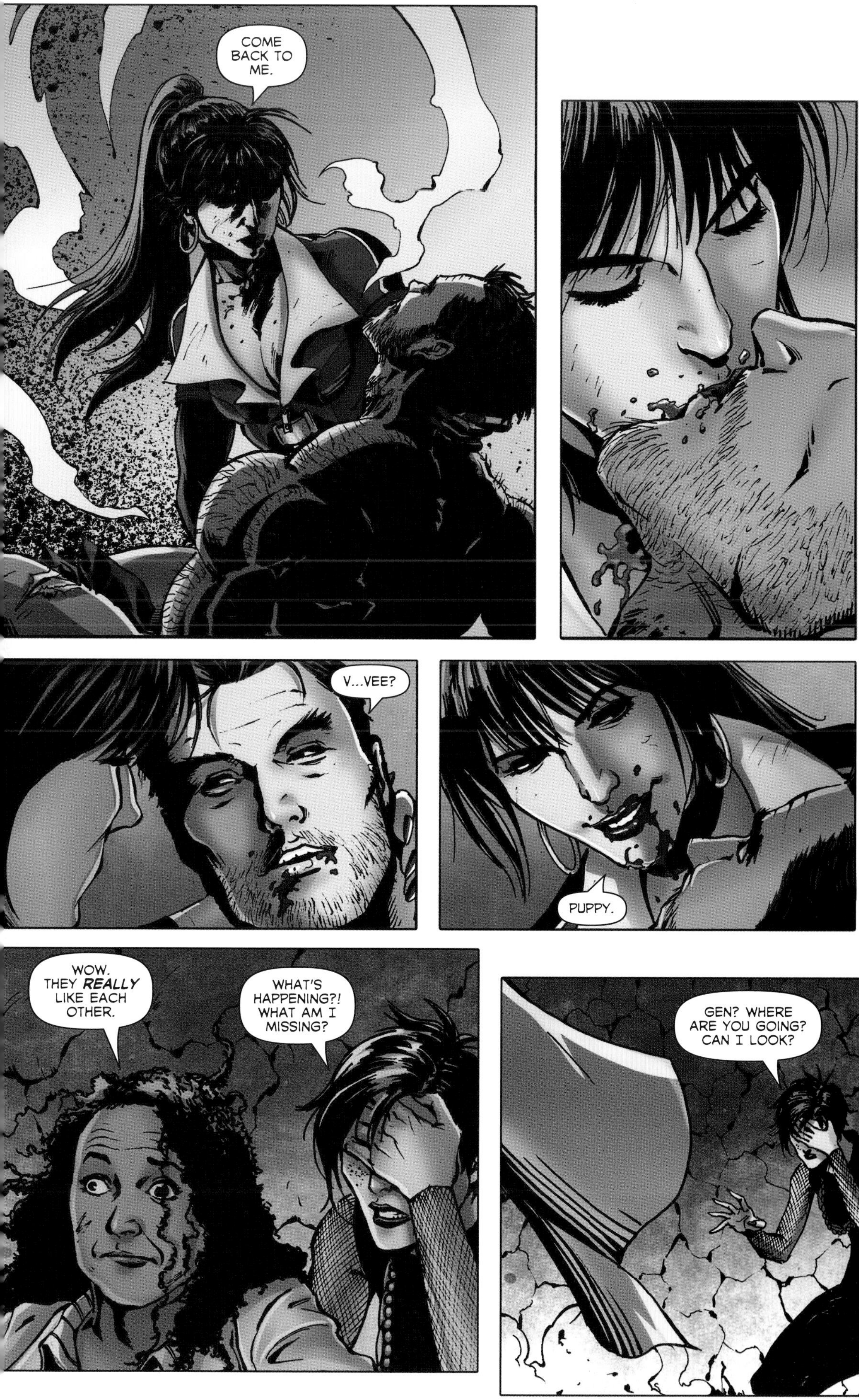
COME BACK TO ME.
V...VEE?
PUPPY.
WOW. THEY *REALLY* LIKE EACH OTHER.
WHAT'S HAPPENING?! WHAT AM I MISSING?
GEN? WHERE ARE YOU GOING? CAN I LOOK?

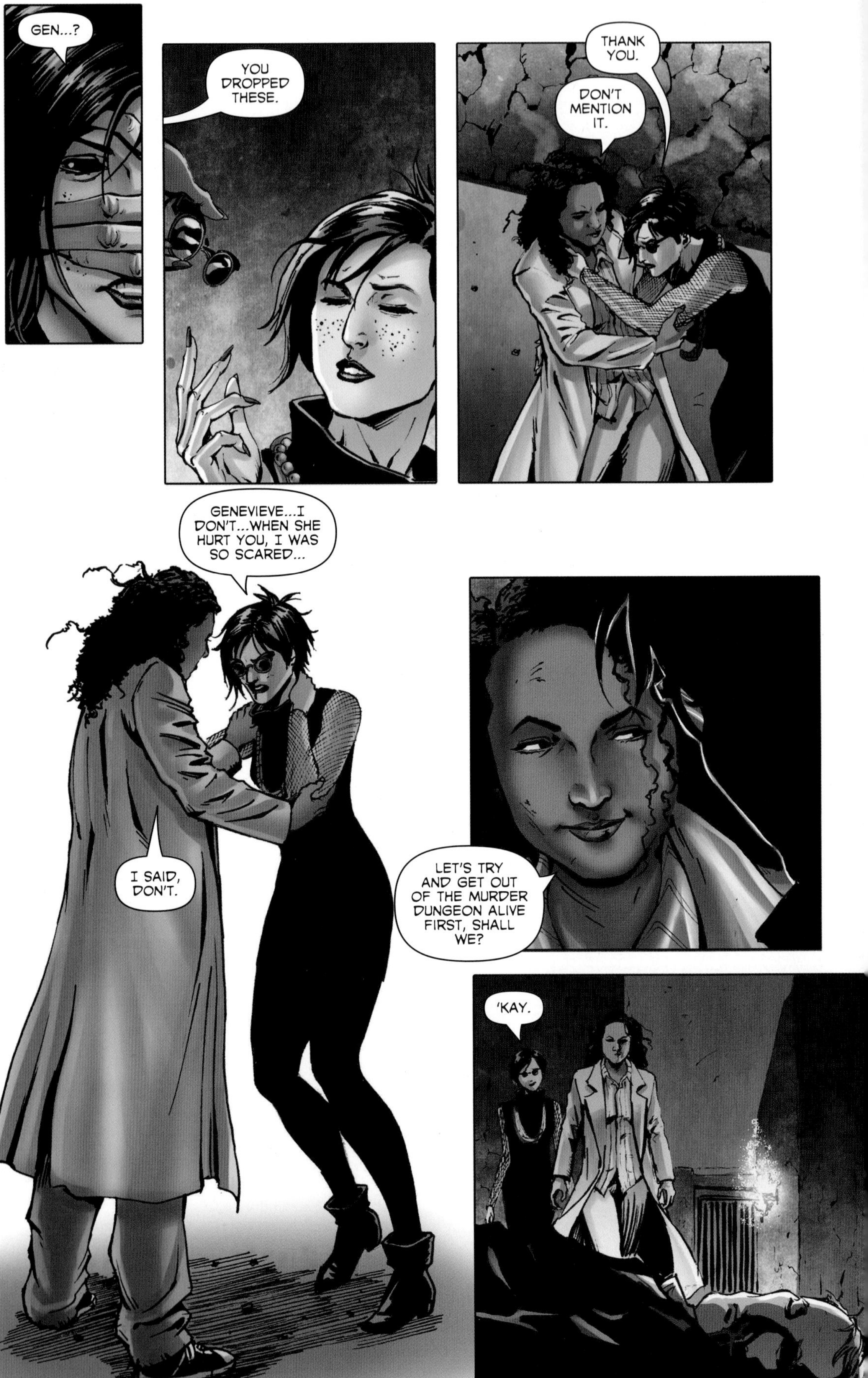
GEN...?
YOU DROPPED THESE.
THANK YOU.
DON'T MENTION IT.
GENEVIEVE...I DON'T...WHEN SHE HURT YOU, I WAS SO SCARED...
I SAID, DON'T.
LET'S TRY AND GET OUT OF THE MURDER DUNGEON ALIVE FIRST, SHALL WE?
'KAY.

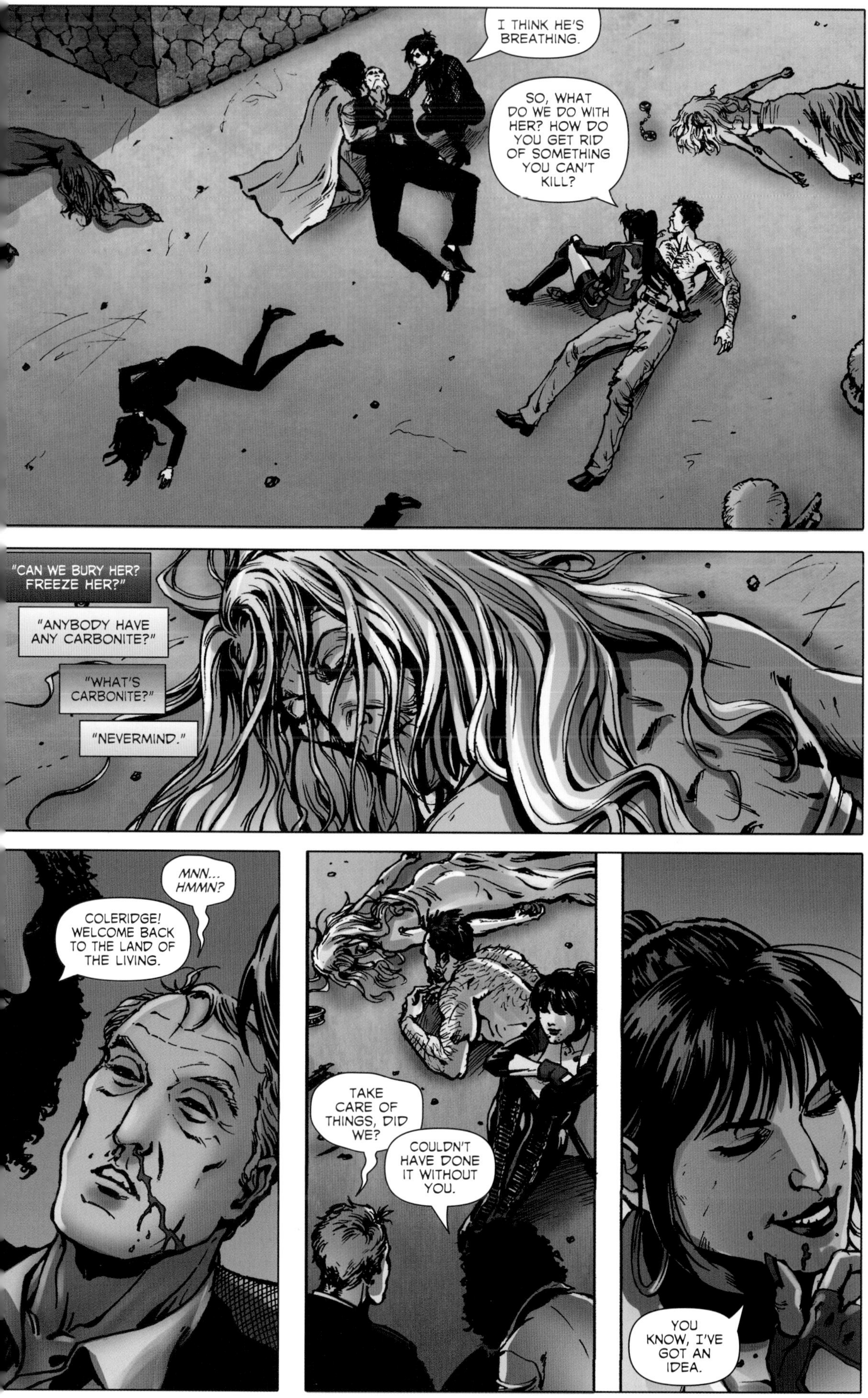
I THINK HE'S BREATHING.
SO, WHAT DO WE DO WITH HER? HOW DO YOU GET RID OF SOMETHING YOU CAN'T KILL?
"CAN WE BURY HER? FREEZE HER?"
"ANYBODY HAVE ANY CARBONITE?"
"WHAT'S CARBONITE?"
"NEVERMIND."
MNN... HMMN?
COLERIDGE! WELCOME BACK TO THE LAND OF THE LIVING.
TAKE CARE OF THINGS, DID WE?
COULDN'T HAVE DONE IT WITHOUT YOU.
YOU KNOW, I'VE GOT AN IDEA.

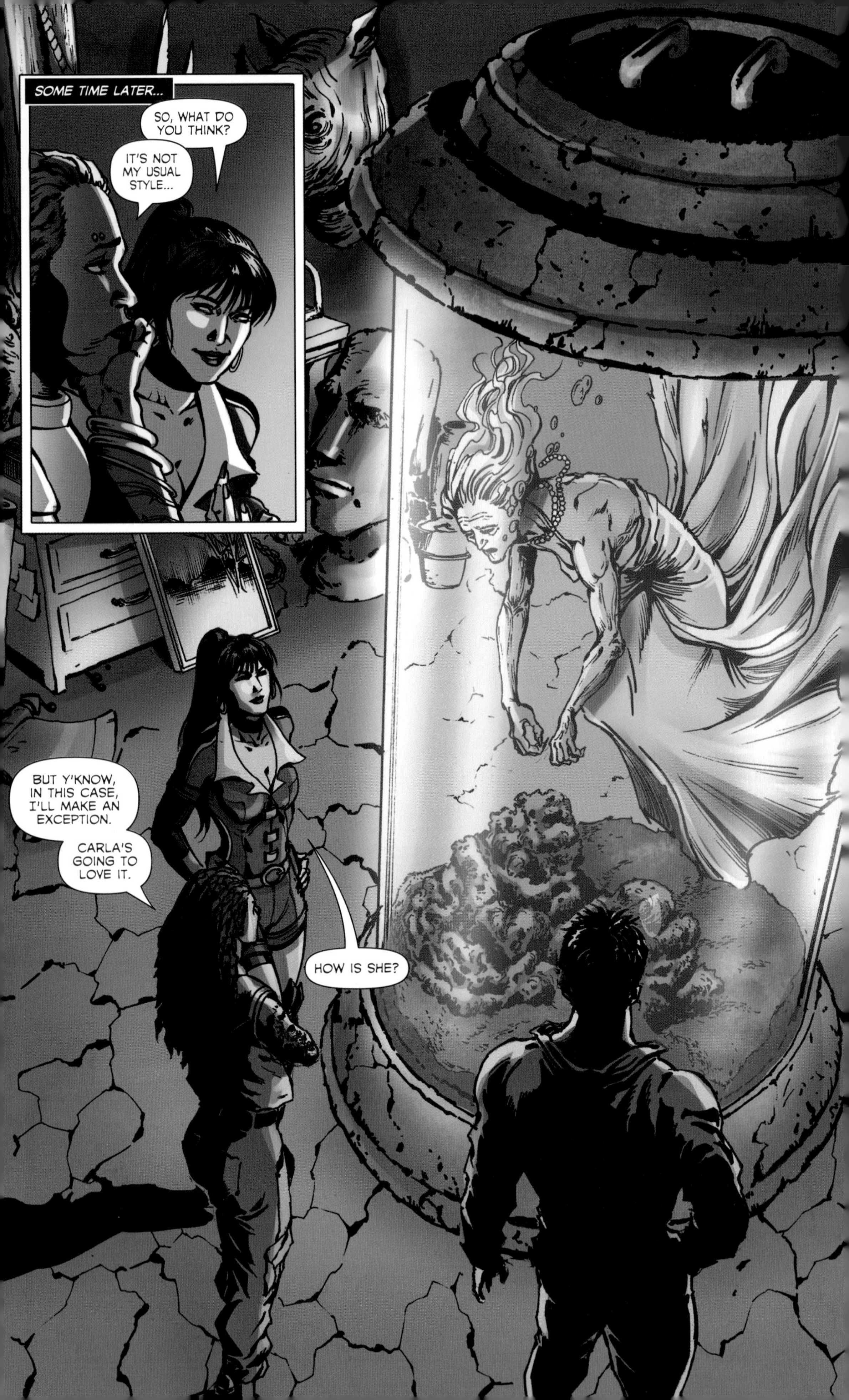

SOME TIME LATER...
SO, WHAT DO YOU THINK?
IT'S NOT MY USUAL STYLE...
BUT Y'KNOW, IN THIS CASE, I'LL MAKE AN EXCEPTION.
CARLA'S GOING TO LOVE IT.
HOW IS SHE?

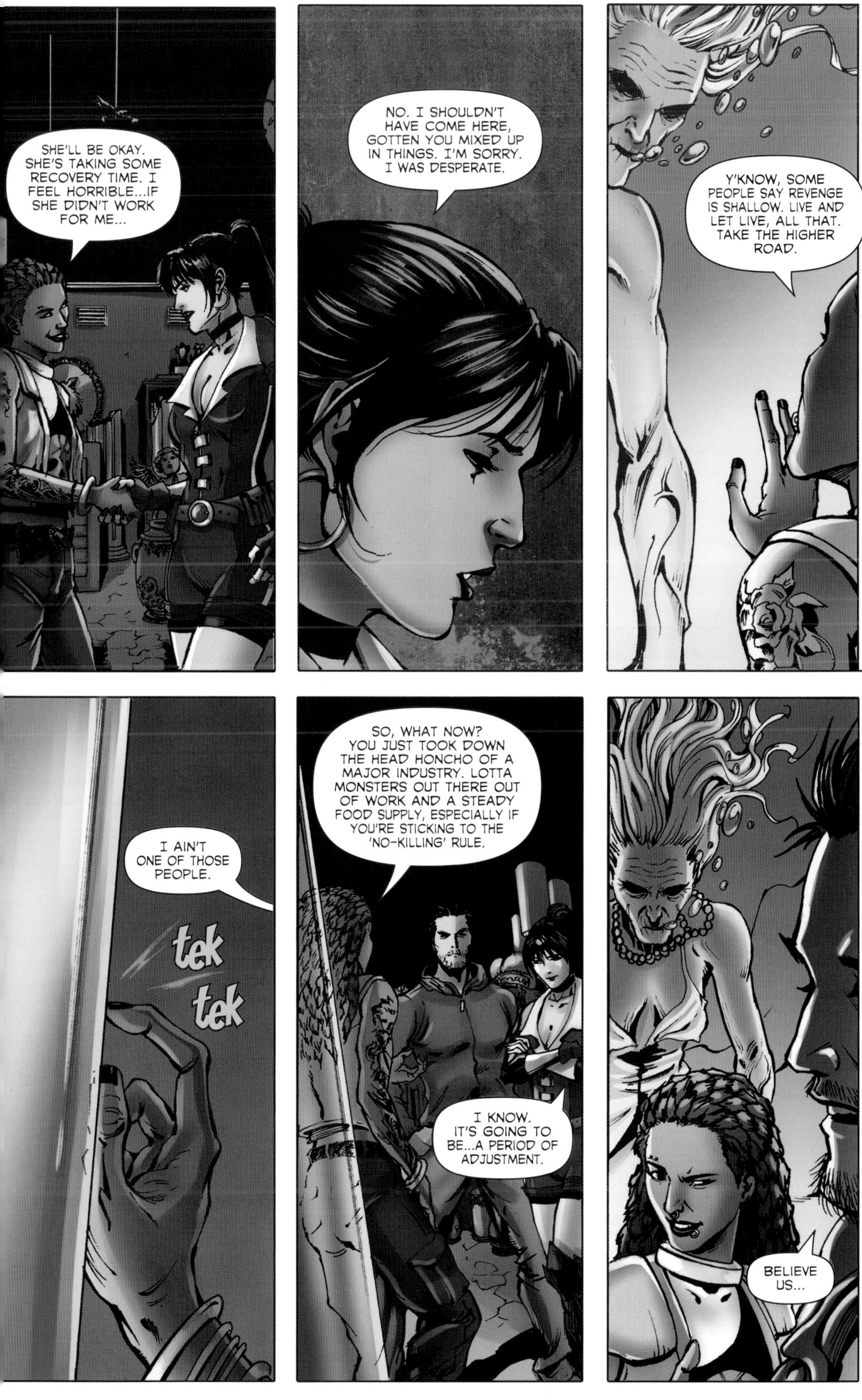
SHE'LL BE OKAY. SHE'S TAKING SOME RECOVERY TIME. I FEEL HORRIBLE...IF SHE DIDN'T WORK FOR ME...
NO. I SHOULDN'T HAVE COME HERE, GOTTEN YOU MIXED UP IN THINGS. I'M SORRY. I WAS DESPERATE.
Y'KNOW, SOME PEOPLE SAY REVENGE IS SHALLOW. LIVE AND LET LIVE, ALL THAT. TAKE THE HIGHER ROAD.
I AIN'T ONE OF THOSE PEOPLE.
tek
tek
SO, WHAT NOW? YOU JUST TOOK DOWN THE HEAD HONCHO OF A MAJOR INDUSTRY. LOTTA MONSTERS OUT THERE OUT OF WORK AND A STEADY FOOD SUPPLY, ESPECIALLY IF YOU'RE STICKING TO THE 'NO-KILLING' RULE.
I KNOW. IT'S GOING TO BE...A PERIOD OF ADJUSTMENT.
BELIEVE US...

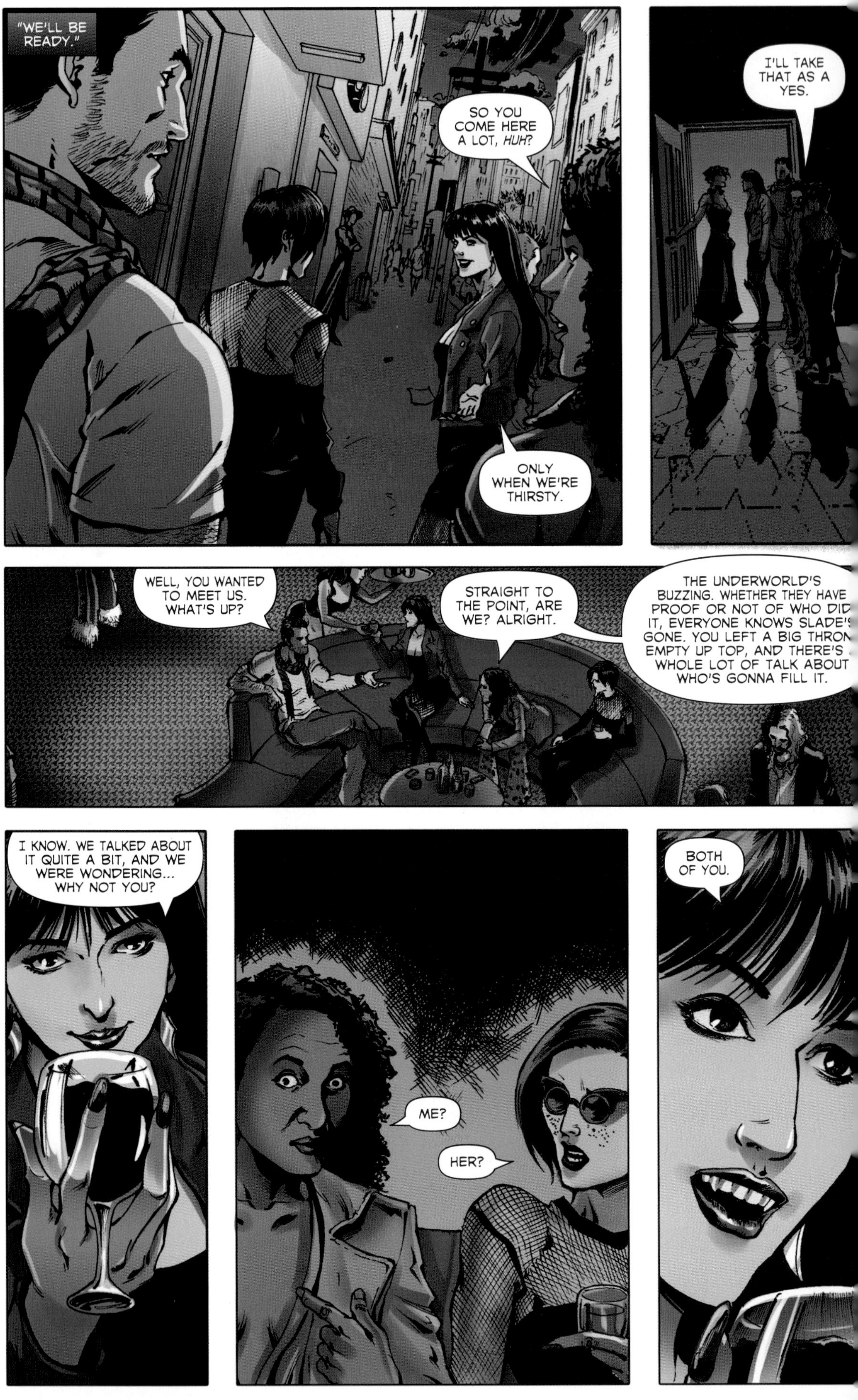
"WE'LL BE READY."
SO YOU COME HERE A LOT, *HUH*?
ONLY WHEN WE'RE THIRSTY.
I'LL TAKE THAT AS A YES.
WELL, YOU WANTED TO MEET US. WHAT'S UP?
STRAIGHT TO THE POINT, ARE WE? ALRIGHT.
THE UNDERWORLD'S BUZZING. WHETHER THEY HAVE PROOF OR NOT OF WHO DID IT, EVERYONE KNOWS SLADE'S GONE. YOU LEFT A BIG THRONE EMPTY UP TOP, AND THERE'S A WHOLE LOT OF TALK ABOUT WHO'S GONNA FILL IT.
I KNOW. WE TALKED ABOUT IT QUITE A BIT, AND WE WERE WONDERING... WHY NOT YOU?
ME?
HER?
BOTH OF YOU.

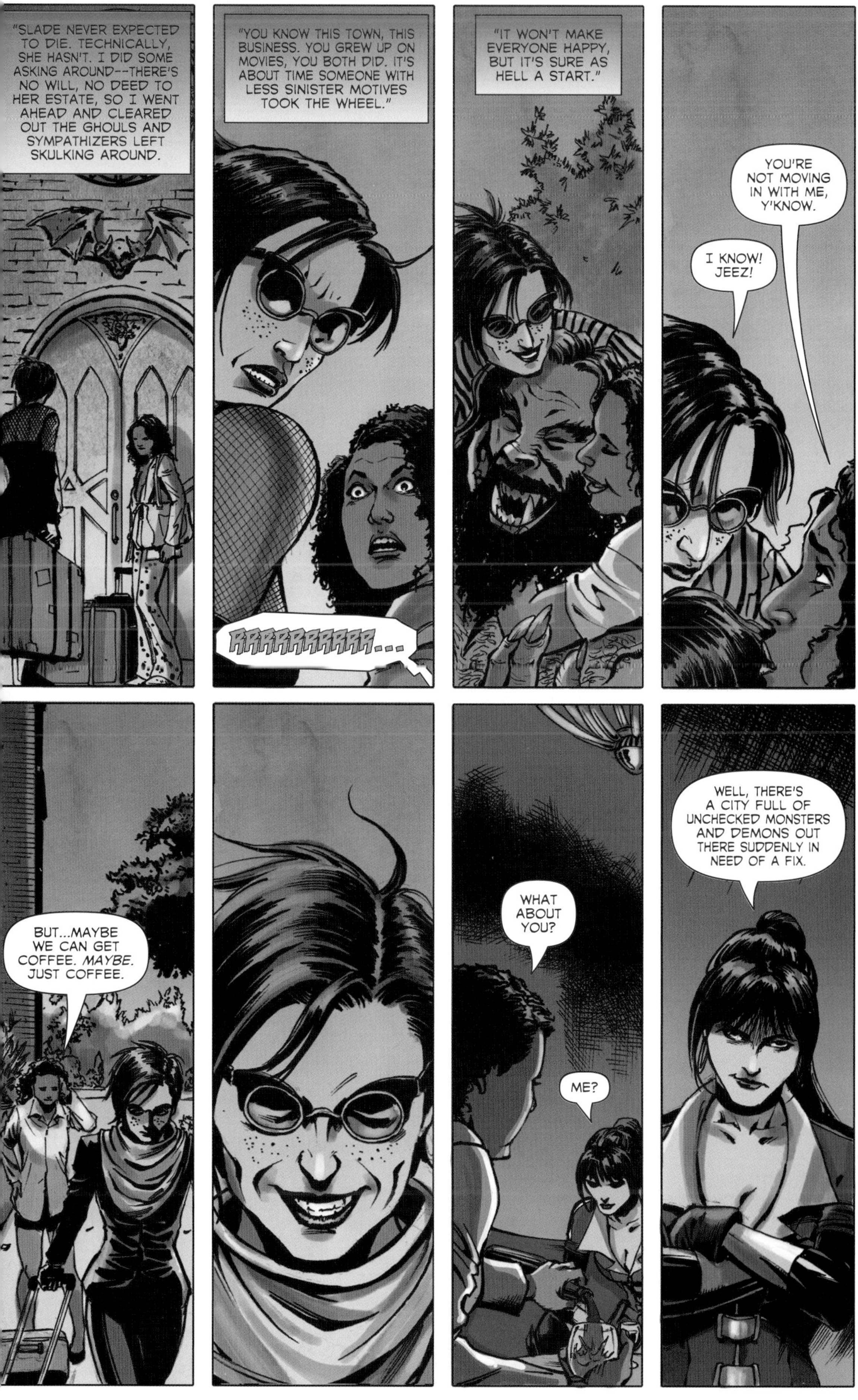
"SLADE NEVER EXPECTED TO DIE. TECHNICALLY, SHE HASN'T. I DID SOME ASKING AROUND--THERE'S NO WILL, NO DEED TO HER ESTATE, SO I WENT AHEAD AND CLEARED OUT THE GHOULS AND SYMPATHIZERS LEFT SKULKING AROUND.
"YOU KNOW THIS TOWN, THIS BUSINESS. YOU GREW UP ON MOVIES, YOU BOTH DID. IT'S ABOUT TIME SOMEONE WITH LESS SINISTER MOTIVES TOOK THE WHEEL."
RRRRRRRRRR...
"IT WON'T MAKE EVERYONE HAPPY, BUT IT'S SURE AS HELL A START."
YOU'RE NOT MOVING IN WITH ME, Y'KNOW.
I KNOW! JEEZ!
BUT...MAYBE WE CAN GET COFFEE. *MAYBE.* JUST COFFEE.
WHAT ABOUT YOU?
ME?
WELL, THERE'S A CITY FULL OF UNCHECKED MONSTERS AND DEMONS OUT THERE SUDDENLY IN NEED OF A FIX.

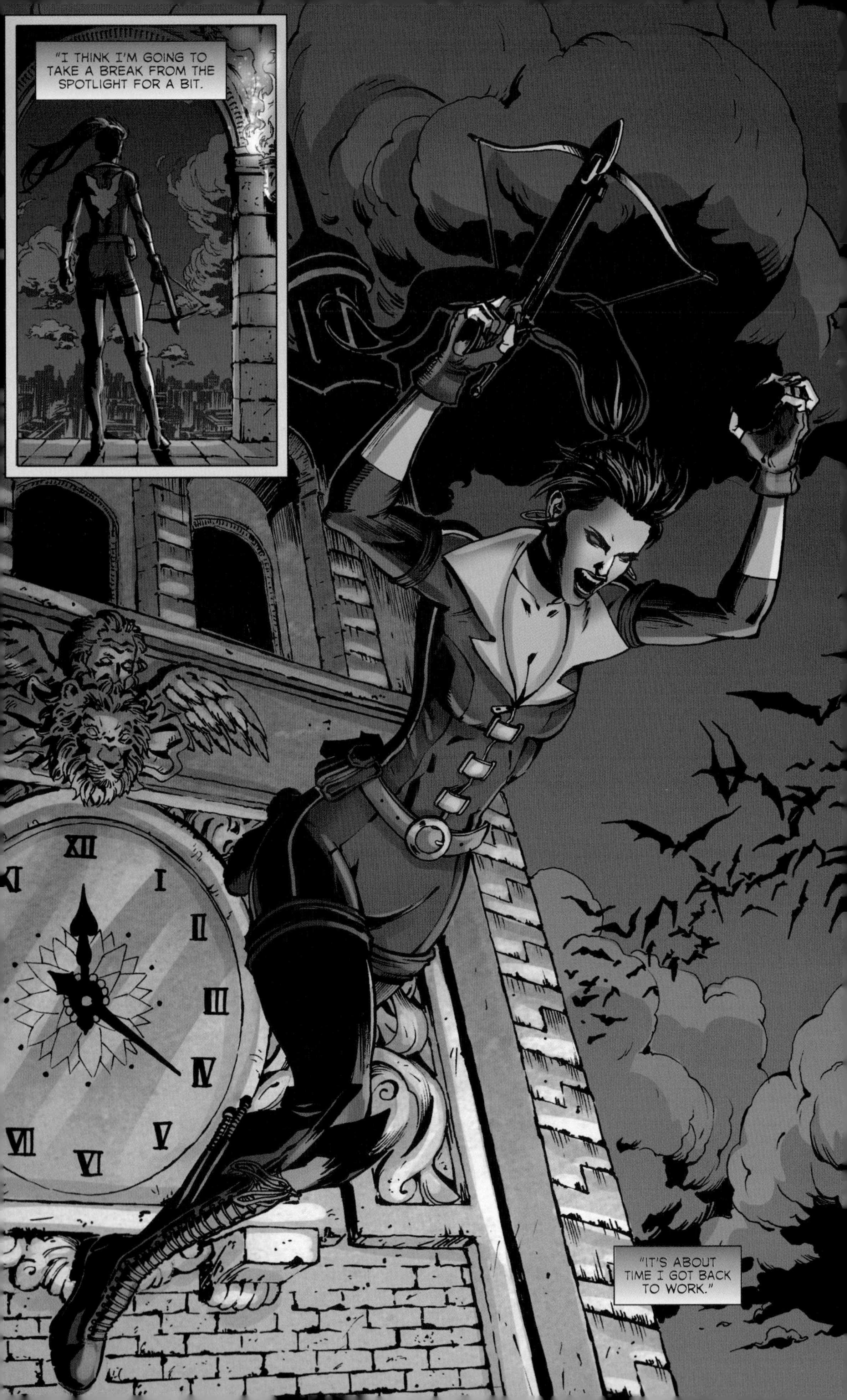
"I THINK I'M GOING TO TAKE A BREAK FROM THE SPOTLIGHT FOR A BIT.
"IT'S ABOUT TIME I GOT BACK TO WORK."

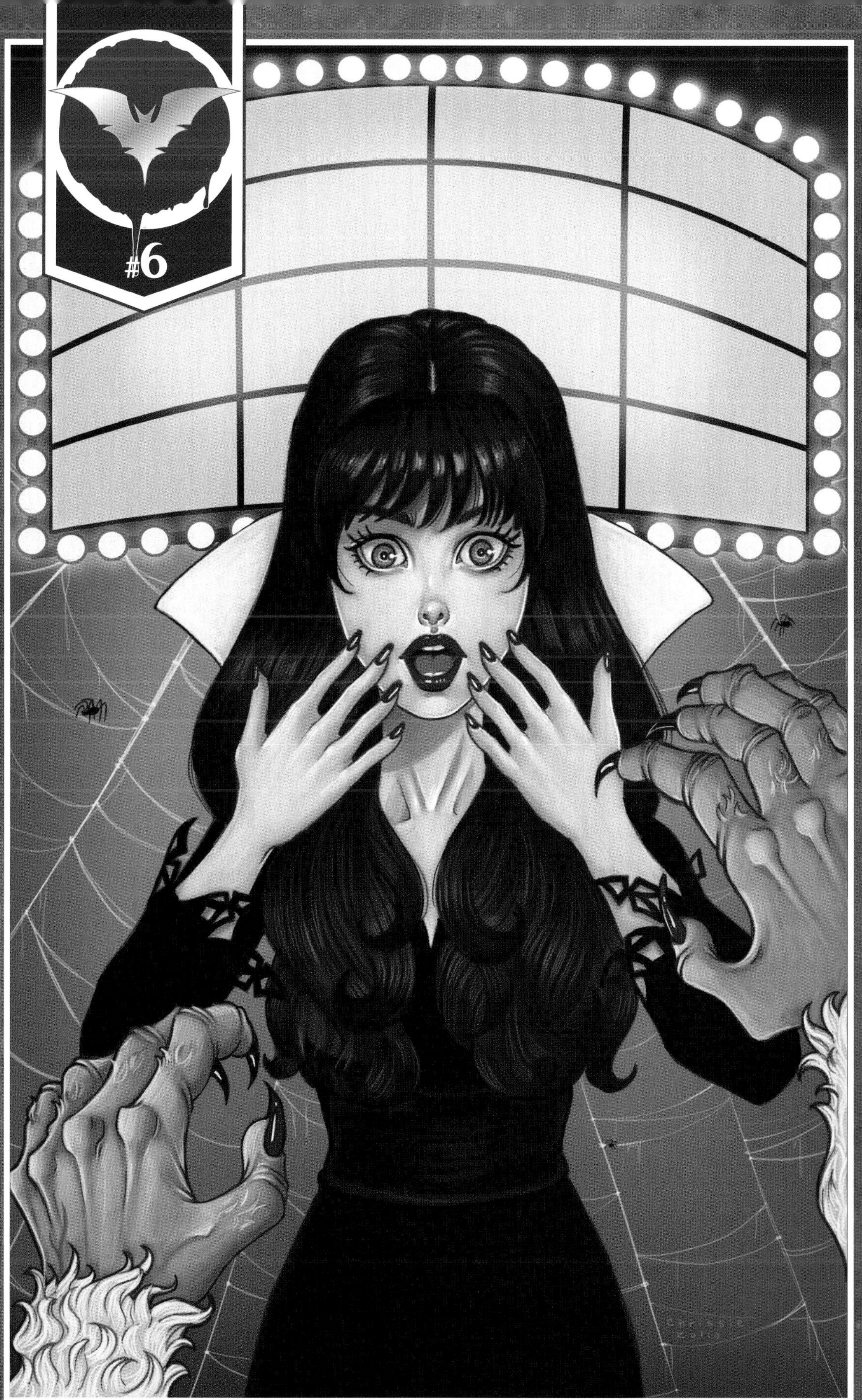
#6
Chrissie Zullo

cover by **Chrissie Zullo**

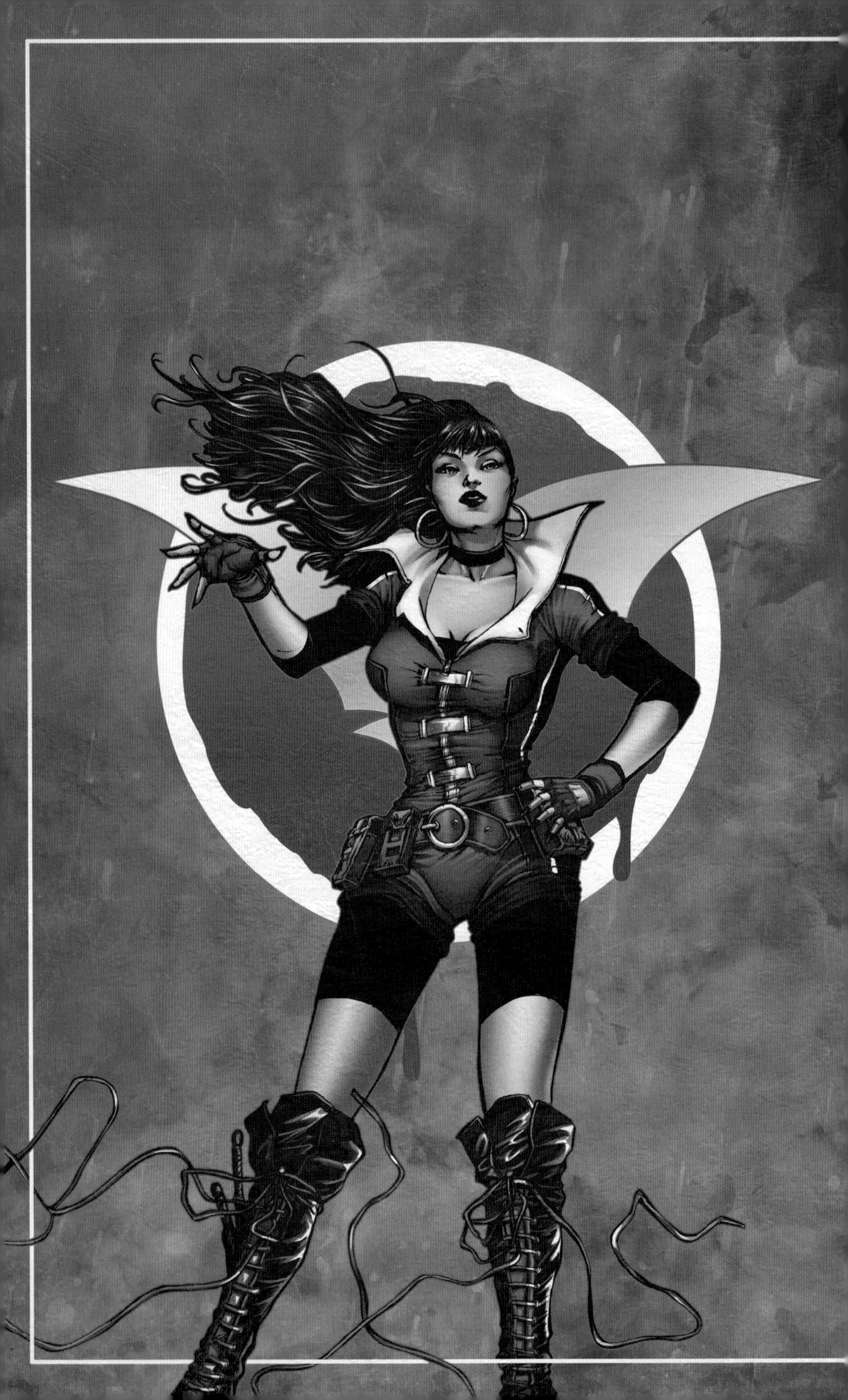

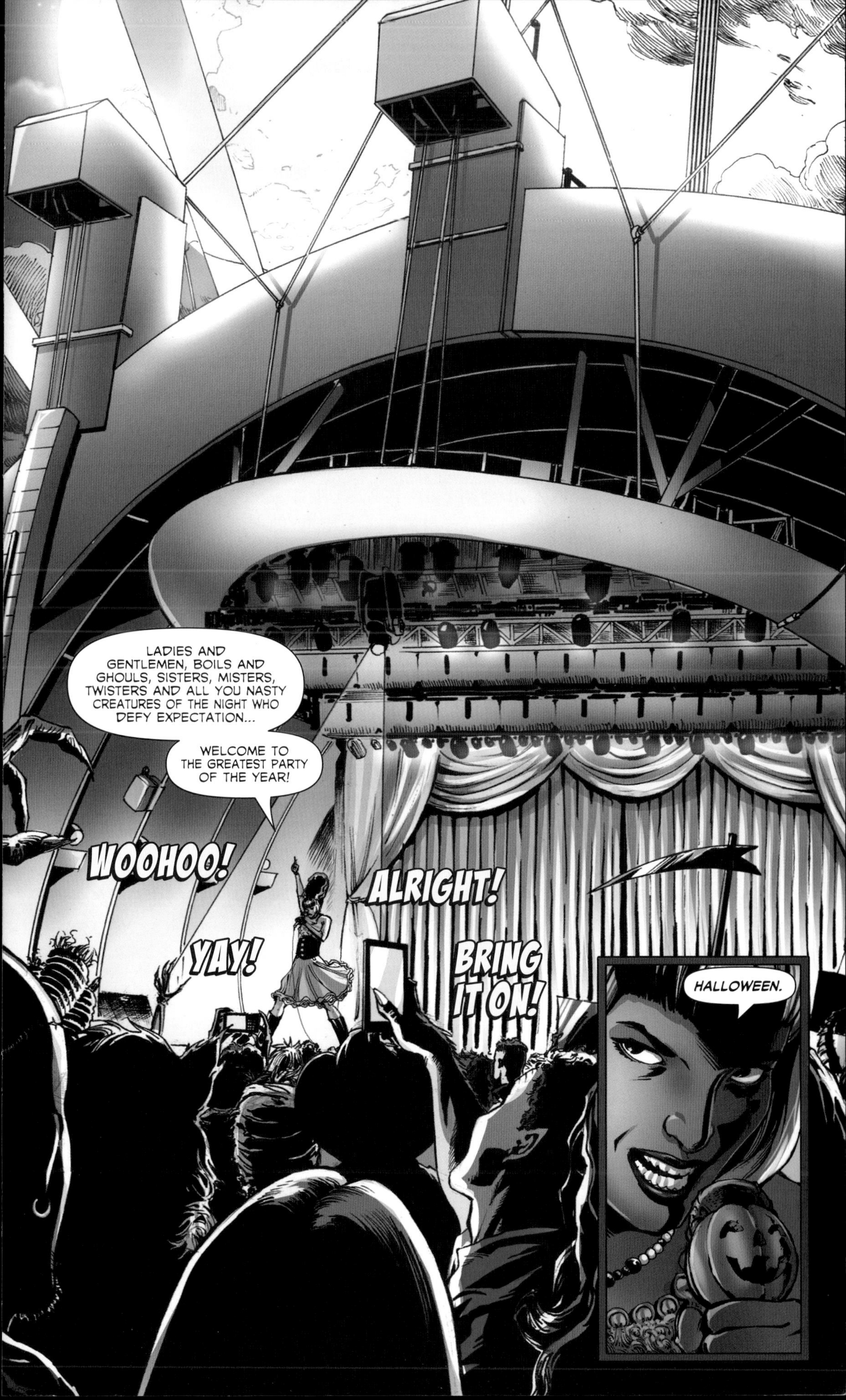
LADIES AND GENTLEMEN, BOILS AND GHOULS, SISTERS, MISTERS, TWISTERS AND ALL YOU NASTY CREATURES OF THE NIGHT WHO DEFY EXPECTATION...
WELCOME TO THE GREATEST PARTY OF THE YEAR!
WOOHOO!
ALRIGHT!
YAY!
BRING IT ON!
HALLOWEEN.

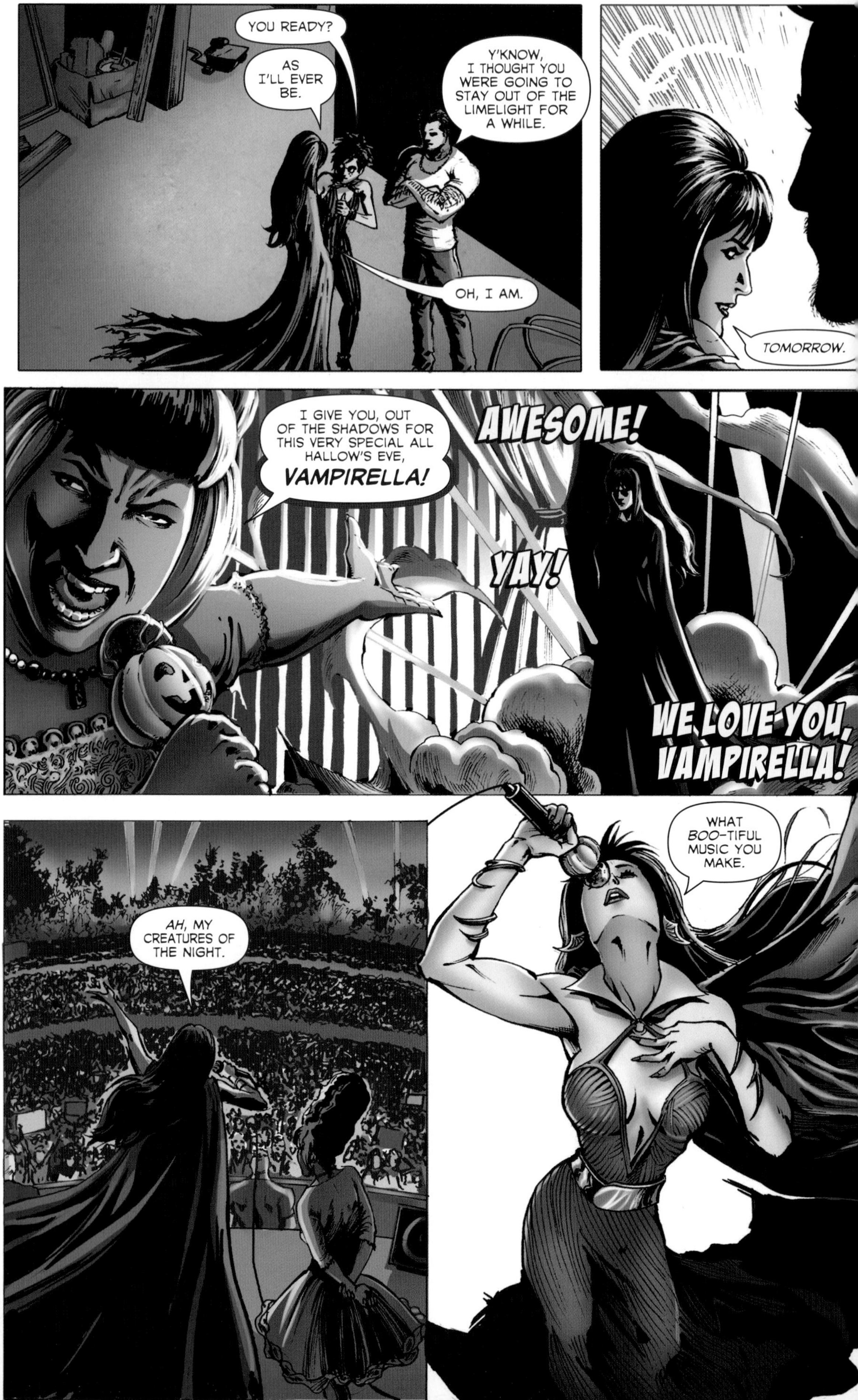
YOU READY?
AS I'LL EVER BE.
Y'KNOW, I THOUGHT YOU WERE GOING TO STAY OUT OF THE LIMELIGHT FOR A WHILE.
OH, I AM.
TOMORROW.
I GIVE YOU, OUT OF THE SHADOWS FOR THIS VERY SPECIAL ALL HALLOW'S EVE, VAMPIRELLA!
AWESOME!
YAY!
WE LOVE YOU, VAMPIRELLA!
AH, MY CREATURES OF THE NIGHT.
WHAT BOO-TIFUL MUSIC YOU MAKE.

THAT GIRL IS A NATURAL, I SWEAR.

YOU'RE NOT SO BAD YOURSELF. I LIKED YOUR INTRODUCTION.

SHE DOES HAVE THEM EATING OUT OF HER HANDS.

SO... WHAT NOW?

WELL, SHE'LL DO A LITTLE TALK, SET UP THE MOVIE, THEN WE'RE OFF THE CLOCK FOR 90 MINUTES 'TIL IT'S OVER.

HUH. YOU GALS WANNA...GRAB A BEER?

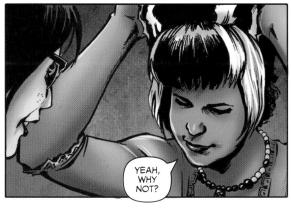

YEAH, WHY NOT?

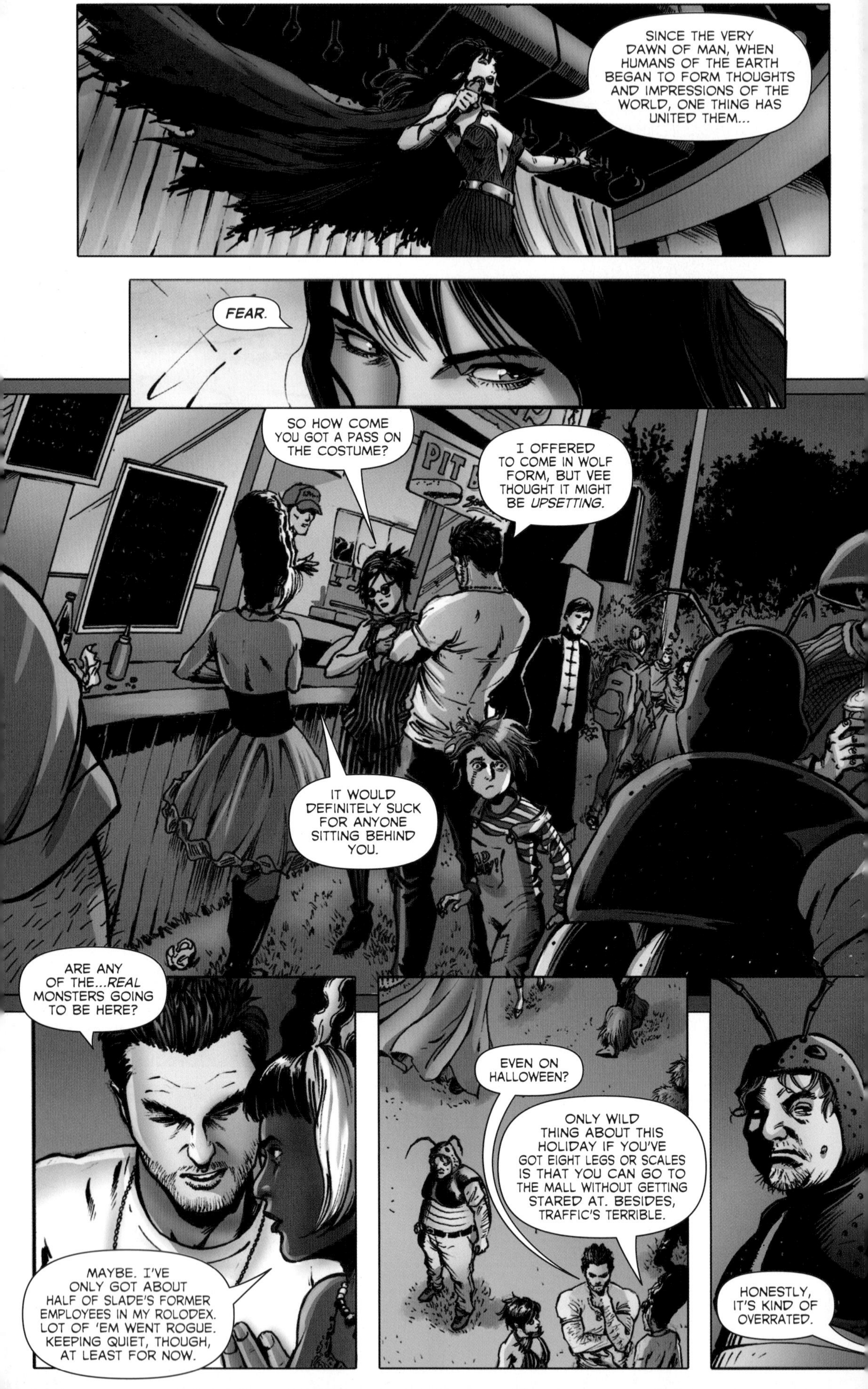
SINCE THE VERY DAWN OF MAN, WHEN HUMANS OF THE EARTH BEGAN TO FORM THOUGHTS AND IMPRESSIONS OF THE WORLD, ONE THING HAS UNITED THEM...
FEAR.
SO HOW COME YOU GOT A PASS ON THE COSTUME?
I OFFERED TO COME IN WOLF FORM, BUT VEE THOUGHT IT MIGHT BE UPSETTING.
IT WOULD DEFINITELY SUCK FOR ANYONE SITTING BEHIND YOU.
ARE ANY OF THE...REAL MONSTERS GOING TO BE HERE?
MAYBE. I'VE ONLY GOT ABOUT HALF OF SLADE'S FORMER EMPLOYEES IN MY ROLODEX. LOT OF 'EM WENT ROGUE. KEEPING QUIET, THOUGH, AT LEAST FOR NOW.
EVEN ON HALLOWEEN?
ONLY WILD THING ABOUT THIS HOLIDAY IF YOU'VE GOT EIGHT LEGS OR SCALES IS THAT YOU CAN GO TO THE MALL WITHOUT GETTING STARED AT. BESIDES, TRAFFIC'S TERRIBLE.
HONESTLY, IT'S KIND OF OVERRATED.

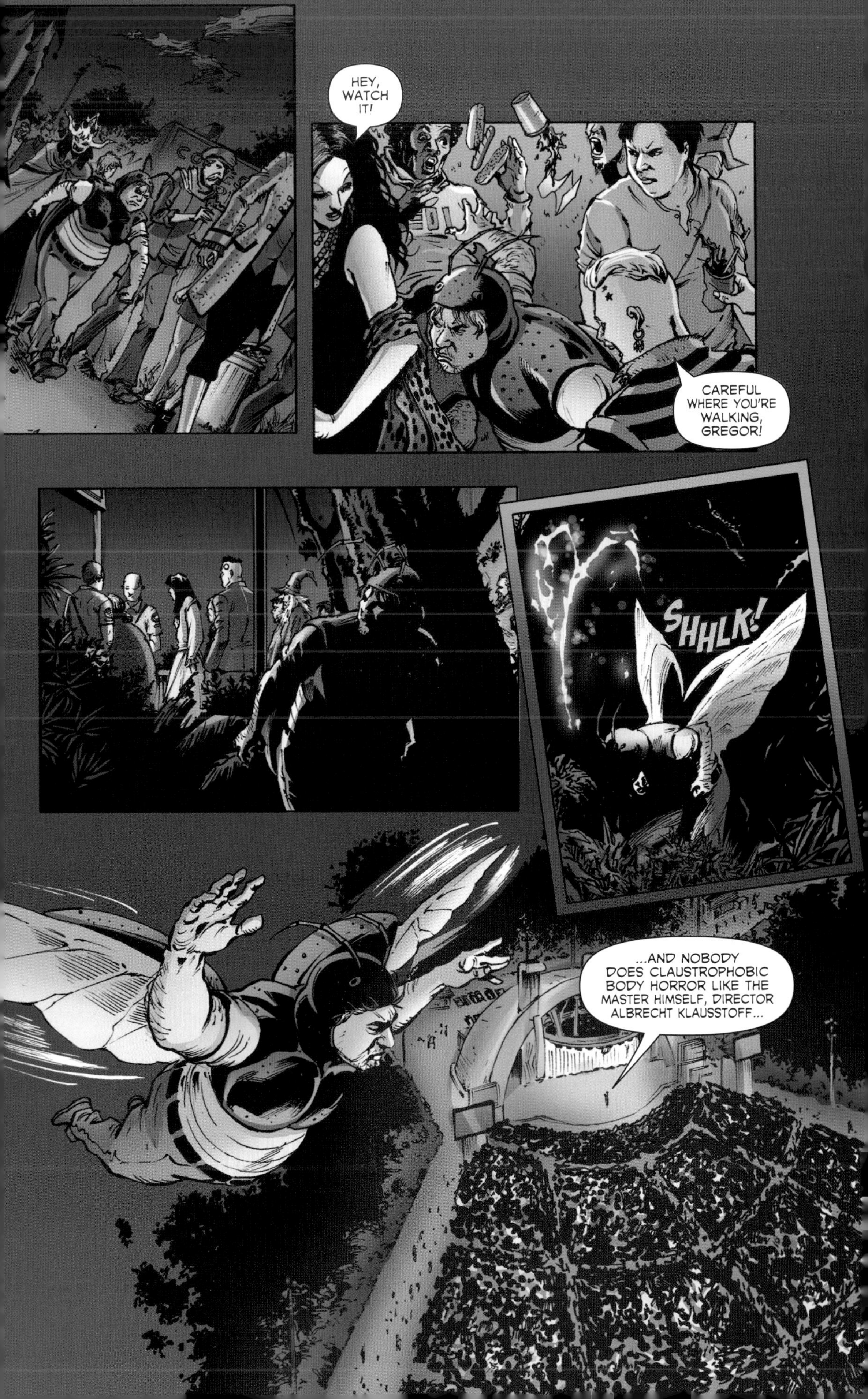
HEY, WATCH IT!
CAREFUL WHERE YOU'RE WALKING, GREGOR!
SHHLK!
...AND NOBODY DOES CLAUSTROPHOBIC BODY HORROR LIKE THE MASTER HIMSELF, DIRECTOR ALBRECHT KLAUSSTOFF...

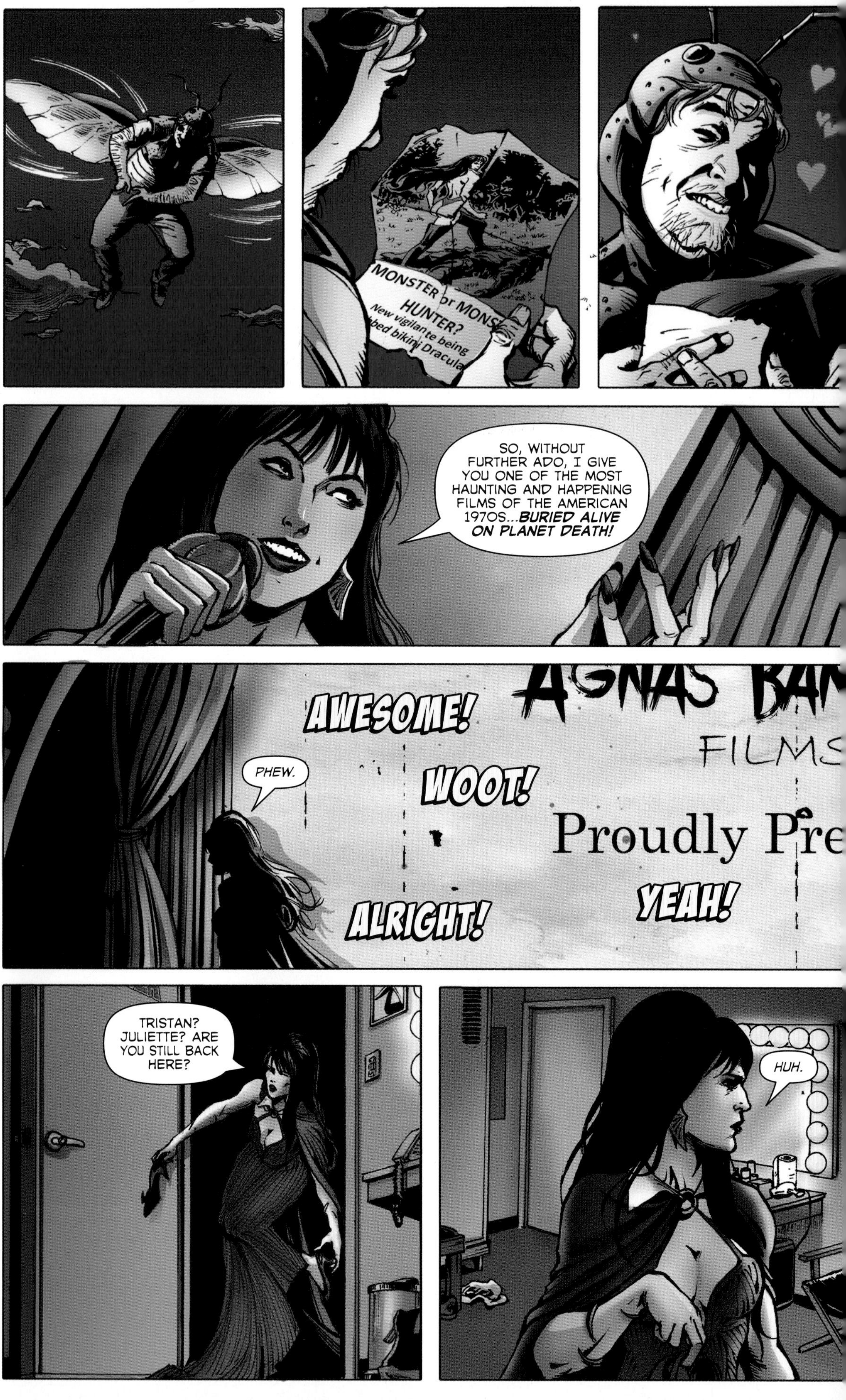
MONSTER or MONS
HUNTER?
New vigilante being
bed bikini Dracula
SO, WITHOUT FURTHER ADO, I GIVE YOU ONE OF THE MOST HAUNTING AND HAPPENING FILMS OF THE AMERICAN 1970S...**BURIED ALIVE ON PLANET DEATH!**
AGNAS BA
FILMS
Proudly Pre
AWESOME!
PHEW.
WOOT!
ALRIGHT!
YEAH!
TRISTAN? JULIETTE? ARE YOU STILL BACK HERE?
HUH.

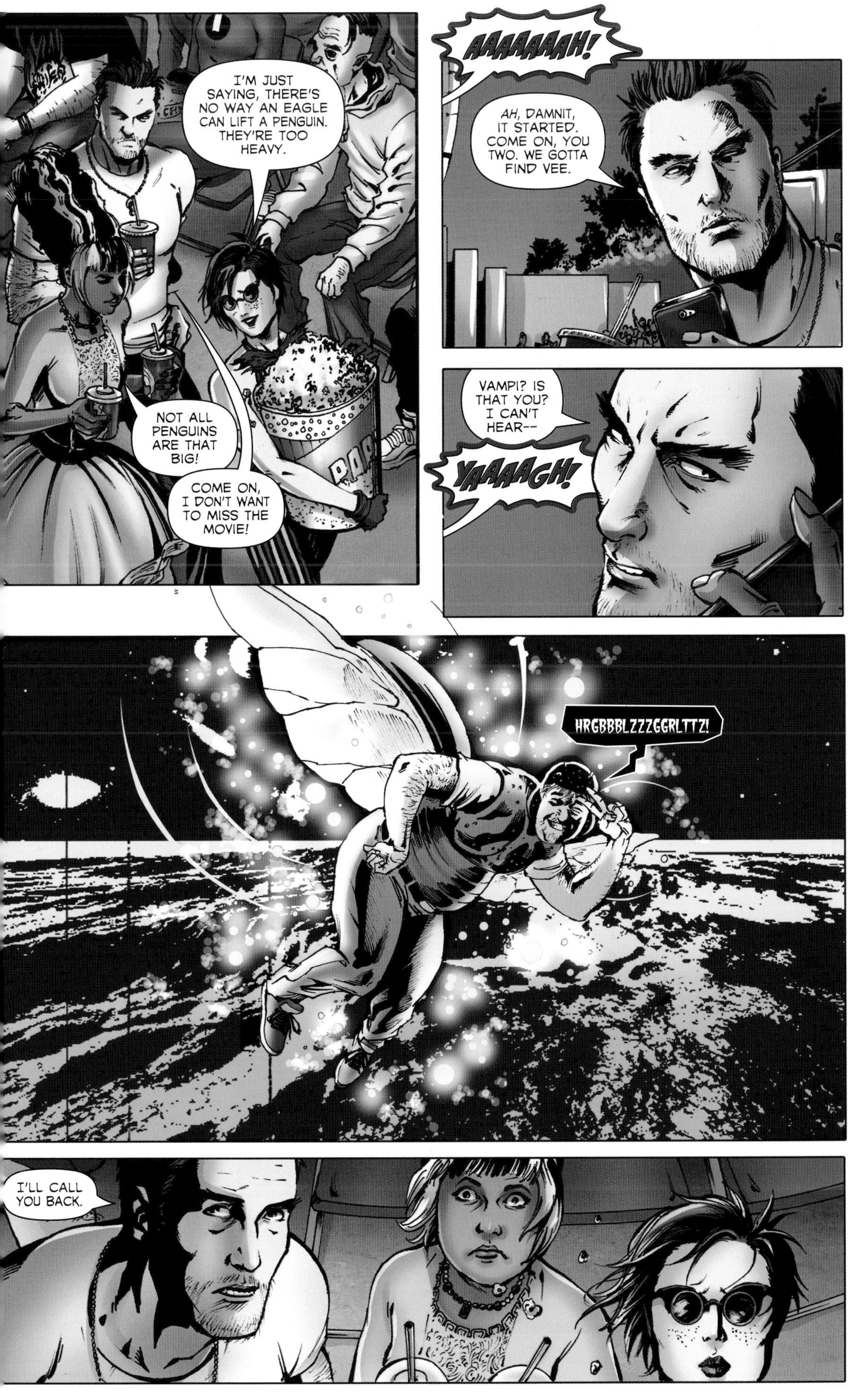
I'M JUST SAYING, THERE'S NO WAY AN EAGLE CAN LIFT A PENGUIN. THEY'RE TOO HEAVY.
NOT ALL PENGUINS ARE THAT BIG!
COME ON, I DON'T WANT TO MISS THE MOVIE!
AAAAAAAH!
AH, DAMNIT, IT STARTED. COME ON, YOU TWO. WE GOTTA FIND VEE.
VAMPI? IS THAT YOU? I CAN'T HEAR--
YAAAAGH!
HRGBBBLZZZGGRLTTZ!
I'LL CALL YOU BACK.

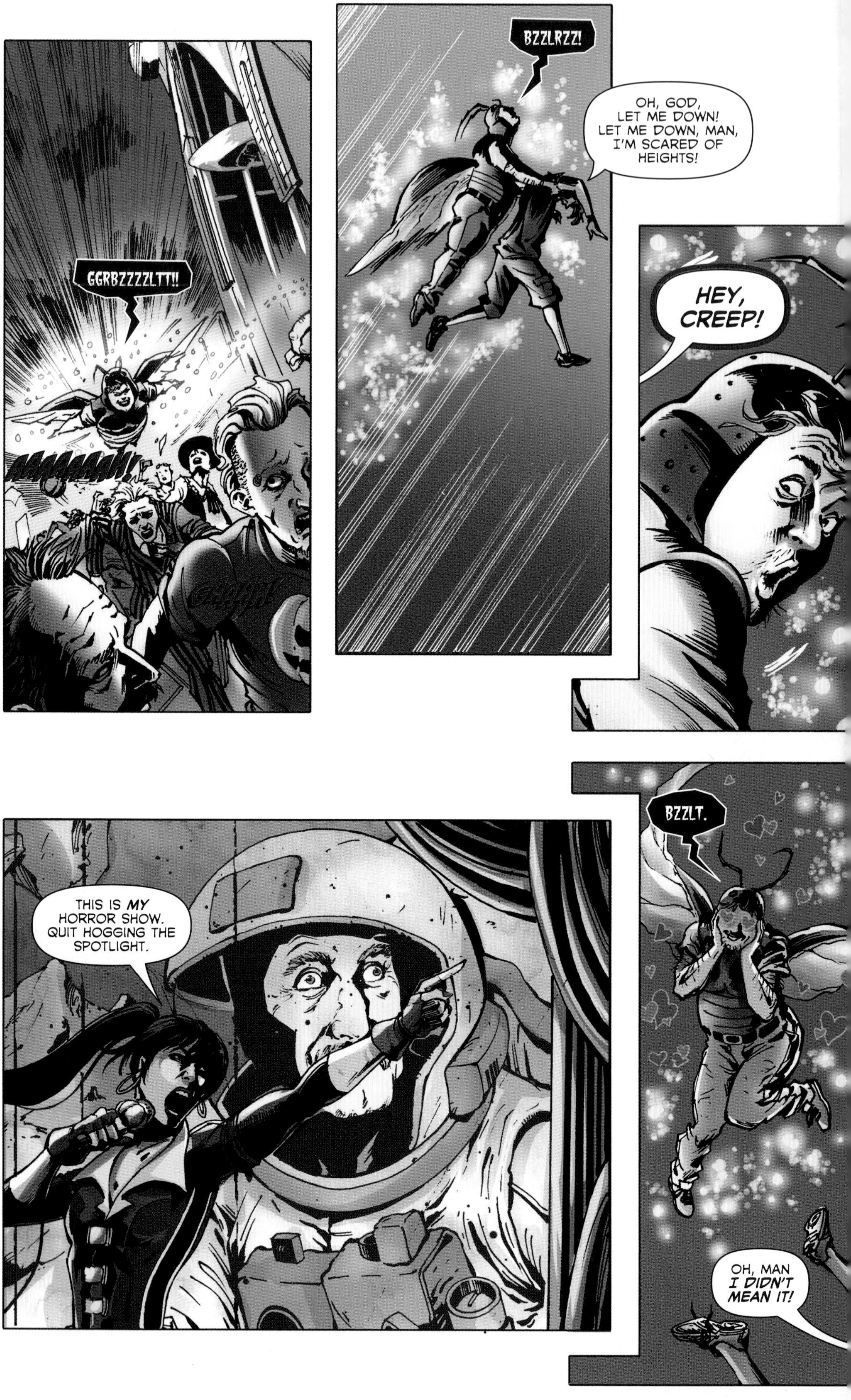
GGRBZZZZZLTT!!
BZZLRZZ!
OH, GOD, LET ME DOWN! LET ME DOWN, MAN, I'M SCARED OF HEIGHTS!
HEY, CREEP!
THIS IS *MY* HORROR SHOW. QUIT HOGGING THE SPOTLIGHT.
BZZLT.
OH, MAN *I DIDN'T MEAN IT!*

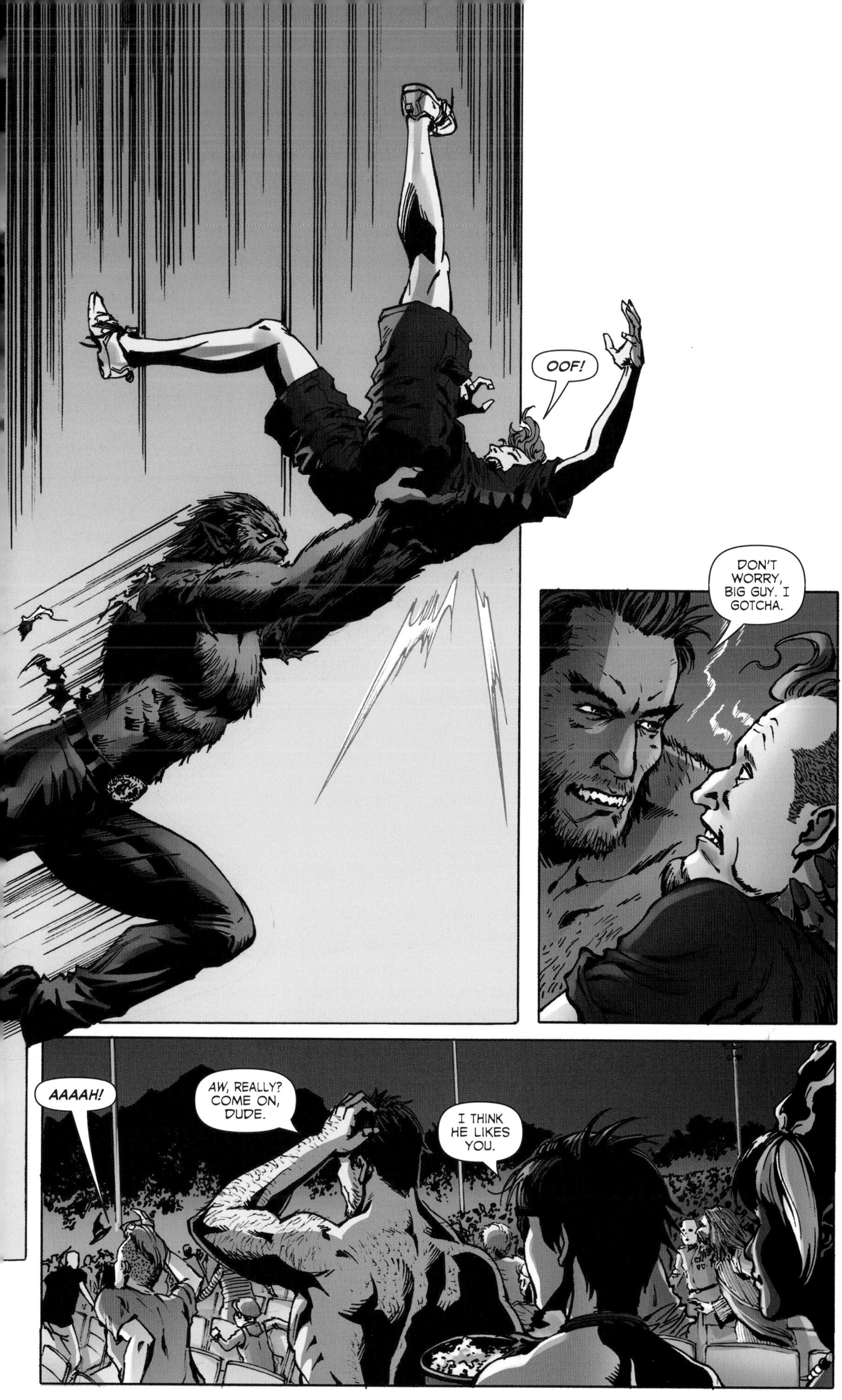
OOF!
DON'T WORRY, BIG GUY. I GOTCHA.
AAAAH!
AW, REALLY? COME ON, DUDE.
I THINK HE LIKES YOU.

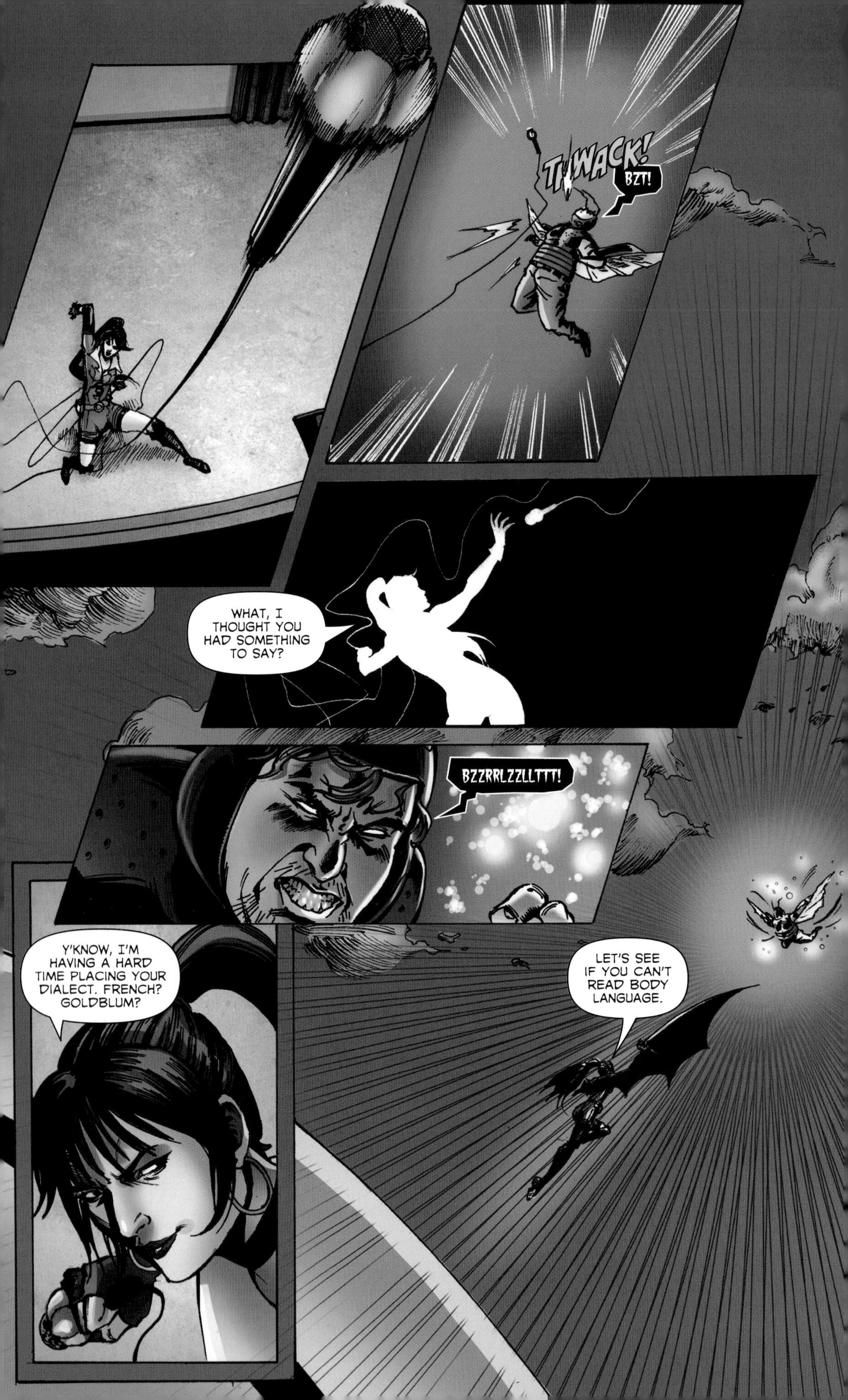
THWACK!
BZT!
WHAT, I THOUGHT YOU HAD SOMETHING TO SAY?
BZZRRLZZLLTTT!
Y'KNOW, I'M HAVING A HARD TIME PLACING YOUR DIALECT. FRENCH? GOLDBLUM?
LET'S SEE IF YOU CAN'T READ BODY LANGUAGE.

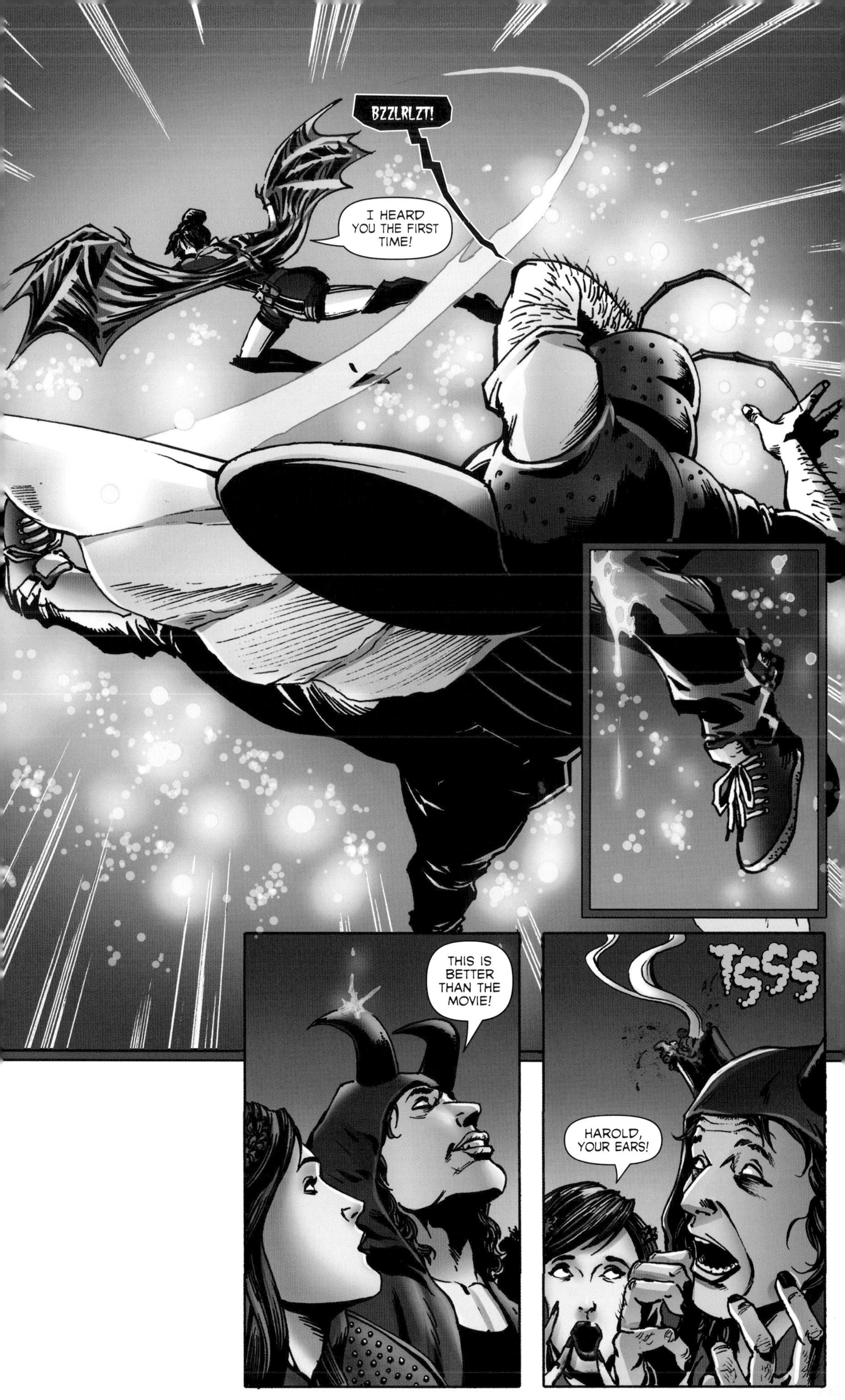
BZZLRLZT!
I HEARD YOU THE FIRST TIME!
THIS IS BETTER THAN THE MOVIE!
TSSS
HAROLD, YOUR EARS!

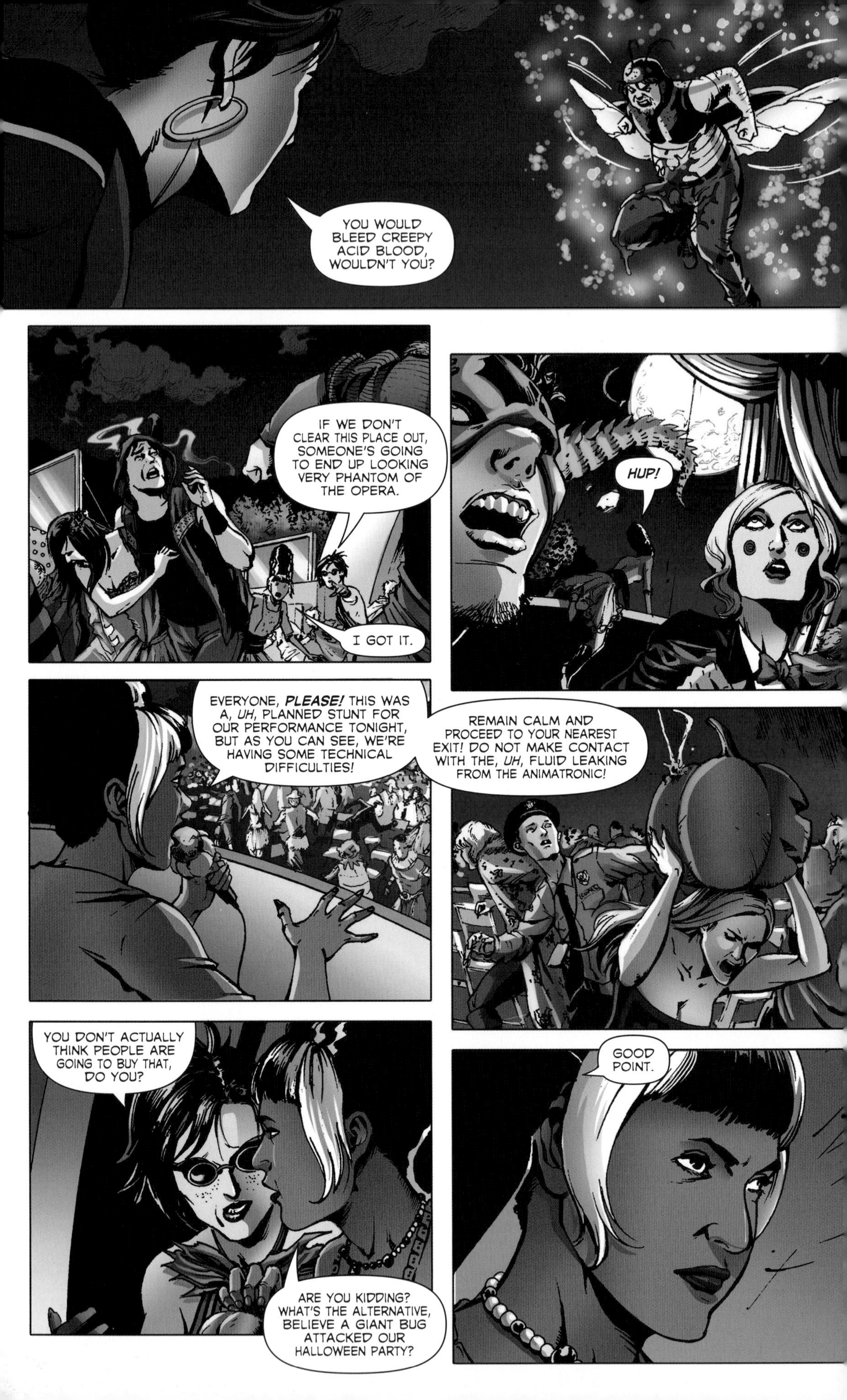
YOU WOULD BLEED CREEPY ACID BLOOD, WOULDN'T YOU?
IF WE DON'T CLEAR THIS PLACE OUT, SOMEONE'S GOING TO END UP LOOKING VERY PHANTOM OF THE OPERA.
I GOT IT.
HUP!
EVERYONE, PLEASE! THIS WAS A, UH, PLANNED STUNT FOR OUR PERFORMANCE TONIGHT, BUT AS YOU CAN SEE, WE'RE HAVING SOME TECHNICAL DIFFICULTIES!
REMAIN CALM AND PROCEED TO YOUR NEAREST EXIT! DO NOT MAKE CONTACT WITH THE, UH, FLUID LEAKING FROM THE ANIMATRONIC!
YOU DON'T ACTUALLY THINK PEOPLE ARE GOING TO BUY THAT, DO YOU?
ARE YOU KIDDING? WHAT'S THE ALTERNATIVE, BELIEVE A GIANT BUG ATTACKED OUR HALLOWEEN PARTY?
GOOD POINT.

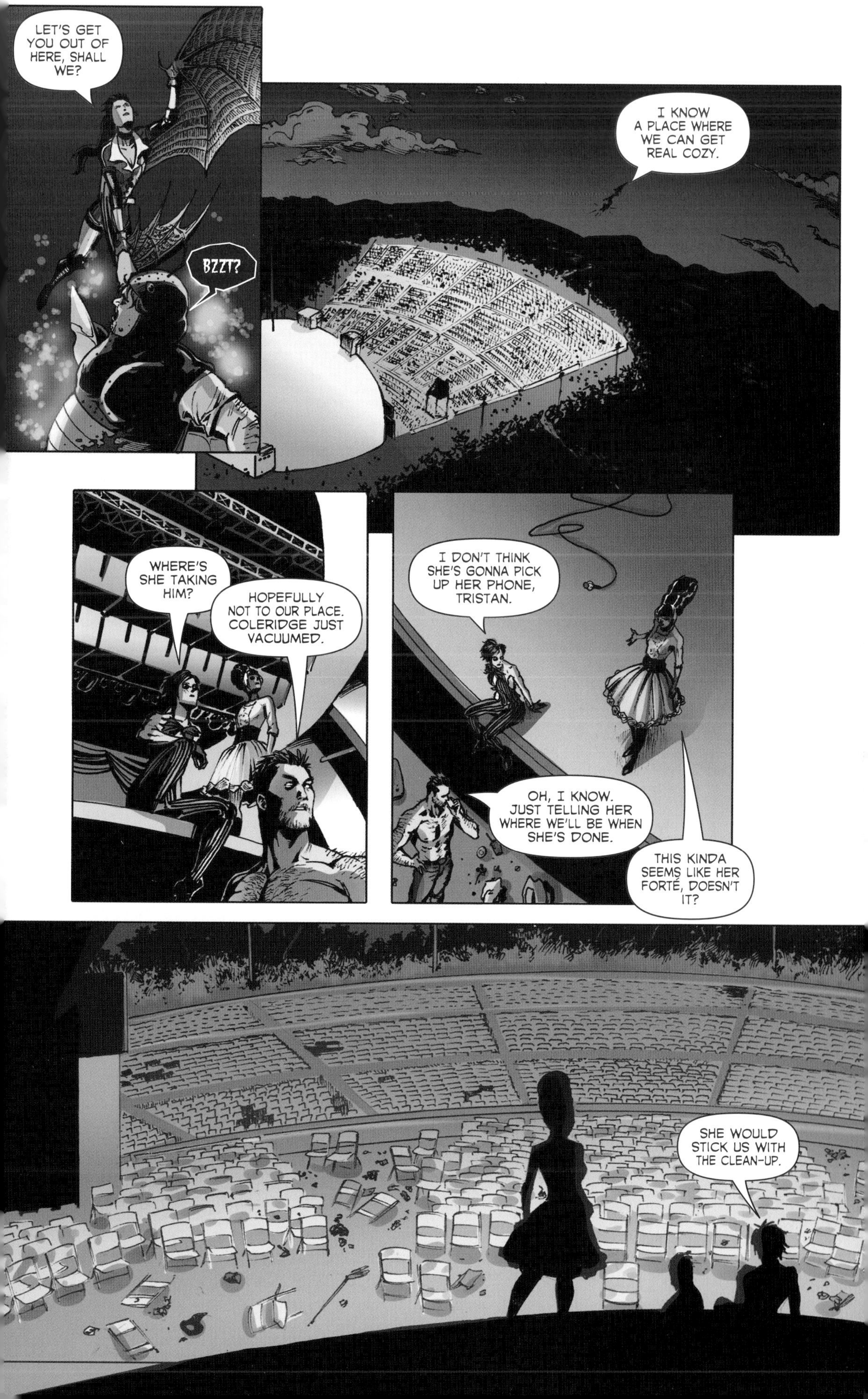
LET'S GET YOU OUT OF HERE, SHALL WE?
BZZT?
I KNOW A PLACE WHERE WE CAN GET REAL COZY.
WHERE'S SHE TAKING HIM?
HOPEFULLY NOT TO OUR PLACE. COLERIDGE JUST VACUUMED.
I DON'T THINK SHE'S GONNA PICK UP HER PHONE, TRISTAN.
OH, I KNOW. JUST TELLING HER WHERE WE'LL BE WHEN SHE'S DONE.
THIS KINDA SEEMS LIKE HER FORTÉ, DOESN'T IT?
SHE WOULD STICK US WITH THE CLEAN-UP.

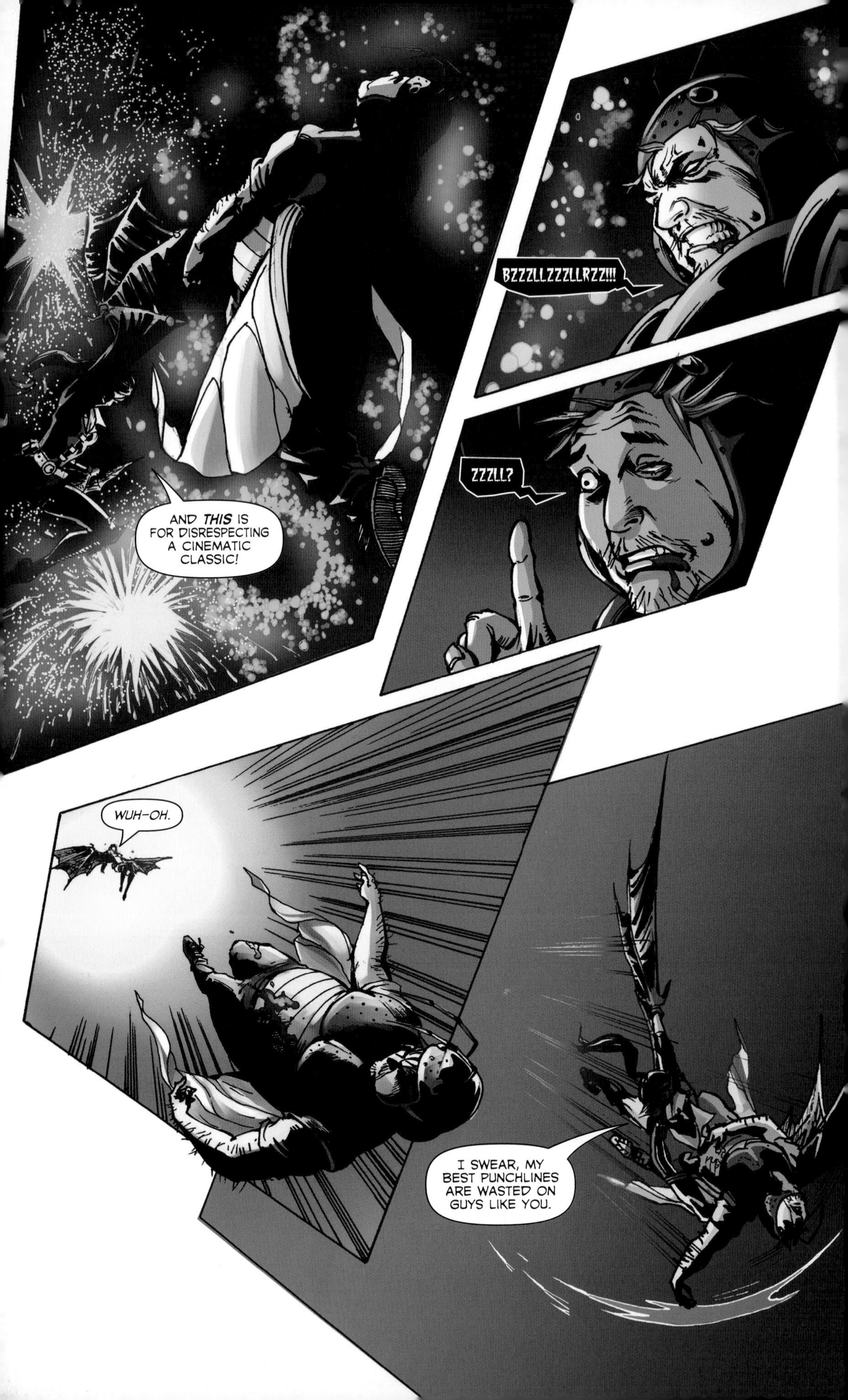
AND THIS IS FOR DISRESPECTING A CINEMATIC CLASSIC!
BZZZLLZZZLLRZZ!!!
ZZZLL?
WUH-OH.
I SWEAR, MY BEST PUNCHLINES ARE WASTED ON GUYS LIKE YOU.

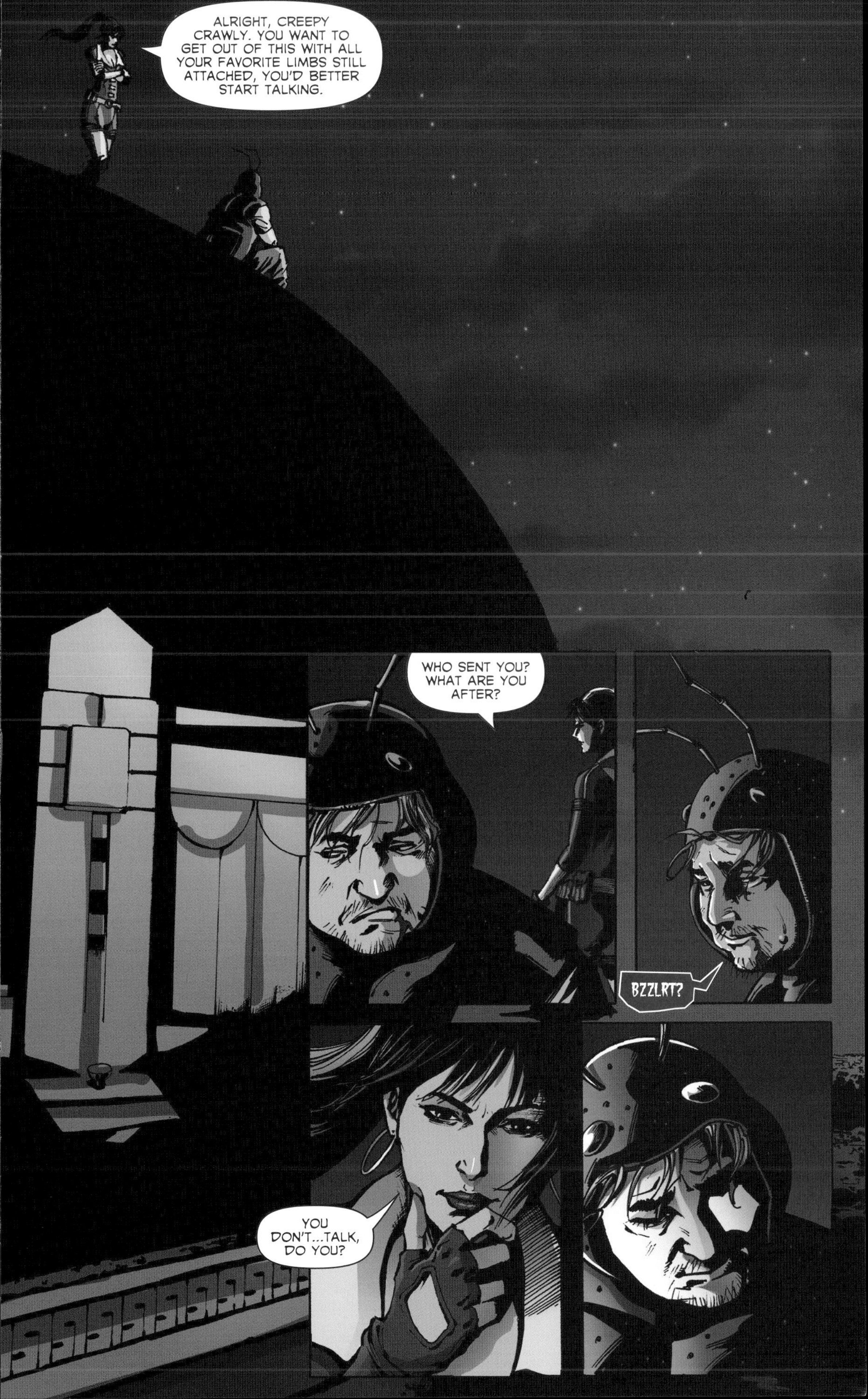
ALRIGHT, CREEPY CRAWLY. YOU WANT TO GET OUT OF THIS WITH ALL YOUR FAVORITE LIMBS STILL ATTACHED, YOU'D BETTER START TALKING.
WHO SENT YOU? WHAT ARE YOU AFTER?
BZZLRT?
YOU DON'T...TALK, DO YOU?

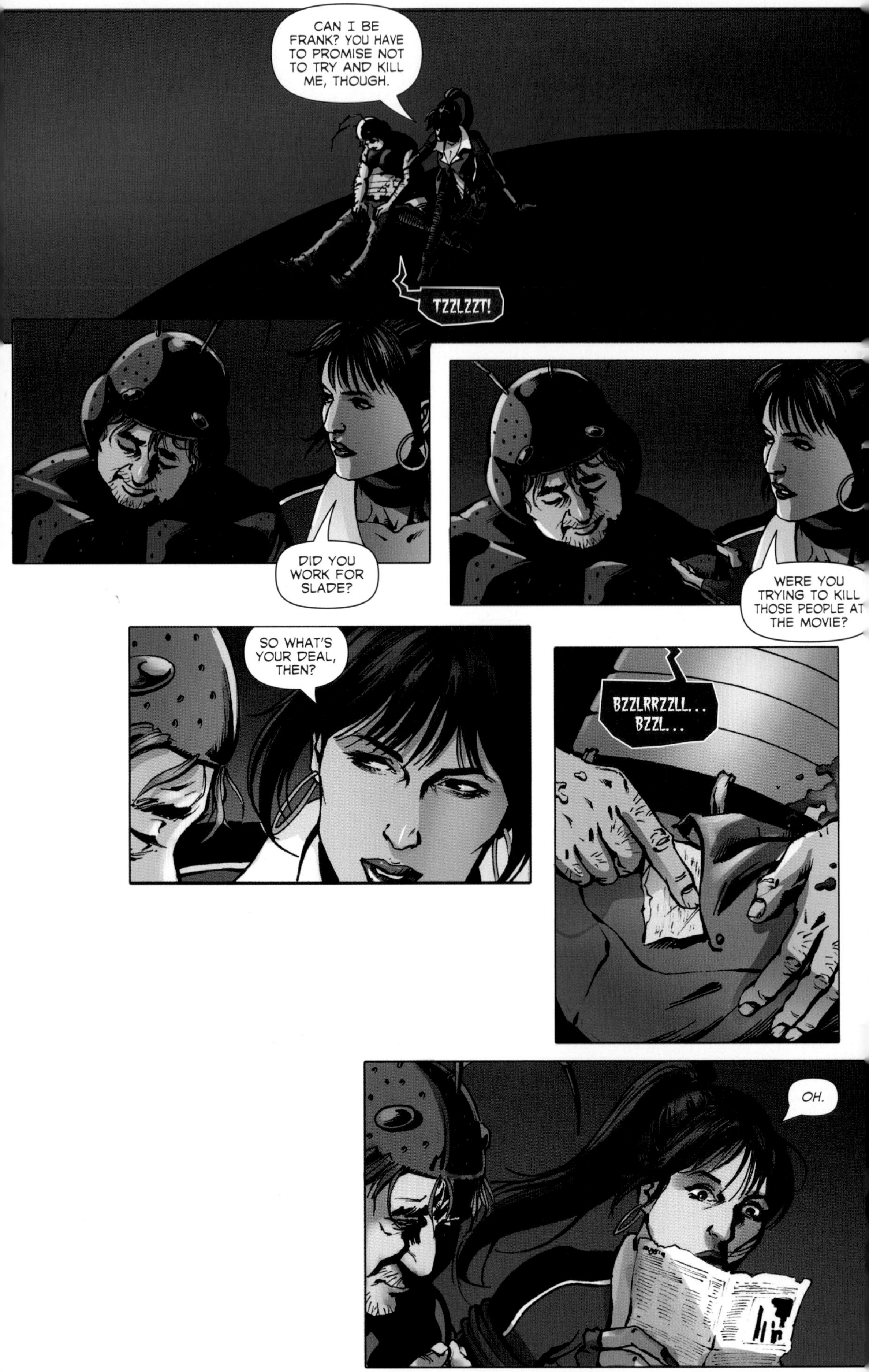
CAN I BE FRANK? YOU HAVE TO PROMISE NOT TO TRY AND KILL ME, THOUGH.
TZZLZZT!
DID YOU WORK FOR SLADE?
WERE YOU TRYING TO KILL THOSE PEOPLE AT THE MOVIE?
SO WHAT'S YOUR DEAL, THEN?
BZZLRRZZLL... BZZL...
OH.

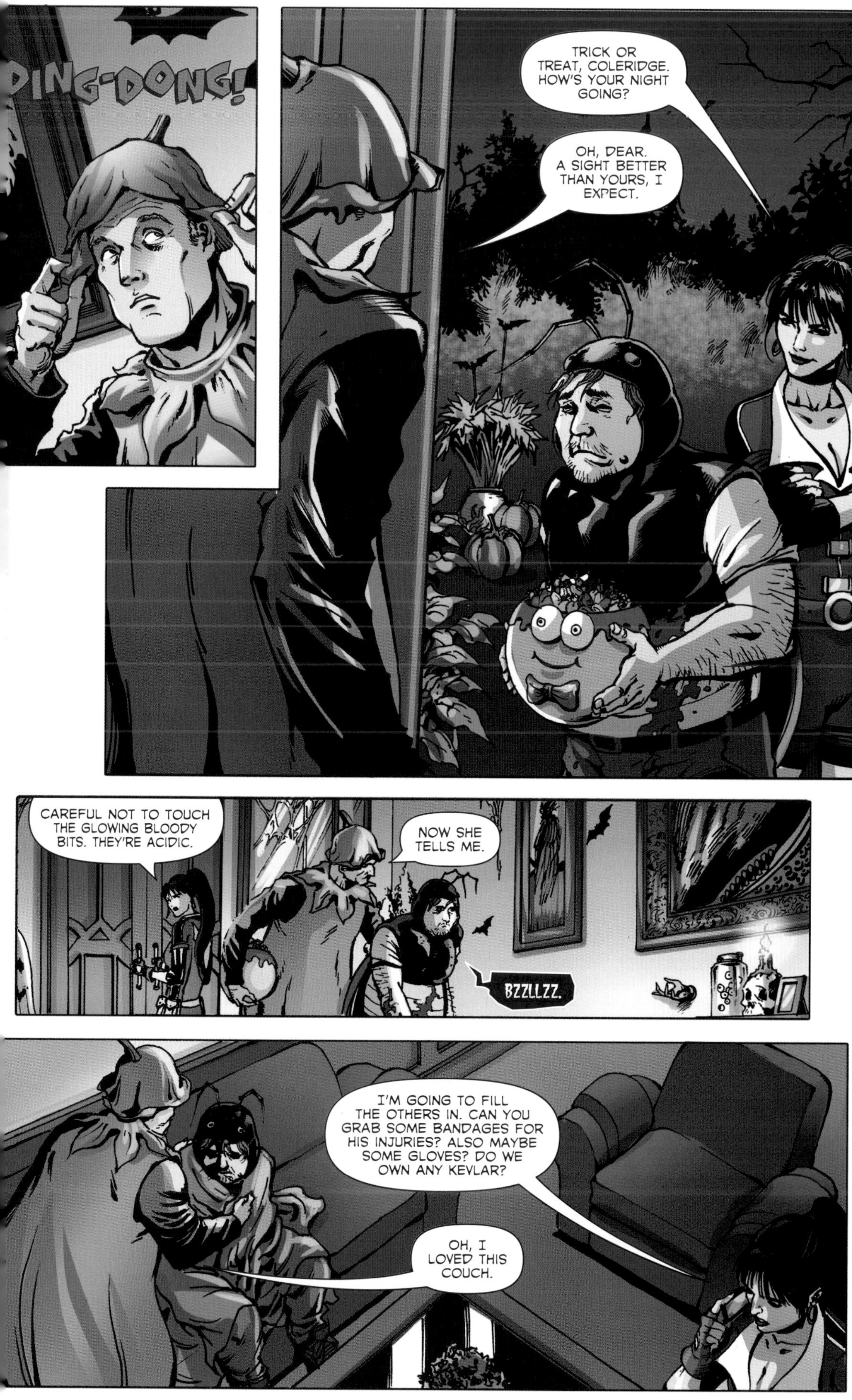
DING-DONG!
TRICK OR TREAT, COLERIDGE. HOW'S YOUR NIGHT GOING?
OH, DEAR. A SIGHT BETTER THAN YOURS, I EXPECT.
CAREFUL NOT TO TOUCH THE GLOWING BLOODY BITS. THEY'RE ACIDIC.
NOW SHE TELLS ME.
BZZLLZZ.
I'M GOING TO FILL THE OTHERS IN. CAN YOU GRAB SOME BANDAGES FOR HIS INJURIES? ALSO MAYBE SOME GLOVES? DO WE OWN ANY KEVLAR?
OH, I LOVED THIS COUCH.

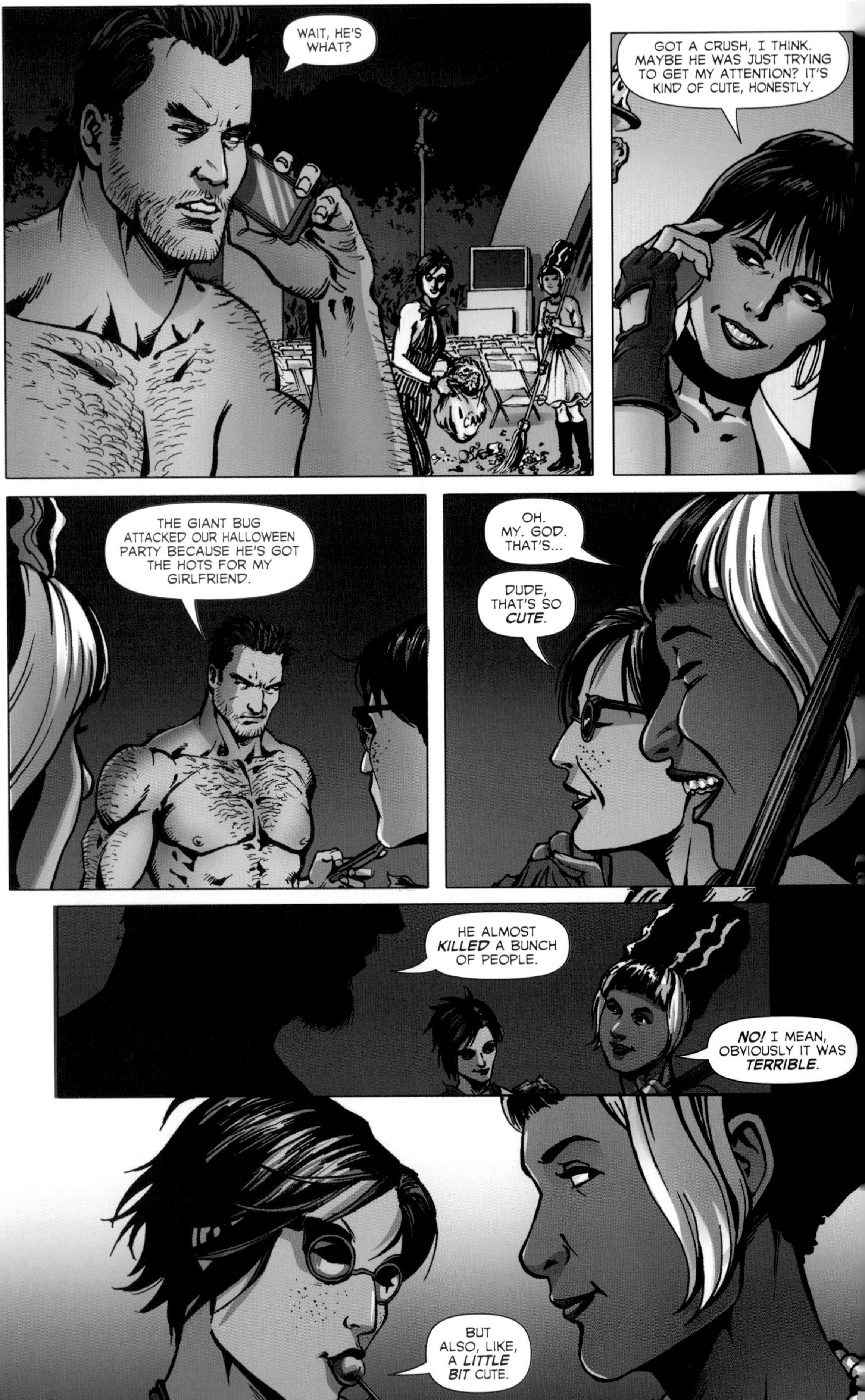
WAIT, HE'S WHAT?
GOT A CRUSH, I THINK. MAYBE HE WAS JUST TRYING TO GET MY ATTENTION? IT'S KIND OF CUTE, HONESTLY.
THE GIANT BUG ATTACKED OUR HALLOWEEN PARTY BECAUSE HE'S GOT THE HOTS FOR MY GIRLFRIEND.
OH. MY. GOD. THAT'S...
DUDE, THAT'S SO *CUTE*.
HE ALMOST *KILLED* A BUNCH OF PEOPLE.
NO! I MEAN, OBVIOUSLY IT WAS *TERRIBLE*.
BUT ALSO, LIKE, A *LITTLE BIT* CUTE.

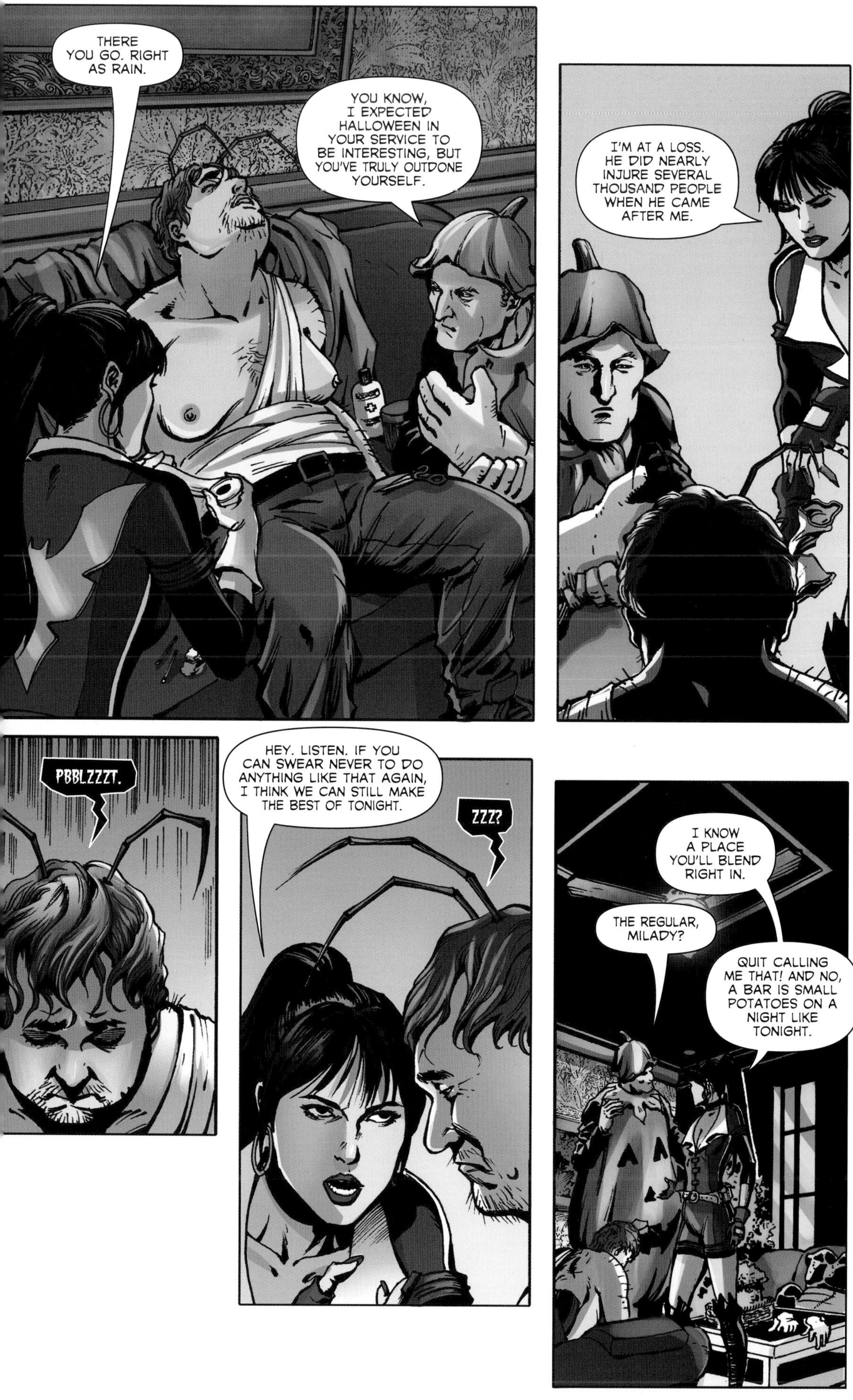
THERE YOU GO. RIGHT AS RAIN.
YOU KNOW, I EXPECTED HALLOWEEN IN YOUR SERVICE TO BE INTERESTING, BUT YOU'VE TRULY OUTDONE YOURSELF.
I'M AT A LOSS. HE DID NEARLY INJURE SEVERAL THOUSAND PEOPLE WHEN HE CAME AFTER ME.
PBBLZZZT.
HEY. LISTEN. IF YOU CAN SWEAR NEVER TO DO ANYTHING LIKE THAT AGAIN, I THINK WE CAN STILL MAKE THE BEST OF TONIGHT.
ZZZ?
I KNOW A PLACE YOU'LL BLEND RIGHT IN.
THE REGULAR, MILADY?
QUIT CALLING ME THAT! AND NO, A BAR IS SMALL POTATOES ON A NIGHT LIKE TONIGHT.

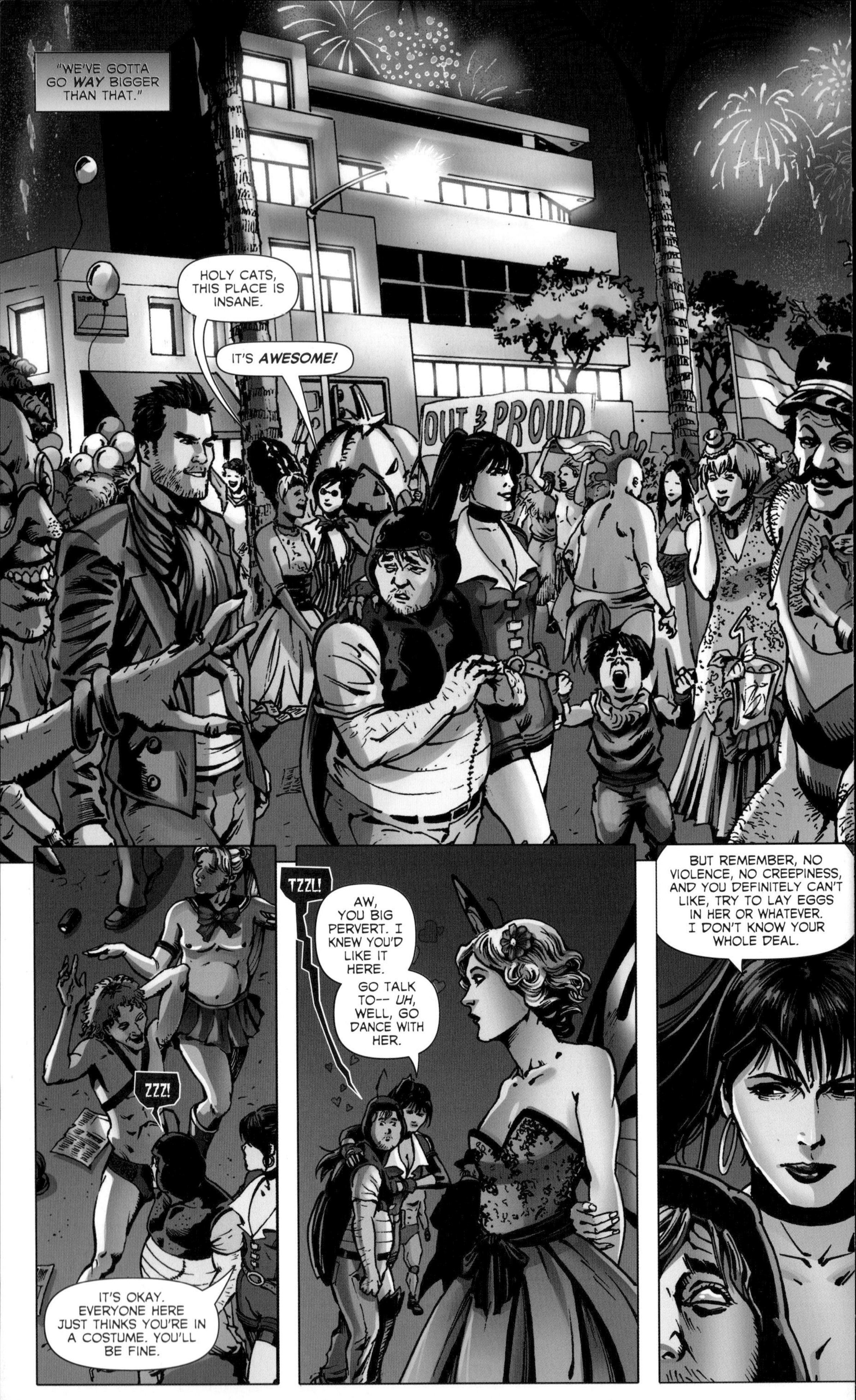
"WE'VE GOTTA GO WAY BIGGER THAN THAT."
HOLY CATS, THIS PLACE IS INSANE.
IT'S AWESOME!
OUT & PROUD
ZZZ!
IT'S OKAY. EVERYONE HERE JUST THINKS YOU'RE IN A COSTUME. YOU'LL BE FINE.
TZZL!
AW, YOU BIG PERVERT. I KNEW YOU'D LIKE IT HERE.
GO TALK TO-- UH, WELL, GO DANCE WITH HER.
BUT REMEMBER, NO VIOLENCE, NO CREEPINESS, AND YOU DEFINITELY CAN'T LIKE, TRY TO LAY EGGS IN HER OR WHATEVER. I DON'T KNOW YOUR WHOLE DEAL.

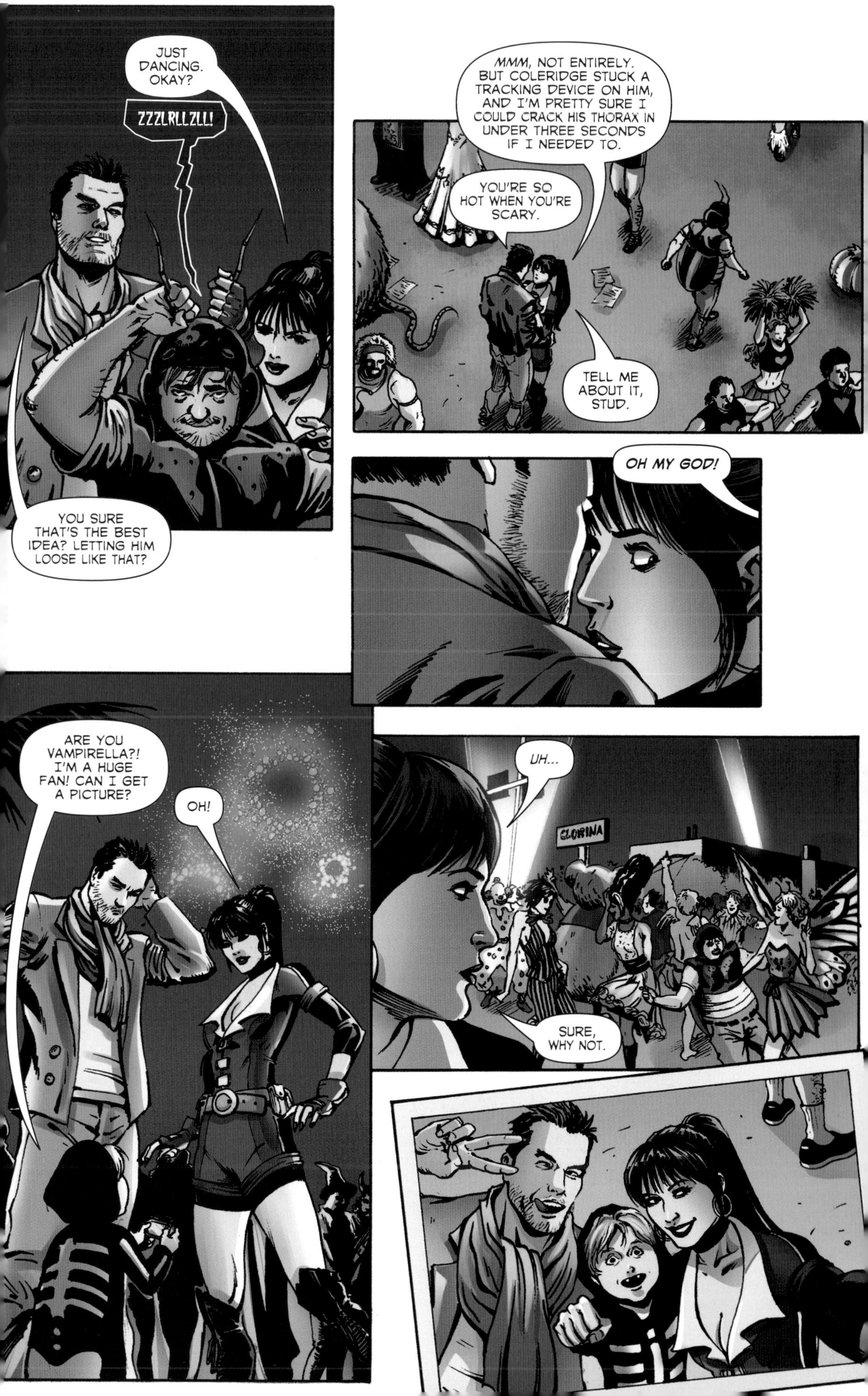

JUST DANCING. OKAY?
ZZZLRLLZLL!
YOU SURE THAT'S THE BEST IDEA? LETTING HIM LOOSE LIKE THAT?
MMM, NOT ENTIRELY. BUT COLERIDGE STUCK A TRACKING DEVICE ON HIM, AND I'M PRETTY SURE I COULD CRACK HIS THORAX IN UNDER THREE SECONDS IF I NEEDED TO.
YOU'RE SO HOT WHEN YOU'RE SCARY.
TELL ME ABOUT IT, STUD.
OH MY GOD!
ARE YOU VAMPIRELLA?! I'M A HUGE FAN! CAN I GET A PICTURE?
OH!
UH...
GLORINA
SURE, WHY NOT.

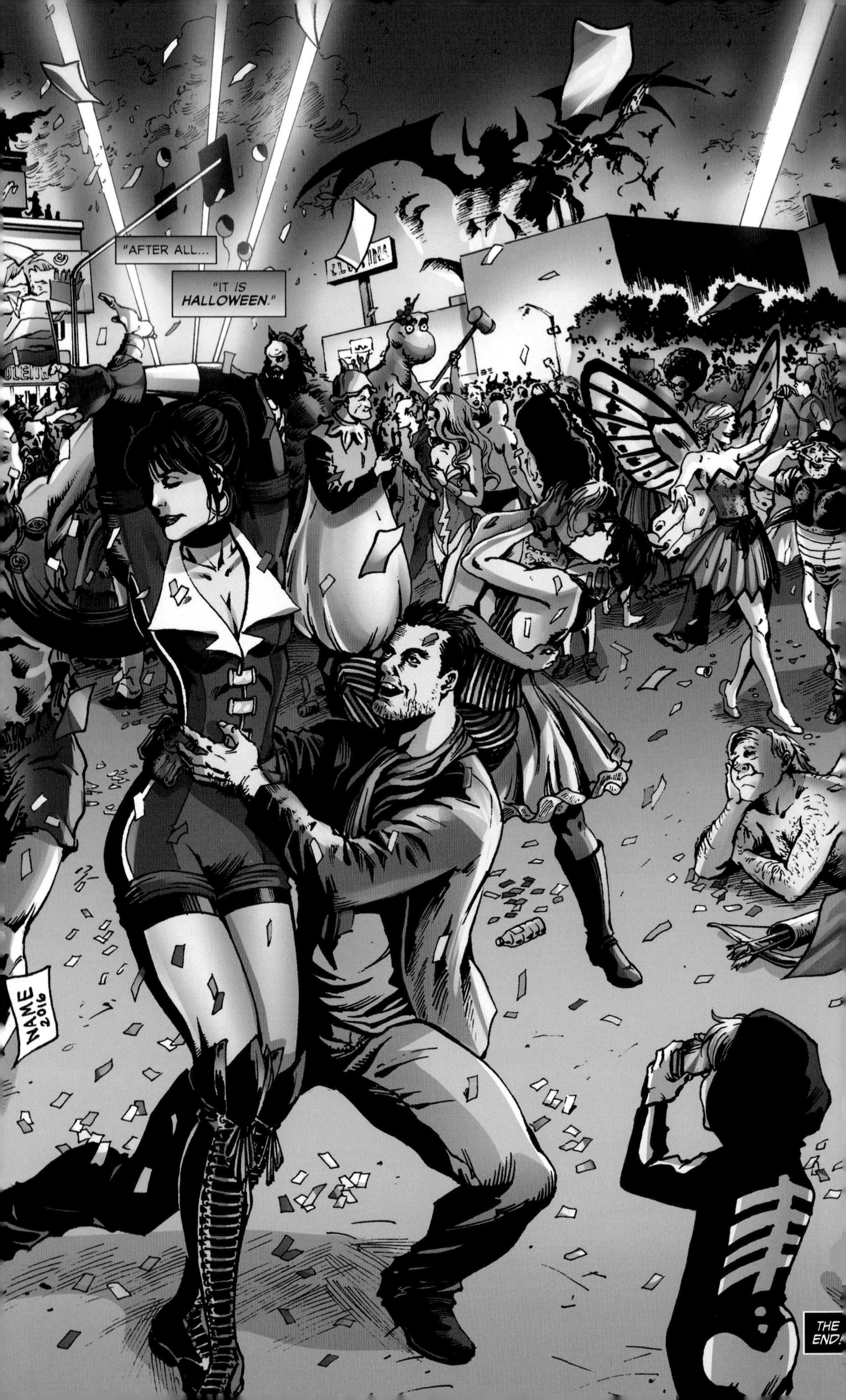
"AFTER ALL...
"IT IS HALLOWEEN."
NAME 2016
THE END!

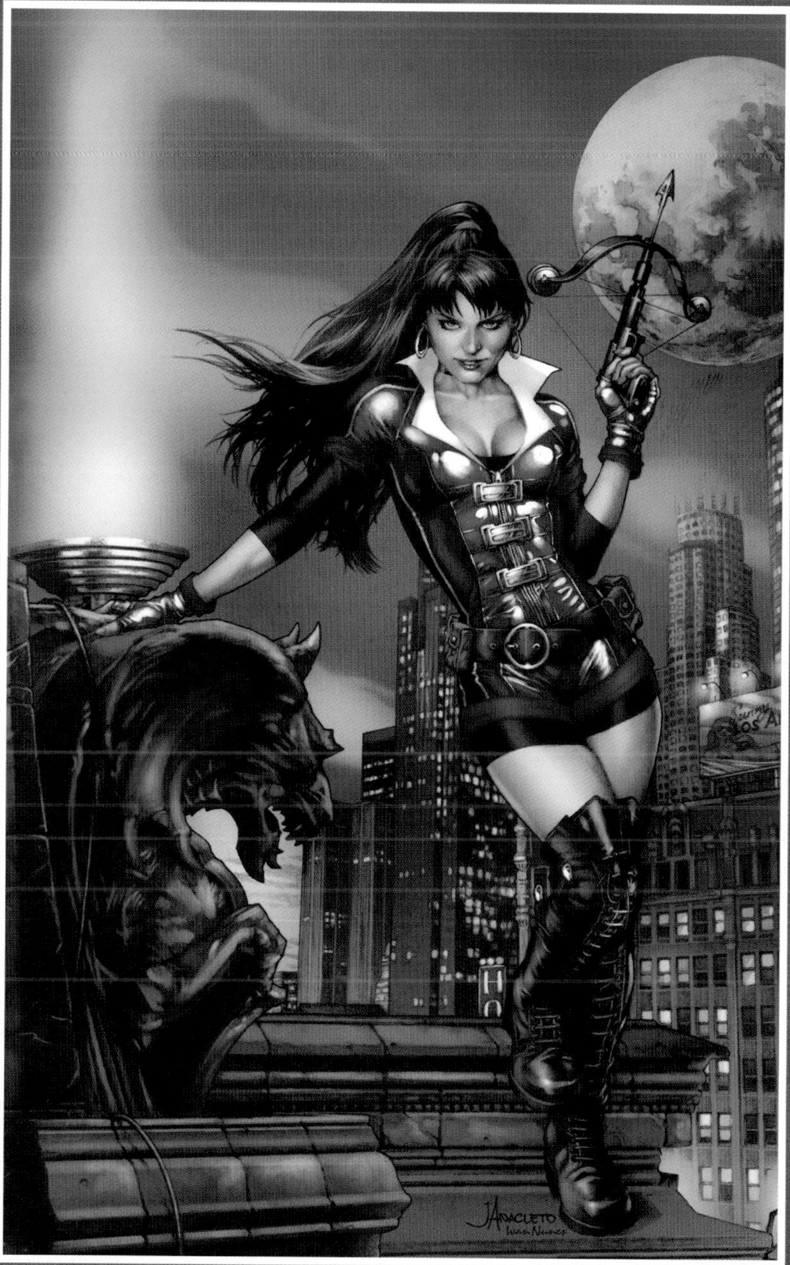
JAnacleto
Ivan Nunes

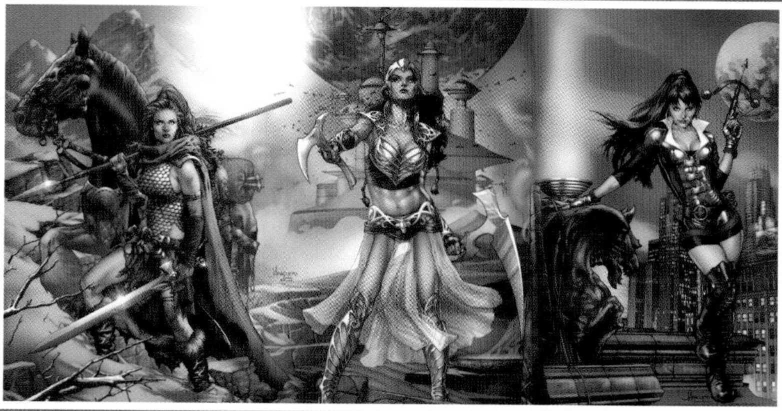

#1 variant cover by **JAY ANACLETO** and **IVAN NUNES**
connecting cover with Dejah Thoris #1 and Red Sonja #1

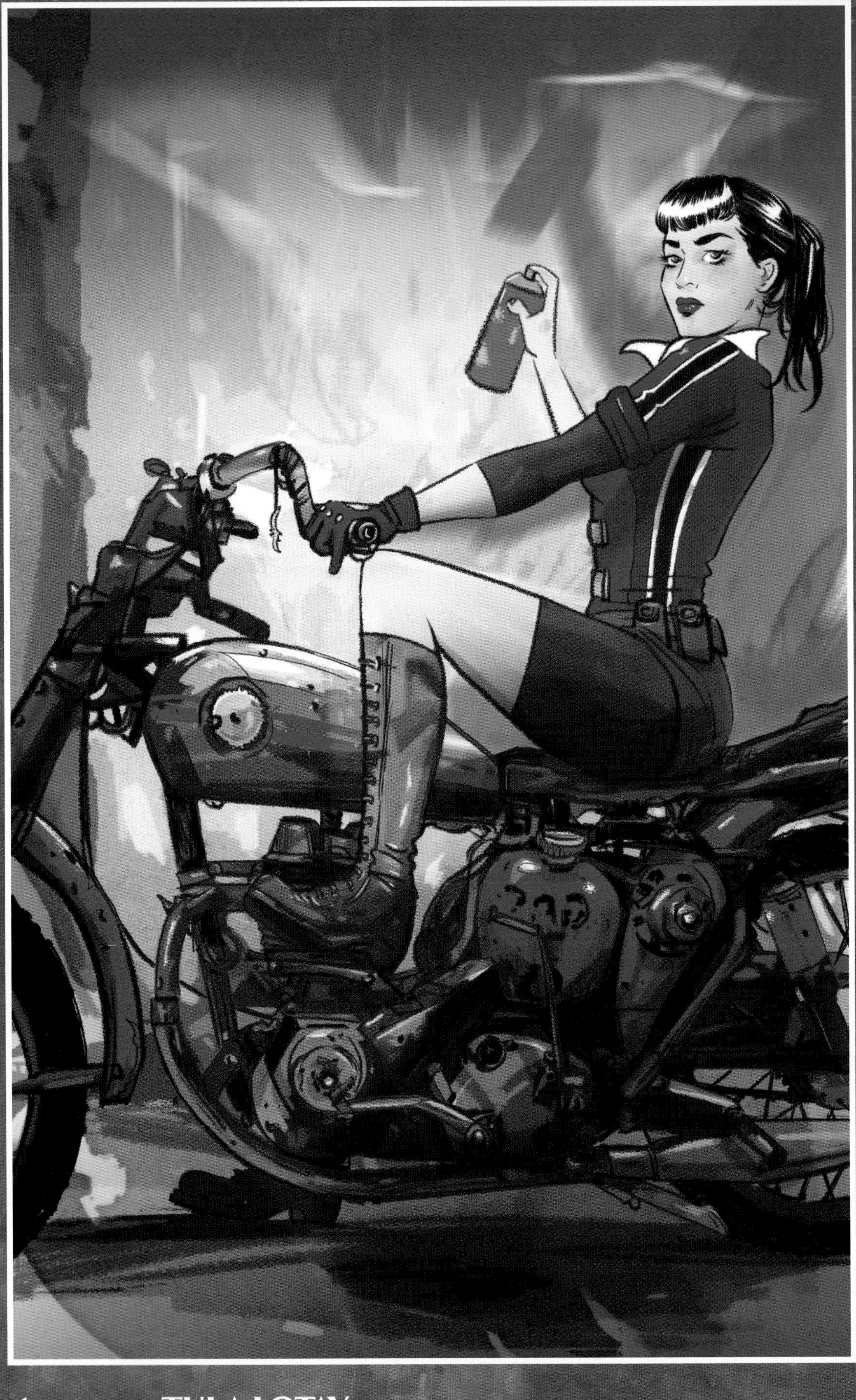

#1 variant cover by **TULA LOTAY**

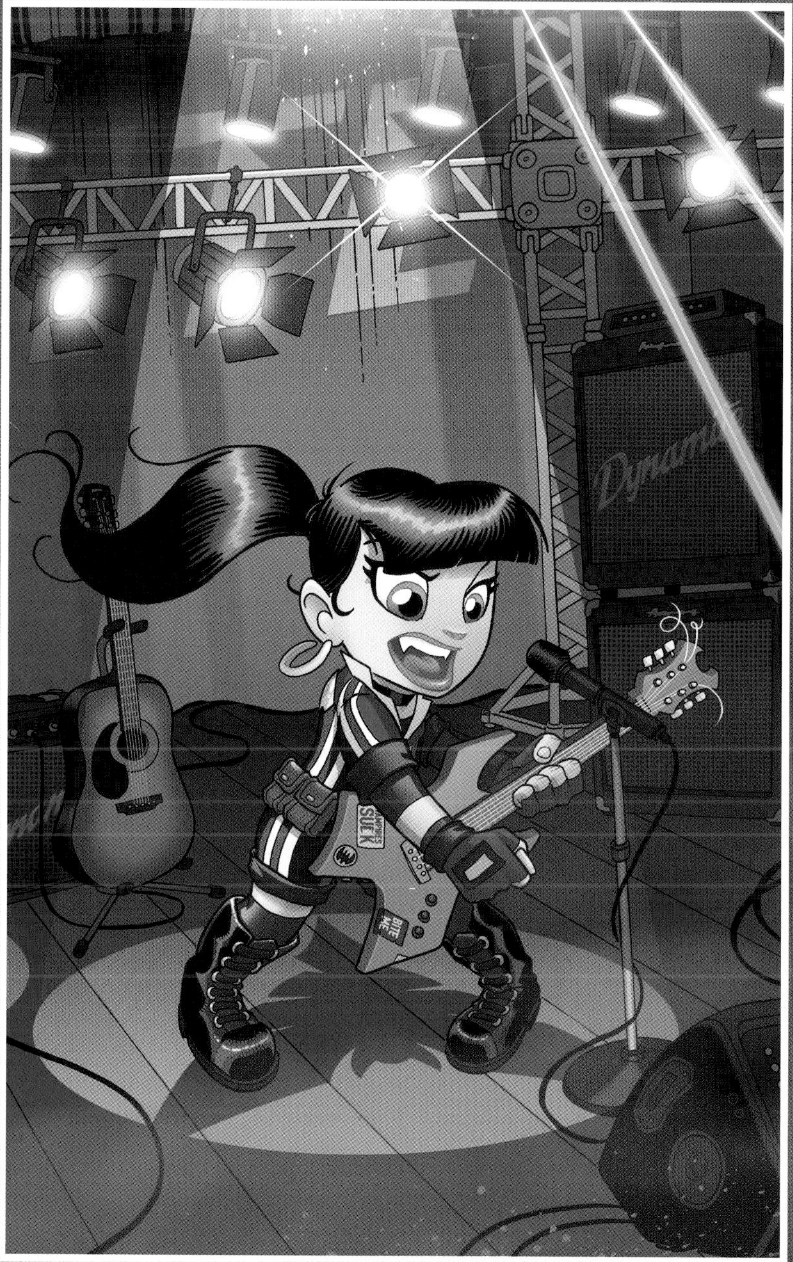
VAMPIRES SUCK
BITE ME
Dynamite

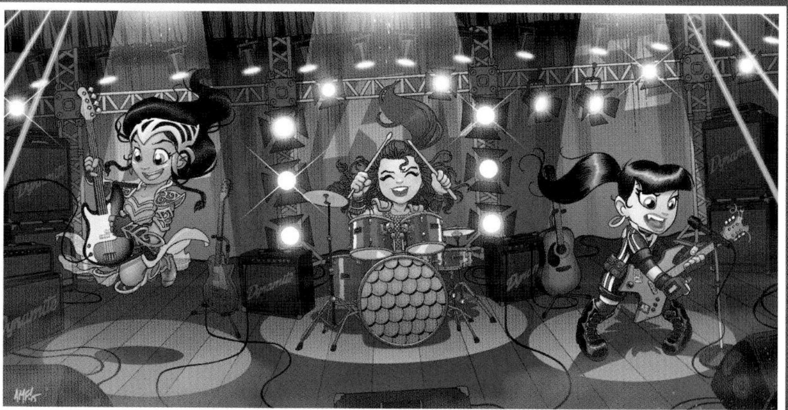

#1 subscription cover by **TONY FLEECS**
connecting cover with Dejah Thoris #1 and Red Sonja #1

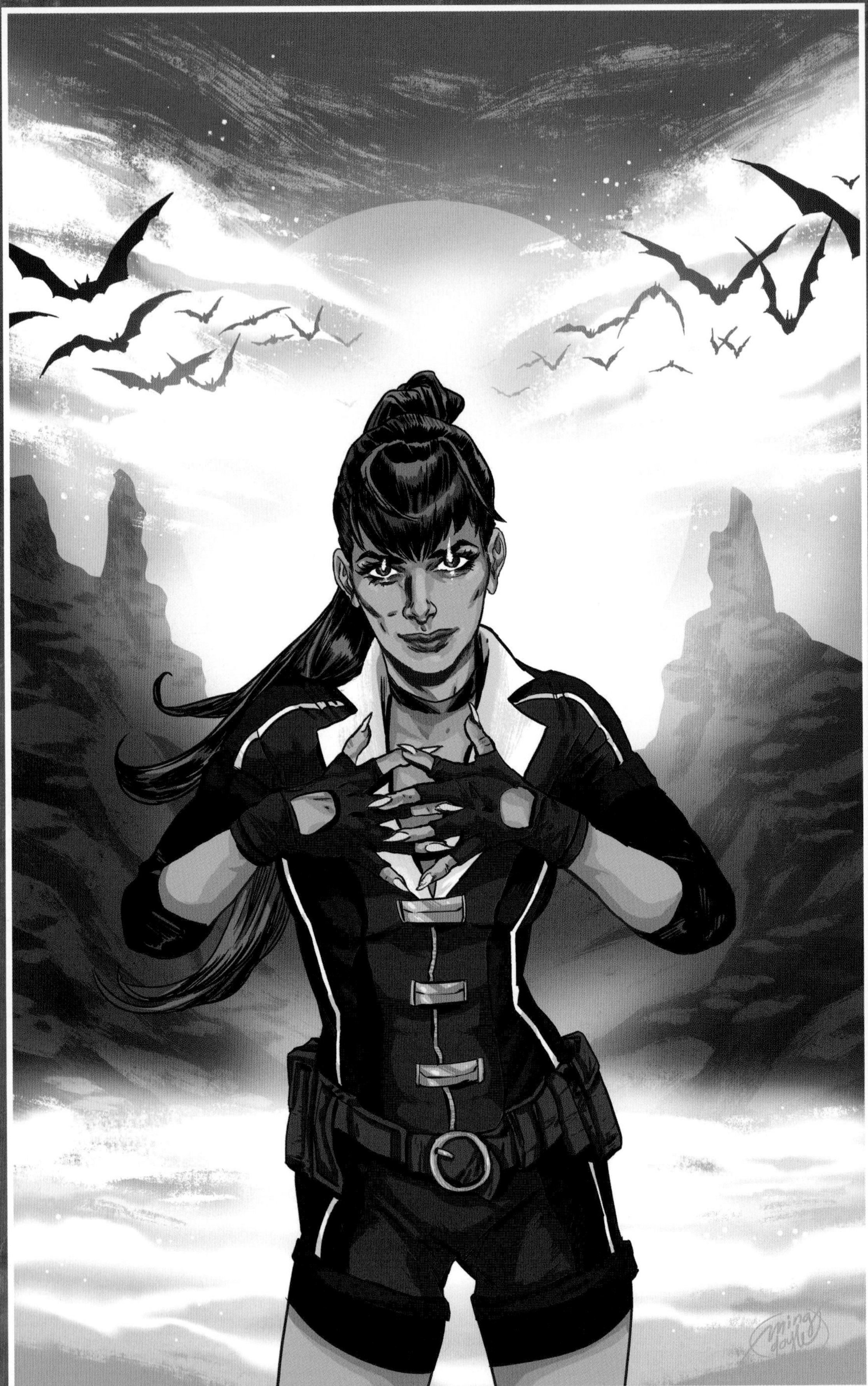
ming doyle

#1 variant cover by **MING DOYLE**

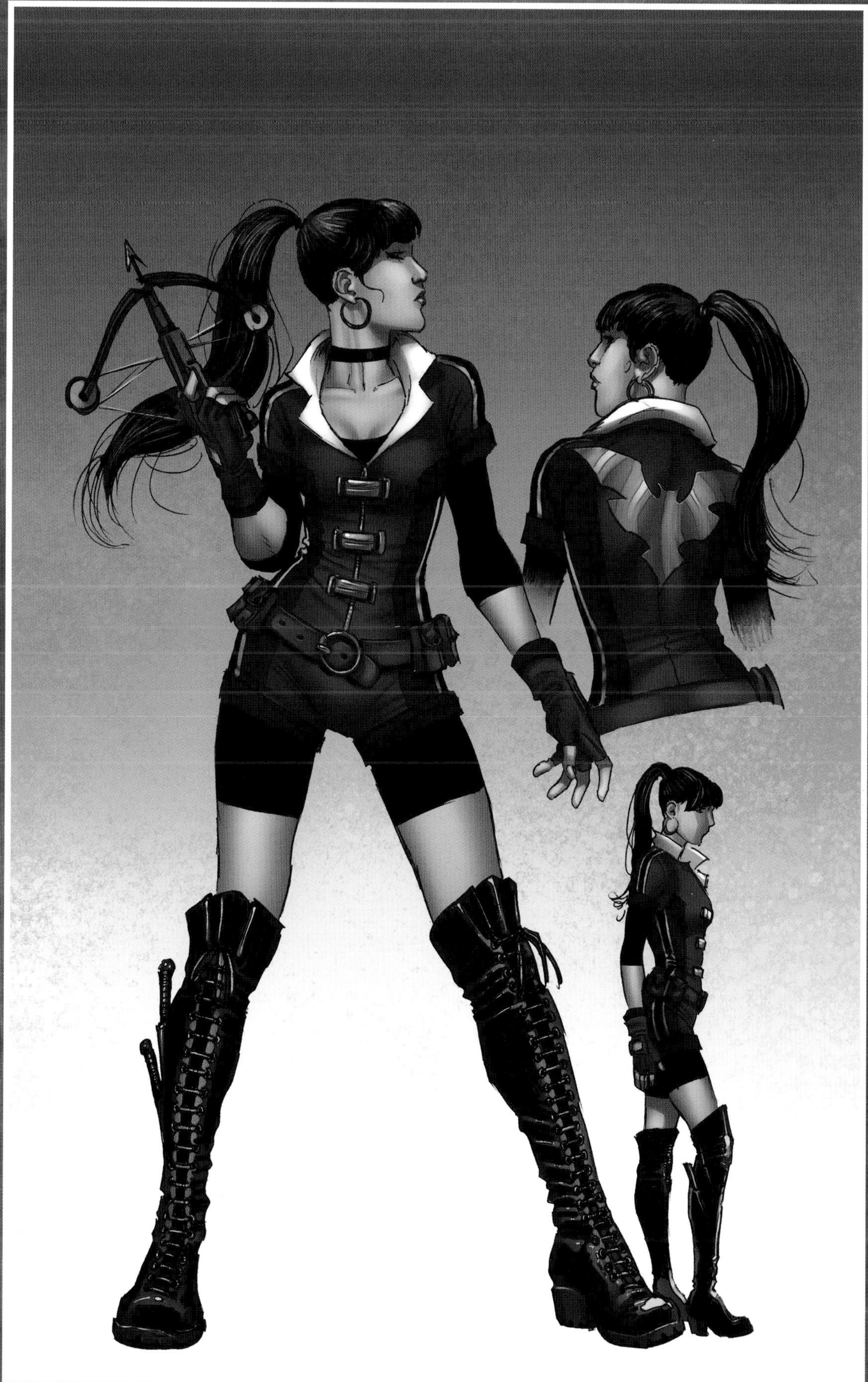

#1 variant cover by **NICOLA SCOTT** and **IVAN NUNES**

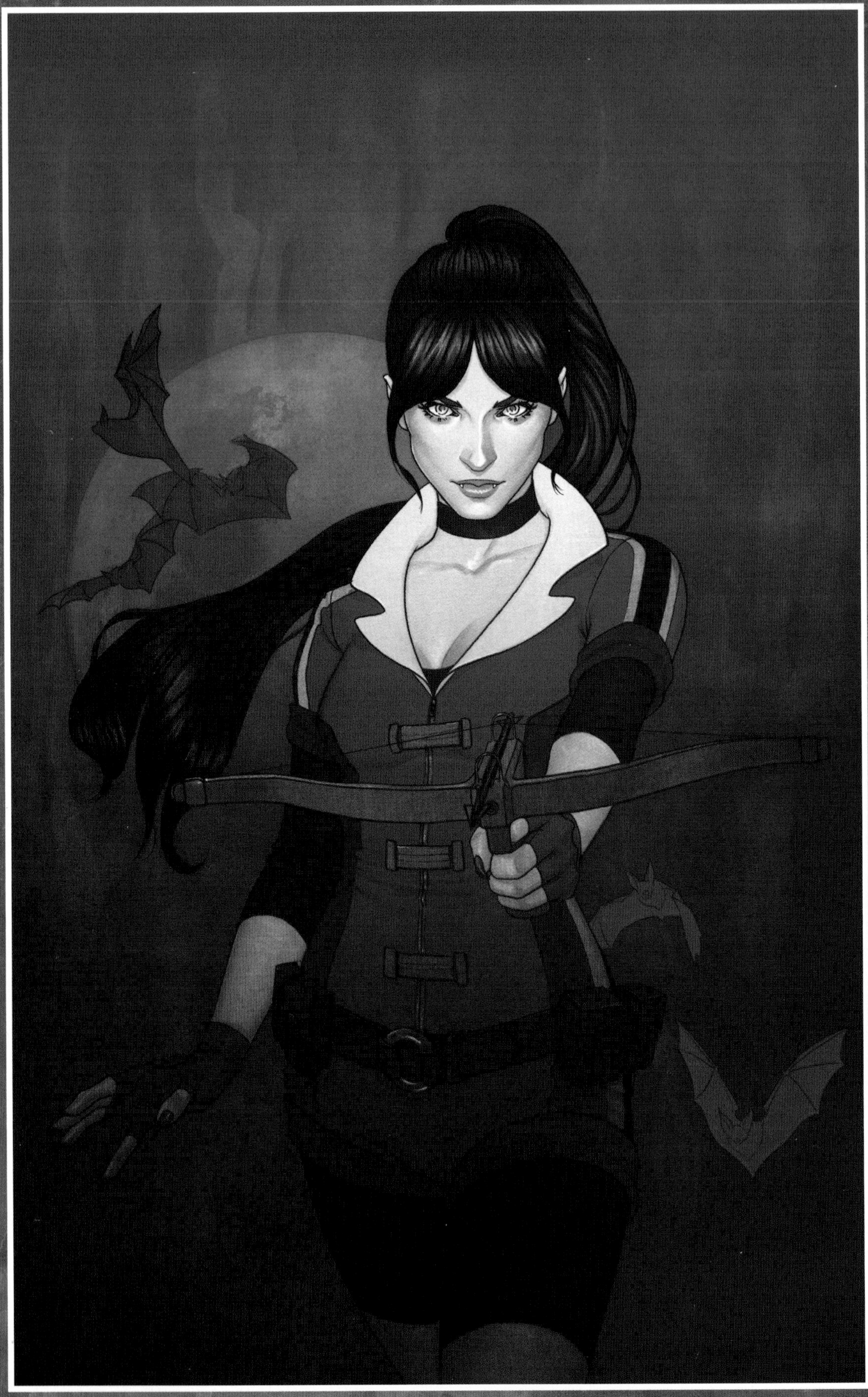

#1 Fried Pie exclusive cover by JENNY FRISON

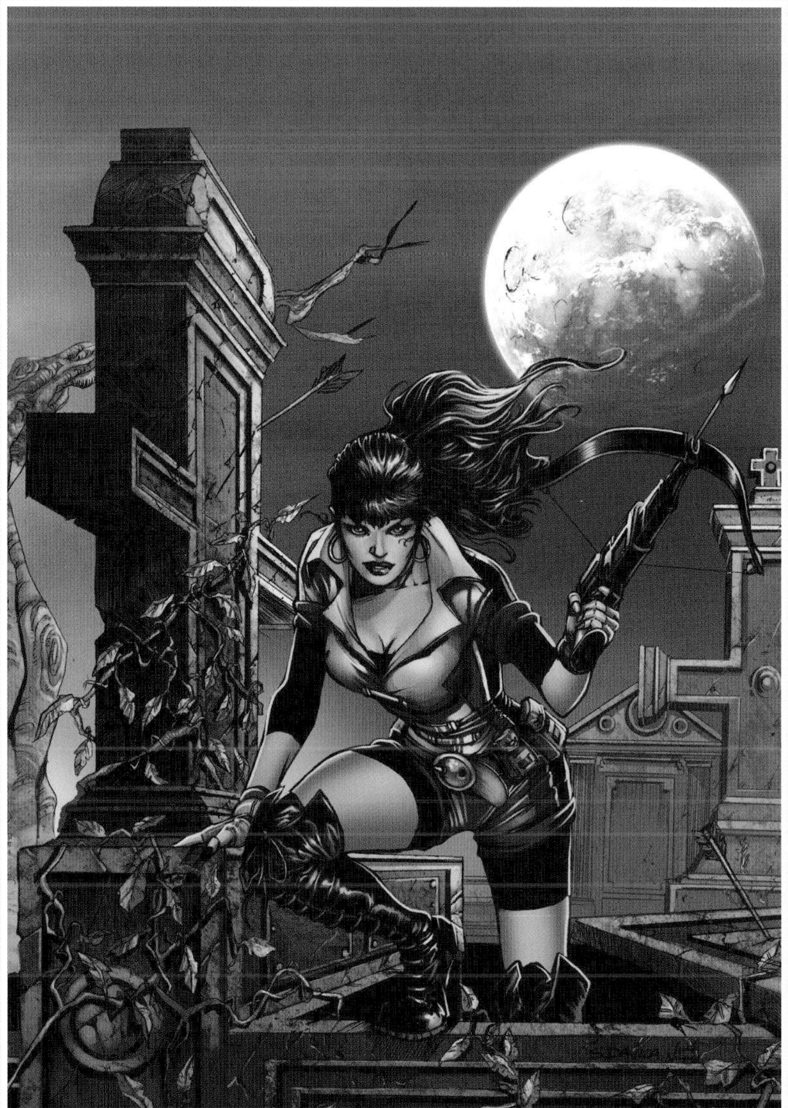

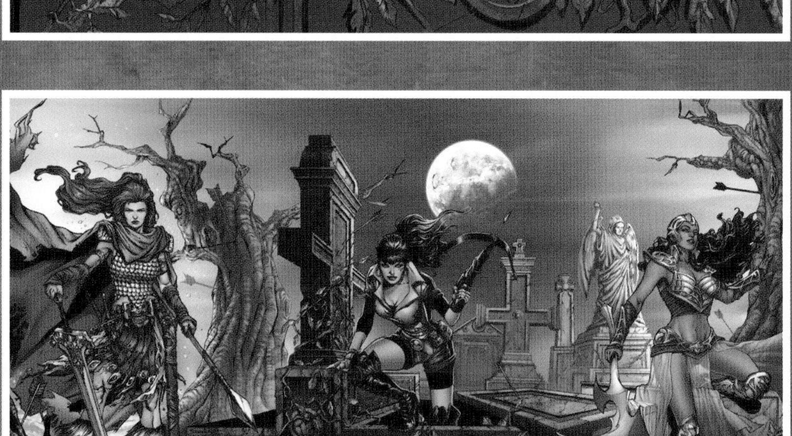

#1 In Your Dreams Collectibles cover by **JAY ANACLETO** and **IVAN NUNES**
connecting cover with Dejah Thoris #1 and Red Sonja #1

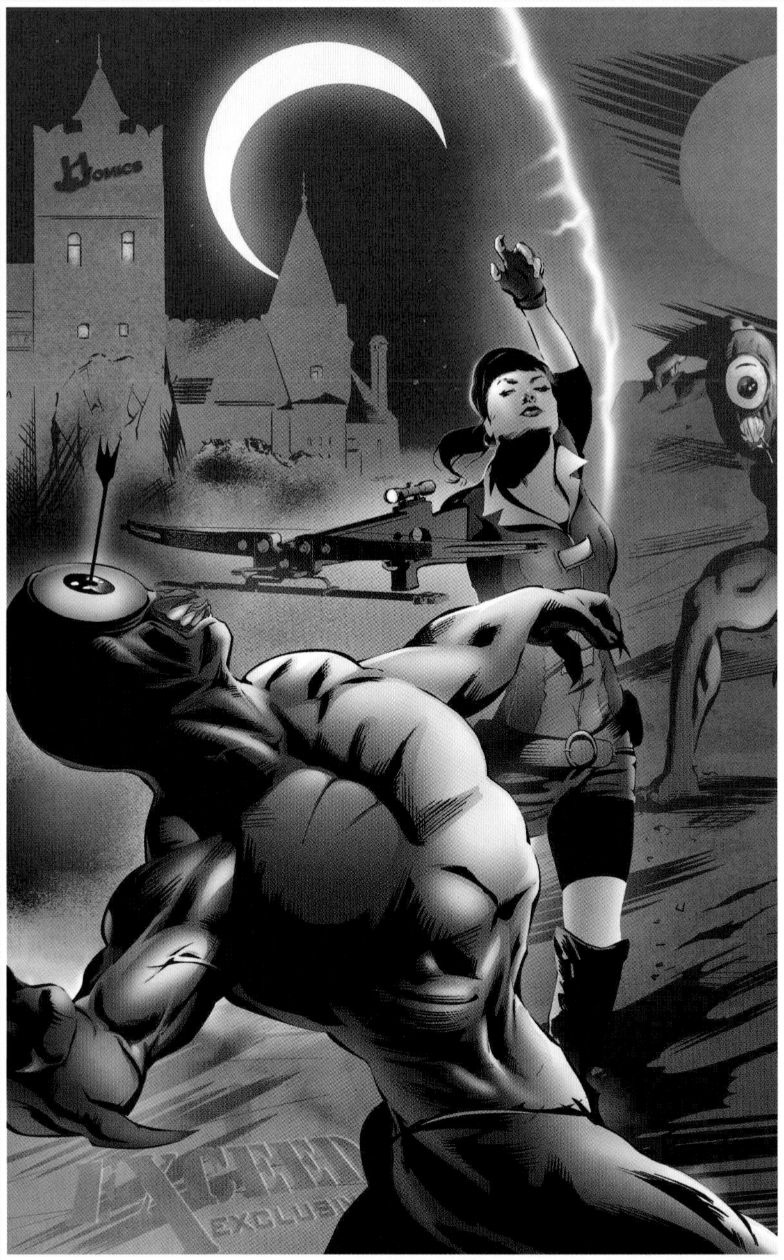

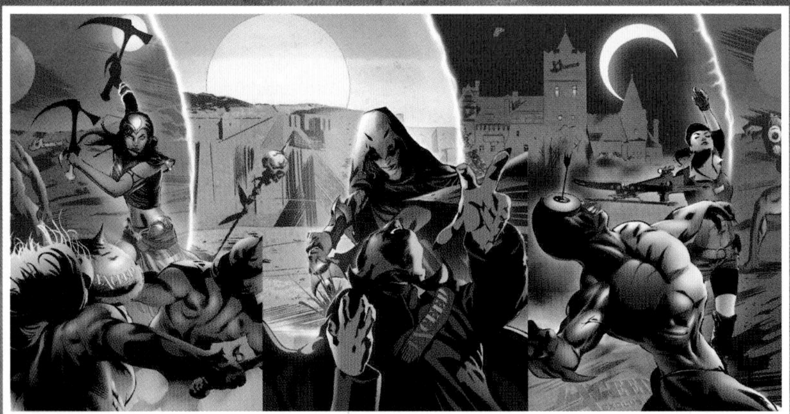

#1 Jesse James Comics exclusive cover by **DENNIS CALERO**

connecting cover with Dejah Thoris #1 and Red Sonja #1

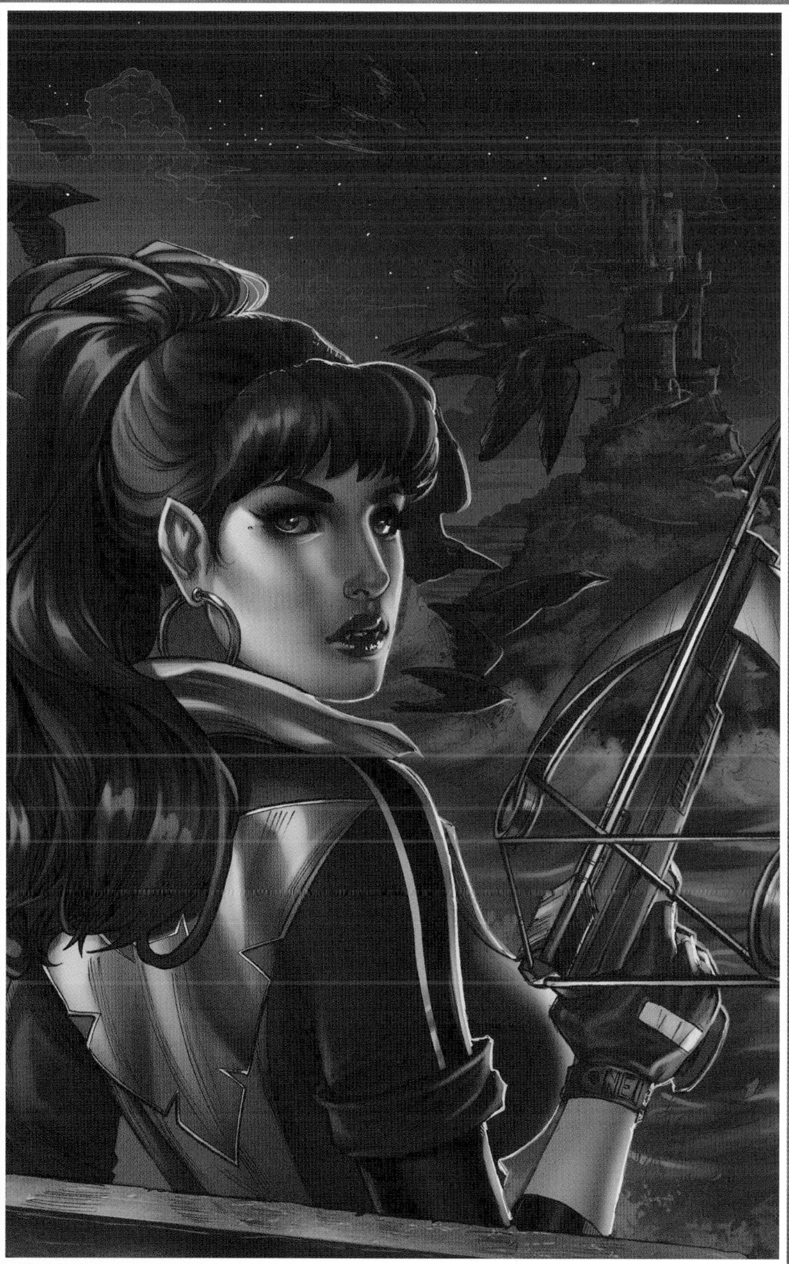

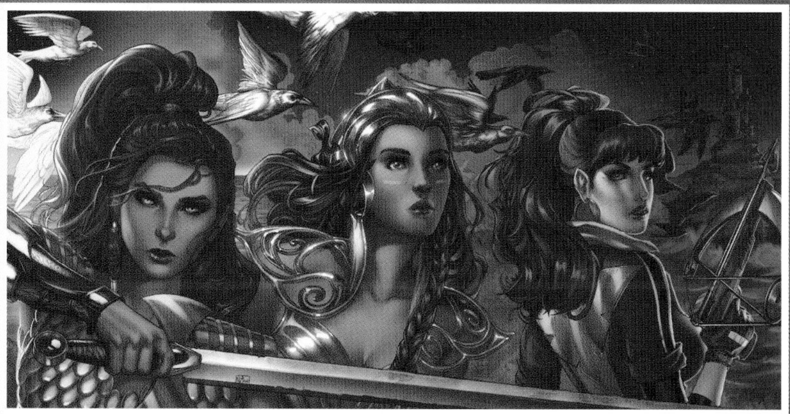

#1 Midtown Comics exclusive cover by **NEI RUFFINO**
connecting cover with Dejah Thoris #1 and Red Sonja #1

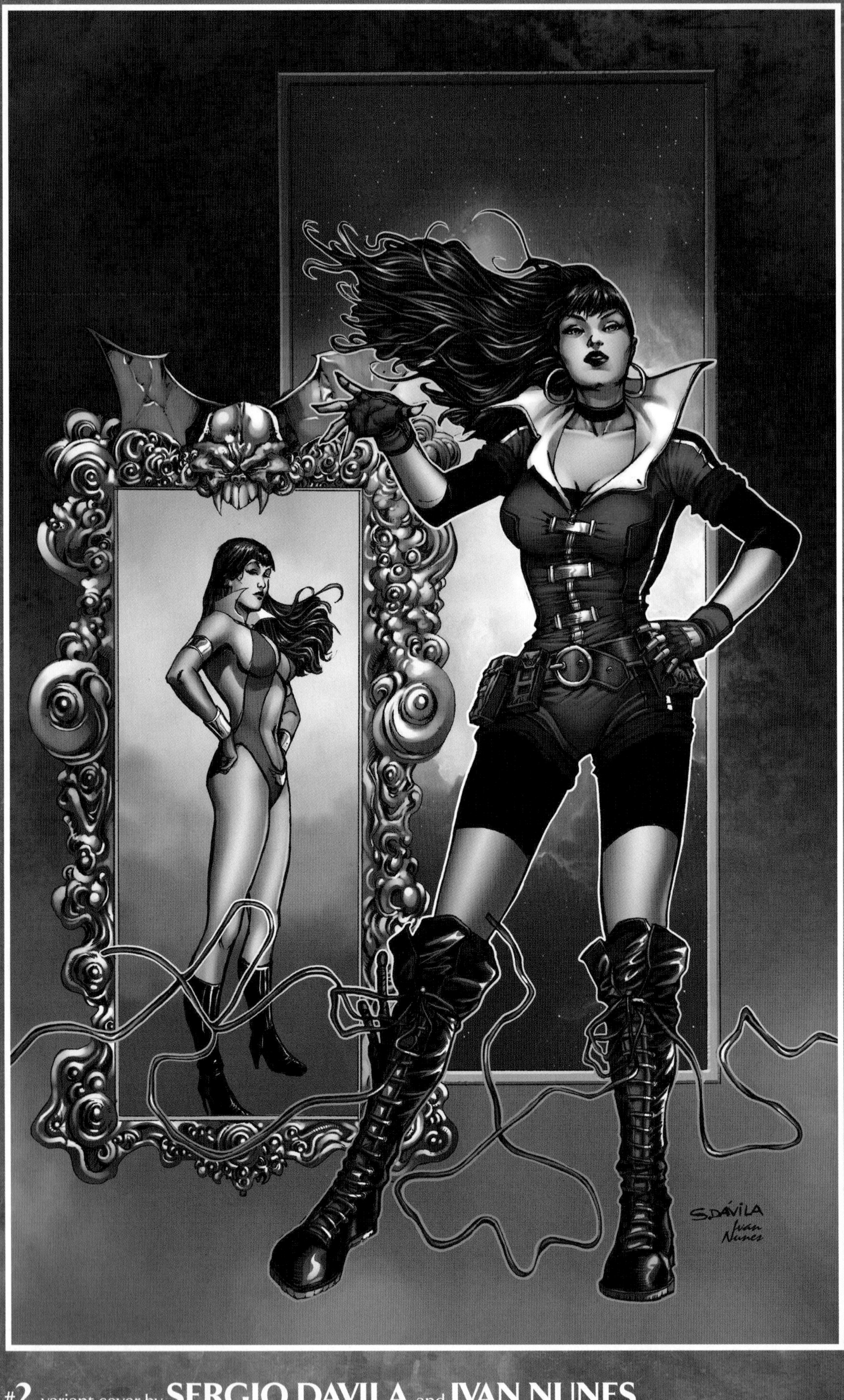
S.DÁVILA
Ivan
Nunes

#2 variant cover by **SERGIO DAVILA** and **IVAN NUNES**

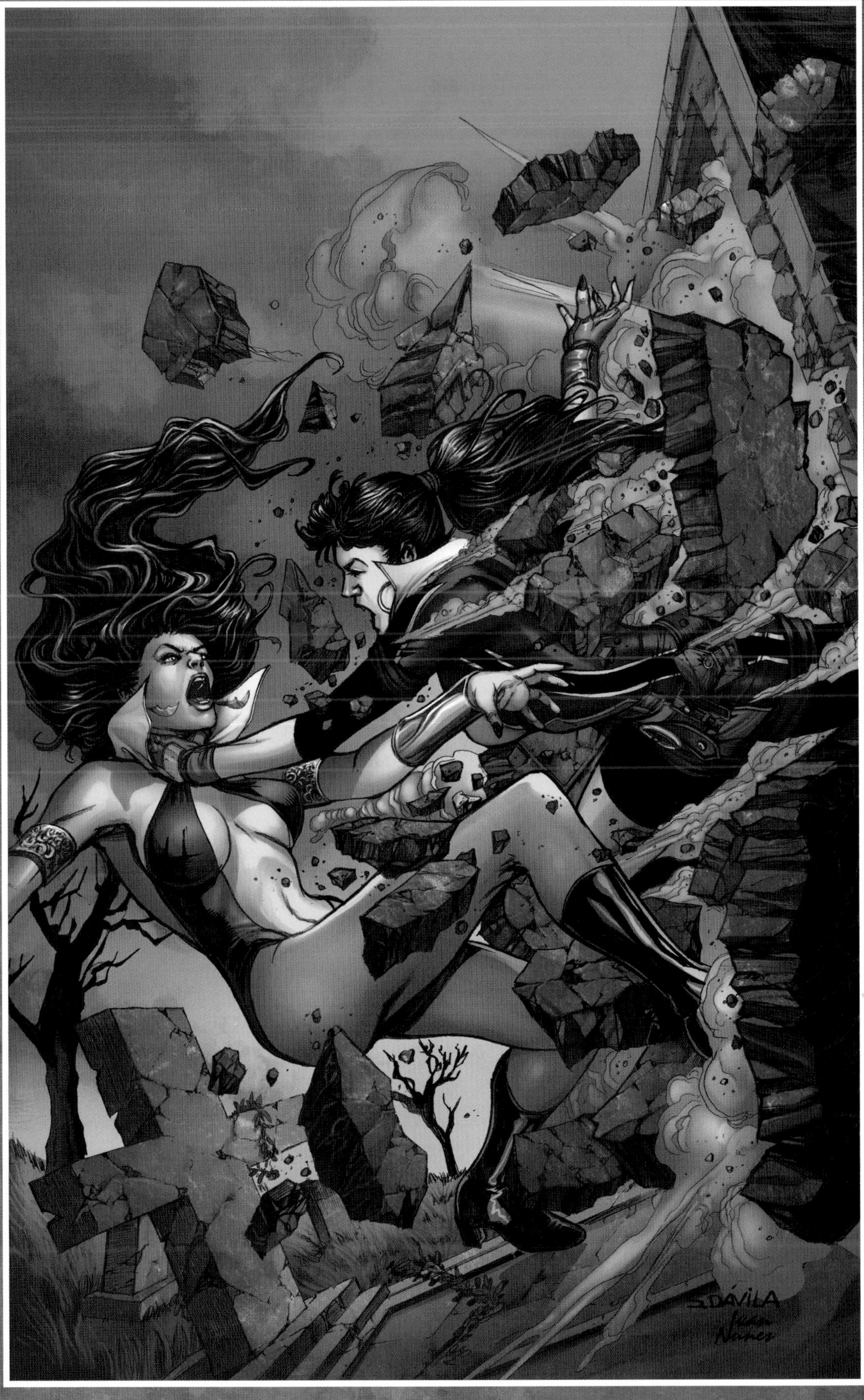
S.DAVILA
Ivan Nunes

#3 variant cover by **SERGIO DAVILA** and **IVAN NUNES**

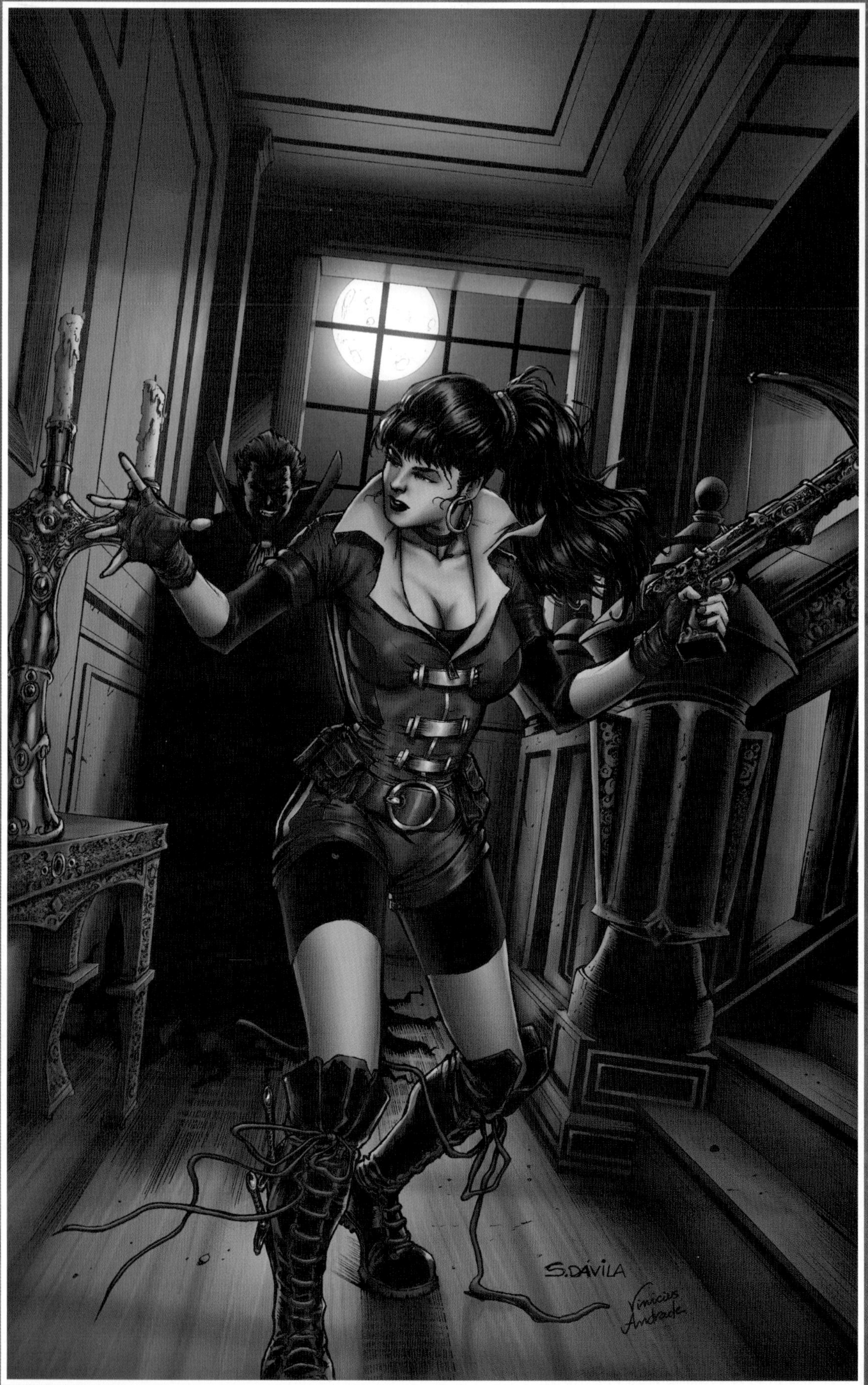
S.DÁVILA
Vinicius Andrade

#4 variant cover by **SERGIO DAVILA** and **VINICIUS ANDRADE**

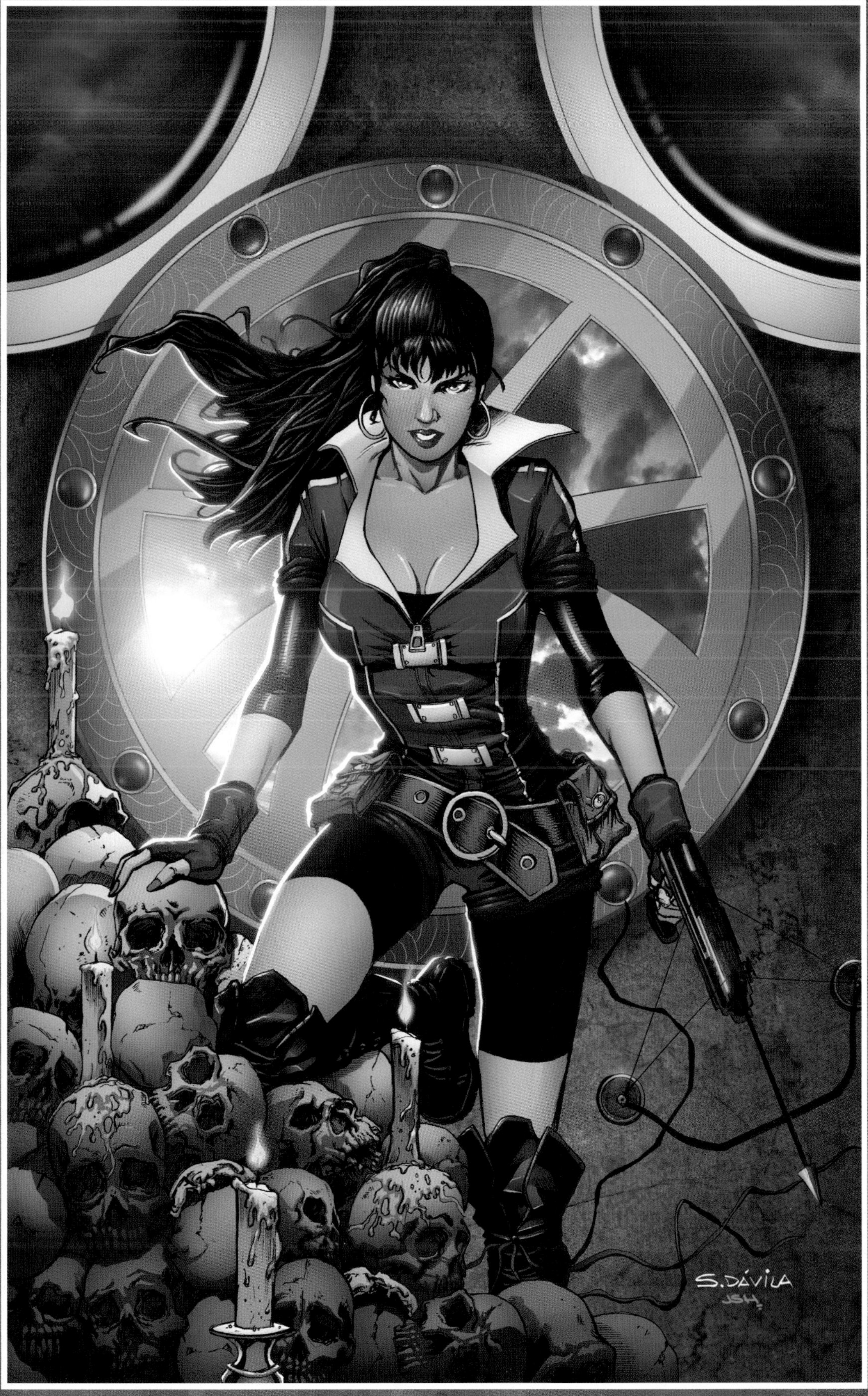
S. DÁVILA
JSH

#5 variant cover by **SERGIO DAVILA** and **JORGE SUTIL**

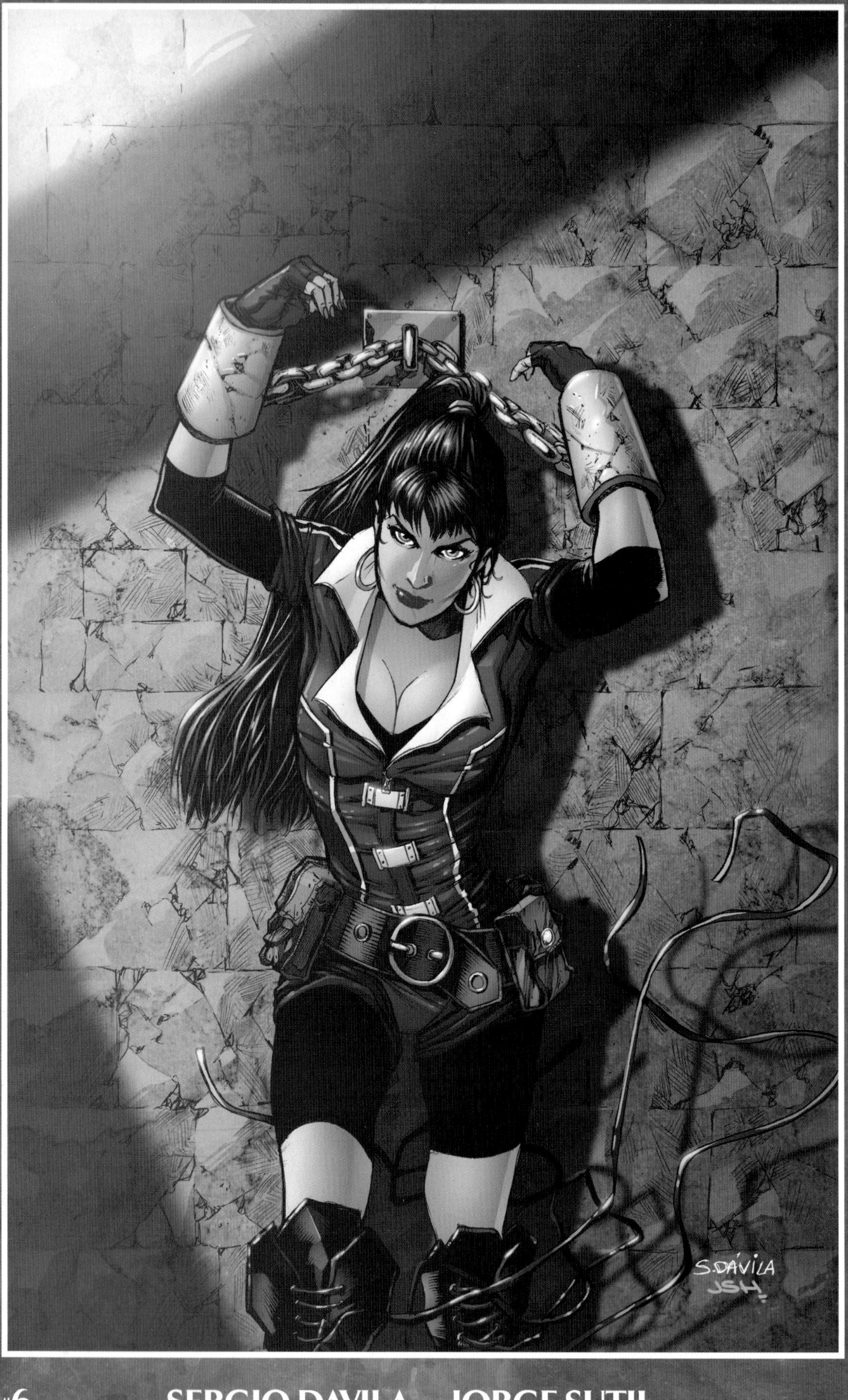
S.DÁVILA
JSH

#6 variant cover by **SERGIO DAVILA** and **JORGE SUTIL**